Cowboy Life

cowboy

life

THE LETTERS OF

GEORGE PHILIP

Edited and with an Introduction

by CATHIE DRAINE

Afterword by Richard W. Slatta

Illustrations by Mick B. Harrison

South Dakota

State Historical Society Press

Pierre, South Dakota

This publication is funded, in part, by the Deadwood
Publications Fund provided by the City of Deadwood and
the Deadwood Historic Preservation Commission.

Library of Congress Cataloging-in-Publication Data
Philip, George, 1880-1948.
Cowboy life : the letters of George Philip / edited and with
an introduction by Cathie Draine ; afterword by Richard
W. Slatta ; illustrations by Mick B. Harrison.
    p. cm.
Includes bibliographical references and index.
ISBN 978-0-9777955-1-2
1. Philip, George, 1880-1948—Correspondence.
2. Philip, George, 1880-1948—Childhood and youth.
3. Cowboys—South Dakota—Correspondence. 4. Ranch
life—South Dakota—History—20th century. 5. Frontier
and pioneer life—South Dakota. 6. Cattle drives—South
Dakota—History—20th century. 7. South Dakota—Social
life and customs—20th century. 8. South Dakota—
Biography. I. Draine, Cathie. II. Title.
F656.P49A4 2007
978.3'033—dc22

                                    22007004290
ISBN 978-0-9777955-1-2

Cover image: Pie-Eyed, 2003, 6 1/2" x 9 1/2", oil,
© by artist Mick B. Harrison

Printed in the United States of America
11 10 09 08 07   2 3 4 5

Contents

Acknowledgements *vii*

Introduction by *Cathie Draine* 1

1   The Open Range (March 4, 1937) 9

2   A Few Days on the Range (August 24, 1939) 45

3   The Ghouls (September 27, 1939) 61

4   Let There Be Light (October 24, 1939) 70

5   Who Knows? (November 10, 1939) 77

6   Happy Landing? (April 16, 1940) 84

7   The Cowman (June 1, 1940) 88

8   The Rooshian Wagon (June 24, 1940) 114

9   The Law of the Range (July 16, 1940) 124

10   Practical Joking (July 24, 1940) 131

11   You Know What That Game of Poker Is (August 1, 1940) 137

12   Plenty O' Nuttin' (August 14, 1940) 144

13   Rough Play (August 16, 1940) 163

14   Old Dishrag (September 1, 1940) 174

15   An Indian Roundup (September 30, 1940) 191

16   The Swinging Cinch (November 27, 1940) 214

17   Fixing the Wheel (December 12, 1940) 231

18   Mostly 'Cross Country (December 30, 1940) 239

19   Working up an Appetite (January 14, 1941) 255

20   Hot Irons on Live Hides (February 24, 1941) 268

21   Ailments of the Range (May 20, 1941) 278

Afterword by *Richard W. Slatta* 297

Appendix 305

Notes 309

Index 353

Acknowledgements

I am grateful to the many persons whose enthusiasm for this project, personal memories of some of the individuals and the times, and research skills assisted me beyond measure. Reid Riner, curator, and Ellen Bishop, genealogist, Minnilusa Historical Society, Rapid City, provided invaluable access to background information, historical records, and texts. Darrel Nelson, interpretation coordinator, Adams Museum and House in Deadwood, and Lili Sjomeling, assistant librarian at the Hearst Library in Lead, were able to provide additional information and a first name for Consul Edwards, a figure in the affair of the buffalo versus the Mexican bulls in Juarez, Mexico. Tara Hicks, Stanley County Clerk of Courts, provided the total transcript of the legal actions surrounding the unfortunate death of Clyde Whiting. The reference staff members at the Rapid City Public Library were devoted sleuths who determined titles and authors of numerous bits of poetry.

The staff at the South Dakota State Historical Society have also been supportive. They include Ken Stewart of the South Dakota State Archives and Patti Edman, Nancy Tystad Koupal, and Jeanne K. Ode of the Research and Publishing program.

Bradford Morgan, good friend and academician, provided soothing counsel on technical writing issues. Justin Eiesland at Computer Repair and Sales in Rapid City was the calm and competent restorative manager of predictable electronic crises. Glen Schut, Jeff Schut, Robert Schnell, and Dick Stoll provided many answers on horse and wagon questions, cattle and horse brands, and general range horse behavior. Robert Johnson, M.D., and Kristine Trautman, D.V.M., offered professional and personal opinion on the matter of the Texas itch.

This project has had stalwart cheerleaders, and I am grateful to them for encouragement, prodding, and enthusiasm. They include amateur historian and good friend Janet Dunlap Rathbun of Rapid City; Scotty Philip's granddaughter Jackie Mack Means of Black Hawk; devoted historian of central South Dakota and long-time friend of the family Faye Longbrake of Dupree; and my husband, LeRoy Draine, whose frequent comment, "I don't see an immediate problem," was consistently motivating.

To the other grandchildren of George Philip goes my deepest gratitude for their absolute belief in the value of these letters and in making them available to everyone. Their generosity in providing material, willingness to share their memories, and consistent encouragement is deeply valued. Margaret ("Snow") Philip in Mount Pleasant, South Carolina, and George Philip III in Freeport, Maine, children of George ("Geordie") Philip, Jr.; George ("Greg") Philip, son of Robert Philip, in Fouqueure, France; as well as I, daughter of Jean Philip Mitchell, have been custodians of our grandfather's letters. We are united in our pleasure in seeing them published.

My task was to present George Philip's experiences intact, as he wrote them. He valued the people and the events he wrote about, found them sustaining and entertaining, and wanted his children to be aware of and appreciate the remarkable characters and period of the open range. One always approaches another's personal experiences with the deepest respect. Any errors or omissions that occur are mine; none is intentional.

Cathie Draine
Black Hawk, S.Dak.
1 July 2006

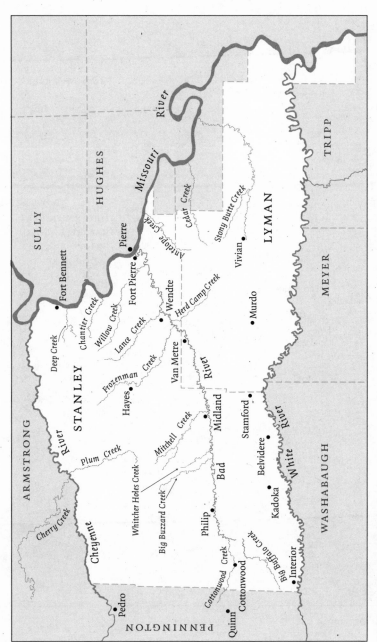

Old Stanley County and Lyman County, 1902

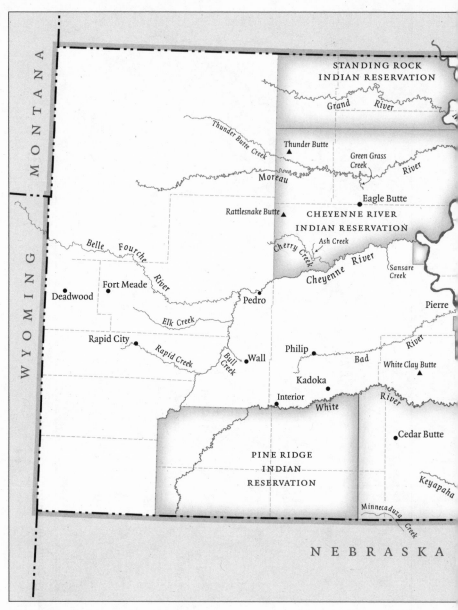

South Dakota, 1901

NORTH DAKOTA

SOUTH DAKOTA

MINNESOTA

LOWER BRULE
INDIAN RESERVATION

River

Creek

Winner

Sioux Falls

ROSEBUD INDIAN
RESERVATION

IOWA

Cowboy Life

Introduction

"Everything that is attempted should be undertaken with some sort of purpose," wrote Rapid City lawyer George Philip to his three adult children, George Philip, Jr., Robert, and Jean, on Christmas Day 1936. At fifty-six years of age, he was preparing to leave a legacy to his two sons and daughter in the form of lengthy letters written over the next five years. "Mine in undertaking this letter, and such others as may follow," he began, "is to chronicle the uneventful story of an unimportant man, and to give to each of you some idea of the experiences an ordinary chap could have in the generation which preceded yours." No one who knew George Philip as a cowboying teenager newly arrived on the Dakota prairies from Scotland or as a respected lawyer and civic leader years later would ever have considered his story "uneventful" or described him as "an unimportant man." George Philip lived fully in his own generation, displaying his belief that, "if we are not too non-conformist, we can sometimes take advantage of the forces that carry us along." And take advantage he did, leaving behind this quite extraordinary record of life on the open range and in the wide-open towns of western South Dakota.

George Philip was born on 16 July 1880 into a large extended family in Auchness, near Dallas, in Morayshire, Scotland. His grandfather and grandmother Philip produced a family of nine children, a number of whom emigrated to the United States. George's father, Robert, was a stonemason who worked in the rebuilding of Chicago after its great fire in 1871, returned to Scotland, married, and died of pulmonary disease, most probably pneumonia, when his son was only three years old. Robert's widow, Catherine Maclaren, struggled to maintain herself and young George, but she was never again "able to establish herself in life, in health, nor in happiness." She died in 1887. Commenting on his orphaned state to his children, George Philip remarked in 1936: "Perhaps one so orphaned never fully overcomes the sense of loss; perhaps such a one values regard of others more than those who through childhood, puberty and adolescence are not subjected to that sense of loss. Who knows? At least, it is likely to give a serious slant in tender years to those who shed their tears alone."

George Philip's Christmas letter to his children covers his genealogy and early years, offering recollections of his youth that are probably typical of most young lads in the highland glens at the end of the nineteenth century. With his pals and a neighbor's dog, he fished, trapped small game, cut birch for firewood, and once successfully dispatched a deer that had broken its leg in a fall. Youthful rambles in the hills soon gave way to serious discussions of the future for young George. The young man himself wanted to go to sea, and eventually his grandmother and his uncles who remained in Scotland determined that he would "join the numberless legion of Scottish trained marine engineers." On his sixteenth birthday, he entered a five-year apprenticeship in the engineering yards of Caldwell and Company on the River Clyde. Work began in the yards at six in the morning with a quick break for breakfast several hours later. Dinner was an hour at midday and then back to work until six, except Saturday when work ended at noon. Combined with demanding evening studies at the engineering high school, this regimen led the young man to realize "that the world would have to struggle along without the mechanical services of one of its poorest engineers."

"It seemed advisable," he recalled in 1936, "to cast about for some means of release from the bonds of an apprenticeship. One with no parents, brothers or sisters in whom to confide, is forced to the necessity of determining without advice the course to pursue, . . . [and] there is likely to be a lack of frankness in dealing with others, and a resort is sometimes had to means that are not the source of too much pride in later years." In other words, he hatched a plot to get out of his commitment. Enlisting the advice of his cousins who were medical students, he arrived at the decision to present the symptoms of tuberculosis. He developed a hacking cough, all the while protesting perfect health. Official after official took notice, and finally the crucial medical examination was held. "I took the flat position that there was nothing the matter," Philip recalled, and at last the examining physician suggested that a leave of absence, perhaps in the Transvaal or the western states of America, might be beneficial. In April 1897, he sailed from the Clyde to America to begin his leave of absence. It was to be a remarkably long year.

Immediately after arriving in New York, the young man hastened to the ranch home of his uncle Alex Philip in Hays, Kansas. One year of recuperation soon became two. In 1899, demands from Scotland that he return to finish the engineering program and the fact that he and Alex Philip did not get along led George to cast about for jobs farther west, and he ultimately arrived at a lumber camp near Grant, Colorado. Only a cousin in Hays knew of his plan to stay out of sight until his majority was reached. Not wanting to make a career of skidding logs, George was pleased when he received a letter via his cousin from his Uncle James ("Scotty") Philip of South Dakota. "I understand Bob's boy is roaming somewhere through the West," the letter read. "If you know where he is, tell him to come up here, and I'll put him to work." The reluctant lumberjack headed immediately to Denver to collect his wages for the trip to South Dakota.

"On arriving at Pierre in the middle of the night," George Philip recalled, "in a town which then could boast of no street light at all, the nearest and most convenient hotel was the old Grand Pacific, long since removed." Looking as if it had never been grand, the hotel "on that particular night . . . was anything but pacific for the reason that there were some cowboys on parade." In due time, Philip started across the river to his future home:

> In those days, the only way of communication and transportation across the Missouri River was by rowboat, for passengers, and the steamship "Jim Leighten" for freight and livestock. Old John Olson was the boatman who transported me, and who enabled me to start my first visit in that quaint frontier cow town, Fort Pierre.
>
> Scotty, whom I had seen but once before, at the wedding of Anne Philip at Hays two years before, happened to be on the street, and I completely surprised him by introducing myself to him. He then took me up to his home, introduced me to his family, where I was then accepted and still remain one of them.
>
> That same day or the next morning I was introduced to Billy Hess, and Fred Ervin. . . . They were in from the roundup outfit camped on Prairie Dog north of Midland, each with a four-horse team, after provisions for the Fall roundup. Acquiring a saddle and a bed, I joined them on their outward trip and launched into what I thought would be my last business.[1]

From 1899 to 1903, when he turned in his saddle and string of horses and entered the University of Michigan to study law, George Philip would work for his legendary uncle.

Scotty Philip had emigrated from Scotland in 1874 at age fifteen. After knocking around the West from Kansas to Colorado, he had arrived at Fort Robinson, where he worked as a guide and scout. He married Sarah ("Sally") Larribee, a French and Cheyenne Indian woman in 1879, and the two of them eventually started ranching along the Bad River near the present-day town of Philip. When the Great Sioux Reservation opened up in 1890, Scotty started a second ranch near Fort Pierre, forming a partnership with the Minnesota and Dakota Cattle Company, known as the "73 outfit" for its brand. Philip also ran cattle under his own L-7 brand, and when the partners quarreled in 1899, Scotty Philip sold his interest in the 73 and shipped in southern cattle and acquired local brands to form his own L-7 cattle company. When his nephew George joined his ranching operation at the turn of the century, Scotty Philip and his family may have had up to forty-thousand head of cattle on the open ranges of western South Dakota. He also bought one of the last surviving herds of buffalo and is credited with helping to save the American bison from extinction.[2] Perhaps it is little wonder that the bulk of the letters that George Philip would write to his children between 1937 and 1941 focus on his early years as one of Scotty Philip's cowboys.

George Philip owed more than his cowboy years to Scotty's influence, however, as the older man also dabbled in banking, real estate, and politics. Scotty had given his young nephew a herd of cattle to get started in the cattle business, but a "smart operator fleeced me out of my herd," George Philip admitted later, and in 1903 he therefore determined to "go to law school and learn how to write a contract so I would never fall prey" again to a clever operator.[3] But admission to law school took the influence of his uncle Scotty who, with the cooperation of officials at the Fort Pierre high school, fabricated a secondary school record and diploma to meet the aspiring lawyer's entrance requirements. George Philip graduated from the University of Michigan in 1906 and received his naturalization papers the same year.

After graduation, Philip partnered with Alvin Waggoner, a classmate at the University of Michigan, and they set up offices in Philip and Fort Pierre. On 30 May 1911, George married Alice Island ("Isle") Waldron of Fort Pierre. Their first child, George Philip, Jr. ("Geordie"), was born in 1912. In January 1914, when Philip was in Sioux Falls getting acquainted with the duties and requirements of his position as assistant United States attorney, he received word of the birth of his daughter, Jean. Robert, the third and last child, was born in November 1914. Three years later, the family moved from Fort Pierre to Rapid City, where Philip was associated in the practice of law until his death. He served two terms as United States attorney for South Dakota under President Woodrow Wilson and twelve years in that capacity under President Franklin D. Roosevelt. As an active Democrat, he also served as close advisor to Governor Tom Berry in the 1930s. His extensive civic interests included the Mount Rushmore National Memorial commission and society, the South Dakota cement commission, the Black Hills Power and Light Company, and the Black Hills General Hospital in Rapid City. He was one of the best-known representatives of masonry in South Dakota, holding the thirty-third degree at the time of his death in 1948. He first joined the masons in Fort Pierre, and his letters reflect his strong commitment to the organization.[4]

When Philip began to write to his grown children on that Christmas Day in 1936, they knew well his professional reputation, his civic participation and contributions. They knew him as a poetry-quoting, suit-wearing, thoroughly urban intellectual. They knew he was a sought-after speaker at political and service-club events. They also knew that he was the center of attention when tales were told at "old-timers" gatherings. But it is quite possible they did not know how well he understood the impact on society of the closing of the last great open range. Barely two generations—thirty-four years—had passed since Philip turned in his saddle in 1903 and began to write about those experiences.

At fifty-six, George Philip had an almost palpable awareness that, for a working cowboy in South Dakota, the decade that straddled the beginning of the twentieth century had been a time like none other. This era, which formed his life and career, came at the end of the open range in the Northern Great Plains. George Philip's writings capture the free, wild, and risky era in which cowboys were loyal, independent, and largely without pretense. Ultimately, that life, bounded only by the demands of the cattle, surrendered to railroads that crawled across the prairies, to the towns that were built to support the trains, to the thousands of miles of barbed wire, to the homesteaders who fenced and plowed the land.[5] But for the cowboys themselves, the values of the open range, its friendships, and the shared experiences remained.

In recreating the era for his children, Philip wrote of his admiration and friendship with individual cowboys such as Bunk White and Tom Beverly. Even though he recalled defending the African-American White against racist attitudes, Philip's letters also refer to the "darky" porter on a train to Mexico and preserve Tom Beverly's naïve solution to the "race problem" in yet another letter.[6] His description of events on the Indian reservation during a roundup probably reflects attitudes held by many at the time that Philip was writing. It would stretch credulity to suggest that he held a bias against the American Indians since his uncle Scotty's wife was of mixed blood, as were his own mother-in-law, Jane Van Metre Waldron, and his wife Isle. Instead, the casual language and tolerance of stereotypes when not directed at people one knew characterized his era.

George Philip was decidedly conscious of capturing and leaving an impression of his generation for his readers to appreciate. "It is impossible for one who knew Tom Beverly in the days when there was a cow country, and there were cowboys," Philip commented, "to call one of the overdressed and underworked drugstore cowboys of this day by that name." The early cowman's "wealth of early cowboy lore, well understood by one who helped make it, was allowed to go to waste when Tom passed on to his reward without leaving his story told for others to come. His views on the great epoch of American life, the cow country, have since been warped out of all semblance to the living truth by pulp magazines, silver screen, plain lies, and even by that modern manifestation of showmanship called the rodeo,"[7] Philip kept his own promise to see that Tom Beverly, almost a tradition on the range, was not totally forgotten after his death. And in the process, he helped to preserve the cowboy era for all of us to appreciate several generations later. Whatever else Tom Beverly may have been, he was clearly a mentor, confidant, and probably a surrogate father to the young Scottish lad coming of age on the vast prairies of central South Dakota.

It seems apparent that Philip began the letters in one state of mind and ended them in another. Initially he wanted to record the time, people, and events that had formed him, but as time went on, he found his health and purpose changing. "When the idea of writing letters occurred to me," he wrote on 4 March 1937, "my intention was to make them much more inclusive than they may turn out to be, for an unusual amount of eye trouble added to the task, which I had expected to be pleasure only. I looked forward to doing a much better job than I may ever be able to accomplish." It was important to him to paint an accurate picture. "The range country was largely peopled by young boys and young men," he wrote in the same letter. "They were not arrayed in the spangles so liberally shown in the movies but in overalls or California pants. . . . They were, in fact, laborers in a hard field. Because of its freedom, it had considerable romantic appeal, but they did not live in the towns such as Hollywood depicts. Instead, they slept beneath the stars or the clouds, when they could get to it, and the rest of the time, they were dirty and sweaty and tired." As the letters progress, they become a gift to himself of meaningful memories. Near the end of the letters, his contempt for Adolph Hitler and his concerns for the war color some of his thoughts even as the letters help to take his mind off the war.

By 20 May 1941, the date of the last letter, not only were his eyes bothering him, but other health problems and sorrows were looming. His two sons would be lost in the war. Major Robert Philip of the United States Marines was killed in the South Pacific on 24 June 1943 when his fighter plane was lost near Monono, Samoa. Commander George Philip, Jr., died on 16 June 1945 off the island of Okinawa when a kamikaze struck the ship he was commanding. George Philip would survive his sons by only a few years. He died at home in Rapid City on 13 March 1948 from the results of a stroke or, perhaps like many others at the time, of the heartbreak of war and family loss. He was sixty-eight years old. His widow Isle, his daughter Jean, and four grandchildren survived him. Remarkably, for a man who spent most of his life in decidedly urban pursuits and experienced only four years on the range, his obituaries gave great recognition and respect to the friendships formed there. His personal memories of the range, which follow, add his own contribution to the cowboying legacy.

After he finished writing the letters, George Philip himself shaped them into a polished whole. The letters were typewritten and corrected in his own hand. They were then bundled together, titles and subheadings were added to most of them, and a set given to each of his children. At least a portion of one letter, the Mexican adventure, was published in Philip's lifetime when he shared it with the South Dakota State Historical Society. Another letter appeared in Bert Hall's classic compilation of cowboy documents entitled Roundup Years.[8] In preparing the letters for publication, I have preserved their order as written, and, other than breaking large blocks of text into paragraphs or combining short ones, I have kept editorial corrections and insertions to a minimum, adding notes at the end to explain or expand on items in the text where possible. Over time, some stories were told more than once, and I have removed repetitions, marking them with an ellipsis, and combined stories. In the interest of focusing on life in early South Dakota, the first letter about Scotland, which is quoted extensively in this Introduction, one about

Hays, Kansas, and those containing his speeches on unrelated topics have been omitted. With these exceptions, the document remains as George Philip wrote it—the story of his generation and his own "ordinary life." At his death, the *Rapid City Daily Journal* eulogized him as "Scottish immigrant, western cowboy, forthright citizen, an eminent lawyer [and] a friend of man. . . . Whether on the range or in the court room or by the fireside, here was a man to tie to."[9]

Cowboys George Philip, Tommy McDonald, Art Woods, and Johnny Cruikshank (from left) posed for this photograph around 1900.

CHAPTER 1

The Open Range

March 4, 1937

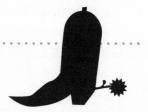

My dear Geordie, Jean, and Bob:

One of the greatest epochs in the development of any country was manifested in that part of America's west, known as "The Cow Country." Migration and settlement took it over piece by piece from the wide-open spaces to the restrictions of community life. The last of the cow country was that part of South Dakota lying west of the Missouri River, with a little strip along northern Nebraska, southern North Dakota, and eastern Wyoming and Montana. That life, and it was a life all unto itself, passed out much too rapidly for people to realize at the time just what was happening.

The range country was largely peopled by young boys and young men. They were not arrayed in the spangles so liberally shown in the movies but in overalls or California pants.[1] Their feminine acquaintances were not the dancehall girls, but much more likely to be bunch-quitting cows none too kindly disposed to their herders. They were not at all the pretty boys of the silver screen. They were, in fact, laborers in a hard field. Because of its freedom, it had considerable romantic appeal, but they did not live in the towns such as Hollywood depicts. Instead, they slept beneath the stars or the clouds, when they could get to it, and the rest of the time, they were dirty and sweaty and tired. The cow country was a law unto itself, and if I ever get the time and the energy simultaneously, I am going to write you a letter on "The Law of the Range."[2]

The great day of the cow country reached its sundown with the homesteader influx. That was true everywhere, and no less true in South Dakota than it was in other places. No one has written the principle of the cow country into better or more inclusive language than the poet Badger Clark in his poem "The Passing of the Trail":

There was a sunny, savage land
   Beneath the eagle's wings,
And there, across the thorns and sand,
   Wild rovers rode as kings.
Is it a yarn from long ago
   And far across the sea?
Could that land be the land we know?
   Those roving riders we?

The trail's a lane, the trail's a lane.
   How comes it, pard of mine?
Within a day it slipped away
   And hardly left a sign.
Now history a tale has gained
   To please the younger ears—
A race of kings that rose, and reigned,
   And passed in fifty years!

Dream back beyond the cramping lanes
   To glories that have been—
The camp smoke on the sunset plains,
   The riders loping in:
Loose rein and rowelled heel to spare,
   The wind our only guide,
For youth was in the saddle there
   With half a world to ride.

The trail's a lane, the trail's a lane.
   Dead is the branding fire.
The prairies wild are tame and mild,
   All close-corralled with wire.
The sunburnt demigods who ranged
   And laughed and lived so free
Have topped the last divide, or changed
   To men like you and me.

Where, in the valley fields and fruits,
   Now hums a lively street,

We milled a mob of fighting brutes
    Among the grim mesquit.
It looks a far and fearful way—
    The trail from Now to Then—
But time is telescoped today,
    A hundred years in ten.

The trail's a lane, the trail's a lane.
    Our brows are scarcely seamed,
But we may scan a mighty span
    Methuselah ne'er dreamed.
Yes, pardner, we are dull and old,
    With paltry hopes and fears,
Beside those rovers gay and bold
    Far riding down the years![3]

Queer Fellows

No end of queer individuals appeared on the range, and it is too bad that they should be forgotten simply because there is no one with a facile pen to record them. The incidents of Cy Hiett alone would make plenty reading without any embellishment of the facts. Indeed, to try to improve on some of Cy's experiences would be a good deal like trying to paint the rainbow or the sunset.

I knew him well and we were and still are good friends. When sober, as he usually was, he was a hardworking, serious-minded cowboy, intensely loyal to his job and to his employer. When drunk, as he occasionally was, he was the very emblem of irresponsibility, engaging in escapades that would put to shame the best efforts of the romancers. For some years he was Scotty's foreman. On occasions he would fall from grace, making a holy show of himself, and Scotty would fire him. By reason of a strange mental quirk by which Cy Hiett, sober, had no knowledge at all of what was done by Cy Hiett, drunk, the incident of being fired was completely obliterated from his mind with returning sobriety, and the first thing Scotty would know, Cy was back out in the country in charge of the outfit, doing more and better work than anybody, wholly oblivious of the fact that he had been fired.

There is a well-authenticated story on Cy, which happened at a time when I was not with the outfit. "The wagon," which was the usual name applied to a cow outfit, was moving into Fort Pierre in the fall, with a beef shipment. When they reached Frozenman Creek, where a large dam had been built by the Northwestern Railway for the accommodation of shippers, at about the point where the road crossing at the town of Hayes now is, camp was made for the night. There was a post office and store called Hayes a couple of miles farther down the creek on the old Deadwood trail crossing. Will Hopkins ran the store, and it is of interest that he still has a store at Hayes.

The mood was on some of the boys, particularly on Cy, to indulge in alcoholics, but the only thing available was Hostetter's bitters.[4] Cy bought a considerable supply and promptly was tight on that insufferable beverage. As was customary with him on such occasions, he spent the night going back and forth from the bed of one cowpuncher to another, waking him up with whispered confidences of a great secret. Each one knew him, of course, and said that so and so wanted him to come over, and so he would go over to so and so's bed, repeating the performance. There was one thing about Cy, he was always self-sustaining and wholly capable of taking care of himself, so much so that when he became intoxicated and thereby wholly useless for any work, everyone simply turned him loose to his own devices.

In the morning, the night-hawk brought in the saddle horses in the fog, which did not lift until after camp was broken. On going out to catch his horse in the rope corral, Cy caught a pony which he had not ridden for a long time because he was very likely to buck, and the sober, serious-minded, hard-working Cy Hiett had not cared to ride him, although he was a good rider when sober, and a splendid rider when drunk. Catching this wild pony and dragging him out to his saddle was something of a task, and no one offered to render any assistance. Almost under any other circumstances such help would have been forthcoming. Cy finally got his saddle on the pony and a bottle of bitters protruded from each saddle pocket. As the other fellows were going on with the serious business of work in hand, Cy got on his pony, which immediately started to buck; away he went into the fog, which closed behind him, and Cy was gone. No one paid attention, nor gave a thought to what might happen to him, knowing that his instinct would land him in the next camp.

The outfit moved on to Lance Creek Holes, and while the boys were eating dinner, preparing to go out and relieve the day herders, along came Cy, the fog having lifted in the meantime. Cy was still drunk, both bottles of bitters were gone, his pony was completely played out, and across the saddle in his lap was a grey wolf he had roped sometime during the forenoon. Cy, of course, not having any recollection of having seen a wolf, far less catching and killing it, could offer no explanation of where he had been or what had happened. It is a safe comment, however, that when Cy took out after that wolf and got his rope down on the wild animal that morning, up until he had him dead on the saddle, there transpired events that would look well in a movie screen but cannot be put there. That picture was wholly lost, even from Cy's mental vision, and the only evidence on which one could build a story at all was on the fact of the dead wolf, the exhausted pony, and the drunken cowboy. It was law of the range to attempt to catch and kill grey wolf every time he appeared, regardless of what might happen to your horse, so Cy was automatically following the law of the range, the spirit of the hunt, and the instincts of a cowboy.

Old Alligator

Not all the horses on the range were gentle. They all had some streak of wildness, and occasionally one came along from which that streak could not be erased. Compared with the great number of saddle horses in the cow country, the number of "outlaws," as the untamable horses were called, was small, but few as they were numerically, they were potent, and everybody knew them by name and number.

Prior to the fall of 1899, Scotty Philip; [M. ("Pat")] Mullen, a banker, and [Charles] Stuebe, a merchant, from New Ulm, Minnesota, were all the stockholders of the Minnesota and Dakota Cattle Company (the 73 outfit). After a row with Mullen, Scotty sold out his interest in the company to Robert W. ("Bob") Stewart (later Colonel Stewart of Standard Oil fame) and Captain Joe Binder, both of Pierre.[5] All, or nearly all of the saddle horses supplying the 73 outfit were Scotty's, so, when he withdrew to run an outfit of his own, he took his horses with him, which left the 73 practically afoot, and that was no way for a cow outfit to be.

Jack Borden of the 73 (Ruth Philip's father) went over to Ross, Wyoming, and bought about one hundred twenty-five head of horses from the Oglala Cattle Company. They were a terrible bunch of horses, but among them were three, Alligator, Face and the third name has slipped my memory, worse than terrible, and Alligator was worst of all. Slim Taggart ("Slobbering Slim") who was riding a wild string for the 73 was given all three of these horses. He could stay on them, but could

MICK
B.
HARRISON

not tame them, nor do any worthwhile work on them. Pat Mullen was out one time looking the outfit over and Slim was riding Alligator. His instruction to the foreman was, "Either fire that rider or kill that horse, or both." Alligator was just a bad, wild horse that nobody wanted to ride, and that very few could ride.[6]

The 73 established a winter camp on Sansarc Creek, with a number of riders in the charge of Cy Hiett, to hold those Oglala horses and keep them from going back to Wyoming.[7] Pete Ashley told me this story. Along in the spring some one brought a lot of whiskey out to this camp, and the boys began to celebrate. Cy, having a lonely streak that day, took a quart bottle full of whiskey and sat off to one side, drinking only from his own bottle. As the party progressed, the occasion grew merrier and such timid spirits as there were became emboldened. Pete Ashley for some time had been trying to get his courage up to the point of riding one of his horses that had not been ridden all winter, and the added encouragement of John Barleycorn got him up to the point where the riding of that horse looked easy. He said, "Cy, I think I'll run in my D P sorrel and ride him."[8]

Cy said, "No, you wait a while. Wait until I finish this quart, and we'll have the horses run in. Then you can ride your D P sorrel and I will ride Alligator." The sober Cy would not get on Alligator if the owners were to give him the whole outfit. Cy, drunk, was now looking for the chance to get on him. Shortly he announced, "Well, that's finished. Somebody run in the horses."

When the horses were run into the corral, Pete caught his D P sorrel and Cy roped Alligator. After plenty of struggle, the two horses were saddled, and Pete successfully gave his horse, which was merely an untrained horse that knew how to buck, the first ride of the season. Then Cy climbed aboard Alligator. The horses had not yet shed off the long hair of winter, and Pete's account of the duel between the drunken Cy and the man-hating Alligator was nothing short of graphic. On horseback at anytime, Cy was capable, and with a "skinful" his equilibrium was uncanny. Alligator did all the things that had made him a terror to the souls of cowboys, but Cy's spurs raked him from the neck to the hip bones, right and left, until, as Pete said, he threw so much of Alligator's long hair into the air with his spurs that it seemed as though a feather pillow had been torn and thrown.

After Alligator's bag of tricks had been exhausted, Cy fought him back to the corral and got off, no inconsiderable task in itself. By this time the blood of battle was commencing to ferment in Cy, and, when he got his saddle off the outlaw, he proudly announced that he could ride him bareback. Suiting the action to the word he was on, and the horse, seeming to feel that now he had all the best of it, repeated his efforts, which in return brought a repetition of his rider's effort and with like result. Poor old Alligator, nearly skinned with the spurs that he could not dislodge, gave up the struggle for the day only. Then Cy "thumbed" him, which means running the thumbs hard up the neck of the horse, and which will nearly always make even a gentle range horse buck, but Alligator had enough for that session and refused to perform. Cy then thumbed him again, this time with such vigor that he sprained both thumbs, so the hunt for too much victory made the struggle end in something like a draw. In later days the sober Cy would look apprehensively at the storied horse he could not remember having ridden.

Rattlesnakes

From that memorable day when Eve in her guilelessness listened to the story that the "varmint" had to tell, and thereby became a sadder, but better-informed girl, poor humans have had great respect of a kind for hissing crawlers. None can say that in that original nudist colony the vocabulary of her who was to be the universal mother may not have been somewhat limited, and that she mistook the vibrating rattle of the pit viper for the dulcet tones she wanted to hear, tempting her to find out what she really wanted to know. Whatever the language, she seemed to understand, and to this day cursing men tread on the head of the snake as a reward for the inestimable benefits he conferred on mankind. Suppose he had kept still. There would have been neither wars nor stratosphere flights, nor even a federal constitution for men to wrangle about, for there would be no men. But he spoke, she listened, and, "Lafayette, we are here."[9]

In nearly all the places where the genus *homo* should be content to make his home, we find the uncles and the cousins of the snake we know the best. They have explored and located everywhere worthwhile. It may be the stylish head of India's hooded cobra. It may be Africa's black mamba, that swift dark streak of poisonous terror, or his brother trimmed in green. The fer-de-lance or his equally deadly brother, the bush-master, may hold the tropical, western hemisphere stage. Some may know that mass of crushing muscle and elastic, which, in violation of the Law of Moses, is satisfied with just one pig for a meal. And how fitting it is that in all the length and breadth of our own United States there should locate the noisiest and most garrulous of them all, the pit viper, whose bony, buzzing extremity has made him to all man the rattlesnake.

He's a sociable cuss, the rattlesnake. When that "race of kings that rose, and reigned, and passed in fifty years," and who were still living on the earth up to 1904, the American cowboy, was in the heyday of royalty in an area "half a world" in western extent, the rattlesnake was often, indeed almost continually, condemned to eternal perdition and the damnation of his soul.[10] A roomy place hell must be to afford even miserly accommodations to the generous consignments made to it in the course of a day, and even in a busy hour, by those roving riders. In those consignments the rattlesnakes were not forgotten.

Still his snakeship seemed to bear no particular grudge and, often in the most neighborly fashion, would establish himself in the bed or boots of the cowboy, whose friendship, even with those gentle advances, was hard to win, and, indeed, was usually denied entirely. Under the door step of a log hut could be heard his vocal tail humming its vibrant song, inviting the high heeled approach that always came, but never in friendship. Someone said he was poisonous, and the cowboy, whose mind ran to other things than science, just took it for granted. Some of them learned to know by bitter experience. If the unlearned, untutored, sunburned cowboy had been dropped into that Garden of long ago he would have chosen Eve and discarded the serpent, thereby proving to the world that he belonged in the class of vigorous and reckless courage.

Nothing long continued is without its measure of romance or of fable, and so it is with his snakeship of the plains, and, let there be no mistake about it, a snake there meant a reptile with a rattle on him. One of the strange friendships cultivated and brought to fruit on the plains is that between the marmot or prairie dog, the little prairie owl, and the rattlesnake. Neither is that friendship completely without its fable. In an earlier day the prairie-dog town might encompass an area as large as a section of civilized land, or maybe more. All over the area of the town could be seen these little land-locked squirrels, each timidly sitting or ranging close to his hole, with each tail nervously twitching as its owner gave his chirping bark. The little prairie owl, whose head has all the appearance of being fastened to his body with a universal joint, stands around on the little mounds, quietly and stupidly watching a visitor. A pleasantry among the cowboys was that the best way to kill a prairie owl was to ride around him and have him twist his head off. The third member of the partnership was the rattlesnake, who lazily sunned himself and disappeared down a prairie-dog hole when disturbed.

The prairie dog must be some distant relative of the squirrel (certainly more closely related to the woodchuck) that got caught in a treeless waste, just as did his roommate the owl. Maybe a geological breathing spell sent them as far below the grass roots as their climbing cousins got above in the branches. The rattlesnake, a ubiquitous American nuisance, missed neither his trees nor their fruits. He was at home in the homes of those who built them, a fearsome moocher whose appetite was regularly satisfied by the young of the prairie dog and the owl. Nature has no court to which an outraged partner can go to effect a dissolution of an oppressive partnership. So the rattlesnake stays on. The partnership was always agreeable to him.[11]

In the winter time the rattlesnake "dens up," or holes up. That means only that they assemble in considerable numbers in favored places and enter into their winter hibernation.[12] There they "ball up," which they do by intertwining themselves into large balls, before they go into that torpor which keeps them from wandering around in the blizzards and getting lost. That is no suggestion that the blizzards are of common occurrence, for they are not, but that they do spread their destructive terror once in a while cannot be denied by the normally truthful enthusiast for South Dakota weather as easily as can the earthquakes by the dyed-in-the-wool Californian. . . .

The Petrified Forest

It was the custom in the range country to keep a very few men on for winter men, and the rest of the cowpunchers were let go until work opened again in the spring. Then, if they were wanted, they would go back with the old outfit, and if they were not wanted they went to work for someone else. During the winter some of them tended bar, some loafed, some gambled, some rode "grub line," and others roamed away. The winter men were usually those who could be counted on to give a fair account of themselves when the going was not so good, and the work harder, or at least more lonesome. Besides they had to be of the class that was willing to do anything that the circumstances called for in the way of work and not quit.

One fall Fred Jones and I were the only ones kept on as winter men, and about the first thing we had to do was to build a number of dams in the gumbo soil of the Missouri River brakes. Fred was about my size, but a bit slimmer. He was a tireless dynamo for work, and many a tired night I saw an example of the vigor of "Rawhide," as some of the fellows called him. While we were in the pink of physical perfection so far as miles and hours of horseback riding mattered, we set a new list of muscles in motion when we were plowing and scraping in the terrible gumbo. The result was two aching bodies, and a couple of cranky young men who were in no mood to be kidded, either by the other. Being well acquainted by experience with the affect of such things, each maintained a respectful attitude to the other.

It never occurred to either of us to take it a bit easy until we got used to the work, for that was not the cowboy's way of going about things. His work was done in a mad fury until it was done, or as long as it was light enough to see. Then when there was nothing to do he rested with lethargy supreme. Such was the condition of our minds and bodies one day as we quit our work at dark to go back to the little shack we called home where we cooked our meals, and slept on the hard, cold floor in a roundup bed. In the dark of the morning we had hitched our four horses to a wagon, which had a triple box on it, for no good reason at all, and a spring seat on top of that. By daylight we were hitched to our plow, and when we had enough plowed up to justify we unhitched the four horses from the plow, and each hooked to a scraper, or slip, with a team. That performance was repeated all day. When plowing we took turns holding the plow and driving the four horses.

On this particular day we happened to plow up a lot of petrified wood in the gumbo. When we quit and started home, both of us perched on the high spring seat, with Fred driving, he remarked, "Say, we sure ran into a lot of petrified wood today."

I answered, "We sure did." I then remembered having heard some fellow on the range tell about a petrified forest in Arizona and, in a moment of recklessness, asked, "Did you see in the last Sunday paper about the big petrified forest they have discovered down in Arizona?"

Although Fred should have known, and did know if he had only stopped to think, that I had not seen a Sunday paper, nor any other, for six months, he answered, "No."

Although I knew better than to kid a tired and cranky man, I said,

"Yes, they found one down there where the trees, sections in extent, are all petrified, solid stone."

An interested, "Is that so?" from Fred gave impetus to my story.

There seemed to be no proper place to call the end, so I said, "Yes, sir, and all the branches are standing out, solid stone, just as they were when they were growing." Encouraged by a profane comment of interest from Fred, I turned my imagination loose, and said, "Even the little twigs on the branches appeared just as they did when the wind blew them about, and the bark, now in stone, was perfect." Greater interest, evidenced by more lurid language from Fred, called for more details of the great discovery, so I said, "Yes, that's a fact, and even the leaves were on the branches and twigs looking just as they did when the sap was running in them, and you can see the veins in the leaves just as plain as the day when they were alive."

I would like to have stopped about there in the interests of personal safety, but Fred's ever increasing interest and strength of language was too encouraging. I said, "They even found a lot of petrified birds in the trees."

Fred said, "Petrified birds?"

I said, "Yes, and every one of them was singing a petrified song."

Quicker than it takes to tell, Fred's adrenal glands, or whatever it takes to make men active and angry, pumped him full, he threw the lines into the bottom of the wagon, jumped off our high seat to the ground, and said, with no diminution in interest, "You Scotch _____ _____. Get down and I'll kick _____ _____ _____ _____ _____ out of you."

On the range you should smile when you called someone that, but Fred did not. Feeling too tired to get off and having no desire for any more exercise that day, I smiled for him, but did not accept his warm invitation. After extending his invitation in every variation of the only two languages he knew, English and profane, but no takers, Fred finally climbed back to the seat with threats of annihilation in the event of a repetition of any such nonsense. He lapsed into silence for the rest of the night.

Years passed, and I went to law school and got admitted to the bar. Fred became a bartender and finally owned his own saloon in Midland, one of the many towns brought to life by the building of railroad lines across the width of the cow country. The Democratic party in the county (old Stanley County, which is now Stanley, Haakon, and Jackson counties) was to hold its county convention at Midland. A lot of us went up from Fort Pierre on the afternoon train. On arriving at Midland, I suggested that we all go over to see my old friend, Fred Jones. Democrats being what they were in those days, we all went over to Fred's. I happened to be the first one in the door, and by good luck Fred himself was on shift tending bar. As I said, "Hello, Fred," he just looked in wonder at the Fort Pierre gang trooping into his place. Then he turned to me and brought up a subject that had never been mentioned except at the time of its original telling.

He said, "I am going to set 'em up for the crowd, but not a word about those _____ _____ birds." Fred set 'em up, and then I told the story, after which business became greatly enlivened in Fred's place.

A Trip to Mexico[13]

During the winter of 1906–1907 in that typical western cow town on the west bank of the Missouri River, Fort Pierre, no end of excitement was generated among the sporting fraternity. Bob Yokum, a former Texan who had been transplanted in South Dakota and who operated saloons in Pierre and Fort Pierre, seemed to be the motivating impulse. His nephew, Billie Harrell, also a Texan who worked for Bob, added to the ferment. Both of them were well acquainted with Tom Powers and Billie Amonett, who were the famous proprietors of the still more famous Coney Island saloon in El Paso, Texas. Also, they were still more acquainted with Felix Robert, himself a matador, who managed the bull ring at Juarez on the south side of the Rio Grande, across from El Paso. Some years before there had been enclosed on the Scotty Philip ranch up the Missouri River from Fort Pierre, under an unusually strong fence surrounding thousands of acres, a herd of native American buffalo. These buffalo, or bison, were about as nearly in their natural state as the presence of any kind of fence anywhere would permit one to imagine.[14]

As local pride always plays an important part in formulating local views, the people of Fort Pierre had come to believe that a self-sufficient buffalo bull could whip any animal that would care to match up with him. But local pride was not indigenous to Fort Pierre alone. It likewise flourished in Juarez, the city whose namesake was the full-blood Indian lawyer who was president of Mexico both before and after Maximilian's unfortunate aspirations to royalty.[15] Those southern neighbors could not believe that the fighting bulls, whose aggressive fierceness they saw exhibited in the bull ring at Juarez each succeeding Sunday, could be conquered by anything but the tinsel-bedecked man with the sword. It was a natural enough development of the argument as to the fighting merits of the native buffalo and the Mexican fighting bull in the frontier town of Fort Pierre, where "I'll bet you" was then no idle phrase, that efforts should be made to end the discussion by a definite test that would decide the bets. Thus it came about that all the arrangements were decided upon to take two of the buffalo bulls from the Scotty Philip herd by rail to Juarez to test their fitness to survive against the bulls of Mexico's choice.

Although the Mexicans may have been able to make their choice of animals for the contest, it was a vastly more difficult task for the northern cowboys to choose their champions. After herculean efforts, such as men of the open range alone know how to make, two buffalo bulls, one about eight years old and the other about four, were corralled, crated and hauled on sleds over the snow to Fort Pierre and then across the Missouri River on the ice to the stockyards at Pierre, which was then the railroad terminus for the cow country. There a box car was fortified and prepared to convey the heroes of Fort Pierre's hopes to the chosen battleground in Mexico. And let not the fact that the box car was fortified and prepared for their captivity be too lightly considered, for the hind legs of a buffalo can teach tricks in kicking to an army mule that before then were beyond the frontiers of his dreams. The extra heavy planking on the interior, sides, and ends of the box cars was no idle gesture, as each end of the car was equipped to house a monarch of the plains, barred off with heavy planking in such fashion that the full width between the side doors was left free to furnish space for the baled hay, and equipment for watering to furnish food and drink for the buffaloes on the long railroad trek from South Dakota's snows to Mexico's sunshine.

And now arose the question as to what manner of men should accompany them. At first it was intended that the men to go were Scotty Philip, who had devoted much time, effort and money to save the bison from extinction; Bob Yokum whose efforts materialized the sporting event; and Eb Jones, a cowman then about forty, who had spent his entire life on the range, and whose activities in the cattle game had not always escaped question.[16] Scotty, who was not devoid of the instincts of a race which invented golf and gave it to the rest of the world so that it would not attend to business, decided that his buffalo bulls were worth three hundred dollars each, and the venture was divided one half to Bob Yokum and one fourth each to Eb Jones and Scotty. As the time for departure arrived a serious blizzard broke, and Scotty decided that his extensive cattle interests demanded his presence at home. His nephew George, who had previously been a rider on the range but who had graduated from the law school of the University of Michigan at Ann Arbor the preceding June and was then engaged in the more or less hazardous occupation of starting a law practice at Fort Pierre, was not so busy that he could not accept Scotty's proposal to take his interest in the venture off his hands, so he became the third adventurer.

As the freight train pulled out of Pierre, South Dakota, on that day in January 1907 in one of those blizzards that are meteorological milestones in that state, the warmth of the stove in the caboose was shared by the trainmen with Bob Yokum, Eb Jones, and George Philip. . . . They thought no farther into the future than the Sunday just a week ahead as they contemplated the contest then to take place in the bullring at Juarez. As with the man who had gone to a distant city and there became unfortunately involved in a poker game, and who could not sleep any of the way home because of the unending monotony with which the car wheels and the rail joints clattered out their reminding song of "jacks and sixes, jacks and sixes," so these men suffered the monotony of the present, tinctured and enlivened by the exciting hopes of next week.

At Sioux City, Iowa, the buffaloes were fed and watered in their well-planked private compartments while waiting for the train to Omaha. The lively curious came in numbers to see real buffaloes that weighed each a ton. They came, looking skeptical of the story which had brought them there, and as they turned to leave, each seemed to echo the sentiments of the intoxicated gentleman who looked long and earnestly at a beautiful salmon displayed on ice in the window of a sporting goods store and, as he turned away with drunken solemnity, muttered, "Well, the fellow who caught that fish is a damn liar."

But the railroad trip was not all monotony. Nothing is. Bob Yokum decided at Sioux City that he should speed on to El Paso and Juarez, there to make the necessary arrangements for crossing the international boundary with buffaloes, and to do whatever else was required to make success easier. Never having been there before, his two companions did not until afterwards suspect that perhaps the hospitable splendor of the Coney Island saloon, and the splendid hospitality of Tom Powers and Billy Amonett, as compared with the rugged individualism of a freight caboose, may have played no small part in Bob's decision. Be that as it may, Bob rode the cushions from there to El Paso.

With storms and Sioux City left behind, the next objective was Omaha, and on arrival in the railroad yards of that city at two o'clock in the morning, the two remaining buffalo attendants sought some rest at a hotel in the brief time between then and 6:30 in the morning, at which hour they were to leave Omaha on a Rock Island freight train. Perhaps to show them that clouds are not clouds clear through, when the train was all ready to leave, the buffalo car was not in the train, and could not be located. Fretting at the delay, and engaging in the national pastime of cursing the railroad octopus, they joined in the almost frantic search for the car, with the result that it was located on a sidetrack about ten miles out, where it had been left by another train crew which had discovered its mistake.

Joining up with the next freight train out, the car was picked up and made a part of the train. Having their buffaloes once more safely in hand served as a signal for rest, and down they laid on the none too downy cushions of a Rock Island caboose. After moving along for sometime and some miles, they were awakened by a trainman who said, "Say, would you fellers like to see the caboose you should have left Omaha in this morning? If you do, look out on the left side of the train when we get to the next curve!" Having nothing else that required much doing at that time, they followed the trainman's instructions, and there in the right of way, smashed to kindling, lay the caboose, the victim of a rear-end collision. That made it a little easier to become philosophical over the delay.

The rail ribbon unwound its miles until arrival at McPherson, Kansas, then a place of much railroad and few people. A thirty-six hour delay, to this day unexplained, at that railroad crossing drove out most of their philosophy. A pool hall offered the only form of entertainment, but as neither of them had even a semblance of skill with the cue, the pool hall man reaped little profit, for it seemed that they could play for hours on a ten-cent game of rotation pool. Time moved on, but seemed to get nowhere. Trains passing through did not pick up the buffalo car. It should not be forgotten that Kansas was then away from the days of Wyatt Earp, Bob Masterson, and Wild Bill and was exhibiting another form of complex, which we may well enough call Carrienationitis, and that state was as dry as a dehydrated bugle blast. As time went on the younger of the amateur pool players more and more suspected that somewhere in that area of constitutional and statutory aridity there was beer. Prompted more by curiosity than by appetite (for Bob's emporiums at Pierre and Fort Pierre had furnished all their grips with plenty of bottled in bond, which was still in the original packages), the suspicion developed into a search.[17]

"Seek and ye shall find," is merely an older version of the maxim that "Equity aids the vigilant." The younger man happened to be wearing at the time a watch charm in the form of a double-headed eagle, and the pool hall men mistook it for the emblem of the Fraternal Order of Eagles, then a very popular secret order among the sporting fraternity. Although neither belonged to the order of the other, a few mysterious passes were indulged, and the pool hall man became convinced that he and his visitor were tied together in an oath-bound brotherhood. He probably thinks so yet. When fraternity was definitely established to the satisfaction of the Kansan, and he had told in graphic detail about a state meeting of the order held at Lawrence the preceding Wednesday where potables were in quantity, the South Dakotan ventured a question as to whether the town of McPherson was as dry as the statutes which governed it. A mysterious look toward the elder man, who was still at the pool table more or less vainly trying to get the balls in the pockets, and a whispered, "Who is that other fellow?" seemed to establish a prima facie case that beer was obtainable. On being assured that, although he did not belong to the brotherhood, the older man was absolutely in accord with some of its principles and entitled to trust otherwise, an invitation was extended to follow him. A faithful and fruitful leader he turned out to be, for in that part of his domain where they came to rest were cases of beer stacked to the ceiling. Beer, real beer, in quantity and in Kansas. Once more philosophy reigned in the bosoms of the buffalo men.

But as all good things must come to an end, so this pleasant association was terminated by a train that came along and picked up the buffalo car. On and on they bumped to and through Liberal and into the flattest part of the earth's surface toward Dalhart, Texas. Here occurred an adventure, born of ignorance and folly, that did not end disastrously. In that stretch, as elsewhere along the way, the presence of the buffaloes on the train excited no end of curiosity, and every stop produced its crop of visitors. As proof of the eternal fact that the world is none too large for those who genuinely seek to become acquainted, the conductor informed his two passengers that he had seen a very large herd of buffalo during a visit he had made to see his brother-in-law in South Dakota during the proceeding summer. Well, who was the brother-in-law? Walter Roush of Fort Pierre. Sure, everybody knew him, and thus were established the bonds of mutual acquaintanceship. This reminded the South Dakotans of what they had in their grips, and although the conductor refused to mingle sociability with professional service, the others did not seem so particular.

At a point where some switching was being done, while Eb lay asleep in the caboose, the younger man got out to stretch his legs. The engineer, whose great physical person fitted well with the size of the monstrous engine he was driving, motioned his fellow traveler and asked him if he had ever ridden on a locomotive. The negative answer seemed to provoke the further question whether he would like to do so. The enthusiastic affirmative showed that here was considered to be an end to, or at least a break in, the monotony, for as the darky porter said, "railroad ride across the plains can be most montonious."

Before there was time to crawl up on the engine, the inviting host said, "It looks like you fellows are pretty stingy."

"How's that?"

"You've got some liquor back there. It looks like you'd give the engineer a nip."

"Sure."

Then came the hurried trip back to the caboose, and the return with a bottle of whiskey. There was a simultaneous pulling out of the train and the cork. That engineer seemed to have an excessive thirst and gave evidence of his belief that an individual quart was required to allay it. The spirits of the engineer went up as those in the bottle went down. He got his young friend over from the fireman's side to sit with him, there to receive instructions on the mechanics and operation of a locomotive engine and to listen to vile songs sung to the accompaniment of the toot-toot-toot of the whistle.

This highly instructive and entertaining program was suddenly interrupted by the appearance of the conductor running furiously forward on the top of the train, over the coal in the tender, and into the engine. An immediate and forceful argument occurred between the Goliath at the throttle and the David from the caboose. When David tried forcibly to take the throttle away from Goliath, he landed sitting in the coal. About this time South Dakota's somewhat perturbed and conscience-stricken representative concluded that this must be a private discussion between the inner family members of the Rock Island, and he withdrew as a matter of courtesy and tact to the fireman's side. Each time the conductor was knocked away from the throttle that enthusiastic engineer "gave her another notch" for the good of the service. A look through the fireman's window gave the northerner an idea of what the fuss was all about, for there in the far distance, squarely between the rails, rose a stream of smoke, and that engineer seemed to be able to do everything with his engine except to stop it. Places intended as stops seemed to flit by in a fog, a real case of "that is a pretty little town, wasn't it?"

The visitor in the fireman's seat then looked back to see what, if any, emotions were being kindled along the train. There, on the lowest step of the engine, hung the fireman, ready to jump. Halfway back along the train hung a brakeman in an unusual state of expectancy, while on the lowest step of the caboose was the other brakeman, apparently feeling about the same. These visions of flight inspired no phenomenal enthusiasm in the mind of him who was taking his first ride on an engine. An engineer and conductor still fighting for the throttle of a runaway engine that now seemed as intoxicated as its master, a long heavy train behind with the crew ready to go, Eb asleep in the caboose, the guest on the engine imprisoned on a monstrous thing from which he could scarcely escape when in repose, and not at all when in motion, and the Golden State Limited in front, combined into a situation that caused him to close his eyes and wish himself back in South Dakota.

It was not a situation calculated to evoke any worthwhile enthusiasm at the moment. Fortunately the engineer on the Golden State Limited had had no such purveyors of immodest courage visit him, and his discretion put him and his train on a side track, not the first occasion of a train giving buffaloes the right of way. The yell of profane defiance from the engineer of the freight train as it swished past the crack passenger train in repose on the sidetrack foretold a visit to the carpet and perhaps back to the farm. But the taming influence of hunger came into play, and the strong man of the rails bowed before it and stopped at a town that had a restaurant to suit him. As the South Dakotan crawled down from his post of complexity, he was heard to mutter, "Well, thank God, I can tell I have had a ride on an engine." To give away, to be generous, may be an admirable qualification, but it is not without its limits. Succeeding incidents were so insignificant in comparison with the engine ride (and there was but one such) that nothing more happened until they drifted into El Paso in the very early hours of Sunday.

As a fight had been scheduled and advertised for the afternoon of that day, reasonably prompt contact was made with Bob Yokum and Charley Burney, the El Paso superintendent of the Mexican Central Railroad. That contact established the fact that no arrangements had been made to get the buffalo car over the border, nor had authority been received from the customs officials, who seemed to swallow hard on the law of the case. That required a trip to the customs authorities where it was necessary strongly to assert and plausibly maintain that to take a pair of buffaloes over the line and then bring them back should mean little in the young life of a young officer of the customs. Whether the theory was sound, or whether the officer wanted to see the fight, has never been entirely clear. At any rate, such was the decision, and no appeal was taken, so it became final.

With the legal handicaps smoothed out, the remaining thing to be done was to arrange for the physical transportation of the car across the Rio Grande from El Paso to Juarez, from the United States into Mexico. In Juarez the first contact of consequence was with the yardmaster, but with such English as was at their command, and no Spanish at all, the men from the North could not make themselves understood. From man to man, up the ladder of officialdom, until the Lord High Commissioner, or whatever he is in Juarez, was reached. A handsome man, wonderfully groomed, he could neither understand nor speak English. An angry fist landed on his desk, and a demand followed for some one who could talk United States. The Spaniard's eye lit up when he observed a ring, and with a smile he said, "Where do you belong to the Consistory, brother?"[18]

The answer came, "At Yankton, South Dakota, but what the Hell has that got to do with getting a couple of buffaloes across the line?"

He seemed to think it had something to do with it, and he introduced himself to the three South Dakotans. He pushed a desk bell, and the underling who answered was told to have Monte come in. Almost immediately Monte, the yardmaster, was in and seemed to have had an amazing education in English in the intervening few minutes. The introductions with Monte completed, he showed his South Dakota brother his Scottish rite ring from which he had lost the diamond that morning in the yards. A few hasty commiserations expressed, and Monte, with his new friends, mounted an engine, with a thoroughly sober engineer, scurried over to El Paso, and in almost nothing flat the buffalo car was spotted at the unloading chute to the bullring. Felix Robert and a host of toreadors of varying ranks were promptly on hand to inspect the new aspirants for butchery in the bullring.

Shortly succeeding the noonday meal came the crowd to the arena to witness a scene similar to that so graphically and forcefully described by Ernest Hemmingway twenty-five years later in his novel *Death in the Afternoon* [1932]. A motley crew was the audience that filed in through the amphitheater of that arena. Mexicans, from princedom to peonage, mingled with the residents from across the river and tourists galore, for that afternoon there were to be four regular bulls, and then a Mexican fighting bull was to compete for honors with a peace-loving buffalo. The South Dakotans and the manager of the bullring were to divide the gate receipts equally, half to the Mexicans and half to Gringos.

To the South Dakotans, except Bob Yokum, the business of bull fighting was something read about, but never before witnessed. A bloody, cruel sport it was considered to be. Nothing was known of the technique of the game, nor of the efforts that had been made through generations of participation in it by enthusiastic devotees to make it an equal contest, or nearly so, between man and beast. The rules are modeled on the habits of the bull, and haphazard or easy killing is not permitted. The man knows the rules and must not violate them, but there are no such restrictions on the bull. Although it may not be a sport suited to the Anglo-Saxon turn of mind, it presents a romantic and thrilling spectacle, from which brutality has been largely removed except in relation to the horses. The president of the bullfight, usually some high official honored for the day, occupies the presidential box with his guests. Then comes the parade in the bullring, with the *matadors*, the men who kill, leading, followed by their *banderilleros* and then their *picadors* in the order of seniority, all decked out in the tinseled trappings of the bullring, which looks gorgeous and romantic at a distance. After the parade is over and salutes are given to and acknowledged by the president, the cavalcade disperses to seemingly appointed places about the ring.

Then the first bull, chosen by lot, is admitted to the ring. After he enters the arched gateway leading from the corrals to the ring, his first experience is to have a small barbed dart, with a small bright flag, stuck into his withers. Being about in the same relation to the usual run of cattle that the wolf is to the dog, the fighting bull seems none too pleased over this initial affront to his dignity. The angered animal is skillfully led to conduct his offense against a picador, a bullfighter mounted on a crow-bait pony, his right leg, which is the one he must keep toward the bull, encased in armor, and armed with a long lance, called a *pic*. With the pic he is expected to withstand the charging attacks of the bull and keep him away from the horse. He rarely succeeds in doing so throughout, and quite usually the horse is fearfully gored and sometimes thrown, a jumbled mass of bull and horse and picador.

Then comes in the skilful work with the capes to get the bull away from the unhorsed picador, nearly always successful. When the rules relating to attacks on the picador have been complied with, the banderilleros come into play. They must first play the bull with the capes then place the *banderillos*, varicolored, gorgeously wrapped wooden shafts about three feet in length with heavily barbed points. They are placed two at a time in the withers, or shoulder tops, of the charging bull by the banderillero who stands squarely in front of him. It is no place for a timid, a cross-eyed, or a club-footed man. Three sets of banderillos are placed in the bull, and by this time he is mad enough to make the acquaintance of the matador, who takes charge at this stage.

After working the bull with the cape, and so close that it seems impossible to escape those dreadful horns, the matador places his bull and gets his sword. Then, with the *muleta*, a small triangular flag on a stick, he plays the bull into a required number of charges, after which, with the bull charging directly at him, and not otherwise, he delivers the thrust. If successful, the bull collapses in his tracks, instantly dead. Up to that moment he has had no right to hurt the bull, although the bull has had full opportunity to do any manner of harm within his power to his annoyers, and no one can justly question the enthusiasm with which he sets out to do that harm. If the bull is unsuccessful he is scientifically and almost painlessly killed. If the bull is successful, a picador, a banderillero, or a matador goes to the hospital or the morgue. Although the game is to kill the bull skillfully and strictly within the rules, it is anything but a one-sided game. On the Sunday in question four bullfights were held, one closely following the other. The temperamental crowd would cheer for the bull or for the man, depending altogether on which seemed to be the winner at the moment. With varying fortunes, some minor injuries to men and serious ones to horses, those four bulls met death in the afternoon in the Juarez bullring.

About then the crowd began shouting its skepticism about the appearance of the northern contestant, when, lo, and behold, who should come in under the arched gateway from the corrals but the larger buffalo bull, the eight year old. The unusual applause evidenced the surprise at the unusual spectacle. Scarcely had he entered the ring when the men who brought him noticed that in his left hind leg the fetlock joint was dislocated, done perhaps when kicking in the boxcar. He walked out and stood peacefully about in the middle of the ring. Just about then a handsome, red Mexican fighting bull was ushered in through the gate. Full of whatever it is that makes things want to fight, he surveyed the bullring, and there saw the buffalo standing three-quartering away from him. It was plain that the buffalo, for no reason at all, incurred his immediate displeasure, and he made a charge calculated to annihilate this object of his wrath.

Something should here be made known that was then within the knowledge of the men who had handled both buffaloes and cattle but was not suspected by the Mexicans, or at least by the Mexican bulls. When a domestic or a fighting bull has occasion to pivot, he pivots on his powerful hind legs. When a bison, whose great weight is distributed over his front legs, is pivoting in fight, he does it on his front legs, swinging his lighter hindquarters away. As this bull charged the buffalo, which continued three-quartering away from him, it seemed certain to the Mexicans, and apparently to the bull, that in an instant the buffalo would be fearfully, if not fatally, gored in the flank. But the buffalo is fitted by nature for survival, and almost at the instant of contact, those hindquarters mysteriously swung away, and his frowsy head met that of the bull full on. As he backed away, it was plain that the bull was a skeptic and that he believed the first blow was a pure accident. His blood told him that he was one of Mexico's choicest bulls. He backed away to the right distance and angle, about the same angle as before, and charged again. This assault was the same as before and with similar consequences, except that this time the buffalo put a little more steam into his punch and knocked his red majesty back on his haunches.

The courageous heart of the bull left him still unconvinced, and, after some little delay, he got himself in position to deliver the charge that would settle the fray. A third time he charged, and with still worse luck. Backing away he surveyed his enemy and seemed to regard him as a foeman more than worthy of his steel. Admiration seemed to be written all over the face of the bull, and yet the will to conquer would not down. He had been the aggressor throughout, and the buffalo had waged only defensive war. Of course, in all justice it should be remembered that the buffalo had been suddenly transported from a cold to a warm climate, he was in entirely strange surroundings, he had ridden cooped up in one end of a boxcar for seven straight days, and he had a dislocated fetlock. If Jack Dempsey had been similarly handled before he went up against the wild bull of the Pampas, a different championship story might have been written.[19] The bull decided to make one more try for glory, and he again maneuvered himself into position to gore that tantalizing flank. The charge was met this time by a greater show of buffalo force, and the bull went down under the impact. That seemed to terrorize him, and the poor creature actually tried to climb out of the ring.

Realizing that which his joint adventurers from the Northwest did not know, that an advertisement in Mexico was a contract with the public, Felix Robert requested the right to turn in another bull with the buffalo. This was immediately granted, and promptly another Mexican bull made his angry entrance through the gateway to the bullring from the pens. A quick look about and he seemed imbued with peeve against the shaggy monster standing strangely three-quartering away from him. His decision was quickly made to gore that flank, and with a confidence born of careful breeding, he proceeded without delay to execute his resolve. By some legerdemain which that bull likely never did understand, a monstrous, well-protected and well-armed head was suddenly substituted for the flank he had in mind. Three runs that bull made, and then, like his red companion of the first encounter, he sought refuge in flight. From then on no coaxing born of bullfighting skill could get him to charge man or beast.

Negotiations were quickly completed for the right to turn in a third fighting bull, and his experience was an exact duplicate of that of the second bull. Three panicky bulls were now careening around the ring with the bullfighters exercising all the wiles of their game to get them to put up some semblance of a fight, but to no avail. About then the buffalo seemed to lose all interest in the show and lay down in the ring with the idea of making himself comfortable. That seemed to arouse the enthusiasm of the crowd, and they lustily cheered the buffalo, which was now nonchalantly resting.

Felix Robert, still fearful of an adverse order from the president of the fight, came running up to his friends from Dakota, and said, "Now I know this isn't very sporty, but the bulls have disappointed me, and I would like to have you agree that I may turn in one more."

One of the northerners said, "Turn in all the damn bulls you wish, just so you give that buffalo room to turn around."

The fourth bull was turned in, and he, with no lack of courage at the beginning, charged as did his predecessors, and did it three successive times. By this time, apparently in resentment at the interruption to his nap, the buffalo undertook to carry the fight to the now thoroughly frightened bulls, but his injured hind leg prevented the display of speed required, and he was unable to catch his opponents in the race, for such it now was. Soon the gate to the pens was opened, and almost magical was the disappearance of the bulls through it and to safety. Shortly the buffalo, too, betook himself to the recesses beyond the gate. So ended the first formal contest between bull and buffalo.

Then there was turned into the ring a bull with brass knobs fastened on the ends of his horns to prevent goring, and a small sack of money tied on his head with a string around the base of his horns. It seemed as though all the children south of the Rio Grande piled into that ring after the little sack of money. Many were tossed but none seemed badly injured, and eventually one small chap got caught on the horns, and before the bull had time to toss him, he had disengaged the sack. And the afternoon's performance was over as the shadows of evening fell across the bullring and the crowd filed out.

A week's stay was then required because on the next Sunday it was planned to have another affair, which was expected to net greater financial returns than the first. The proceeds from the first fight were enough to pay for the buffaloes and all the expenses of the trip, fortunately. El Paso, Texas, formerly famous for gun men of the John Wesley Hardin type,[20] was sufficiently interesting in itself to justify a week's visit even if one were to discount the equally interesting Mexican city across the Rio Grande. Juarez, with its cock fights, its gambling halls, and other forms of stormy amusement correctly calculated to draw the money from the folks away from home, was not a place in which time was expected to hang too heavy. One of the places of interest was the jail of the city, built in the sixteenth century by the Spaniards, with its tremendous walls of solid stone masonry and its company of armed soldiers standing guard, and the observer would never be led to believe that a wooden pistol would be a sufficient vehicle of escape.

The hordes of bullfighters were a unique group of loafers six days in the week and active showmen on Sunday. Well-armed Mexican *rurales*, or mounted police, with their turnip-horned saddles, looking like men who would be greatly amused to see a bullet-riddled man fall, added a touch of romance to an already wholly romantic picture. Here and there, too, would be pointed out the American who could not go home. At least one of the northerners, perhaps in a spirit of caution, made a genuine, friendly acquaintance with United States Consul Edwards, who hailed from Lead, South Dakota, and who seemed especially pleased at the chance to see folks from home.[21] Anyway, it is not always a poor idea to have friendly connections with those in authority.

On the El Paso side of the river were many unusual personages to be met, especially if one were not too unwilling to mingle with the guests at the Coney Island and Gem saloons. In the Coney Island, a place famed in the annals of the Southwest and operated by his two good friends Tom Powers and Billy Amonett, the famous Pat Garrett, then collector of the port of El Paso by appointment from Theodore Roosevelt, was not an infrequent visitor. Garrett, with his gunfighting friend Tobe Driskill and other cowboys on the rampage in Dodge City when it was the end of the trail [1878], had been cowed into submission and arrested before the cold gray eyes and effective pistol of Wyatt Earp. At a later time [1881], as a New Mexico sheriff, Garrett had also been the law's instrument of death for the notorious Billy the Kid. In 1907, no one suspected that Pat Garrett would meet his death in the next calendar year at the point of an opposing pistol and that his funeral sermon should consist of Robert Ingersoll's speech at the grave of his brother, read by his friend Tom Powers. Interesting places and people they were and no mistake.[22]

But to pierce the veil of the future into the next calendar year seems to be little if any more difficult than to see clearly to next Sunday, and so it was in this instance. The first fight, as carried out according to schedule and advertisement, was to have four regular bullfights and then a fight between the buffalo and a bull. For the next Sunday the program was for four bullfights, and then the younger buffalo bull would be fought by the men in regular bullfighting procedure. A lot of badinage and bluffing was carried on as to the relative merits of bulls and man and buffaloes. El Cuco, who seemed to be the Babe Ruth of the Juarez bullring, was the man given the doubtful post of honor as matador, and his was the job to administer the fatal thrust to the buffalo bull. A highly popular man, a jovial companion, and a courageous fellow, he knew by heart everything that a bull could be expected to do in the ring, and it never occurred to him that a buffalo might not consider himself bound by the rules governing the ring conduct of mere bulls.

A bull charges straight, while a buffalo is likely to go into battle feinting and jabbing with those dangerous horns of his after the manner of a skillful boxer. While a bull pivots on his hind feet, the buffalo makes his swing on his front feet. A bull does not kick, while a buffalo seems to delight in damage done by those outstandingly capable hind feet. Moreover, the thin skin that protects the spinal cord and vital organs of the bull is not the character of the buffalo's protection, which nature has designed for the survival of the buffalo. One should not be led into the thoughtless error that the hump on the buffalo is caused by curvature of the spine, for indeed his spine is just as straight as that of any bull, beef or fighting. The upper prongs of the vertebrae are elongated to about a foot at the height of the hump, filled in with muscle or steak, and hence the preference for that part of the animal by those who in earlier days used him for meat. Over that part of him nature has placed on the full-grown animal a tough hide about an inch or more in thickness. Over that thickness of skin is placed an almost impervious blanket of matted, curly, woolen hair, six inches or more through. Still more, the great height of the buffalo makes him a far better target for the heavy rifle of the expert hunter than for the slender sword of the matador.

All through the discussion of the probabilities of the next Sunday, El Cuco had all the coolness of complete confidence of a brave and skillful man. His confidence was communicated to his friend, Felix Robert, who in the warmth of discussion said, "I'll bet you $500.00 Cuco kills your buffalo."

Bob Yokum, who was a sport if he was anything, retorted, "Hell, I'll give you a better bet than that. I'll bet you $500.00 the buffalo kills Cuco." So the bet was laid, but the mystery was never solved, nor the bet paid.

At last the long awaited Sunday came, and with it a paying crowd that filled the great arena to capacity to witness a bullfight presided over by the Governor of Chihuahua as president of the fight. Then came the fiasco. After the cavalcade had made its pretentious entrance, the salutes were given and acknowledged, the first bull was let into the arena, and what should he be but the beautiful, red fighting bull that had first fought the buffalo on the preceding Sunday. No amount of coaxing could get him to believe that his adversary of the week before was not somewhere in that ring. Without regard to men or horses, capes or pics, he persisted only in his search for the most accessible spot to climb the walls. Said to be one of the best specimens of the fighting bull ever exhibited in the Juarez bullring, he had left only the instinct and desire for escape. He was finally run back through the chute into the pens, and another bull was let in to take his place.

Then followed an experience said to have been unparalleled in the annals of the bullring. Three other bulls were successively let in, and each in his turn refused to fight and could not be prevailed upon to charge horse or cape. It must be remembered that the advertising had said four bullfights. At this point, Felix Robert, realizing that the fight was going flat, went running to the ringside seats of the three Dakotans and said, "I don't know what I am going to do. My bulls won't fight, and I never saw anything like this before."

Not realizing the dire financial possibilities, one of the Dakotans said, "Don't blame us if your bulls won't fight."

"But," said Felix, "the President will call off the fight and make us return the money."

That presented a more dismal prospect than some of the Dakotans could enjoy, and one said, "Well, what do you propose to do about it?"

"We'll turn in the buffalo and see if he will fight," said Felix.

The Dakotan answered, "Just have one of your men stick a sword or one of those pics in the buffalo, and by God, he'll fight."

Amid the hubbub of disgruntlement from the crowd, the younger buffalo was admitted to the ring, and he came in just looking for trouble. A few skillful and careful passes were made at him with the capes, and he seemed to discard all his passive good humor. At this time a tremendous uproar came from the crowd, and all eyes seemed glued on the president's box. A blackboard with a lot of writing in chalk on it, none of which meant anything to the three northerners, hung in front of the box.

Felix Robert said, "They have called off the fight and ordered the money refunded. I'll go and see what I can do." He hurried to the president's box, where he seemed to be discussing the matter with agitated eloquence, but to no avail.

Down in the ring was the courageous Cuco, with a banderillo in each hand, petitioning the president that if he would not let him fight the buffalo at least to let him plant the two banderillos in him. Much less privilege than that would please most folks acquainted with buffaloes. The president's answer was that, unless Felix Robert would quit talking to him and Cuco get out of the ring, in addition to ordering the money refunded he would fine each of them five hundred dollars and suspend Cuco as a bullfighter. There a buffalo was spoiling for a fight, and Cuco aching to fight him. But the president was adamant, and the crowd filed out of the amphitheater, each receiving back his entrance money, aggregating thousands of dollars. It was a stormy, angry scene, and the mystery remains: could Cuco kill the buffalo, or would something permanent happen to Cuco?

Three disappointed Dakotans crossed the international bridge to receive the stimulating sympathy of their friends in the Coney Island. Early the next morning a deal was made with an El Paso butcher, or maybe it was made that night, to buy the two buffaloes at $200.00 each and hang them up in his shop as an advertising stunt. Over to Juarez went the four of them to get the buffaloes for the butcher and found Felix in a corner saloon in none too good humor. When they got to the little abode that Felix Robert used for his office, with several impressive appearing rurales strategically placed, the Dakotans heard the amazing news that Felix did not intend to give up the buffaloes. They were to be his from then on. The fact that Bob Yokum had been suspected of making eyes, or something, at the beautiful Mexican wife of a matador did not seem to lend any peaceful atmosphere to the negotiations, so he had to be completely eliminated from the discussion.

Expressed reluctance to the loss of their buffaloes seemed to make matters no better, and the two remaining negotiators were startled to hear Robert say, "Well, I lost $1500.00 in expenses on yesterday's fight. I am going to sue you fellows for that amount, and I am going to put you in jail until I get ready to sue you."

One look at the savage six shooters of the rurales lent conviction to his argument and made calm thinking a virtue. One could probably escape any evil effects of the six shooters by marching peacefully to that terrible fortress used there as a jail. But then, when would Felix Robert get ready to sue them? That was an impressive question in a country like Mexico, where time seemed of little moment, and where the Anglo-Saxon right of *habeas corpus* had no place. The only silver lining to the terrible cloud cast by the thought of that jail was the man from Lead, American Consul Edwards, who could be used if necessary. Acting on the Presbyterian belief that a soft answer turneth away wrath, the negotiators expressed no end of sympathy with the manager of the bullring at the loss sustained and the sorrow, to which all were party, caused by the refunding of the money. The deal proceeded to the final compromise of Robert taking his pick of the buffalo and the butcher taking the other. The older buffalo was selected by Robert, and the butcher, a good sport, agreed to take the younger one.

The rurales were then dismissed, the three Dakotans and the butcher returned to El Paso, and the two hundred dollars was paid, the trans-action being finally closed in the hospitable grandeur of the Coney Island. A real homey place the Coney Island seemed on that occasion, after the distressing business surroundings of the morning. The experiences filed away in the storehouse of recollection and the goodbyes said to the friends in El Paso, the three men took transportation back to the snows and the blows of South Dakota, their bullfighting days over forever. Still they wondered who would have won that bet. Could Cuco kill the buffalo, or would the buffalo have killed Cuco?

After the first fight Eb Jones and his younger companion had visions of the sporting life, and they agreed to a rather ambitious program in which Bob Yokum refused to join because his business interests in Pierre and Fort Pierre demanded his return. The plan was that after the second fight, the results of which they did not doubt so far as the buffalo was concerned, they would take the two buffaloes to Chihuahua and fight them there against any and all comers, man or beast. After exhausting all the sporting and financial possibilities there they would go on to Mexico City, where [Porfirio] Diaz then held sway. When that city was conquered, they would take their buffaloes and go on to Madrid.

"The best laid schemes o' mice an' men gang aft agley," but plans must be made even if they fail of fruition.[23] Several years afterwards at one of the Gas Belt Expositions, an annual event formerly held in Pierre, one of the group met a lady who was quite thrilled over a visit she had made that day to see the Scotty Philip buffalo herd. She then told about being in El Paso and going to Juarez on two successive Sundays to see some fights in which buffaloes participated. When she learned that her listener was there too, she asked him if he knew what had become of the remaining buffalo. He admitted that he had lost all interest in the animal and did not know. She then told that several Sundays later, after his leg had fully mended, the big buffalo was advertised to fight a bull in Juarez. A specially constructed pen had been built of four-by-four timbers in the center of the bullring, with a chute leading to it from the pens. The buffalo was run into it, and a fighting bull followed. In the fight that ensued, there was neither escape nor flight, and the bull was fought and killed. A second bull and then a third shared the same fate. Then a fourth bull was run in, and when the buffalo killed him, he broke the pen shoving his slain opponents through the side. According to her story there was no refunding of the money that day.

She was then asked what eventually became of the buffalo, and she answered, "I don't know, but the story I heard is that they took him to Chihuahua and fought him there against the bulls. Then they took him to Mexico City and fought bulls with him there, and the last I heard of him it was said he was in Madrid."

Maybe the lady had the story straight. Who knows? But still the question, forever unanswered, is: Could Cuco kill the buffalo, or would the buffalo have killed Cuco?

Frontier Medicine

The first winter I was in South Dakota a persistent cough made me wonder what was the matter, until a little self-inspection disclosed an unusually long uvula, which hung into the throat, causing a constant tickle. Having no acquaintance with doctors prior to that time, and supposing that they were all somewhere near even in knowledge and skill, I went in to see old Doc Dickey, who kept no office but could usually be found back of the prescription case in Jim McGarry's drugstore. There I found him looking unsanitary as usual. Telling him my desires for surgery, he made me sit in a rickety old kitchen chair, with my head thrown backward, mouth open and uvula exposed to view. Scotty happened in at that time and made remarks about my choice of physicians that shocked me but did not appear to disturb Doc in the least. Scotty's suggestion that I go to Pierre and see Dr. Ruble, who knew something about medicine, which Dickey did not, was not enough to divert a youngster who was still timid in the presence of professional men.[24] So, Scotty went out.

Doc reached over the prescription case and got an old pair of scissors and a whetstone. Spitting on the stone and sharpening his scissors, Doc proceeded to visit with me, spitting and sharpening, spitting and sharpening, while I made an effort to conceal my terror. Finally getting the scissors sharpened to suit him, he wiped them off on the leg of his pants, which lost nothing in appearance in consequence. Then he said, "Put your head back and open your mouth."

Dismayed and afraid, but without the courage to break away, I obeyed. Doc reached the scissors back into my throat and made the initial swipe at the offending uvula, with the result that it was cut halfway through, and said, "Huh, we didn't get it that time." He certainly drew first blood in no uncertain style. His command, "Well, open her up again," put my head back over the chair, jaws wide apart. He inserted the scissors again and took another swipe with like result, more blood and discomfort for me. Doc said, "Open up." I opened up, and Doc went half through the uvula again. That seemed almost too much, so Doc said, "We'll fix it next time," and he produced a pair of pincers with which he reached into the bloody recesses of the throat, took hold of the lower end of the uvula, pulled it forward over the tongue, reached in with his scissors and this time cut it off above all the other wounds. Doc said, "All right that is a dollar."

He was paid and the patient left for home, spitting a bloody trail along the way. When I arrived at home, my cousin Clara inquired the reason for the very apparent situation. With a kindness habitual to her, she immediately set about to make some hot tea.[25] The first swallow of that steaming hot tea was almost as terrible in its torture as the wayward scissors of Doc Dickey. Prompt recovery bore testimony to healthy youth and discounted the need of ether and Listerine. Such was surgery in the good old days as practiced by some. The operations may not have been successful, but the patients got well.

Another visit to Doc Dickey occurred one summer when we were holding a herd of bulls and cows on Plum Creek (Bad River Plum). Most of the time we were down the creek from the old Deadwood trail, and later we moved up the creek above the trail crossing.[26] Plum Creek is the last creek one crosses going north from Midland just before turning east to go to Hayes. The present bridge is exactly at the Deadwood trail crossing. Although the country looks, and is, different now, the place on the face of the earth about which I am talking is right there, where it was my bad luck in getting a cow out of a plum patch, which was a job not always calculated to give peace to one's soul, to run a plum thorn between the bones in my forearm. Cowboy surgery, which consisted of digging around with a pocketknife, did not prove successful in extracting the offending thorn. Days added to days passed, and the arm got sore and sorer, until finally it was swelled up, painful and useless from blood poisoning.

Billie Hess, who was boss at the time, told me to go to Fort Pierre and see a doctor. That was at the noonday meal, and it was fifty miles to town. I don't remember who all were there, but Hugh Burgess, Harry Read and Posey were.[27] My going to town provoked discussion of the best means of transportation because there were all kinds of horses. It was finally decided that I should ride old Tamarack, a blaze-faced bay horse that was not in my string. Tamarack was an especially tough and long-winded horse, but when he had a few days' rest it was a feat of combined contortionism, hypnotism, agility and legerdemain to get on the old devil. He was the hardest horse to mount that I ever saw, but once you were on him it was a marvel to watch him unwind the miles. After dinner I caught Tamarack and put my saddle on him, the first time he had been saddled in several weeks. All hands turned to and held him while I got on him with that quite helpless arm. It never entered the mind of anyone to question that Tamarack was the right horse to carry a man with a blood-poisoned arm to town, and he was. Consideration in those times meant doing the practical thing.

About sunset that evening Tamarack and I galloped into Fort Pierre, and it is no exaggeration to say that by that time anyone could have mounted Tamarack forward or backward. As soon as I got him in Dave Crippen's livery barn (it was always first in order to take care of the horse), I went directly to Jim McGarry's drugstore, and Doc Dickey was there, standing back of the showcase. As soon as he was told of the situation, he said, "Roll up your sleeve and let me see it." As soon as this was done he grabbed an antiquated lance, and, without even the formality of cleaning it on his pants, he plunged it into my forearm as I stood with my elbow on the showcase and arm upraised. He stood behind and I in front of the showcase.

Having difficulty locating the thorn, in spite of a lance that carelessly roved through the muscular construction of my arm, Doc noticed that I finally began to wilt. He said, "Sit down on that chair," and I had just about enough strength to obey. Doc got a big swig of brandy, which he poured into me with reviving effect. Then he told me to resume my position on the operating showcase, retrieved his lance, and after further devastating exploration, he got the thorn. I paid him the demanded dollar, without even the formality of wrapping my arm, and I left cured, but wondering if surgery could not be made over into a more gentle art.

Comedy or Tragedy?

Pollyvoo, a Parisian, whose real name was Paul Clogenson, found his way to the range country and became a very competent cowhand. He worked for Doug Carlin and for some of the Duprees on the Cheyenne River. The Duprees were owners of the buffalo that ranged that part of the open range at the turn of the century, and which Scotty bought from Doug Carlin, the administrator of the estate of his brother-in-law, Pete Dupree.[28] Pollyvoo went to work for Scotty about the time of that purchase. Claiming special knowledge of the buffalo, and I believe he had it, he was given the job of looking after them in the winter. He had a saddle horse named Flaxy, and between them they seemed to know just what to do with the buffaloes. He had a good barn and corral for Flaxy and a cold, board shack for himself, the same one occupied by Fred Jones and me when we heard the petrified song.

Pollyvoo's main weakness seemed to be an obsession that everybody wanted his job, when in fact its lonesomeness made it unattractive to most. On one occasion when I was loafing around Fort Pierre, Scotty asked me to go out and help the Frenchman butcher a cow. I rode out and told Frenchy my mission, so we ran in the cow that was to be butchered on that cold winter day. When we got this Texas cow in the corral, she was as wild as the joker and the one-eyed jacks in what passes today in the high society as poker. We went to the house to get the butcher knives and the 30-30 rifle and returned to the corral for the butchering.

Conceded to be the better rifle shot, I took the rifle to shoot the cow, which was standing in the center of the corral, tossing her head, and showing every willingness to sheath one of those long horns in anybody, no favorites. Taking a bead on that tossing head, I fired, and down went the cow. Pollyvoo, who had been sitting on top of the corral waiting for just that, was almost immediately sticking the knife in the cow's throat to bleed her. At the first stab of that knife, a highly incensed cow was on her feet declaring war on the French, and Pollyvoo beat a rapid and strategic retreat to the corral fence with those horns about close enough to pick his hip pockets. The lack of dignity produced loud and hearty merriment from me. All that made Pollyvoo as much out of patience as the cow. His obsession immediately took control, and with angry oaths, he declared that I shot the cow high on purpose and just stunned her, to allow him to get killed so as to get his job.

The realization of this awful purpose so angered him that he promised to let my guts out on the snow, and he started for me with the butcher knife. Thinking that my intestines where they were better suited my purposes, I raised the rifle and told him in effect that I would postpone the shooting of the cow until after he was effectively shot. About fifteen feet apart we stood, he with the butcher knife in his hand and I with the rifle pointing at him. In that position we argued our respective points of view, and the 30-30 and I finally convinced the Frenchman that the shot was really meant to kill the cow, but the tossing head allowed the bullet to go a couple of inches too high.

We decided to butcher the cow instead of each other, and the next shot fixed matters so that the Frenchman could bleed the cow without any protest from her. By the time we had her skinned and cut up, we were good friends again, and Pollyvoo was told with convincing definiteness that I would rather herd sheep than hold his job. The whole incident was a bit tough on the cow, but there were no other casualties.

On November 1st, 1903, I turned in my string of horses and quit the range. That was caused very largely by the range quitting as such and becoming peopled with all kinds of human beings, who were determined to make it a farming country and own their own farms.[29] What a dream that was, and what a nightmare it became for so many of the dreamers. . . .

Affectionately,

Dad

CHAPTER 2

A Few Days on the Range

August 24, 1939

My dear Geordie, Jean, and Bob:

If you will take a map of western South Dakota, you can see where the acts set forth below occurred, and, inasmuch as the facts are set down as accurately as memory serves, it may be of interest to know where they transpired.

In the summer of 1901, all of western South Dakota was still "a sunny savage land/Beneath the eagle's wings," where hundreds of thousands of cattle and horses roamed the open range and fattened on the free grass of the public domain. The free and easy days (speaking in an economic sense) were not yet ended by the filing of homestead entries on Uncle Sam's land acquired in many ways, all somewhat dishonest, from the Sioux Indians. In those days a cattle outfit established its headquarters where it pleased and let its cattle roam where they would, knowing that alert cowboys with the roundup outfits would look after them and see that they were turned toward their own range. . . .

In that summer the L-7 outfit, which paid me on the union basis of the day, $40.00 a month and one hundred sixty-eight hours a week if need be, established its headquarters under some sort of arrangement with the authorities of the Cheyenne River Indian Reservation on Thunder Butte Creek, which runs into the Moreau River from the north, and not far east of what was then the west line of that reservation.[1] Outside men, "reps" as they were called in cow country jargon, were the riders who represented their own outfit while riding with other roundup wagons. Often times they did not see their own outfit for long stretches at a time, and when they did get back to the home wagon, they might well expect to be sent soon to another roundup operating somewhere on the range. Although I knew that the outfit was headquartered on Thunder Butte Creek, and that any cattle picked up by me had to be "thrown" or "shoved" towards that place on the face of God's green earth, I had never been in the Thunder Butte area and had never seen Thunder Butte.

Now what is Thunder Butte? Without attempting any explanation of the geologic forces that laid it down, that caused it to emerge from the waters, and caused its erosion to the shape it bears in our age, suffice it to say that to the east of the creek that bears its name, about thirty-five miles northwest of the present town of Dupree, the county seat of Ziebach County, on the divide between the Moreau and Grand rivers, it presents a noteworthy landmark. It is a great cone rising from the open prairie with its upper part off, presenting a flat rock top. To say it is sheared off is an inaccuracy because the flat top presents the surface rock that saved that part, as the rest of the countryside eroded over the ages, and sent its silts down the rivers to form other Thunder Buttes that will some day arise out of the waters of the Gulf of Mexico.

The top, as a rough estimate based on recollection over the years, is perhaps about one hundred fifty feet across. At the base, where it begins to rise from the surrounding prairie, it is about a mile in circumference. Rising as a fairly sharp cone, it is grass covered for about half its height, and there gets rocky and steeper. The higher one ascends, the rougher are the rocks. The east side then presented the best climbing possibilities, and as one reached a point eighteen feet or so from the top, he was confronted with a rimrock, roughly perpendicular, except that at the extreme southeast corner there was what unbridled imagination might call a path over and through the rocks. The south side of the butte was rocky and steep for practically its entire height, and from a point immediately south of what by courtesy was called a path, extended a V-shaped gully for a long way down the butte. In brief such was Thunder Butte.

Among the boys on the range there were many stories of experiences on the butte, as well as traditions borrowed from the Sioux. The main story of the butte was that of being trapped on top by the rattlesnakes and having to stay there until the dark and cold of the night, when the imprisoned cowboy could make his way back to the pony that he left early in the day about a third or half of the way up the butte. And let it not be forgotten that a well-trained cow pony would stand there for a long time. Many like myself regarded those stories with a degree of unbelief that would do credit to the school of Tam O'Shanter.[2]

Until well along toward the latter part of September, it was my job from early spring to rep with outfits that worked on the Rosebud and Pine Ridge reservations, along White River, on the Lower Brule reservation, and the Bad River country. Reaching the end with a roundup outfit that quit working north of the White Clay Buttes, at a point between where the towns of Murdo and Van Metre now stand, I was left with quite a bunch of cattle (a throw back) to be taken to the Thunder Butte country, a hundred miles away. There was nothing but disinclination to prevent it because there were no fences nor other obstacles, natural or artificial, and the cowboy did not dare encourage in himself disinclination to travel long distances across country. So, with a considerable herd of cattle and my string of horses, about ten in number, one of them packed with my bed and all other belongings, I took a beeline for Thunder Butte, a little to the left of the North Star.

A couple of days later, off in the distance to the east of me, and early in the day, was a rider who appeared to be trailing some cattle and horses northward. A sharp gallop over to him quickly disclosed that it was Jimmie Harrell, who was working for the same outfit and was headed for the same place. It did not take long to get Jimmie's throw back in with mine, and that meant company and cooperation for both of us. The lone prairie can get lonesome enough at times. Later on in the day Jimmie and I spied a rider away to the west of us as we were coming into the Minneconjou water shed. He seemed to be driving cattle and a string of horses northward. Such things were the subjects of careful notice on the range, so, after an exchange of ideas with Jimmie, I galloped over to investigate. Well, it was Hughie Burgess,[3] another rider for the same outfit, who like Jimmie and myself, had been repping with an outfit on the southern portion of the range and was now throwing back what cattle he had gathered to Thunder Butte. It took small time to get Hughie's stuff in with ours. Our lonesomeness was gone and our work was easier.

It is seldom that the cowboy is pictured at his work. Sweaty, dirty, tired, often sleepy, and sometimes frightened young men, who worked dreadfully long hours at times and in every sort of weather, are so often pictured as over-dressed, over-manicured, over-armed and under-worked Romeos that one is forced to wonder who on earth hired those and for what class of work. But we three made our way across the prairie as fast as careful treatment of cattle, from which it was intended that their owner would make money, would permit. Eating where and when we could, and going without when we could not, we reached and crossed the Cheyenne River and in due time came to the Bear Creek ranch, home of Joe Langlois, about a mile or so east of where the town of Dupree is today. Jimmie Harrell was one of old Joe's four sons-in-laws. The others were Eb Jones, Quill Ewing, and Babe LaPlante. With Langlois's hospitality, typical of the frontier, we were all made welcome at Joe's home, and with a good supper after dark and a good breakfast before daylight, we were off on the last leg of the trip. That was the last time I saw old Joe Langlois, for he died soon after.[4]

By shoving the cattle along all day, . . . we reached the Moreau River after dark and found it in flood, running bank full. That was not considered a deterrent to crossing in those days, so the cattle were herded into the flood, went over, and were turned loose. Then the saddle horses, three of them packed, for each of us had a packhorse, were put in, and then the three riders followed and swam their horses across. Incidentally, it may be mentioned that the Moreau in flood is a miserable river to cross. Of course, no one of them is easy.

Safely across the river and the saddle horses rounded up, there was nothing to do but to hit for the ranch headquarters, which consisted of a log house and a round pole corral. Men and packs were dripping muddy Moreau water when we rode up in front of the log hut and unsaddled and unpacked. Jimmie and Hugh had put in a good share of the summer at the ranch, and they knew the way, so no time was lost, and we got there along about midnight and found Billy Hess, the foreman, Happy Jack, Posey, and Slim Sargent asleep in their roundup beds on the floor.[5] A light, a fire, a meal ended the trip. It is not set down here as anything unusual but to show the usual thing in the life of the young man on the range, particularly after he got to be a rep.

The Texas Itch

Let those who never had disturbing occasion to obey its commands make light badinage or slighting remarks about the Texas itch.[6] "He jests at scars who never felt a wound."[7] That very spring large shipments of southern cattle to Fort Pierre brought also some Texas men to work on the range. Although Texas was the original and the greatest cow country from the end of the war between the states until the state was put up in barbed wire packages, it had ceased to be open range, and the boys who came up from there were fence-line riders, windmill tenders, cotton pickers, and the like. South Dakota, the last of the free range, looked good to them, and they came. Some of them, or at least one of them, that spring was afflicted with Texas itch. Most of the fellows, including your humble servant, got it early and kept it late. In the struggle to avoid getting it, only a few of the cowpunchers were successful.

What about this itch? It was bad. When the victim was cold or wet, it was inactive, but let him begin to warm up, and then, whether up or in bed, afoot or on horseback, there was a single urge and that was to get off to one side, take down his pants and drawers (union suits were not worn on the range) and go to work, scratching until the blood came. Then he could go back to work.

We had not been together long until we learned that each of us had acquired the curse of the range country that summer, the Texas itch. Why it should be called by that name I never knew, unless it was that every other place had made a timely denial of paternity and Texas was guilty of laches.[8] Be that as it may, Hugh, Jimmie and I were then members of that great fraternity, The Mystic Knights of the Scratch. It so happened that Billy Hess, Posey, Happy Jack, and Slim Sargent had managed to steer clear of it.

A few days before Jimmie and I had joined forces on the prairie, as told above, he had been in Fort Pierre, and Dr. C. J. Lavery gave him a prescription for itch medicine, and he had it filled in a can that held nearly a quart.[9] Hugh and I on the trip begged and coaxed and cursed to get some of the itch medicine, which Jimmie was using on himself to good purpose, but Jimmie, who would have shared his last dollar or his last crust with either of us, was adamant in his determination that his itch medicine should salve no other person than his own. Moreover, he kept it packed in his bedroll, and that was the cowboy's castle, where neither search nor seizure, just or unjust, was permitted. But more of that later.

The four fellows at the ranch knew that Hugh and Jimmie had the itch, so they were told in no uncertain way that, "You can sleep in your wet bed or stand up in the corner, just as you damn please." Slim Sargent looked down from his six feet three and told me that if I did not have the itch I could sleep with him. Cold and wet, no man was freer from the itch than I at the moment, and Slim was so assured. Accordingly I took off all but my wet undershirt and drawers and rolled in alongside Slim.

With a warm meal in me, and the warmth from Slim's body warming me from the outside in, it was not long until my vigorous young body got warm, but returning warmth brought with it the distressing necessity for a finger nail massage on my itching lower extremities. Standing out against the urge until all the resolution in my soul was worn away, I broke the news by saying, "Slim, it's no use. I must get up and scratch." Suiting the action to the word, I stood up on the dirt floor, dropped my drawers and went to work. Slim got up too, and in militant mood. There was only one window in the hut, but through it a beautiful peaceful moonlight shone down on Slim and me as I was bent over scratching, while Slim towered over me with fists clenched, inviting me to engage in fisticuffs in combinations of language that it is shameful for any one to know.

If he had ever had the Texas itch, he would have known that no man could have been coaxed from his scratching to engage in a mere affair of honor. When Slim realized that his gentle invitations were spurned, he went back to bed, leaving me to my purposeful operations. After my itch was curry-combed to a fair degree of subsidence to the accompaniment of Slim's expositions of my family tree, he said, "_____ _____ _____ _____ _____. You have done it now anyway, so you might just as well sleep here the rest of the night." I did so and was glad afterwards to know that some miracle saved Slim from the itch.

Rattlesnakes on the Butte

The next morning, after spreading beds and contents on the bushes and the grass to dry, I tried to get some information from the boys who had been there all summer as to whether there was any truth in the stories that had been circulated among the cowpunchers about the assembly of rattlesnakes on Thunder Butte. With one accord they assured me that the stories were nonsense. They had been up on the butte many times, but not lately. In fact any time they had lost any of the saddle or work horses they would go up on the butte, from the top of which they could see the bottom of every draw for fifteen miles around, and thus spot every bunch of horses in that part of the country. They were sure there were not as many snakes in the country surrounding Thunder Butte as there were down on the Big and Little Prairie Dog Creeks, north of Midland. They were telling the gospel truth, but a status is not permanent.

This day was a Sunday, which made no difference on the range. It happened, however, that there was nothing to do, and the cowboys could do nothing just as diligently as they could do any part of their strenuous work. No amount of persuasion could get Hugh or Jimmie to go on to the butte. It could go places, one in particular, and I could go with it, but they were going to rest. Billy Hess, Slim Sargent and Happy Jack all agreed to go, so a picketed horse was saddled and someone ran in a bunch of saddle horses. Each of us caught a horse, saddled, mounted, and rode up to the east side of Thunder Butte, only a few miles away. Riding up the east side of the butte as far as the footing was good for the barefooted (unshod) horses, we dismounted and left our bridle reins hanging on the ground, the sign to the well-trained cowpony that he is to stay there until his rider returns.

As we got off our horses Happy Jack said to me, "I'll bet you a box of cigars that you can't go to the top without stopping to rest."

"I'll bet you" was a common, but not an idle, phrase. The bet was accepted and my ascent began. There was nothing difficult about climbing the butte provided it was not done with exhausting enthusiasm. The way grew rockier near the top, and for the last thirty or forty feet, it was all rocks that had fallen at one time or another from the rimrock crown. Following what a generous imagination would call a path at the southeast edge of the rimrock, it was no trick at all to climb the butte and to do it without a rest. On reaching the top I looked down to see how the other fellows were coming along. A little more than half way up the butte, they were lashing away with their quirts at rattlesnakes, which apparently were out investigating. I had seen no signs of snakes and had accepted the assurance of the other fellows that there were none on Thunder Butte. We did not then know that in the fall the snakes from far and near denned in on that secluded eminence. It was then about 9:30 or 10:00 in the morning of the last day in September, a sunny day, and about time for the snakes to sun themselves.[10]

Perhaps in order to appear facetious and matter-of-fact about it, I yelled out to the others, "Come on up. There are no snakes here."

"Brr-Brr-Brr-Brr."

Here and there on the top the sound called my attention to about a dozen snakes up sunning, but before I could get at any of them with the quirt slung on my wrist, they dropped into the wide cracks that seamed the cap rock. On looking down into those cracks, it is no exaggeration to say that the butte itself seemed to be weaving back and forth. Soon it dawned on my sluggish consciousness that the stories of the snakes were true, and that another cowpuncher was marooned on top of Thunder Butte. If alone, it meant staying there until the cool and the dark of the night made descent possible. Any part of the descent could have been made with care, except over the alleged path over the fifteen or eighteen feet of rimrock, but there a fellow would have had little chance to protect himself. Then it became a problem for the three men down on the side of the butte to furnish a way down for the fellow who had been shortsighted enough to get on top.

At one place on the east side there was a hole back in the rimrock with some rosebushes at its outer edge or mouth, and on these bushes were resting about half a dozen of the graceful blue racer snakes, prairie cousins to the black snake. Out beyond the bushes, and about in line with the rimrock, was a small grassy plot, maybe seven feet across, and free from rocks. Rendering lip service to the fellows who were killing snakes as they came slowly up the slope, I could see the advantage of the little level grassy plot, but there were snakes making their way back and forth across it. After what seemed a long time, but was in fact quick work, the three men reached the grassy plot, cleared it of snakes, and extended profane invitations to the man on top to jump, which he did, landing safely.

Billy Hess and Slim Sargent, being old enough to have sense, although in the fall of the year all cowboys denied that any of them had any sense at all, went back to their horses, killing such snakes on the way back as presented, for the man on the range always was willing to go to quite a bit of trouble to kill a rattlesnake. It may be that they knew that nature never intended man to play a good hand, because she never deals one, but nature does intend that a poor hand should be played well, and they calculated that their poor hand had been played well enough in that experience, and they were retiring without casualties. However, Jack and I worked our way over to the south side and sent large, flat, circular stones hurtling down its steep side, where untold numbers of snakes were out taking a lazy look at the noon-day sun, for it was now about that time. Soon tiring of the fun of seeing snakes and pieces of snakes hurled into the air, and also of the vile imprecations hurled at our heads by our two friends now safely seated on their horses, we worked our way down to them and mounted our own ponies. Instead of going back the way we came, we went around the north side and down the west side of the base and on to camp, encircling the butte. On the way around we got off and killed snake after snake headed toward the butte.

Happy Jack and Billie Hess complained bitterly of the odor (the snake smell) up on the butte. Slim insisted he never noticed it, and I am certain

I did not. Many claim to be able to detect the smell and can give convincing proof that they do, while others cannot.[11] Before we got to camp, Billie Hess and Slim became nauseated and threw up pitifully from off their horses. About the time we got to camp and started to get a bite of dinner, Happy Jack and I, too, were sick, so preparation of food for us was suspended.

It is my candid belief, in retrospect, that if a blanket of some modern deadly gas, fatal to reptiles, could have been laid down on Thunder Butte that day, a host of rattling pit viper descendants of Eve's counselor would have been gathered in, to the benefit of a large surrounding territory. How many that would be is problematical, but from the way they were balled up and huddled together on that large and lonely rendezvous that day, a hundred thousand, two hundred thousand, three hundred thousand would not be out of reason in my opinion. I have many times stated without any thought of exaggeration that a quarter of a million snakes were on that butte that day.

A few years ago, when Col. W. R. Pope was commanding officer at Fort Meade, near Sturgis, we, with Mr. and Mrs. Robert S. Hill and Mrs. Eva Wortman, were invited to dinner at their home at the fort. While there the colonel told of his earlier days as a lieutenant, when he was sent to western South Dakota to assemble the Ute Indians, who had left their western reservation and come in a body to settle with the Sioux.[12] After quite a discussion he got around to Thunder Butte. Then he fell to questioning me: Had I ever seen it? Had I ever been near it? Had I ever been on top? What season of the year? On being told that I had been on top on the last day of September, he cautiously ventured the question, "Did you see any snakes?"

At this point Mrs. Hill laughed and said, "Colonel, go ahead and tell your story. We want to see if it is like the impossible snake story George has told us about that butte."

The colonel was visibly relieved and said, "Well, I have told this story many times, and nobody will believe it, although it is the gospel truth." Then he told a story about going on top to survey the surrounding country on the first day of October in the Ute year (I think 1907) and being held prisoner there by rattlesnakes until a few soldiers of his command saw his predicament and cleaned off the snakes so that he could jump off the rimrock, just as Billy Hess, Slim Sargent and Happy Jack had done for me a few years before. Whatever may be the fact now with Jack-

MICK
B.
HARRISON

ley on the job, do not let anyone convince you that the rattlesnakes "in shoals and nations" did not, in former days, make winter headquarters on Thunder Butte.[13]

Off Repping Again

The next morning, after health reasserted itself, the boss, Billie Hess, told Jimmie Harrell and me to get our strings (assigned saddle horses) and go to the mouth of the Cheyenne River to Ed Delehan's wagon,[14] which was to work from the mouth of the Cheyenne River up to Pedro and then down the divide between the Cheyenne and Bad rivers to Fort Pierre and ship beef from there. Quickly catching out our horses and packing our bed horses, we were on our way for the long drag to the mouth of the Cheyenne River. Changing horses anytime we wanted to rope one that had not been ridden that day, we made good time, and in early dusk we joined up with the outfit, turned our horses loose, unpacked our beds, and got ready to interview the cook, often a touchy gentleman, but one whom every cowboy was willing to vote a gentleman, at least, to his face.

There seemed to be a lot of excitement, and riders were galloping back and forth between the camp and the other side of a small hill about a quarter mile to the south. As I was getting my bed off my packhorse, one of the fellows rode up to me and said, "George, don't turn that horse loose. Saddle him up and come over where we are."

Not having any special urge for a horseback ride at the moment, I said, "Why?"

He answered, "We have found a rattlesnake den, and we had killed a hundred and eleven just before I left. Come on over."

I said, "That is just chicken feed. I saw my snakes yesterday." I did not go.

The roundup started the next morning, working up the Cheyenne River. After dinner (noon) just as the outfit was all ready to go, Terry Singleton got on a horse that started to buck in accomplished fashion, and Terry was doing a fine job of riding him when suddenly the horse sunfished too far and landed flat on his side, cracking Terry's head against the ground. The horse got up, but Terry did not, so after making our best efforts to bring him to without success, it was decided to leave him there. Like the show, the roundup must go on. A tepee was taken from the bed wagon and set up over unconscious Terry. His uncle, Henry Singleton, afterwards sheriff of Haakon County, who was with the roundup, stayed with him. A couple of horses were picketed for them and their saddles, etc., left there.[15]

A doctor must be had, so Jet Calhoon, who was riding a big U-necked gray horse to which the number of miles on the ride meant little, started off for Fort Pierre, more than fifty miles away, to get Dr. Lavery.[16] Late next afternoon Jet caught up with the outfit farther up the Cheyenne River and told us that Dr. Lavery got out there about noon, and Terry, who had been unconscious for twenty-four hours, had just commenced to come to. The next day Terry and Henry caught up with the wagon and announced that he was all right, so the incident furnished no more conversation.

It should not be forgotten that I still had the itch; that Jimmie had the itch medicine, which he would not share, still carefully stowed in his bed. The outfit worked up the Cheyenne to Pedro and then moved out to the divide and commenced working east towards Fort Pierre, where I hoped to get some itch medicine just like Jimmie's. One noon when we were camped on Sansarc Creek, a rider came out from Fort Pierre with word to me that Scotty had bought out George Jackson's interest in the JR– [J R Bar] cattle, which he had previously owned with Bill Hayes, and instructed me to take a saddle horse and a pack horse, go to the JR– ranch, tally out the JR– cattle, and stay there alone that winter. (Incidentally I did not have to stay alone, for Bill and Mrs. Hayes came out to the ranch, with their daughter, Mary, who was then a baby. But those were my instructions.)[17]

Lead us not into temptation. Here was I with the itch, and there was Jimmie's bed with the medicine. I would be batching on a ranch all winter. He would be in Fort Pierre in a week and could get plenty more. He was nearly cured anyway. A good deal of rationalizing was done in a very short time, and then I violated one of the most binding provisions of the cowboy's code and raided Jimmie's bed. I stole his itch medicine. By the time the cowboys with Ed Delehan's wagon were ready to spread their beds that night, I was over the hills and far away, and so was Jimmie's itch medicine. When he got ready to apply it to his ailing parts, he discovered it was gone. It took no Conan Doyle to deduce a proper conclusion from the well-known facts that the medicine and I were both gone.[18] According to reliable reports that came to me, Jimmie's wrath was as boundless as the damage he promised to do to me with a six-shooter the first time we met. It was effective itch medicine, and in a reasonable time it cured me.

Quite a few years passed before I again saw Jimmie. The country settled up, and the cowboys had to change into a different class of folks. They had to settle down somewhere because there was no more range, and there could be no more cowboys ever again. To a Gas Belt Exposition in Pierre in the fall of 1909, I believe, I went over from Fort Pierre, where I was then practicing law, in company with A. L. Bodley, who was working for the Robertson Lumber Company, and Dr. T. E. Bowen, who was a practicing dentist in Fort Pierre.[19] In the densely crowded lobby of the Locke Hotel, I spied Jimmie some distance away and hailed him.

At first he seemed as delighted to see me as I was to see him. We worked our ways through the crowd, and just as our hands were about to come together in friendly grasp, Jimmie pulled his hand back, a look of anger came on his face, and he said, "You ____ ____ ____ ____ of a ____. You stole my itch medicine."

Jimmie didn't smile when he said it, but it made me laugh heartily. I said, "Oh, well, Jimmie, let's shake hands anyway. We're both cured of the itch." Jimmie grudgingly consented, but he still wanted to do something about it.

The code, which protected his bed as sacred, had passed into oblivion, and its place was taken by prosaic statutes including the statute of limitations. The incident passed off with Jimmie only partly reconciled. Years passed with only occasional stories of crimination of me by my friend Jimmie. About 1935, when Jimmie, still living in the spirit of the old days, was gambling in Deadwood to earn a precarious living, his daughter, Loretta, wanted a position as a stenographer. I saw that she was employed in the United States attorney's office and located at Deadwood. When she wrote me a note of thanks, she said in the letter, "Dad is delighted because I got the job, and he told me to tell you that the itch medicine deal is all forgiven." It took a long time to earn full forgiveness for that violation of the cowboy's code, but I cured my itch. . . .

The cow country, or the open range, died about 1904 when the homesteaders had taken a good part of the country. The cowboys died with it, and they never can live again. Their world is gone. The cow country was both an epic and an epoch that lasted less than forty years. The only purpose in writing this at all is to give a sketch of about three weeks of life on the range, with what little light it may cast on an extinct species, the real cowboy, who bore no resemblance to the silly, rootin'-tootin' make-believe of the stage, the screen and the rodeo.[20]

Rattlesnake Butte

About five years or six years ago, during a deer-hunting trip in the southern Black Hills at Bob McAdam's ranch, Tommy McDonald, Bob McAdam and I were visiting about old times. Tommy and Bob were boyhood acquaintances dating back to the time when Tommy's older brother Alvin and Bob and his older brother Mack were voluntary boy explorers of the now famous Wind Cave. Alvin was the young man who, after he and the McAdam boys quit their joint exploration, went on and on, leaving his marks almost everywhere in that underground labyrinth until his death in early manhood.[21]

Tommy and I had known each other well when we were young men. Then he was riding on the range for Billie Borst[22] and I for Scotty Philip. . . . Bob and I had been good friends for many years, so it is not hard to believe that there was no shortage of gossiping material, and the evening hours did not drag slowly. Each reminded the other of many things, and a lot of breeze was shot about. Tommy, in reminiscent mood, told of an experience he and another young cowpuncher had up on the Cheyenne River Indian Reservation, when he was up there repping with Narcisse's wagon. Narcisse Narcelle was a half-breed Sioux, who at one time was wealthy in cattle and horses. Anyone with a gifted pen and knowledge of the facts could certainly tell a stirring story about the "Savage" as he dubbed himself.[23]

Tommy told how he and his companion were on circle, which meant the way the cowboys gathered in cattle for a roundup by spreading out fan shape and then gathering all the cattle seen on the way as they converged to the handle of the fan. The roundup was to be made on the west side of Red Scaffold Creek, near Rattlesnake Butte. This butte must not be confused with Thunder Butte, about forty-five or fifty miles to the north. The two buttes are very much alike in immediate appearance, with the difference that Thunder Butte arises from a divide, while Rattlesnake Butte comes up from the level bottomland along the creek. The former is so much more striking, but the latter is much more unusual.

It so happened that Tommy and his pal did not strike any cattle, and they were empty handed as they came by Rattlesnake Butte. As Tommy told his story, not one of the three knew, and I do not know now, whether that butte was a rendezvous for rattlesnakes as its more noticeable brother to the north assuredly was. Being young and full of whatever fills youth, and having some time on their hands while waiting for the other circlers to come in with the gathered cattle, the thought of climbing the butte quickly suggested itself, so that decision was soon made.

They rode up the side as far as it was convenient for the horses to carry them. Dismounting, one or the other suggested taking the horses up on top, if possible. Tommy described in graphic detail how they pulled and pushed their horses over the large rocks that seemed insurmountable obstacles, and how finally, by dint of sweating and swearing, the two boys and the saddle horses were on the flat top of Rattlesnake Butte. He then told how he and his friend got on their horses atop the butte, and as the other riders went along its base with the cattle, the boys on top waved their hats to them.

Tommy's story ended there, and I said, "Well, well, and you were both riding white horses."

He gave me a sharp look, banged his fist on his knee and said, "By God, I have told that story over and over in the last twenty-five years, and I never could remember who was up there with me. Anyway, George, we sat on our horses on top of Rattlesnake Butte, didn't we?"

If rattlesnakes rendezvous and hibernate on Rattlesnake Butte, as I have been informed they do, I have no knowledge of it, never having been on it at the right (or wrong) time of the year. However, I am not a skeptic on rattlesnakes, and proper evidence would make me a true believer.

This letter makes no pretense to literary merit and is written for no other purpose than to afford in days to come a glimpse of days that were.

Affectionately,

Dad

CHAPTER 3

The Ghouls

My dear Geordie, Jean, and Bob:

In a life of varied experiences, such as the frontier fringe of existence usually affords, being an official grave robber was my lot only once. Looking into old Indian graves in the hope of finding buried elk teeth and other trinkets is deemed unofficial and does not count.[1]

When the country west of the river in South Dakota commenced settling up, and the railroads built across what was then Stanley County, the Chicago, Milwaukee & St. Paul Railway Company established the town of Stamford.[2] It should not be forgotten that Stanley County then was composed of what is now the territory of Stanley, Haakon, and Jackson counties, and it was no inconsiderable pasture for the boys to ride in. Although never on the expansive scale of Texas, one cannot but be reminded of the Harvard class in Southwest American history in which the professor asked the question, "Can anyone tell me whereabouts in Texas is Crockett County?" A young man with a Texas drawl finally announced that he knew. When the professor told him to enlighten the rest of the class, he very modestly stated, "It's in the northwest corner of my grandpa's horse pasture."

No one has yet successfully disputed that Stamford, in its original settlement, was composed of more incompatible ingredients than any community in the west. Although it has long since settled into moribund quietude, the day was when its troubles, from murder to every other activity punishable by fine and imprisonment, kept the court calendars crowded, and sometimes almost drove the lawyers to distraction.

Such was the community that was startled on September 21st, 1906, to learn that Clyde G. Whiting had been killed by an explosion occurring in his stove. (I had been admitted to the bar less than sixty days at the time and made my first talk to a jury in defense of the man charged with his slaying.) The excitement quickly settled down, and the authorities of Stanley County, under the leadership of John F. Hughes, for many years circuit judge of the Sixth Judicial Circuit of the State of South Dakota headquartered at Fort Pierre who was then states attorney, and an intelligently pugnacious one, pursued the inquiry into the cause of Whiting's death. No man with an eye for leisure would care to put in his spare time trying lawsuits against John F. Hughes.[3]

The investigation resulted in the arrest of a new settler, Gus A. Tusha, who was charged with murdering Whiting by placing an infernal machine in his stovepipe. Judge L. E. Gaffy of Pierre, J. H. Johnson, and I were retained to defend Tusha, and we did so at the July 1907 term of circuit court at Fort Pierre, with Judge Lyman T. Boucher (old Bouch) presiding.[4] The information was filed against Tusha on my twenty-seventh birthday, July 16th, 1907. It was a hard place to cut one's eyeteeth as a trial lawyer, but maybe it worked.

Shortly prior to the time of trial, counsel for the defense learned that my good friend, Dr. J. M. Walsh of Fort Pierre (who, incidentally, ushered each of you into the world for whatever that is worth),[5] was employed by the state to conduct an autopsy on the body of Clyde G. Whiting, which had then laid in the graveyard at Murdo for about nine months. That was back in the days when the automobile was still an amazing curiosity. It was reasoned that Dr. Walsh would go west from Fort Pierre on the afternoon passenger train, probably going as far as Van Metre, and there hiring a team to take him over to Murdo. It then became a matter of carefully watching the movement of Walsh, because someone representing Tusha should be somewhere in the vicinity of the autopsy.

In a day or two I spotted Walsh and Dave Giddings,[6] a deputy sheriff, going toward the depot about in time for the westbound afternoon passenger train. I, too, went to the depot and visited with them on the platform. When they got on the train, I got on and made arrangements to sit in a double seat with them. After a little sparring around, we quickly set each other at ease as they found out that I was going as far as they went and no further. Walsh and I were always good friends, and a little thing like one catching the other off base was no strain on our friendship. Then the conversation on the trip occasionally turned to the treatment they were to accord me during the autopsy, such as making me lie quiet in the coffin while they performed it, tying me up to a fence post with a string of the dead man's guts so that I could not interfere with their work, and much more of the same sort. All of this was wasted effort because, while it never occurred to me that Walsh's nerve would fail him under any such circumstances, it certainly did not enter my head that Dave Giddings would still be on his feet after I should go down.

They soon told me their plans, which included having Dutch Van Metre drive them from Van Metre to Murdo with a team and buckboard. Dutch, who was your mother's uncle, I knew very well, having ridden with him on the range.[7] He was waiting with the team. Dr. Walsh got into the front seat with Dutch, and Dave and I took the back seat, and away we went over the cross-country trails to Murdo. There were no roads then. A lot of inconvenience and discomfort in those days was hidden underneath a barrage of raillery or, that forgotten name, joshing. No small part of the conversation on the way over was devoted to a discussion of the dire things that were going to be done to me for injecting myself into their plans. We suffered no inconvenience on the ride because we were young and knew no more comfortable way of cross-country travel than in a good spring wagon or buckboard.

On arrival in Murdo our first job was to hunt up the undertaker who had interred Clyde Whiting the previous September. We found him at home, sick enough to refuse to go with us, but he sent his young helper, who knew the cemetery as well as he did, according to his recommendation. Dr. Walsh commandeered a pick and a couple of shovels, and away we went to the cemetery. Every man in the party was equipped with overalls except me, and my hurry in leaving Fort Pierre was a little too precipitate to permit acquiring full equipment. Dr. Walsh also knew Dutch's inclination to wet his whistle under any and all circumstances if the wetting fluid (quality immaterial) was available, so he purchased a quart of whiskey from a saloon in Murdo. Thus equipped we reached the cemetery.

While the undertaker's helper was making a survey to determine the right grave, Dutch pulled the cork, sampled the contents of the bottle, and pronounced them good. By the time each of the rest of us had taken a little sample, the undertaker's helper had located the proper grave. Dutch and Dave, being dressed for the occasion, did the digging, and soon they reached the casket, which lacked quite a little of being six feet under the sod. To add effluvial discomforts to whatever others there might be, let me interject the information at this point that the level of the ground waters in that cemetery, in those days of more plentiful rainfall, was just about to the top of this casket. Of course, none of us knew Clyde Whiting, nor could we have recognized him after soaking for about nine months in that grave even if we had known him well in his lifetime.

There was an unfailing mark of identity, however, and that was the plaster of Paris filling in the skull, a large part of which had been blown away in the explosion that caused his death. In order to lay him away in some form of orthodox appearance, the undertaker, prior to burial, had in effect given him a plaster of Paris head. Consequently, we knew we would recognize him. When the coffin was laid sufficiently bare to allow removal of the lid for identification purposes, that was done. One good look at the remains convinced each of us that the woman who was buried in that simple wooden coffin, as was the vogue of those days, was not Clyde Whiting. One look, too, was enough for Dave Giddings. With a heave that would have done credit to a volcano, Dave cleared his insides with one spout, forgetting completely the things he had promised to do to me.

We now had a job of reinterment on our hands, and it was done with a good deal of dispatch. In forceful, but inelegant, language, of which Dutch and I approved if we did not in fact join in, Dr. Walsh told that undertaker's helper to locate the right grave and be quick about it. Dutch and I filled up the desecrated grave, and Dave, in the meantime, had laid down in the spring wagon hoping for early death or recovery. By the time we got the grave filled in, the helper and doctor had located the grave, and taking turns, the four of us dug down until that sepulcher disclosed its casket, lying in about the same depth of water as the first one. Removal of the lid disclosed the ghastly remains of a man, whose uninjured head had been buried with him.

That was almost too much for Dutch, who rushed for the whiskey bottle and brought a smile to the angry and disgusted face of Dr. Walsh, as, looking at the bottle and shaking it vigorously, he said, "Jesus Christ, Doc, you forgot to write the directions on this label." It is well that he had forgotten because the size of the drink Dutch took would never have been prescribed by Dr. Walsh. It was almost too much for the undertaker's helper because he began casting his food to the ants and expressed a profound desire to lie down alongside Dave.

I was all ready to forget that anything had ever happened to a man named Whiting, but doctor had a job to do, and he was never the man to falter. Also, he was being paid for doing this particular job, but there was no chance that the experience would enhance my fee for defending Tusha. With masterful profanity, doctor told what he thought of undertakers in general, and Murdo undertakers in particular. If I was silent at the time, it was not because I was in disagreement on the subject with my friend. Sick and sorry that he ever took up that business, but spurred on by the domineering tauntings of Walsh, the young man then made an especially careful survey and, after pointing out the right grave, went and laid down with Dave in the wagon.

Dutch, doctor, and I gave hurried reestablishment to the second grave. Just before starting in on the third one, for fear that Dutch might have the temptation to take another such drink, doctor and I each took a good swig, and so did Dutch. About the time we were halfway down with our digging, a sudden prairie thunderstorm struck with a downpour of rain, quickly followed by intense hail. We ran to the wagon and got under. Dave and the undertaker cared very little whether they were in or under the wagon, but they did climb down. The harnessed horses had been tied to the wheels when we first stopped, and, although they made a good bit of fuss during the hailstorm, they were still there when it was over.

When the sun came out, and it was now getting late in the day, almost sundown, we finished the digging in the third grave. Soon we were down to the coffin, sure this time that we were right, and, with that assurance in mind, we prepared to open the lid.

"The best laid schemes o' mice an' men
   Gang aft a-gley."[8]

So it was with us, for on opening the casket we found that its occupant did not have a plaster of Paris head. The sight inspired doctor and me with anger, but it seemed to fill Dutch with horror or terror.

He grabbed the whiskey bottle and started off across the prairie at the top of his speed. He appeared to have but one thought, and that was to get away from there. Forgetting that he was in an enclosure, and not noticing the barbed wire fence surrounding the cemetery, Dutch hit it full force with the top wire about at the waistband of his pants. The lower half of him hung down inside the cemetery, and the upper half hung down on the outside. It was an inconvenient position for one to get

rid of his dinner, and everything else, but Dutch was equal to the occasion. His position was so inexpressibly ludicrous that it restored a measure of good humor to Walsh and me. By the time we effected Dutch's release, we were ready to hold a council. We were fully determined that we were not going to dig up every grave in that cemetery, and we knew there was the possibility of having to do just that if we relied on the guesswork directions of the undertaker's helper. So we decided to go in to Murdo, get our supper, round up the undertaker regardless of his illness, and get him out there.

After filling in the third grave, we hitched up the team and went to

MICK
B.
HARRISON

town. By now, all but Dave and the undertaker's helper were dirty and muddy spectacles. After attempting to clean up, without enough success to make us vain, we had our supper. Dave did not eat, and the helper went home and to bed. After supper, doctor, who by this time was in no mood to be denied, went to the undertaker's home and brought him back with him. By this time it was dark, so we added two lanterns to our other paraphernalia, and Dutch, doctor, the undertaker, and I started back to the cemetery to outghoul the ghouls.

On arriving at the cemetery, which was still soft mud and soaking wet from the hard rain of late afternoon, the undertaker inspired us with new confidence because, sick as he was, he seemed to know just what he was doing. He was too sick to do any work, and Dutch was almost that, but when that undertaker pointed out to us the spot where we should dig, we set to it with all the enthusiasm of disciples of a water witch or a doodle-bug. Before long we reached the coffin, and quickly we removed the lid. Eureka! There it was. A plaster of Paris head in all its putridity.

Then it became a question of no mean proportions to figure out how to get that coffin and contents out of that mushy grave and up to the sod surface where Dr. Walsh could hold his belated autopsy by the light of a lantern. It must be remembered that whatever was done had to be done by doctor and me because illness had overcome all the others. Lifting the head end a bit at a time until it was leaning up against the upper part of the end grave wall, I got up on top, and doctor stayed down at the feet to push. After I got up and got a good hold on my end, we acted cooperatively with doctor giving the heave-ho. That went fairly well until I backed into a part of the piled dirt thrown from the grave, lost my footing in its muddy surface, and started to fall into a sitting position.

Tightening my grip almost to desperation on my end of the coffin for fear it might slide back into the grave, I grasped so tight that the coffin, evidently a glued affair, collapsed in my hands. There I was, sitting in the mud, more or less gently grasping the plaster of Paris head of Clyde Whiting in my lap. Doctor was busy enough at his end without any such misfortune as mine, and he, not being able to see just what was happening, thought I was failing to do my part. The language he used to me would not cause anyone hearing him for the first time to suspect that he was my friend. I soon got myself adjusted, and we slid the coffin and contents out on the grass.

That autopsy in the dark, by lantern light, on remains in that condition was gruesome enough. What the state wanted the inquest to show were pieces of metal other than sheet iron or stove metal to prove the infernal machine. Although pierced through every organ from the waist up with metal now deteriorated to rust (every particular of every organ was being examined by Walsh in detail, while I sat at his side and wrote his notes), nothing was discovered that could not originally have been metal from stovepipe or stove. There was no proof in the body of infernal machine. There was other proof later put in at the trial.[9] After minute inspection, and when nothing further remained to be done, we replaced the pieces in the coffin as best we could, went to Murdo and to sleep. The next day we drove back to Van Metre, caught the afternoon train to

Fort Pierre. It may have been an experience worth having, but not worth repeating.

Later, on a trial, Tusha was acquitted. That's the story of the grave robbing.

Affectionately,

Dad

CHAPTER 4

Let There Be Light

October 24, 1939

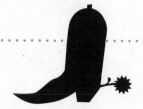

My dear Geordie, Jean, and Bob:

President Roosevelt has said something to the effect that the only thing we have to fear is fear itself.[1] Most of our troubles come from fears born of ignorance. If only we could survey our problems from the viewpoint of knowledge instead of the much more frequent one of ignorance, most of our troubles would vanish into nothingness, like the mists of the morning. In fact, almost all the things we worry about never happen.

The mountains, the woods, the lakes and streams produce romance. They also produce superstitions and follies, which could never gain headway on prosaic plains. The mountain men are the ones who know the whereabouts of fairies, the methods employed by witches, the whole gamut of eerie lights, and what they foretell. The patron saint of sailors did not suffer neglect at the hands of the distributors of spooky lights. St. Elmo's lights or St. Elmo's fire has brought little comfort to the sailor lad as he saw its dim, phosphorescent glow adorning his masthead or yardarm when the weather was in storm, or just about to break into storm.

To the cowboy, about as far away from anybody's ocean as it was possible to get in America, St. Elmo's lights were well known, but not by name. To him they were "balls of fire" as he saw their awe-inspiring ghostly luminosity in the fearful darkness of storm-impending night on the ears of his horse and on the horns of the cattle around which he rode as he stood his guard. There was little in his experience that held a less pleasant prospect for the young cowboy as he lay sound asleep in his bed on the ground than to have one of his fellows slip up to him about ten minutes to midnight and say, "George, get up. It is time for third guard." Up he comes and grabs his hat and his boots from under his pillow.

His fellow then says, "There's balls of fire on their horns tonight."

The boy just awakened pulls on his hat a little tighter, jams his feet into his boots, says, "Oh, Christ," and disappears into the darkness in the direction of his tethered night horse and the storm.

Neither the cowboy nor the sailor could give a satisfactory scientific explanation of St. Elmo's lights, nor balls of fire, but each knew that he was likely to have to ride out the storm, the one on his ship in a wind-swept sea, and the other on his pony in the dark reaches of the night, holding running cattle. The fear that filled each then was not born of ignorance, but of the knowledge of what that storm might mean for him. The balls of fire were not spooky, but terrifically real, and they were not romantic. To the mountain man they might mean ghosts or witches, warlocks or banshees, or even fairies, but to the plainsman or the sea-men, they were as plain as signposts marked "Danger—STORM."[2]

To the uninformed, unusual lights have especial significance, just as the comets were considered pestilential by the ancients, even of recent days. Even the "borealis race, that flit ere you can point their place,"[3] hold superstition and fear for many, although it is hard to understand how those beautiful folding curtains can be considered to hold aught but beauty.

That reminds me of Bob Withers.[4] Bob was a husky, young fellow, a native Texan who had worked on a Texas cattle ranch. He longed to get away from the cramping influence of barbed wire and windmills and get out on the open range. That meant going to South Dakota, in the western half of which the open range still held sway. One spring (1903, I believe), Bob got a job on a trainload of cattle being shipped north by Scotty Philip, as one of many train loads, and a string of horses after arriving in Pierre. A powerful young giant, and a bit unsophisticated in the ways of the open range, Bob caught on rapidly and, indeed, had very little to learn. He already knew how to ride, rope, and work many hours on end. He was not afraid of work, but like everybody else, he was afraid of the unknown, the fear born of ignorance.

It must have been in the night of the 30th of October 1903 because there could in the nature of things be about one day between then and the first of November that year, when I turned in my string of horses and quit forever the profession of rider on the open range. It was well to do so then because almost overnight the world of the cow country passed away, leaving no evidence that it had ever existed, except in the recollections of those who had participated in the doings of a young society in a young world. But all that has little to do with the experience of Bob Withers.

On this particular night Cy Hiett and I were standing second guard on a beef herd that was to be shipped, and was shipped, from Fort Pierre on the first day of November. Second guard was admittedly the curse of the cowboy's life, although none of the four night guards was anything to be sought after.

In order that you may know what I am trying to tell, let me explain briefly the handling of a herd when everything went in the normal fashion. Immediately after breakfast the nighthawk, the rider who held the saddle horses all night, drove the bunch into the rope corral. That was at the crack of dawn, and immediately the day herders caught their horses for the forenoon's ride and went out to the cattle herd, taking it over from the last guard. They held them until dinnertime and moved them along to about the point where the wagon (meaning the whole outfit) would camp for dinner. That would mean approximately the noon hour. Immediately after getting dinner the next set of day herders, who would hold the herd that afternoon and the next forenoon, would relieve the day herders who would hurry in to camp, eat, change horses and help break camp for the afternoon move.

Those day herders held the herd until they were relieved after supper (usually about six o'clock) by the boys who went on kilpecker—that meant anybody because usually none were assigned to it.[5] To be regularly on kilpecker marked the willing hand, and to dodge it marked the loafer. That group of riders handled the herd and worked them on to the bed ground. There the cattle were rounded up fairly compactly and held quietly until they began settling down for the night. The first guard came on at eight o'clock and consisted of two riders, unless it was a very large herd or an especially unruly one, in which case the number might be increased. As soon as first guard took over, all the others turned in. There were two things that the cowboys could be entrusted to do at every available opportunity—eat and sleep, and well they should, for sometimes they were short of both, and nearly always short of sleep.

First guard held from eight till ten, and the plan of it was to ride around them at a walk or a slow trail trot, the riders going in opposite ways and therefore meeting twice each round. Many, in fact most, of the boys "sang to them" as they rode around them. Only a confirmed optimist would consider that the singing held any promise of operatic excellence, but it covered a wide range, from attempts at sweet religious music to songs of the grossest vulgarity.

At about ten minutes to ten, one of the boys on first guard rode into camp to awaken second guard. This was done by quietly slipping up to the men of second guard, the location of whose beds on the ground had already been located before going on guard, shaking the sleeper, and saying quietly, "John, get up. Second guard." John came out of his bed quickly, grabbed his hat and his boots from under his pillow, put them on quickly, walked into the darkness to his picketed night horse, mounted and rode out to the cattle, usually about a quarter-mile away. Then John and his fellow second-guardsman took over and held till twelve, when a similar performance brought on the third guard, which held until two in the morning. Then in the same way as before, last guard came on at two and stood guard until relieved by the day herders. That was the arrangement in ideal conditions, barring storms, restless or frightened cattle, stumbling or falling horses, and all of the hundred and one things that might upset the situation and send the frightened cattle running and the equally frightened cowboys riding like mad in the darkness.

Well, Cy and I were standing second guard on this particular night on a beef herd, bedded down at the head of the Missouri River breaks, adjoining a point on the west bank of the Missouri River, about eighteen miles above Fort Pierre and known as the Yellow Hawk landing. That cold, crisp October night, clear and beautiful, stands out in mellow memory among the nights spent on the range. The heavily breathing cattle were hugging the bed ground in perfect behavior. Although there was no moon, the night was so clear that our trained eyes could see at all times that everything was right, and that not an animal was stirring.

Then Cy and I stopped riding and did that which is really frowned upon by the best traditions of the range, we "augered on guard." Auguring, in cow country parlance, meant becoming interested in a personal conversation when there was work to be done. But neither Cy nor I could be justly condemned on a general charge of auguring at any time, and we should not be on that night. The light was such that every animal in the herd was plainly visible, and each clearly showed himself at peace with all the world. It was not cold enough to be uncomfortable to us in coonskin coats.[6] We were neither too tired nor too sleepy to enjoy life in its enjoyable phases.

In one way nature was doing her level best that night to make a show, for from zenith to horizon, from east to west, the entire northern sky was bursting forth the glory of the aurora borealis. The northern lights were showing all their royalty of color. Everywhere those beautiful northern curtains of the night were swinging and swaying, rising and falling in all the wonderment of the merry dancers, and all the other luminous, if not fluorescent, phenomena that the lights can display. Two cowboys sitting on their night ponies on guard, at peace and in love with nature, were contentedly watching one of her best shows, with a lighted northern sky in front of them and with a peacefully sleeping beef herd behind them.

Thus ticked away the minutes of that night guard, thrilling the viewers with the beauty of the scene. Although there are those abroad in the world who not only see with appreciation the beauties of the northern lights, but actually claim to be able to hear the hissing sound they make, Cy and I could see all the beauty of it without hearing the hideous handicap of a hiss. Perhaps we were men of the plains, realists, lacking imagination. Anyway we could see and admire without hearing and fearing God's illuminated curtains, the northern lights.

The boss of our outfit was Jesse Knight.[7] As the watch showed the approach of midnight, and as sleep was just as precious to us as the scene of the heavens afire with northern lights, I rode into camp to awaken third guard, one of the pair being Bob Withers. On reaching camp I slipped quietly up to Bob's bed so as not to awaken any who should not be awakened. Shaking him and saying, "Bob, get up. Third guard."

Up he came, reaching for his hat and boots. All at once he witnessed the fiery fury of the northern sky. Instantly, and in terror, he shouted to Jesse Knight, the boss, himself a former Texan, "Lo'd God, Mister Jesse, Lo'd God, Mister Jesse," and began to run across the prairie in the opposite direction from the frightening glow.

Thinking that he was having a nightmare and that he would ruin his feet with cacti unless stopped, I quickly caught him and told him to wake up. As he importuned me to let him go, I finally shook him and said, "Wake up, you damn fool. What is the matter with you?"

In genuine fright he asked, "What is it? Is it the end of the world?"

Then realizing that the Texas boy had never seen the aurora borealis, I told him it was just a swell display of the northern lights. Logically enough he then asked, "What are the northern lights?"[8]

That question left me as badly stumped then as it would now, but, having seen them from boyhood, they held no terror, no forebodings,

MICK
B.
HARRISON

nothing but beauty for me. My calm assurance in the face of this un-known quieted Bob down to the point where he put on whatever garb he lacked. His night-guard partner needed no special attention from me because he was up and dressed, ready to go before Bob was, having been awakened, as was everybody in camp, by the horror-breathing experi-ence that Bob had. By the time two o'clock had come, when it was his job to call the last guard, he was accustomed to the northern lights. But, although still unlearned as to their cause and effect, as to them he had no fear born of ignorance.

My old friend Cy Hiett, who, drunk and sober, had more hair-raising personal experiences than any individual on the range, now lives near Eagle Butte, a man of about seventy. Jesse Knight now lives at Fort Pierre, an old-age pensioner. Where Bob Withers is goodness knows. I am sure that, wherever he is, he still remembers his first view of the aurora bore-alis, and that Cy, too, has not forgotten the night.

Affectionately,

Dad

CHAPTER 5

Who Knows?
November 10, 1939

My dear Geordie, Jean, and Bob:

The subject of education is one that has disturbed the calm of individuals and likewise has rocked families, communities, states, and maybe nations to their foundations at times. We have all heard the demagogic bombast about the "little red American schoolhouse," but seldom have we heard the ozone crackle with proper caustic comment on the "little read American schoolbooks."

Many believe that our duty to the generation pursuing on our heels is fully discharged if its members are exposed to learning, and that to play through high school and to pretend to listen during four years of college is the equivalent of an education. At any rate, that all too frequently caters to the conceit of the generation that foots the bills. "I sent all my children through college" is often said with too much pride, as we can all see when we take note of the great number of graduates who might just as well have been sent through college in hermetically sealed barrels, avoiding even the chance of exposure to education. It does, however, enable some parents to stick their chests out farther than they properly belong. After all, education is the acquiring of a degree of information about the world in which we live that will enable a person with the will to do to cope with the conditions of the life in which he is cast.

My old friend Bill Hurst was raised in Fort Pierre and spent his life west of the Missouri River in South Dakota, occasionally reaching over into Wyoming ("W'oming" as Bill called it). He was a highly competent man of the open range, and he knew how to do almost everything in that line of life. Bill was a good rider, a good man with a horse; he knew how to handle cattle; he was a competent teamster, a fine cook; and, above all things also, he was perfectly willing to work on a basis of hours that would shock John L. Lewis into a cerebral hemorrhage.[1] Bill knew all the brands in the surrounding plains and where and to whom they belonged. Strangely enough, he could run a brand on an animal with a running iron,[2] and he could read it after it was on, but his complete illiteracy prevented him from reading it off or putting it on paper. Indeed, he was one of those individuals who must be paid in cash because of inability to endorse a paycheck. There is no question that Bill was highly able to meet and overcome conditions that might arise to confront him in the cowboy's life on the open range.

When I first knew Bill, he had become a roundup cook, and he was an exception to the rule that cooks were cranks, for he was always good-natured, maybe because he could not read and it took a lot of nonsense to upset him. Of all the people on a roundup, there was none more important than the cook. Called by the last guard, he was the first man up. How the cook could do all he did is beyond my knowledge, and even beyond my imagination. By the time the nighthawk came in with the saddle horses, the cook had breakfast ready for the outfit whether there were ten men or fifty. About then (the first graying of the dawn), he would sing out his, "Roll out. Come and get it or I'll throw it out," and the camp became electrified with activity.

Every rider would roll and tie his bed and lay it by the bed wagon to be loaded later under the direction of the nighthawk, who drove the bed wagon. Then he would grab the wash bowl, wash, get his dishes, eat, throw his dishes in the dish pan, and ride off to catch and harness the work horses used to draw the mess wagon and the bed wagon. Then the saddle horse he expected to ride that morning was caught, saddled and left standing untied, with hanging bridle reins. By that time the cook was washing the dishes, always with a volunteer or two (and usually the same ones) drying them. All of this was always swiftly done in fast motion. Often moving twice a day, setting up and breaking camp, the cook always was, and will continue to be, a mystery man to me. It is small wonder that the cook was the best-paid man with the outfit, including the boss. I digress only to show the character of the work, and all of that Bill could do. So he was well equipped to handle the problems of the life in which he was cast, and consequently well educated.

Frequently at the commencement of a roundup, a man would just go along with the roundup, doing what he could in the way of work, riding horses of the outfit, but usually not very good ones. They were so often persons seeking experience, perhaps for the novelty and perhaps for the information. They were accepted only into the outer fringes of the fraternity, and sometimes they were kidded unmercifully by some of the yarn-spinning cowboys, who could take unfair advantage of an embryo novelist and consequently get a lot of nonsense into seriously intended writing.

Just why he came, and where he went, I never knew, but one fall a man by the name of Harleigh came to ride the range for a month on a beef roundup and get some cowboy color. Harleigh was a fine fellow and without any airs. He was a Bostonian, a graduate of Harvard, a civil engineer, etc. Like Wes in *Out Our Way* he wore laced boots,[3] which surely had little to recommend them compared with the well-fitting, high-heeled boots of his temporary associates. He could drag out a Ha'vard "a" until it seemed that his tonsils must permanently disappear down his throat. To Bill Hurst, the long-drawn "a" in Harleigh, to which he was wholly unaccustomed, made the name sound like Howley, reminiscent of coyotes and gray wolves. In all good faith, Bill called him Howley and surveyed him with interested curiosity. The fact of college degrees meant nothing to Bill, who, in range vernacular, considered Howley "pretty damned harmless on a horse." Two examples of education were coming into head-on collision.

After the beef cattle were gathered, and the animals to be shipped were in a day herd, now called a beef herd, there was nothing to do except the leisurely job of trailing the herd to the shipping point, Fort Pierre, on the Missouri River. One day as we were approaching the Missouri River brakes, northwest of Fort Pierre and at the east end of the Giddings Flat, the boss decided he would camp that noon at the poplar grove, where there was a good spring with enough water for the cook, leaving the cattle and the horses to water in the Missouri River.

Accordingly, the outfit was piloted to the poplar grove, and camp made there. The pilot was the foreman, or some one assigned by him to the task of taking "the wagon" to the next camping point and setting up camp. After camp was broken up, the mess wagon loaded with tent, food and cooking paraphernalia, the cook stove loaded in the two-wheeled stove wagon hooked on behind the mess wagon, the bed wagon loaded with the beds, individual tepees, the stakes and rope of the rope corral, and each man's picket rope and stake for night horses, the pilot led the way on horseback; the cook followed driving the four-horse mess

wagon; the nighthawk came along driving the two- or four-horse bed wagon, as the case might be; and the horse wrangler brought up the rear with the saddle horses. That cavalcade constituted what, in cow country parlance, was "the wagon." So, you can see that taking the wagon across rough country often without a trail, and always without bridges, was more of a problem than for a farmer boy to get into his wagon and drive out to the field.

On this particular occasion, when the wagon reached the poplar grove, the cook and I unhooked and unharnessed mess-wagon horses, assisted by Bill's friend Howley who had come along for the ride. The bed wagon was pulled into proper place to allow setting up the rope corral; the corral was set up by the horse wrangler and the nighthawk; and the wrangler went out to the grove and dragged up a rope load of wood for the cook and chopped it up, which was an orthodox part of his job. The camp was set up, a fire started, and Bill got ready to feed his crew. When there remained nothing to do in the way of setting up camp, I proceeded to do that which every cowpuncher did at every possible opportunity (not all cooks permitted it, but Bill did) and that was to eat a lunch.

While I was digging into the mess box for cold biscuits and whatever was available, Howley got on his horse and started back in the general direction of the beef herd. Standing in the tent opening with his feet wide apart and hands in pants pockets, intently watching the receding form of the civil engineer on horseback, Bill made a picture that is as clear to me today as it was at the moment. Suddenly swinging to me, Bill said, "By God, George, that Howley is a iggerant son of a gun, ain't he?"

The force of the remark, slightly expurgated (modified for the purpose of this letter), has not diminished with the passing of the years. It struck me, a careless kid cowpuncher at the time, that Bill was stating a great truth. Here was he, wholly unlettered, standing almost on the west bank of the Missouri River, with the world he understood and could handle to the west of him, and in that world Harleigh was practically valueless. He did not know enough to enter into the usual run of conversation, and certainly none of them (his then associates) could understand (perhaps could not pronounce) his calculus and logarithms. A complete reversal of respective superiorities would be accomplished by crossing the Missouri River, and Bill would be out of his world. Yet in the life in which Bill moved and had his being, all too soon to vanish into the misty nothingness of a dream, it was true enough for Bill to say, while that life lasted, that the man who knew books and slide rules was, compared to him, "a iggerant son of a gun."

Affectionately,

Dad

CHAPTER 6

Happy Landing?
April 16, 1940

My dear Geordie, Jean, and Bob:

In this day and age, and probably in all ages past, people are disposed to address each other in the vernacular of the time, the place and the company. Now it is a token to express the wish for a successful termination of business in hand, whether that be a fight or a frolic, in the sky man's words, "Happy Landing." For the cowboy who must needs "stay with him," there was no such thing as a happy landing. Certainly Jimmie Schneider's landing was not a happy one. The cowboy had to stay on his horse or else.

On one spring roundup, working up Bad River with the Bad River pool wagon, run by George Jackson, all the riders were getting ready one morning, to start out on circle to the north and to the south of Bad River.[1] We were camped at the mouth of Plum Creek, running into Bad River from the north, between where are now the two railroad points of Wendte and Van Metre. As we were not going to move that morning, we were not put to the business of breaking camp. There was that much that did not have to be done.

Although I knew every man with the outfit I have no independent, clear recollection of any except Harry Briggs and Jimmie Schneider. Harry Briggs had been born and raised in that west river country and quite regularly rode with the roundups, gathering his own cattle and those of his neighbors along Bad River.[2] He worked with, but not for, the big cow outfits and was a fine hand who rode his own string of good horses. Incidentally, it often made one wonder how the saddle horses acquired their individual names. Often the reason was quite simple and came from the characteristics of the horse or some brand he bore, but sometimes the mystery of the name was unexplainable. Harry's top horse, a big, fine bay and a splendid cow horse, went under the euphonious cognomen of Synonymous. Parenthetically, let me state now that all the yarns spoken and written about the big rides the cowboy made on his favorite mare are the veriest nonsense, for nothing but geldings were ridden or worked on the range.

Jimmie Schneider was a Sioux City boy who had done a lot of work around the Sioux City stockyards as well as on the range. Among his other qualifications, he was a good bronco rider, and that spring he was riding for John Holland, a rancher who lived up on the Missouri River, just below the mouth of the Cheyenne River.[3] John Holland's horses were not proverbially gentle, and there were several in Jimmie's string which were far from it. Especially was this true of one big bay that did a hard job of bucking nearly every time he was ridden.

Having a long, hard ride in mind for that morning, Jimmie very properly selected his hard-bucking bay because the long ride always took the tuck out of the bad horse, and no rider was disposed to save him or give him leisure. You will often hear those who are deficient in measurement of time, or means of measurement (experience), tell about a horse bucking for five minutes, ten minutes, fifteen minutes, even an hour. I have seen many, many bucking horses, and often times in that business a young man had his own private rodeo along with him, and right between his knees. I am sure that I never saw a horse do a concentrated job of bucking that lasted a minute, and I seriously doubt if any horse could do it. He would make those terrible jumps at the rate of about three a second, and all the power of his mind and body went into the job he was doing. If a horse made as many as thirty jumps without tapering off into crow-hopping, breaking into a run, or rearing up with seeming intent of falling over backwards, the cowboy on his back knew that he had been somewhere—and so did the horse. Those thirty jumps may have seemed long to each of them (and it would be long), but the chances are that the wild performance was commenced and completed in ten seconds.[4] Of course, he might break and run for a while, and then buck a few more jumps, and keep that up for a good while. But the business of bucking was furious and it was fast.

When Jimmie got his horse saddled, and putting a saddle on some of those horses was no job for a mollycoddle, he crawled in the middle of him. That horse put on a show to which we with the ringside seats paid no admission, and which enhanced Jimmie's income not one penny, for it was all in the day's work. He made a good ride, as could well be expected from the good rider that he was. Having got that poison out of his system, the big bay stood there with the other saddled horses until all were ready to mount and get going on circle.

Jimmie, thinking that he knew his horse and that the contest was over, was sitting unconcernedly and carelessly on his mount, when without the least warning, that horse went into action again, and with the first terrific jump he threw Jimmie to the end of the bridle reins. There was no happy landing in those cases, and certainly none in Jimmie's, for when he came down with spread-eagled arms and legs flat on his back, he landed squarely in a cactus patch, which reached slightly beyond the outermost limits of the man no longer on horseback.

First aid was always quick and heroic in that life, and he had scarcely landed when Harry Briggs and I were off our horses and at his side. George Jackson said, "You two fellows stay there and help pull the cacti out of him," and we did. George really did not say "cacti," but he should have said it. Then all but the three of us left on circle.

We got Jimmie pried loose from the cactus bed and onto a rolled out roundup bed, face down. Longitudinally from the high heels of his boots to his Stetson hat, and in all his latitude, Jimmie's clothes were fastened to him by hundreds of spines of the cactus plant. We had no conveniences, no tweezers, nor even pliers. After we got him stripped to a point without bubble or fan, and that is no easy job when the man is like a pin cushion, especially for the poor soul being undressed by valets none too gentle, Briggs got from the jockey box of the wagon the big nippers that were used to trim the hoofs of the saddle horses, and I took my knife, and we went to work on our surgery.

Stoic that he was, and he was supposed to be, Jimmie groaned in agony and cursed his benefactors, who in turn cursed him. By the time the cook had dinner ready, and that meant a much longer half day than the union scale, we had pulled with the nippers and dug with the knife every sticker out of the person of our co-rider, and we had also cleared his clothes of them. There was no analgesic balm, no soothing lotion, and no Mercurochrome or other disinfectant in that life, so Jimmie just put on his clothes and that afternoon was riding again, but not the hard-bucking bay. He deferred that ride a couple of days.

Many years had passed and I had lost all track of the whereabouts of Jimmie Schneider. One day as I walked along the street on the south side of Main Street in Rapid City, about in front of the Morris dry-goods store, Victor Jepsen was standing on the sidewalk facing me and talking to a man whose back was to me.[5]

Just as I came up to them I said, "Hello, Vic."

He said, "Hello, George. Just a minute. I want you to meet a friend of mine, Mr. Schneider."

Each recognized the other instantly, and Jimmie, as he took my hand, said, "Good God, Vic, don't introduce me to this fellow. He and Harry Briggs sat on my back for half a day once and pulled cactus spines out of me with hoof nippers and a knife."

Vic looked at me and said, "Well, you have told me about that experience. So this is the fellow."

The remedies in those days were almost as tough as the disease.

Affectionately,

Dad

CHAPTER 7

The Cowman

June 1, 1940

My dear Geordie, Jean, and Bob:

Letters to you about older days, not so far distant in point of years but tremendously distant in point of human experiences and the possibility of repetition, would be as gaping as two missing front teeth if they contained no account at all about Tom Beverly, who in his lifetime was almost a tradition on the range, and who after his death was quickly forgotten.

Some other members of the Beverly family, his immediate relatives, lived at Ellis, Kansas, the early home of Walter P. Chrysler, in the glorious nineties, but only one, Frank Beverly, a half-brother, a locomotive fireman on the Union Pacific out of Ellis, was known to me.[1] Because of some difficulty with his family, the nature of which was never known to me, Tom threw in his lot with the Texas cattle men, and, at an early day in the history of South Dakota's range cattle industry, he "came up the trail." Even yet, when men who knew him get together, they are likely to be unanimous in their verdict that Tom Beverly was as good a cowman as ever operated on the range. It is still the small talk custom on such occasions to tell how Tom could "hind foot" the calves, meaning the deadly accuracy with which he could rope calves by both hind feet to drag them up to a branding fire. Orlin Holcomb was another expert in that same department of the cattle business.[2]

Maybe a word of explanation on that may tend to enlighten you about an experience of men which you are never likely to see except in greatly modified form. In the work of the general roundup, or spring roundup, one of the necessary tasks was the branding of the calves. In the roundup made twice each day, all the cows with unbranded calves would be cut out and placed in a separate group, known as the "brand-ing bunch." They would be driven to some place along a creek conve-nient to firewood. There some wood would be cut and a big branding fire started. The cows and calves were compactly bunched and were so held by mounted men. The branding irons were brought out from the wagon and promptly heated in the branding fire. Some of the branding irons were stamp irons, meaning by that that the entire brand was made up and could be put on the animal at one operation. For instance, the brand 73 could be made into a stamp containing both figures, or it could be made by having separate figures, or it could be "run on," which meant that some cowpuncher would trace it on the animal with the red-hot end of the branding iron.

As soon as the irons were heated, and they usually were by the time the fellows got there with the cows and calves, the job of branding began. One man would be designated to rope the calves, and that called for skill, not only in catching the calves, but also in definitely identifying the mother, for the calf was branded with the brand carried by its mother. The man doing the roping would drag the caught calf up to the wrestlers at the fire and would call out, for example, "Flying V." The man handling the irons would then brand the calf with the brand announced by the roper. No one checked the brand on the mother, although that would often be an easy task because she indignantly followed the calf right up to the men. Tom Beverly was a master at this type of roping. He did the minimum of stirring up the cows and calves; he never fought with his horse; he always cast a small loop without swing or flourish; and with uncanny frequency he caught the calf around both hind legs.

Several fellows were assigned as wrestlers, "rasslers," and to them it was most important whether the calf was roped by the hind feet or by the neck. If it came in caught by the hind feet, it was helpless, and one wrestler would catch it by a front foot with his hands, turning it over if need be so that the brand called out by the roper could be put on the right side or the left according to the proper placing. In the case of a left-side brand and a calf caught by the heels, one wrestler would catch hold of the animal's left front foot, pulling it up tight and putting his right knee on its neck. At that instant the other wrestler (there were always two to an animal) threw himself down in a sitting position on the ground, grabbing the left hind leg, pulling it back, holding it tight to his side, and at the same time shoving the right or lower leg, as the animal lay on its right side, as far forward as he could with his right foot, and the high-heeled boot fitted admirably into that performance. Thus the calf was held as solid as if he were in a vise when two hardy young men had hold of him.

A different technique of wrestling was required when the roper caught the calf by the neck. In such a case a wrestler caught hold of the tightly stretched rope, usually near the horse, and rapidly ran down the rope with his right or his left hand depending on which side should carry the brand, and he quickly reached the neck of the jumping, bawling, fighting calf. Let us suppose again a left-side brand called out by the roper. In that event the wrestler ran down the rope with his right hand on it. On reaching the calf, he would take a firm grasp on the rope around the calf's neck, lifting hard on the left flank with his left hand, and with celerity the calf would be thrown a wind knocker.[3] Immediately the other wrestler would grab the upper hind leg, holding it back hard against his side and pushing the lower leg hard forward with his booted foot. In that way it was held fast for the branders, and the rope was immediately cast off by front or hind wrestler, depending on whether the roper had caught it by the head or the hind feet. They were never caught by the front feet for branding. The roper wasted no time in going back for another.

With the animal firmly held, the branders put on the proper brand, and the "knife man" cut the proper ear mark belonging with the brand, cutting wattles if such went with the marking,[4] and altered the bull calves into steer calves, and all this was done in less time than it takes to tell it, for work was fast motion in that life. Then the calf was turned loose and with its mother went at once into the bunch. (Long before Rocky Mountain oysters became the dish of epicures in fancy cafes and at prices that would stagger their imagination, the cowboys had theirs for nothing, cooked to a delicious pop-open stage in the branding fire). Thus it went on until every calf in the bunch was branded and otherwise marked and mutilated. Then those that belonged in that part of the range were turned loose, and those that belonged elsewhere were taken along in the day herd. That was the orthodox way of branding on the roundup, and Tom Beverly was one of the few sufficiently skillful with the rope always to make the work of the wrestlers least difficult.

The second night guard I ever stood was with Tom Beverly, and the cattle ran with us, causing us no end of trouble, after having been bedded down right where the waterworks tank of the city of Philip stands today and has stood for years. It makes one think of the words of Badger Clark's "The Passing of the Trail":

Where, in the valley's fields and fruits,
   Now hums a lively street,
We milled a mob of fighting brutes,
   Among the grim mesquit[e].

It was in 1899 that I first met Tom, when we were both working for the 73, he as an old seasoned hand, past his heyday, and I as a cub, a greenhorn, a tenderfoot. To my own surprise in looking backward, and contrary to the usual experience, I immediately became a great friend of Tom Beverly and also, which may be a little beside the point, of Billy Pressler, who was the dashing type of cowboy and a real hand who knew all about the game.[5]

When I knew Tom he was on the downhill slope of life. His life had been varied. In the nineties he had run a big cow outfit for an English concern, the BXB Cattle Company, which had its headquarters about where the inland town of Bixby now is in Perkins County, South Dakota.[6] Tom then was at the height of his glory and recognized even in the big cattle centers of San Antonio, Kansas City, Omaha, Chicago as one of the best cowmen that ever was on the range. He had a wife and a couple of daughters. Life should have been easy for him, and it would have been but for an unfortunate weakness for liquor. He was not a steady drinker and would stay strictly teetotal for long periods, then the craving overcame him, and he would stay drunk for five or six months at a time, mooching drinks after going broke, getting delirium tremens, and becoming a local nuisance in the town where he happened to get drunk.

So far as I know he was the first exponent of the terrible art of taking the first drink in the morning, when he was so shaky and nervous that he would spill every drop from his whiskey glass as he tried to raise it to his mouth. His plan was to take the long black silk handkerchief that, as a cowboy, he wore around his neck, place it full length around the back of his neck, having hold of an end in each hand. With his right hand, still holding the handkerchief, he would reach down and get hold of the glass, and then by pulling on the end of the handkerchief held in the left hand, he would raise the glass to the level of his mouth. After about three drinks ushered into his nervous, drink-maddened system in this fashion, Tom was off for the day. And yet, after extraordinarily protracted drunks, during which he always lost his job, Tom would somehow right himself, get another job with some cow outfit, and get back out on the range where he knew how to do everything, and how to behave himself to boot.

Philosophy

Tom was a philosopher of no mean parts, but no one on the Harvard faculty would ever be tempted to adopt his style of expression. One time as he and I were making a ride together, he fell to discussing the race problem in this country, with especial reference to the Negro problem. To my professions of ignorance as to the question or its solution, Tom said, "No, George, this country has not seen anywhere near the end of its colored race trouble, and there's only one solution for it."

The fact that he had a solution interested me and prompted my question, "Well, Tom, what is that solution?"

He said, "Well, the only solution is to breed 'em down to a light brown saddle color." There may be many scholars who can put many more words into a discussion of it, but it is doubtful if any one of them could more tersely and pithily state the theory of amalgamation of races.

Tom's unfortunate habits were the cause of trouble in his family, and it is pitiful but true that Tom's wife and daughters who lived near Hermosa were not on terms of utmost amity with him. He was not blind to the reason for it all, nor did he endeavor to pass the blame to where it did not belong. He realized that where an intelligent and sensitive person might rebel against his slavery to drink, one of duller perceptions might weigh his good qualities with only small regard to his failings. When he was giving such questions a mental chewing over, he would ride along, if circumstances permitted, humming a tuneless tune to himself or singing meaningless words. . . . Suddenly, if he was with one to whom he cared to unburden his thoughts, he would turn to his companion and say, as he said one time to me, "George, if I ever get married again do you know what I'll do?"

Naturally, my answer was in the negative.

"Well, by God, if I do ever get married again I am going to marry a wife who will know enough to raise kids and fry meat, and no more." Domestic felicity weighed heavily with Tom, but maybe that status, coupled with mediocrity, would not be as pleasing to him as it seemed at a distance.

On another occasion, after a period of silent riding, Tom swung part way around in his saddle and burst out with, "George, did you ever notice how often the finest girl in a neighborhood will marry some damned, no-account _____ _____ _____?" On my concurrence with his view, Tom said, "Yes, it is altogether too bad, but it is true that far too often the finest girl in a community is just like a butterfly. She'll fly all around the finest flowers in the garden and light on a horse turd." He might have been more elegant in his remarks but scarcely more expressive. His comments on the habits and customs of the cattle, the horses and the men of the range were no less enlightening.

Tom knew that I, figuratively, sat at his feet to listen and to learn, and he made me his pupil and his friend, just as did Billy Pressler, another cowboy about whom I must write you one of these times. Tom knew, and none knew better, that punching cows was work, hard work, hazardous work. Of course he did not realize how quickly it could vanish from the earth, so he wanted to educate those he thought were willing to learn how to help the owner of the cows make money from them, which after all was the underlying purpose in everything proper that was done on the range. Tom was an advocate of proper conduct on the range and considered that the six-shooter, or the rope, was fitting reward for those who ran off horses or cattle, changed brands, ate another outfits' beef, or did the unethical acts that made bad manners on the range. Yet, ironically enough, Tom was jailed in Rapid City on a charge of grand larceny, alleged to have been committed by him and Faye Gentry. Nothing came of it, so Tom must not have been guilty. If he was, booze did it.

It was an education for me to know him and to hear his philosophy, just as it was for King Taylor of Sioux City, who came out to be a cowboy and undertook to tell the rest of us about *Ben Hur*, written by General Lew Wallace while he was governor of the territory of New Mexico and under threat of death from the six-shooter of Billy the Kid.[7] After strutting his stuff about the book, guessing that no cowpuncher had ever read it, he was amazed to have his impressions of it corrected by Tom, who had read the book and understood it better than King did. A wealth of early cowboy lore, well understood by one who helped to make it, was allowed to go to waste when Tom passed on to his reward without leaving his story told for others to come. His views on the great epoch in American life, the cow country, have since been warped out of all semblance to the living truth by pulp magazines, silver screen, plain lies, and even by that modern manifestation of showmanship called the rodeo, in which the actors are often good riders of the bucking bronco but perhaps could not tell which end of the cow carries the horns. . . .

One Night

Many people seem to believe that cowboys, or freighters, or frontiersmen of any sort were all cut off the same bolt and were all of one kind, which is about as far off the mark as an estimate can well be. There were at least as many types as there were persons. I say at least because often there would be several types of individual rolled into one, and my old friend Tom was easily one of these.

During the winter of 1899–1900, my uncle Scotty Philip, who had sold out of the 73 cattle outfit the fall before, established himself in a large way in the range-cattle business by putting in a big outfit of his own. Of course he had a goodly number of cattle on the range carrying his own brand, L-7, and many horses. In the late winter, after arranging with Tom Beverly to take charge of the outfit as foreman, he put in the balance of the winter and early spring buying southern cattle to be shipped to Pierre, unloaded and branded there, and then taken west of the Missouri River to be turned loose on the range. It became Tom's duty to assemble and equip the mess wagon, the bed wagon, and all that necessarily went with them to make up what would be the "L-7 wagon," as I have previously explained to you. Also he had to hire a crew of men. One of these men was Ira Miller, a fine reliable fellow.[8]

Scotty told afterwards that while in San Antonio, Texas, on this trip, he was asked by an old-time cattleman as to whom he had selected as his foreman. When Scotty told him that it was Tom Beverly, the man said, "Well, Scotty, you have the best cowman on the range as your foreman, provided you can keep him sober, but you just can't do that."

Scotty's answer was, "By God, I'll keep him sober all right."

Alas for such well-intentioned assurances, at that very time the scene had changed. Tom had been sober for many months and strictly teetotal. Having got the outfit together and on hand waiting for the first shipments to come in, there was nothing to do but to loaf around Pierre and Fort Pierre until they came. The gnawing temptation got too much for Tom, and he took a drink in a Pierre saloon. That brought on the explosion, and for a couple of days he was boiling drunk around Pierre and landed in the Locke Hotel with delirium tremens, which always happened to him.

It so happened that I was on the west side of the river, at Fort Pierre, when word came that Tom was having "the snakes." All the other fellows seemed quite matter-of-fact about it, and, while they regretted the foreman's fall from grace, they followed the principle that every man should look after himself, no matter what the situation. My feelings in this particular case were different. I loved old Tom; I wanted to get him sobered up before the cattle began to arrive, and especially before Scotty got back. I wanted him to continue as foreman. Also I had the lack of knowledge that went with having made the acquaintance of that life only the year before and also the enthusiasm and illusions of nineteen.

I got Tom to the west side of the river and undertook the job of sobering him up. That task brought some disillusionment. After several days of doing a pretty fair job as a dry nurse for my friend, which meant only keeping him to such a moderate degree of drunkenness that he did not get the snakes, I went to a dance in the old Hollenback Hall on the east side of Deadwood Street in Fort Pierre, a building long since gone up in smoke. Everything was going along merrily at the dance, until, like the interruption of the ball before Quatre Bras and Waterloo, someone jolted me with the news, "Your old partner is down in George Gordon's saloon just raising hell."[9] My sense of duty to him being much greater than any sense of social obligation (and that was the law of the range), I immediately left the dance hall, the ladies and all, and went down to George Gordon's saloon.

What I had been told in the dance hall about Tom's conduct was a model of understatement. He certainly had that saloon by the ears, and great was my joy to know that his six-shooter was safely rolled up in his roundup bed in our camp up Bad River a couple of miles, just above the mouth of Dry Run. That gentle soul, when filled to the limit of his skin with "inspiring bold John Barleycorn,"[10] and seeing snakes eighteen feet long playing tiddly-winks with pink elephants, was as wild as the wild cat, but no one knew exactly what made him wild. No others could see the pictures so vividly and so harshly imprinted on his brain. When I walked into that saloon, he was cleaning house, with everybody who had remained in the place, and they were few, keeping a respectful distance. I called his name and it seemed to clear the phantoms from his brain.

As I walked up to him and caught him by the arm, he put a hand on my shoulder and said, "Georgie, the old man's pretty snaky tonight."

I said, "That's plain, Tom, so you better come with me." With no further word he walked out with me to the utter amazement of the folks in and about the saloon, who had been trying to handle him.

We walked along the street on the occasional pieces of board sidewalk in a beautiful, full-moon spring night until we came to Dr. Lavery's office, in the back of Fletcher's drugstore, where the back end of the Fort Pierre National Bank building has stood for more than thirty years. The gleam of his kerosene lamp disclosed that the doctor was still at his office, and a call brought him out. It took only a few words of explanation for the doctor to understand Tom's predicament and mine. Retiring and soon reappearing, the doctor said, "What are you going to do with him?"

My reply was, "I am going to take him up in Scotty's basement and put him to bed. His roundup bed is on the floor there, and we will sleep there."

Doctor laughed and said, "Are you sure you are going to sleep?"

Missing the point of the doctor's joke, I gave him my mistaken assurance that we were going to sleep.

Doctor then said, "You may have a tough time of it with him. Here are some pills, and, if he gets too wild for you, give him one of them, but not more than one at a time, and not closer than an hour apart. There is enough poison in one of those to put him out three times over if he were not so filled with whiskey. Then, if he looks like he is going to die on you, give him a good shot of this." This was a bottle of brandy; so, armed with my brandy and my pills, I escorted the groaning, shaking, drunken cowman up the street, and it was no easy task.

The only conversation he offered was when he would put his arm around my shoulder and say, "Georgie, the old man is pretty snaky tonight."

I would say, "Yes, I know it, Tom, but you will have to be good."

He always made the same reply, "I'll be good for you."

With no small effort, but with no spells of delirium tremens, blue devils, pink elephants, snakes, or whatever you choose to call those horrifying visions of alcoholism, we reached Scotty's house, which was built on the slope of the hillside in such a way that on the south west there was a grade door on the level of the basement floor. In we went, and my bedroll was plainly visible on the floor in the moonlight streaming in through the door and a small window alongside. Quickly as the bed was unrolled, it was not any too soon, for there came the impact between Tom and one of his visions, the forerunner of a horror-breathing night.

Forty years have not served to dim that picture. Efforts to soothe with persuasive talk were as useless as the sharp command, for one cannot be soothed or commanded when those fearful sights are so dreadfully and dangerously visible to a disordered brain. Every little while some woman crossed his vision, as could be noted from his moaned, "poor woman," but it was not until far into the night that the identity of his mother was disclosed. Soon sensing the uselessness of all efforts to pacify the poor man when those hideous spells were on him, I realized that the only thing was to fight it out with him. It was easy to tell, as we lay on that bed, that his shouts and screams of terror meant the coming of another spell. As he jumped up to escape those dreadful, nonexistent dangers, I would fasten both hands in a choking grasp on his throat. With the fear and strength of madness, Tom, who was much larger than I, would toss me about as a terrier would a rat, but I was huskier and better fitted for such a task then than now. Tom was not fighting me; he was not fighting at all but trying to defend himself and to escape from tormentors. With me hanging on to his throat, he would soon choke down and sink to the floor. Then I would drag him over onto the bed on the floor and let him gasp himself back to life, while I rested and panted.

After one especially trying struggle, as he lay there panting for breath, I remembered Dr. Lavery's pills, so I got them out and decided to give him one. At the moment, he was exhausted and in no position to refuse. Sitting there all ready to administer to the momentarily helpless man the pill poised between my fingers, the thought that if he were to die as a result of the pill made it seem better to accept the ordeal of battle through the night because I would never feel right if Tom died as a result of my unwillingness to go through. Quickly I put the pill back in the box, stepped to the grade door, and threw that box just as far out into the night as lay within my arm's strength. About that time Tom was resuming activity and seeing things. My course was now plain. With no relief from medication, for the medicine was gone, I accepted the challenge (I would gladly have refused it) and got old Tom around the neck.

When we got down after that spasm, my mind turned to the rest of Lavery's medicine, the bottle of brandy still in my hip pocket. Maybe my need for it was greater than his, for he needed no alcoholic stimulant. Be that as it may, I took a good snort of the brandy and sat down to await developments, which soon came. After each struggle, a good stiff hooker of the brandy set me up for the next. By the time the bottle was empty, a good bit of pink had been painted on my clouds, Tom's devils seemed fewer and farther between, until he was little more than a man with a terrible hangover. So about five o'clock in the morning, the hour when the saloons opened, if they had not forgotten to close, the two us, with neither one highly sober, walked downtown to George Gordon's saloon to see what the genial gentleman in the white apron could suggest and administer for our welfare.

To insure that there would be no repetition of that awful night (it was not so bad along toward morning), after leaving word at each saloon that Tom must not be given any more liquor in my absence, I got the necessary horse power and packed my bed out to the camp, a couple of miles up Bad River. Then I came back to town to wait and to ride herd on the erring foreman. As nights go, that was memorable in the sense that it is not easy to forget.

Van Moore

A few days after the night above described, and while the sobering of Tom was still in progress, he and I were sitting on the front porch of Scotty's house in Fort Pierre facing about the west end of Main Street, which was Bad River road, a trail which really went from the head of the river to the mouth. As we were sitting there chatting, perhaps on the evils of drink, an Indian appeared riding bareback on a white horse. There was an Indian camp about five miles up Bad River, stretching for a mile or two along the river and known as the White Church, by reason of the fact that there was such an edifice there among the Indian homes. Sometimes it was spoken of as the Indian village. The Indian on the white horse was coming from that direction. He was putting his horse through on a good gallop and emitting what seemed to my untutored ears the howl extraordinary.

To me it seemed a laughable performance, but Tom looked serious. To my statement, "That Indian certainly has a skinful," he replied, "No, no, something bad has happened out at the Indian village. That is the Sioux death wail."

Soon, following the Indian on the white horse came another Sioux, Paul Prairie Chicken, an immensely corpulent Indian whom we both knew.[11] He followed the first one downtown. Van Moore, a half-breed Indian from the Moreau River country up on the Cheyenne River Indian Reservation, had been drunk and creating a disturbance in Fort Pierre, and he had left town heading up Bad River in the company of a white man, George Tackett, earlier in the day.[12] Tom suggested that we get on our horses, which were saddled in Scotty's barn not over a hundred fifty feet away, and go down to get the facts of what happened.

We saw the bareback white horse and Prairie Chicken's horse standing in the street immediately in front of Fred Rowe's store, so we dismounted there and went in to the store. It then developed that the first Indian was Frank Tincup, with whom I was acquainted, but who was a stranger to Tom, and he was telling the people in the store that Van Moore had shot to death old lady Tincup, Frank's mother. Beyond the facts that Van Moore and George Tackett had come out there boiling drunk, that Van Moore had shot Mrs. Tincup, and that he had disappeared, there was nothing either Frank Tincup or Prairie Chicken could tell, except that Chicken wanted to borrow a rifle from Fred Rowe.[13] That loan was quickly made, but no one there had much confidence as to Chicken's capacity as a gunfighter. In fact there was no such confidence at all.

Tom turned quickly to me and said, "Georgie, are you afraid to go out with me and get Van Moore?"

If God will forgive me for the one I told on that occasion when I said, "No," in answer to that question, the forgiveness of any others should be easy.

Tom was a realist if nothing else, and his next question showed it, "Have you a gun?"

"My six-shooter is out at camp rolled up in my bed."

"Well," he said, "mine is out there too, so we will stop at camp long enough to get them and go on up the river after Van Moore." In as nonchalant a manner as nineteen can affect, I announced that the arrangement suited me.

We got on our horses and rode out to the camp, where we unrolled the beds, got our guns and put them on. Away we went up Bad River, and before long were at the Indian village. Not finding any Indians, although we stopped at several of their log houses, we decided to go on up Bad River to the home of old man Owens, a hardy, old Civil War veteran, to find out if anyone there had seen the murderer of old lady Tincup. By this time a beautiful moon was riding high in the sky, flooding all the landscape with light. Fording Bad River at the upper end and of the Indian village, we went right into the cottonwoods with which Bad River was then lined for its full length. The trees met over the trail, with here and there splashes of moonlight reaching the ground. Two riders came toward us through the trees, and almost instantly a metallic click-click told me that Tom's single-action Frontier Colt was cocked. About that time they came into a patch of moonlight, and at once I recognized one of the riders as Elias Owens, and the other was George Tackett.

I told Tom not to shoot, that I knew the men, and after making me state that I was sure, he seemed assured. By the time we met up with the two riders a second or two later, they proved to be on their way down the river to see how the Indians were getting along. They told us all the Indians were huddled into the Indian house farthest down the river, while the old lady's body lay in the house farthest up the river. Inquiry developed that old man Owens had seen Van Moore going up the river after the killing. Van was riding hard and took a shot at old man Owens. The old man, who had arrived at the stage where his eyesight was pitifully poor, happened to have a rifle with him, and he shot twice at Van Moore, and thought he hit him with the second shot because Van went far down on the neck of his horse. It developed, however, that he did not hit him and that the rider was merely trying to make himself inconspicuous.

Elias and George knew where the old lady's body lay, so they took us to the house. After we had lighted the lantern we looked over the scene of the struggle. The body lay on the dirt floor of the little log house, fully clothed. We assumed she had been shot, because we found some empty shells just immediately outside the door. We knew, too, that she had been beaten savagely over the head with a six-shooter because that was all too evident. Her clothes were somewhat torn, but not especially disarranged. She was lying on her back. Through a tear in her dress the left shoulder seemed to be bitten, and in her right hand was some of her murderer's black hair. The report of the inquest held the next day showed that she had not been shot at all, but in fact been beaten to death by a revolver and then ravished. Seemingly, just to hear the noise, [Van Moore] had stepped to the door and had emptied his pistol, rode around the Indian village some more, shooting and yelling wildly, and then started up the river.

Tackett told us that he and Van had left Fort Pierre together, both intoxicated; that he had sobered up by the time they got to the Indian village, but Van appeared to get worse. George quit him, and went up to Owens's place. Then Van and an Indian by the name of Spotted Crow, a worthless hanger-on, who was not in the habit of overlooking an opportunity to get drunk, had stormed around the village together. It was never shown that Spotted Crow (Old Spot) was doing anything more than hanging around in the hope of getting a drink. Neither did it ever appear that he was present at the time of the killing.[14]

Tom then told Owens and Tackett to direct us to the home where the Indians were, and they did so. When we got there the house was packed almost solid with wailing Indians, and in the group were our friends, Frank Tincup and Paul Prairie Chicken. Inquiry for Van Moore brought the search to a dead end when the Indians said the last they had seen of him was when he and Spotted Crow were creating a disturbance in the neighborhood.

Tom's view was that Van Moore and Spotted Crow were still together, and probably at Spotted Crow's house, which was off towards the hills, as they were called, meaning the high breaks of Bad River southeast of Fort Pierre, northeast of the Indian village and about three miles from either place. I knew Spotted Crow better than Tom did, and my conclusion was that he had probably gone home and that Van Moore had gone some other way. Tom knew Van Moore better than I did, and I can well remember the determination in his tone when he said, "I want to meet up with Van Moore tonight. I know him from long ago, and it is a grudge with me. I can remember when that _____ shot my horse through the neck when I was taking a BXB beef herd to Whitewood to ship." . . .

It seemed certain that Tom was anxious that we should come in contact with Van Moore that night. My wishful thinking was that he had made good his temporary escape. After getting all the available information from the Indians, and it was very little, Tom said, "Now we are going over to Spot's place, and we will find them both there. Tackett, you were in with Van Moore at the start, so you come along. Prairie Chicken, you have a rifle, and we may want an interpreter, so you come along too. All right, let's get going."

So the four of us mounted and started down the river, through the timber, in the moonlight, for Spotted Crow's place. The house was back a mile or more from the river on a gentle slope from the Bad River bottoms to the hills on the south and east. As we left the bottoms and started up the slope to the house, it seemed to me that the moon had never before shone with such a fierce white light. If Tom was right and if Van Moore, a dangerous and desperate man at bay, was actually in that house, he could have picked off each of the four of us in turn, and we would not be able to make any effective return of fire.

Had he commenced firing, just how hard I would have made my horse go down that slope is problematical. I might have stood my ground. We

cannot tell. Our progress seemed ridiculously foolhardy to three members of our party, Prairie Chicken, Tackett, and me, but Tom was determined. Almost miraculously we rode up to the door of that Indian hut without awakening any of the sleepers, even the dogs. At Tom's direction, previously given, Prairie Chicken had his rifle in readiness, and I had a six-shooter in my hand and a prayer in my heart that there would be no occasion to use it. Tom had his gun in his hand, and I still believe he wanted to use it. Sitting on his horse at the door, Tom called for Spotted Crow.

Instantly there was a commotion of barking dogs, combined with the excited chatter of three Indian women who came to the door. Poor

Prairie Chicken was so rattled and scared that he was talking Indian to us and English to the Indians. Tom's demands that Spotted Crow and Van Moore come out, and do it now, were answered by Spotted Crow coming out, and by assurances from him and from the three women that Van Moore was not there and had not been there at all. Still not satisfied, Tom insisted on searching the little, one-room log house, so he got down off his horse, pistol in hand and went in. To me that appears now, and appeared then, the most foolhardy piece of conduct that ever came under my immediate observation. Looking around, and compelling one of the women to light a lantern to make sure, he finally satisfied himself that his man was not there.

When Tom came out of the house, he gave some orders that are engraven on my memory. He said, "Spotted Crow, you _____ _____, you get up here behind me on Wildcat. George, you get right behind me, and if this _____ _____ makes a move to get away, you shoot him. Now, Chicken, you tell me what he has to say, and, Spot, you tell me all about this deal, and just how you fellows killed old lady Tincup."

The cavalcade was formed with Tom out in front on Wildcat and Spot up behind him. I was riding behind Tom's horse. Tackett was a little to my right, and Prairie Chicken a little in front of me and to my left. Spot began to tell his story, which, when interpreted by Chicken did not suit and brought angry and profane denunciations on its falsity from Tom. Spot was surely anxious to please and immediately gave another and different version of the affair. That made Tom angrier and more profane. Spot was willing to tell anything that would pacify Tom, who was not in the mood to be pacified or to believe Spot, no matter what he said.

Tom finally said, "Spot you _____ _____ _____ _____, you tell me the truth, or by God, we'll hang you from the Bad River bridge."

As a matter of fact Spot could talk better English than Prairie Chicken, but his nerves were not in such condition that he could do a decent job of English by that time. After Chicken had interpreted that gentle hint, a useless ceremony for the accused man understood, Spot really became garrulous in Indian, in the hope that some story he would tell would appear satisfactory to Tom Beverly. He seemed to have no luck, and that experience informed me of the menace of procuring stories and confessions by third-degree methods.

Of course my thought was that Tom was bluffing with the story of the hanging. Imagine my horror when we got into town and were on the bridge across Bad River, which divided and still divides Fort Pierre into two parts, and when Tom reigned up his horse, took down his rope, and said, "Now, Spotted Crow, you _____ _____ _____ _____, you get down off this horse, because this is where you hang."

No part of the night's performance had been exactly to my liking, but this was the worst of all, lynching a man by hanging within a hundred fifty yards of the sheriff's house. I protested savagely against any such high-handed administration of justice, being fully convinced that Spotted Crow had nothing to do with the killing of Mrs. Tincup, a conclusion later developed to be entirely correct. Although I have many times since argued for the life and liberty of men facing the chance of penalty for their misdeeds, it is not likely that I ever put more enthusiasm into the task than that night while arguing for Spotted Crow's life about three o'clock in the morning on the Bad River bridge.

Finally Taggart and Prairie Chicken recovered enough from their stupor to join forces with counsel for the defense. Tom was obdurate and insisted that the only proper course was to hang him. He thought we were falling down completely on the job, but of course he could not hang him alone. He finally reluctantly consented to my proposal that we turn him over to Mart Kennedy, the sheriff.[15] Accordingly we rode up to Mart Kennedy's house, which was about halfway between the bridge and Main Street, and got the sheriff out of bed. Mart insisted that he had no warrant for Spotted Crow, nor any right to take him. Finally, at my earnest insistence, he put Spot in jail and turned him loose next day. That was not what one would call a really restful night, but Tom and I went out to camp and to bed.

In a day or so the southern cattle began coming in by train loads, and we had so much work to do in the Pierre stockyards and in the stockyards on the island that we could give not a bit more of our time to Van Moore or any other extraneous interest. We were holding cattle in the day time, branding them in the yards, holding them at night with all the other grueling work that goes with receiving large numbers of cattle at the railhead, and getting them ready for the range. Many of the incoming cattle were sold to other cattlemen, and we had to handle and brand them, too.

As soon as Scotty showed up, he learned from some source, maybe from many, the class of party Tom had staged. Realizing then that his foreman, who could handle cattle so admirably, was no match for John Barleycorn, although he insisted on challenging him periodically, he demoted him to the rank of a cowhand, and put Ira Miller on as foreman. Ira was a fine fellow, and he was the man with whom I stood my first night guard, west of Midland on the north side of Bad River, across from the mouth of Brave Bull Creek.

What Became of Van Moore

Perhaps it would be out of place not to tell something of the subsequent history of Van Moore, who really contributed to the making of some law history in South Dakota, although all of that has nothing to do with my old friend, Tom Beverly, because he never saw Van Moore again.

After leaving the Indian village, Van Moore rode up Bad River and arrived at old Bill Brown's place, near where the railroad town of Capa is. Showing that his horse was just about played out, and convincing old Bill that he had to go on, he borrowed a fresh saddle horse. My friend Fred Ervin, now a railroad conductor out of Sioux Falls, then a cowboy, said to me that after Van got the fresh horse from Bill Brown, he hid in a clump of timber on Bad River, about the mouth of Prairie Dog Creek, the creek which drains the large, level stretch of country northerly from Midland. He stayed in hiding there for two days. Then, according to his own story, he made a night ride north to the Cheyenne River and hid there from dawn to dark of the next day. That gave his horse a good chance to rest and feed. The next night he made a night ride north to the Moreau River, to the home of his mother, Mrs. Dolphus.[16]

Acquainting his old mother with what he had done and she insisting that he should surrender to the law enforcement officer, he agreed to do so provided she would turn him over to the Indian agent at the Cheyenne River Agency, and not to any of the cowpunchers or officers in Stanley County.[17] At that time that county consisted of the territory now comprising the counties of Haakon, Jackson, and Stanley, with the county seat at Fort Pierre. (Parenthetically let me state that in that area at that time there was not a foot of roadway, except such as may have been dug into the earth with wagon wheels, and not a single bridge was over creek or river in all that expanse, except the Bad River bridge in Fort Pierre, which Tom wanted to use as a gallows for Spotted Crow.) Accordingly, his mother took him into the Cheyenne River Agency and turned him over to the agent, who, in turn, delivered him over to Mart Kennedy, the sheriff of Stanley County. Soon he was prosecuted on a charge of murdering Mrs. Tincup, and believing that on a trial the jury would convict him and provide the death penalty, Van Moore entered a plea of guilty. Judge Loring E. Gaffy sentenced him to imprisonment in the South Dakota state penitentiary for life.

A few years passed and the world had changed. The homesteaders, taking advantage of unwise land-settlement laws, had portioned out the range among themselves in quarter sections. There was no more cow country, there was no more cowboy, and there never could be again. As the world was changing, I made an effort to adapt myself to circumstance, and, by a lot of gall and some good luck, after the Law School at the University of Michigan had kindly put its stamp of approval on me, I was admitted a member of the bar of South Dakota in July of 1906. A year or so later, when Van Moore wanted to get out of the penitentiary, he employed William G. Porter, who, I think, was at the time United States attorney for South Dakota or recently had been.[18] Porter made an application for a pardon for Van Moore, and when the hearing on the application was had before the board of pardons, I went to Pierre to look the situation over. After Porter got through extolling the virtues of his client, I asked to be heard, and the chairman of the board, the then presiding judge of the supreme court, asked me whom I represented. My response that my interest was only that of a citizen of South Dakota who wanted to tell them a story got me permission to address the board, and that gave them a picture of the other side of Van Moore. The result was that the application for pardon was denied. A later application met the same fate.

Then Van Moore, through Porter, made application to the Supreme Court of South Dakota for his release by *habeas corpus* proceedings on the ground that the murder had been committed on an Indian trust allotment in Stanley County, and that the federal court, and not the state court, had jurisdiction to punish for the offense. The Supreme Court of South Dakota, in an opinion written by Judge McCoy, held that the state court did have jurisdiction.[19]

Time moved on, and I was serving as assistant United States attorney for the district of South Dakota, when the Supreme Court of the United States, speaking through Mr. Justice (now Chief Justice) Hughes, decided the Pelican case, which was similar in its facts to the Van Moore case. The Pelican opinion took the opposite view and held that an Indian trust allotment within an organized county was part of the Indian country and that the right to punish for a murder committed thereon was in the federal courts.[20] Porter at once sued out a writ of *habeas corpus* in the district court of the United States asking for the release of Van Moore.

I went to Judge J. D. Elliott and told him the facts and circumstances, and he said that he could see nothing for him to do but to turn Van Moore loose because the state court that sentenced him had no jurisdiction to do so.[21] He agreed to hold the matter up until I should take the case up with the Department of Justice, but the department replied that he was just an Indian who had killed another Indian and that he had probably been punished enough. Of course the fellow who wrote that letter did not know anything about the murderer. He had not seen the terror-stricken Indians at the Indian village, and he had not, with more fear than enthusiasm, hunted for Van Moore through the night. Anyway

Van was turned loose and returned to the Cheyenne River reservation. Not long after his return, he went horse hunting one day. Later, his horse returned, but from that day to this, not a sign has ever been seen by anybody of his saddle, blanket, or bridle, nor of Van Moore himself.[22]

Buffalo George, a former cowboy, a hard citizen, who had served several penitentiary sentences for larceny of livestock, was in the pen with Van. Buffalo and I were good friends, really good friends, on the range. Without any solicitation on his part, I was helpful in getting a pardon for Buffalo. It was not my intention ever to disclose my part in it to him, but he learned it on that mysterious, but wonderfully effective, source of information, the prison grapevine. Well, Buffalo was released and went to work for Stanley Philip near Fort Pierre.[23] He took a several days' holiday, and no one knew where he was, nor did he tell. It was about the same time that Van went horse hunting.

One summer night, after I had moved to Rapid City (which I did in February 1917), I was in Fort Pierre visiting in the hardware store of my old friend Fred S. Rowe, who was always in the habit of keeping open until late. About ten o'clock, as Fred was getting ready to close the store, in walked my friend Buffalo. I was delighted to see him, and, when Fred closed the store, Buffalo and I went out and, in the fashion of an older day, sat down cross-legged on the sidewalk for a good visit. Thus we sat in that nice, summer night, visiting away until the train for Rapid City went west at three o'clock in the morning. As we sat there visiting, Van Moore went through my mind, and I said, "Say, Buff, did you kill Van Moore?"

In the most nonchalant way, he said, "No."

I said, "You're a damn liar, Buff, you did kill him."

He said, "No, I didn't kill him. I'd just as soon tell you if I did." Then after a pause he asked, "Did you know that Van Moore threatened to kill you?"

I said, "Doc Redfield (Dr. C. C. Redfield of Rapid City, who was warden of the state penitentiary when Van Moore and Buffalo were in prison there) told me that Van had threatened to kill three men when he got out, and I was number one, but I never said anything about it."

Buffalo said, "He told me he was going to kill you, but, hell, I wouldn't worry about a thing like that if I were you."

I have not worried about it from that time until now. No matter what others thought, I liked Buffalo, and he liked me. His friendship was the fundamental kind that could develop in natural, rather than artificial, society.[24]

More of Tom Beverly

Pardon the digression, but there seemed no escape, and now we come back to my friend Tom. He had been in the cow country a long time, although it is doubtful if he was over forty-five, which was an ancient age for a cowboy. That game was started young, and, if he was as old as forty-five, it is easy to believe that he was a range rider for close to thirty years when I knew him. I last saw him in 1900. It is my recollection that, as a very young rider, he had known Wild Bill Hickok in Kansas, and he could grow eloquently profane in telling the miserable qualities of that cold-blooded killer.

One day while we were loafing in camp, Hughie Burgess got to telling an account of Wild Bill's encounter with the McCandlas gang in the Rock Creek Station in southwestern Nebraska in 1861. Bill Hickok was killed in Deadwood in 1876, and, if my calculation is right, Tom must have been about twenty or twenty-one years of age at that time, so at least some of his personal friends may have run afoul of Wild Bill when he was a town marshal in some of the cow towns of Kansas. Anyway, when Hughie got done, Tom cut loose with testimony about Wild Bill, which could never be used as a working hypothesis to prove any theory that he was a gentleman in anybody's language.[25]

One of the most fascinating discussions was to hear Tom and Cheyenne Bill, another old-timer about the same age and experience as Tom, argue the merits and demerits of the rawhide rope and the hemp rope. Cheyenne Bill used a rawhide rope of his own plaiting, between fifty and sixty feet long, while Tom used a hard, hemp three-eighths rope, between thirty-five and forty feet long. Bill was no mean performer, and Tom was an expert. We would hear that when the rawhide rope was wet it would stretch so far that it would play out a steer to run far enough to take the slack out of it. On the other hand we would hear that when the hemp rope was wet it got so hard and uncontrollable that it would take two men to put a loop of it on a resin weed. The arguments in favor and against each were legion, but the fact remains that either one of those worthies could place a loop about where it belonged.

Bill was a hard and fast roper, meaning that he tied his rope hard and fast to his saddle horn. Tom was a dally-welter roper, meaning that he caught his animal with the end of the rope free and "took his dallies," which meant that he wrapped the free end of the rope around the saddle horn. The dally was the more skillful way, but most of the cowpunchers tied hard and fast for the very simple reason that they were not good enough with the dally. Those respective methods furnished basis for no end of argument between the two. Another eternal question between them was whether the range horses or the sheep did the greater damage to the cow range. Tom thought the sheep was the more harmful and Bill the horse, and away they would go again. Of course that was discussion by experts, and the rest of us could sit around and learn something each time the two old boys got going.

Tom had spent practically all his life in the rattlesnake country, and it was common talk in the cow country that you can mistake something else for a rattlesnake, but you never mistake a rattlesnake for anything else. One morning when the outfit was camped on Prairie Dog, Tom, getting up in the early dawn, pulled a boot out from under the edge of his tarp (the tarpaulin on his bed) and reached his hand in for the sock. He gave a scream that startled the whole camp, and it would have done credit to a young picnicking female with an ice cube down her back. The cause of the scream was a rattlesnake in his boot. That called for careful expulsion of his snakeship, and, when that was done, the snake developed into a toad that seemed to have taken a fancy to Tom's boot.

Only once was I ever able to tell Tom something about things on the range, and that was accidental. We learn that the young of rattlesnakes are born live, not hatched from eggs as are the young of some reptiles. But how about the mating? Well, one day as I was riding alone in the Prairie Dog Creek country, the warning rattle of a snake caused me to look and, after locating the source of the noise, to get off my horse, quirt in hand, to play the role of executioner. The snake was always easily killed if one had him away from a hole and had a quirt. A good snap on the head with the popper of the quirt rendered him unconscious, and then to tramp the head not gently but firmly into the ground with a boot heel finished the job. It was most easily done when you got him moving along, instead of coiled. On this occasion, instead of finding one snake, there were two, joined together in the mating act and wholly unable to pull apart. Having no special emotion for the love life of a rattlesnake, I dispatched the two of them, being a bit more cautious than would have been thought necessary if there were only one.

The next day it happened that Tom and I were riding along together well up on Bad River on the Wilburn Flat about the place where Dick Wickert was killed by lightning when working a roundup, a little to the northwest of where the railroad town of Powell now is.[26] The strange snake incident of the day before was told to Tom in all its details, particularly the difficulty of pulling them apart after they were killed. After I finished the story, Tom said, "Georgie, it's all right to pick a load into a tenderfoot, but, Good Lord, I was punching cows before you were born and have lived in a rattlesnake country all my life. Now you tell that story to some young fellow, but don't pick on an old stager like me. If you are going to string somebody, always pick the right man."

I was thoroughly abashed at the reception given to the recital of this incident, which had so interested me. Just then—Brrzz—and I rode a few feet to one side to kill the snake giving the warning. Imagine my surprise and delight, too, to find an exact repetition of the experience of the day before. Two snakes were firmly fastened together in love's embrace. I got off and told my skeptical friend to come over. He rode over and watched me tantalize the two love-locked snakes, which could not get apart, and soon they were duly killed. Then pulling hard on one, with the other held firmly under a boot heel, the lady and the snake were pulled apart. I can still see the picture of old Tom, with his hands resting on the saddle horn, as he leaned forward over his horse's withers to watch the whole show, and when it was completed, I can still hear him say, "Well, by God, after all these years on the range, I never saw nor heard of that until today, and you have seen it on two successive days. I guess a fellow never should think he knows all about anything." I never saw the like except on those two occasions.

Along in the latter part of the summer, it became necessary for Ira Miller to let old Tom go. Ira had not wanted to run the L-7 outfit, nor even to work steadily. He had developed into the nester class, which meant a man with a place of his own (up near the Forks of Bad River) and a small bunch of cattle. Also, he was sweet on Eva Wilburn, the daughter of a neighboring rancher, and was going to marry her, which he afterwards did. So Ira had interests beyond being foreman of a big cow outfit. Tom brooded over his demotion and seemed to hold Ira responsible for it. Ira was blameless. John Barleycorn was the only one responsible.

One day as the outfit was working on Mitchell Creek, which runs into Bad River at Midland from the north, we had a bunch of calves to brand. Tom, who always did the roping in such cases when he was present, had gone to Midland and got himself well oiled up on Hostetter's Bitters, which he bought at Charlie Russell's store. That was the last straw so far as Ira was concerned, and he decided Tom was through. Choosing one of the best-understood methods of firing a cowpuncher, Ira said to Leo Hollis, "You get on Big Enough and catch those calves."[27]

Big Enough was a large bay horse, one of the best cutting horses on the range, and was in Tom's string. No man, not even the boss nor the owner himself, had the right to ride, or even to touch, a horse that was in a cowpuncher's string. We all knew what it meant, but Leo did as he was told. While Leo was busy roping the calves and the branding was going on, Tom arrived from Midland a few miles away. Midland then consisted of Russell's country store and the Hall House. Tom was a bit drunk on bitters, and when he saw Leo Hollis on his top horse, Big Enough, he became thoroughly indignant.

He said, "What in hell are you doing on that horse. You get off there now."

Ira said, "I told him to get on that horse."

Tom turned his horse away, then turned back and said to Ira, "Can I have a pack horse?"

Ira said, "Sure," and the deal was closed.

When we got through branding and went to camp, Tom had his saddle on his own private horse and his bed on a company horse. Ira gave him a check for the wages he had coming. Tom shook hands and said goodbye to each of us, got on his horse, and leading his pack horse, started west for Rapid City. That was the last time I saw him. He was gone but not forgotten. Also gone were all the high hopes with which the hazy horizons of the range had beckoned to him years before. His last chance for cowman greatness was shattered when he squandered the opportunity Scotty gave him when he put him in charge of a big outfit once again.

During the winter of 1901–1902, news came filtering down to the Missouri River country that Tom Beverly was in a jam with the law at Rapid City. The story and the fact was that he and Faye Gentry, a cowpuncher from the Belle Fourche River country (I knew Faye quite well), had been arrested on a charge of stealing some cattle belonging to John Reddick.[28] They were tried at Rapid and were acquitted March 14, 1902. Charles T. Buell was the state's attorney who prosecuted him. The charge in the information stated the date of the larceny as November 15, 1901. Looking back from this angle, it is a matter of sincere delight to me to know that there was not sufficient proof to justify conviction of my friend.

From the time of his trial onward, Tom's career was notable for nothing, unless it be for surrender to his besetting weakness. He was never again able to establish himself in the good opinion of the big cattlemen. Indeed, although they did not know it clearly, the cattlemen were soon, pitifully soon, to be converted into fence riders, doing their cowpunching with a claw hammer and a saddle pocket full of staples.

As shown by the record of a lawsuit brought against John Clower and three other saloon-keepers of Rapid City, Tom Beverly died in Rapid City on April 29, 1905, as the result of a continuous, month-long drunk. Poor Tom!

> Owning his weakness, his evil behavior,
> And leaving, with meekness, his sins to his Saviour.[29]

I loved the man and cherish his memory, which, thank God, is not a memory of his last month of life. He was a marvel out in the wide-open country and a mess in town.

It is easy to picture him yet out in the country, big man that he was, riding his fourteen-inch seat saddle, when almost all others used a sixteen-inch seat, and with his feet incased in size 5-1/2 high-heeled boots, jauntily set in his iron stirrups. He was not in any sense the grandstander or the fool when he was at business on horseback. . . . Well worthwhile was the Tom Beverly I knew. Peace to his ashes and rest to his soul.

Affectionately,
Dad

CHAPTER 8

The Rooshian Wagon

June 24, 1940

My dear Geordie, Jean, and Bob:

No matter what precautions we take, our footprints on the sands of time are almost sure to be obliterated, and, unless we are careful conservationists, the sands themselves will wash away. So it is with the story of the cow country. . . . Most of the men who participated in the work of the cow country have neither the capacity nor the inclination to make a written record of those days that can never return, days which they took in their stride, and the work of those days was to them just the day's work. Most of them are disinclined to tell the story to those who know nothing about it, and who will reward the teller with an outward skepticism to conceal their inward ignorance. Having no great gift of pen, and none at all of imagination, all I can do is to record in letter form some little incident that happened, and then set around it, as best I can, the circumstances that produced the incident, and in that way give you some kind of a picture, accurate so far as it goes, of life and work in the cow country. . . . The cow country was an epoch, and one could well wish for a Scott or a Twain to give it life in the printed page. . . .

It happened in the fall of 1900, at a time when I was out on my first job as a rep. The L-7 outfit having separated itself from the 73 outfit, ... was expecting to winter all of its cattle, as soon as they were gathered up, in the general country along the western side of the Lower Brule Indian Reservation, along the Missouri River, and on Cedar and Antelope Creeks. That is down the Missouri River from Fort Pierre. Billie Hess, the foreman, told me to go with the Russian wagon, which was working the country to the northwest of Fort Pierre.

To say "Russian wagon," without further explanation, would leave out too much. On Willow Creek, about twenty to twenty-five miles northwest of Fort Pierre, there was then a colony of Russian settlers. They were not of the Mennonite type of Russians. They had no peculiarities of dress nor thoughts of common ownership of property. Each of them owned cattle, branded with his own individual brand, perhaps several thousand head when all were grouped. They had no community government of any sort. Although each was the captain of his own ship, or maybe I should say string, and the master of his own soul (no other status was recognized on the range), they did seem to have that "Follow-my-leader" principle that now is so prevalent in some parts of Europe and so disastrous to the peace of all the world.[1] As a result, one of their number, Alex Meers, was generally looked upon as their spokesman and their leader. The younger members, who had the cowboy philosophy of independence of thought and freedom of action, must have been something of a trial to Alex, who was usually called by the cowboys as "King o' the Rooshians." But Alex was a good fellow and went right along on the ways of the country. All the group talked the English language and were highly assimilable.[2]

In the fall of 1900, in order to facilitate the gathering of their own cattle and the shipping of their beef, they decided to run a roundup of their own, with Alex Meers as foreman. Alex had followed the roundups, and he knew what it was all about, as well as others of the young Russians. Running a wagon meant a general invitation to reps (the representatives of other cow outfits), and I was sent by Billie Hess. There were quite a few reps with the outfit, some representing big outfits and some representing themselves. Old John J. Hilger of Pierre, a merchant whose business has been continued all these years and is now the Hengel clothing company, and who was a considerable cattle owner,[3] had a string of horses on this roundup ridden by Bunk White.

Now who was Bunk White? Bunk was a colored cowboy, originally from Texas, and a top hand. But for the injustice that nature did to him in wrapping up that much cowboy in a black skin, his recognized capacity as a cowhand would have landed him in charge of almost any of the big outfits. All the men of the range who knew him, and nearly all of them did, were forced to admit that as a roper in the great outdoors, and as a bronco rider in the same place, he was without a superior. No one did, nor should, complain of his diligence as a worker. Neither did any one attempt to suggest that he did not know the cow game. Bunk knew, and he knew that he knew. Many who were frankly inferior to him in every department of the business of the cow country disliked him with a cordiality that must have been born of what has since come to be known as an inferiority complex. Anyway, Bunk was a black so-and-so to many of the cowpunchers who were really not in his class. To me he always seemed like a good hand, who was expert in all departments, and who was not much blacker by nature than the rest of us were with the sun.[4] Moreover, he was always a good fellow with me, and we were close friends. The color of his skin was of less consequence to me than the color of his liver.

This roundup worked up Bad River from its mouth, then out across country, taking in Plum Creek, Lance Creek, Willow Creek, Chantier Creek, and up the Missouri River to about the mouth of the Cheyenne. One day when Bunk and I happened to get paired off on circle, we raised a gray wolf on the head of Chantier Creek. (Just what the proper French pronunciation of the name of that creek is I do not know, but to me, as to every other fellow who ever rode that part of the country, it was "Shanty" Creek. That had nothing to do with this gray wolf, which cared little for scholastic refinement of geography.) It was almost an obligatory duty for the cowboy to do what lay within his power to catch a gray wolf any time one came within his vision, even to the point of riding his horse to death.

The gray wolf, or the lobo, was a dreadfully destructive animal in a livestock country. We still hear stories about their skill in designedly hamstringing an animal, but based on observation of his work, my view is that he never had such specific intention. He was a large and fierce animal with heavy shoulders and amazingly powerful jaws. Suppose he took in after a two-year-old steer; of course the quarry would try to get away. On getting close enough to his prey, he would bite, and if he got a good hold with his big mouth, savage teeth, and powerful jaws, he would jerk a pound of meat out of the hindquarters of the harried animal. I saw one such animal still alive, with no wolf in sight but with enough of a meal eaten out of its hindquarters to expose the entrails in part, but without severed hamstrings. Although still alive, it was helpless and could not survive. It died before I left it. If the jaws of the wolf had happened to land on the hamstring, he would have cut it.

Bunk and I took in after the wolf we had seen, and we maneuvered as best we could to wear him out and still have something left of the horse-flesh under us. Working on him by turns, we hoped to wear him down so we could catch him, but this wolf was gaunt and hungry, or "ga'nt" as a cowhand would have it. When in that condition, a gray wolf was very fast on foot and unbelievably long winded. We never did get close enough to that particular wolf to take down our ropes and try to get a loop on him. We finally lost him in the brakes of Shanty Creek. . . . Chasing a wolf on horseback was no frolic, but a fierce contest of speed and endurance over rough terrain. If you caught up with him, your job was to rope him and drag him to death. If the catch was round the neck, you could so handle the situation as to give him some terrific jerks at the end of the rope. Of course you want to remember that those horses did not love the lobo, and sometimes there was the problem of reconciling the pony to the situation. If you could raise a wolf that just had a full feed, he was easy to catch. A feed to a wolf meant everything he could hold, and in such circumstances he was easily winded.

I can give a unique experience of my own on another occasion to illustrate my point. On a blazing hot day I was on day herd on the slope between Eagle Butte and the Cheyenne River. My horse was a ten- or twelve-year-old long-legged sorrel, very well trained and gentle. On such occasions, and with a really gentle horse, it was a common practice to take the bit out of the horse's mouth and leave the bridle hang on his neck. The cattle were all lying down, grunting and resting in the hot sun, and it was not yet time to move them along toward the next camp and the bed ground. My horse, old Bar X, named for one brand he bore, was standing there at ease, with the bit out of his mouth, and I was sitting on the ground in his shade with my back against his front legs. When it seemed too hot for any form of activity, here came a wolf cutting through the edge of the herd and within fifty feet of me, showing plainly from his puffing and panting and clumsy gait that he was full of meat. He had not noticed the horse or me until I jumped up and landed in the middle of old Bar X, taking down my rope.

Those horses were all broken to neck rein, and the fact that I forgot to put the bit in his mouth bothered neither Bar X nor me from the moment he realized that my point of interest lay just a little to the left and a short way behind that wolf. By the time I was swinging a loop, old Bar X was laying up alongside that short-winded wolf. It is doubtful if we had gone over two hundred yards before I got a good chance for a throw. Although I was of no special consequence as a roper, by good luck and the skill of a good horse, the first loop thrown settled squarely round his big neck. Old Bar X and I galloped back and forth across that prairie until I was sure the wolf had gone to his own hell.

Then I dismounted, put the bridle bit in the mouth of old Bar X, took my rope off the wolf and went on about my business. Every circumstance had to be exactly right to get it done that way. Many and many a hard chase the cowboy took, without getting even fairly close to his wolf. It was nothing romantic, not even fun, just part of a hard job. Occasionally it meant hard luck for the wolf; almost always it meant a heart-breaking run for the horse and a long ride for the fellow on him. Incidentally, there has not been a single gray wolf in South Dakota for years. The last one was old Three Toes, trapped up in Harding County in the early twenties, and a good riddance that was. The gray wolf cannot survive in civilization like his sneaking cousin, the coyote.[5]

Memory does not serve to tell all who were on that roundup. Big Mouth Thompson was the cook, and he, in a voice that could be heard rumbling to the next divide, was in the habit of reviving our drooping spirits with an astonishingly lewd song apparently dedicated to a "Sweet Ida Williams, who lives in Glendive." Poor Big Mouth, he was afterwards blown beyond recovery in any part by a charge of dynamite that he thought he could handle. Guy Moulton of Pierre, Harry Briggs of Bad River and Fort Pierre, Harry Hoyt of Fort Bennett, and a goodly number of others were on the Russian roundup.[6]

One day when we were working a roundup on the north side of Chantier Creek, Bunk was turning a fast-running steer. The young horse he was riding slipped and fell, something the young horse was more likely to do than the older, better-trained and seasoned cow pony. Of course falls were so frequent as not to excite comment. Almost invariably the rider cleared himself of the falling horse and just waited at the scene of the fall until some other fellow caught the horse and returned it to him, for a horse that fell always ran away on getting to his feet. He might be so well trained scarcely anything else would make him run away with a saddle and bridle on him, but he would run after a fall.

I happened to be close by as this horse fell with Bunk, and I was horrified to see that his left foot was caught in his stirrup, and his spur was tangled in the hind cinch. As the horse got to his feet and started to run, he began kicking at the form following him and attached to the stirrup. I made a frantic run to catch the runaway horse by the bridle reins, and just then the spur strap broke, releasing Bunk's foot. Through the tail of my eye, I saw him start to get up, so I gave chase to his horse and caught him. When I returned his horse, we gave voice to the usual courtesies, "Are you hurt, Bunk?"

"No." The incident was then forgotten. The cowboy was not supposed to be hurt if he could get to his feet and no bones broken.

Another incident took place a day or so later in which Bunk was one of the leading actors. Although it all happened and passed in less time then it takes to tell it, in looking back at it from the vantage point of later years, it seems one of the most dramatic moments in my experience. Alex Meers, the wagon boss, after breakfast one morning decided to ride over to his home to see how the folks were along. He told where to camp the outfit for noon, where to work the cattle that were rounded up, and then told Bunk to lead the circle. . . .

Although Bunk was a splendid cowman who knew exactly what to do and how to do it, he was a Negro. That brought two customs of the range into head-on collision. The tradition of the Texas men that no one could "take orders from a nigger" was considered proper custom on the range, and on the other hand, the wagon boss was in complete charge. In case the wagon boss failed to appear when the cattle were rounded up, the task of seeing that the roundup was properly worked fell on the shoulders of the circle leader, and on that morning Bunk held the job. We started off on circle, and the leader told the men off, a couple now and a couple then, to drive everything in the line of cattle in the area to the gathering place, the roundup.

Of course the leader, with whomsoever ever else he selected, took the longest ride, "went 'round the outside, went 'round the rim-rock." On this occasion I went around the outside with Bunk, and, as was almost invariably the case, the circle leader and whoever was with him were last into the roundup with our cattle. About that time the wrangler brought out the saddle bunch, and each of us roped out a fresh mount, a cutting horse. Then we compactly bunched the cattle, and Bunk told me to go in. That meant to go into the bunched roundup, which is held by riders stationed around it, and cut out whatever cattle there were in the roundup that should be put into our day herd and taken along for distribution to other points on the range. Each "rep," or outside man, with the outfit was entitled to his turn in the roundup to assure that none of the cattle he represented were left.

All efforts at horsemanship seem mild to one who for years was accustomed to observe good riders on good cowponies doing their stuff on the range. Without considering trick and fancy stunts, standing up on the horse, going under and over, standing on their hands, and all that

MICK
B.
HARRISON

sort of thing, but just giving thought to the matter of riding astraddle of horses broken to ride, there perhaps never were better horseback riders on the face of the earth than the cowboys of the North American range country. When my horse began to tire, and it did not take very long to work a horse into a lather when he was cutting out, I came out to make room for another fellow to be ordered in by the boss.

Since Alex Meers had not returned, and Bunk was circle leader, he was boss in spite of himself. It certainly never had occurred to me to take offense when Bunk had ordered me in. When I came out and set myself in position to help hold the roundup, Bunk was directly across from me, and I saw him ride up to Harry Hoyt, and of course I expected to see

Harry go in to the roundup and go to work cutting out cattle. Instead, Harry's hand went up in menacing attitude, holding his coiled rope. Almost instantly several riders were with them and stationed back of Harry. Knowing that something was wrong, but not knowing just what, I galloped quickly around and got alongside of Bunk and asked him what was the matter. His worst swear word was "Dad blame," and he said, "Dad blamed if I know, George. I just told Harry he could go in to the roundup and get his stuff. He said that no black son of a _____ could tell him what to do, and he said he would rope me and drag me to death."

I said, "Well, Bunk, by God, there will be nobody get at you from behind."

Almost quick enough to defy the eye, Bunk's rope came off the saddle fork and sizzled into a loop. Without at any time taking his eyes away from Harry, with his loop all ready, Bunk said, "Now, you dad blamed basta'd, I'll give you the first three throws."

Well was it for Harry that his common sense prevailed, for in my opinion Bunk was too good a horseman for Harry to catch him in three throws, and too good a roper for Harry to escape being caught if he took the throws. I have never thought that it showed anything but good sense on Harry's part to back away from the offer of Bunk, although he was very foolish to have set the incident in motion in the first place. He knew that Bunk was merely doing his duty under the law of the range. In less than a minute, everybody was busy at his work and the whole matter was forgotten. It could have been a tragic duel.

This roundup finished on the head of Willow Creek, and I was required to take all the cattle I had gathered to a point on Stony Butte Creek, about forty or fifty miles away, a little north of where the town of Vivian stands today. All the L-7 cattle were to be taken to the Fort George Bottoms on the Missouri River above the Lower Brule Agency and there turned loose. It was about Thanksgiving when the Russian roundup disbanded, and I started off across country with my string of horses and a good-sized bunch of cattle. A few days later I turned those cattle into the herd the outfit was holding on Stony Butte Creek, a little way south of the butte. If memory serves me right, I was next to the last of the fellows to get in. Posey came in a day or two later, and then we were ready to start with the big herd for the Missouri.

The men I recall being there were Billy Hess, the wagon boss, Fred Ervin, Posey, Hughie Burgess, Harry Read, and Al Martin was cook. Scotty came out from Fort Pierre and Pat Oakes came with him, and one morning in early December, we broke camp in a snowstorm and started for the Missouri River.[7] We had scarcely started when the storm became a fury, and it continued unabated until we turned loose near the Missouri River three full days later. How we managed to go along in the right direction without losing any horses or cattle, or even men, has always been a bit of a mystery to me. Of course it was excelled by the exploit of the actor Frank Bacon in his play *Lightning*, when he said that he drove some swarms of bees across the plains to California and never lost a bee. We were not that good, but we did well enough for the job we had.[8]

It would be interesting to know what became of the Russians in that colony. They are all gone, run out by the homesteaders' migration, and for many years I have not heard any word about any of them. Poor Bunk lost his mind and was sent to the State Hospital for the Insane at Yankton. He recovered, was released, and went to California, where he was the last I heard of him, maybe twenty years ago.[9] If he is not dead now, he is a mighty old man, but, in his day, he could rope 'em, he could ride 'em, he could do anything that was needed to be done on the range.

Affectionately,

Dad

CHAPTER 9

The Law of the Range

July 16, 1940

My dear Geordie, Jean, and Bob:

In the case of *Nashville, Chattanooga & St. Louis Railway v. Browning*, decided by the Supreme Court of the United States on May 20th, 1940, Justice [Felix] Frankfurter had this to say about law: "It would be a narrow conception of jurisprudence to confine the notion of 'laws' to what is found written on the statute books, and to disregard the gloss which life has written upon it. Settled state practice cannot supplement constitutional guarantees, but it can establish what is state law. . . . Deeply embedded traditional ways of carrying out state policy . . . are often tougher and truer law than the dead words of the written text."

Although there were statutes and court decisions stating what acts were and were not proper to be done in the state of South Dakota during the years when most of the west-of-the-river country was open range, with courts and public officers to enforce those laws, underlying all that was the law of the range, unwritten, understood, and supreme where the men of the range held sway. Those men served on the juries, and the written law was to them of no consequence when it violated the rules that were required for the proper government of human conduct on a frontier fringe.

Any man could go to his neighbor's home on the range when no one was there, eat anything he could find, feed his horse, sleep if it was that time of day, take a fresh horse if he really needed it; and he need have no fear that anyone could successfully charge him with unlawfully breaking and entering the house or with any sort of unlawful taking of his neighbor's horse. In that highly individualistic state of society (and yet communal in a sense), he had the right to take that which he really needed, and the jurors selected from the men of the range would enforce such right, no matter what judges or lawyers thought or said about it. The "dead words of the written text" made no appeal to those men when set by the side of the live needs of life itself. But it was the law of the range that the ranch visitor, under no circumstances, had the right to leave any dirty dishes. Also, it was the law of that life that he must leave as much chopped wood as he found, even if he had to go a considerable distance to haul in a rope load of wood and chop it up. The hay used by his horse, if any, he could not replace and was not expected to. No matter how far away the water hole, he was expected to leave the water bucket full. There was nothing on those ranches that was not needed, and no one was lower in the esteem of those people than was one of whom it could be said, "The son of a _____ would steal a bridle bit" or "would steal your spurs."

After filling his actual needs, a person was expected to ride away without having a single thing that he did not bring with him, except what was in his stomach or in that of his horse, with the further single exception that, if necessary, he could have a fresh horse under him. Every man knew that everything on the meagerly equipped place was needed for the survival of the owner or his men. Nothing must be suffered to be done by anyone that would increase the hazards of survival. Locks were unknown and unneeded. It was not considered necessary to leave any recognition of your visit nor of thanks for the courtesy, and pay was out of the question. But when the country got civilized and settled up, you would not dare to leave a bridle bit or spurs, or anything else for that matter, where it could be the subject of the cupidity of the civilized horde. . . .

That does not mean that all were always honest, because not infrequently some of them would lapse from such grace as they had and make off with a bunch of cattle or, as was more likely, with a bunch of the more mobile, faster, and easier-handled range horses. That was dangerous business and was contrary to the law of the range. Heaven help the fellow who got caught at it, because if he lasted until he faced a jury, he was almost certain to be convicted if his jury consisted of men of the range. Of course, even there, former favors played their part.

One of the stock jokes on the range was about eating the other fellow's beef. Let a 6 L man drop into a U Cross camp for a passing meal, and he was almost sure to be asked how he liked the taste of 6 L beef. He would then take another bite and say, "Oh, I didn't recognize it. I never

ate any before. It seems to taste a good deal like U Cross meat. I'll tell the boss to try some one of these days."

Such raillery always went on, but each side knew that it was the law of the range, scrupulously adhered to by the big outfits at least, that under no circumstances should they ever kill and eat anything but their own beef. In the handling of livestock, the big outfits were almost fanatically honest, and they impressed their rules of conduct on the minds of their riders in unmistakable fashion. The men carried out the rules always on the South Dakota range.

Winston Churchill, the British prime minister, says in his book *My Early Life: A Roving Commission* that the hours spent on horseback are never wasted. However close that statement may be to the truth, it is certainly a verity that by the time the snow came flying around and a fellow had to kick his way as best he could into a pair of frozen boots if they happened to be wet, without a single exception every fellow on the range would be willing to insist that he had wasted all the time he spent on it, and in the selection of the world's greatest brainless wonder the only one who could compete with him for the place was some other cowpuncher. Of course as the day wore on, if it happened to be sunny, he would revise his opinion of himself and his kind, especially after his pony got the kinks out of his backbone caused by a cold saddle and a colder blanket. Their personal pride might soar in the sunshine, but it was surely at a low ebb on a dark morning in the fall.

The one thing that more than all others chilled the marrow of the range hand, no matter how well inured he may have been to the business, was lightning. He could neither defend against, nor escape, its blows. He feared his own futility. A dispute is frequently waged as to whether profanity derives from fluidity of expression or from poverty of language. The question is one that is of little interest to me, and whatever be the answer, it can be admitted that for picturesque and sincerely intended profanity the young men of the range should be entitled to Class A rating. It was interesting to hear the flow as they went about their work, but when the clouds hung low and the fiery streaks with their instant and ear-crashing detonations cleaved the sky, the fellows went on with their work, but with no profanity.

The horror of the boys at the conduct of Win Goddell, a roundup cook, when he went outside of his mess tent during a terrible thunderstorm, defiantly shook his fist at the cloud that might hold deaths, and profanely dared it to strike again and closer, had to be experienced, for it cannot be described.[1] Frightened boys would do their duty in holding frightened horses or frightened cattle when the bolts of death were threatening, but none wanted to meet death with profanity on his lips. But let the storm pass and all safe, and then the boys returned to normalcy, blithely cursing everything in sight. It is just a variant of the old jingle:

> The devil got sick, the devil a saint would be.
> The devil got well, the devil a saint was he.[2]

One of Scotty's pet stories was of the bishop on a trans-Atlantic steamer with all passengers battened down under hatches in a serious storm. Inquiring of a passing officer whether there was imminent prospect of disaster, the officer said, "No. As long as you can hear those sailors topside swearing we are riding out the storm."

Time passed, the storm grew worse, and the bishop's fears increased. The greater noise made it more difficult for him to hear, so, sick and frightened, he crawled on his hands and knees to where he got his ear against the hatch and listened for a long enough time to make sure. Then he turned and started back to his berth with a look of thankfulness lighting his face as he said, "Oh! Thank God, they are still swearing." Around a cow outfit in a thunderstorm, that could be slightly paraphrased into, "Thank God! They are swearing again."

On the range a man's past was entirely his own. If he chose to discuss it, then he let it be the subject of such inquiry as anyone cared to make. On the other hand, if he chose to seal it, no one was permitted to indulge his curiosity as to what lay behind. Under the law of the range, a man's secrets were his own unless he cared to share them, and no questions were asked.

A man's personal belongings were denied to the curious if he packed them in his bed. In every roundup bed was a "war sack," usually a wheat sack or so-called seamless sack, in which he kept his clothes and any little personal belonging he had with him. The Anglo-Saxon maxim that "A man's home is his castle" was fiercely true in the cowboy's case, but, as such, the only home he had was his bed. That was why Jimmie Harrell threatened to shoot me for raiding his bed and stealing his itch medicine.[3] The law of privacy, the law of the range, called for complete sanctity of a man's bedroll.

It was the duty of every man working on the range to turn his neighbor's cattle towards that point on the range generally considered as their home range. It was forbidden to drive them farther away from that range or to allow it to be done. Those rugged individuals realized the need of the cooperative state, paradoxical as that may seem now.

It was a rule of good manners, but frequently violated, not to ride, particularly for a long ride, the horse of another outfit. That rule did not apply when permission was granted by the owner. Nor was it necessary, in order to abide the rules, to return the horse. All that was required was that he should be turned loose in good condition. He would be sure to work back to his own home range. It may be of interest to note here that when Zay Jeffries, now the most famous graduate of the South Dakota State School of Mines, decided to go from his home at Fort Pierre to Rapid City to enroll at the Mines, he got an old saddle, blankets, and bridle, borrowed a saddle horse, tied his few belongings on his saddle, and started out. Riding across in about three days, he sold the saddle, blanket, and bridle and turned the horse loose.[4] Soon the horse was back close to Fort Pierre.

The saddle horse was an integral part of the cowpuncher. Each without the other was like the odd half of a pair of scissors, but get them together and then it was plain that the horse and his rider constituted the cowboy. Each man with a cow outfit was assigned about ten head of saddle horses, and they constituted his string. No man, including the wagon boss, or even the owner of the outfit had the right to touch one of the horses in a cowpuncher's string. With his consent and not otherwise, a horse from his string could be borrowed for the use of another. In fact one of the gentle ways of firing a rider was to assign one or more of his horses to another rider. In such case the discharged man drew his pay from the wagon boss, packed his bed and left the outfit.[5]

Among the requirements of the cowboy's code was one which compelled the boss to ride up to a man and tell him what he wanted done in a normal tone. There was no shouting of orders tolerated, and this was fully understood by cowmen, whether giving or taking orders. It may have been due to a sense of pride based in self-importance, and it may have been a courtesy requirement due to and from those highly mobile individuals—men on horseback. Of course the rule was subject to exceptions, and when the going was too tough to permit the courteous approach, the shouted word was considered in proper form.

One thing that was deeply engraven in the cowboy's code was the treatment of the women folks of the range. It was always understood that no molestation was permitted, and the law of the range required that the women must always be safe—in cowboy phrase, "just as safe as if she were in God's pocket." Rough fellows many of them were, and it could hardly be fair at this far distant day to wrap them up in a mantle of personal chastity, but they would neither do nor permit a damage to the character or reputation of a woman placed in their charge. This does not mean that they would out-Joseph Joseph, but it does mean that they would protect, with a real protection.[6]

"Who is my neighbor?" was never much of a question on the range. To do all the things that were required to be done with the horses and the cattle was accepted as axiomatic, and the property of one who was despised was treated with the same consideration for the code of the range as was one's own. Probably the owner would be the object of profane bad wishes, but his livestock got exactly the type of care accorded to the cattle and the horses of a dearest friend.

"Deeply embedded traditional ways of carrying out" their way of life was the range-dweller's code, and that code was adhered to more strictly than the rules are observed often in milder society by the law-abiding elements of that society. This cannot be considered a written code but just a glimpse here and there of a way of life, a life that has vanished from the earth with no possibility of return. . . .

Affectionately,

Dad

CHAPTER 10

Practical Joking

My dear Geordie, Jean, and Bob:

The stories of the old days on the range are likely to be too one-sided. On the one hand you are likely to see depicted on paper, on the stage, or on the screens people who never knew what it meant to have streaks of sweat through the dust on all exposed parts, or boots that lacked a shine, or clothes that were not beautifully clean and well pressed. On the other hand the story is likely to tell of never-ending hardships, danger and work. A good deal can be said about the difficulties of the life, but it surely had its compensations in play and good times. One of the forms of amusement was the practical joke, now almost obsolete, and many were its manifestations, with the perpetrators laughing in unholy glee and the victim cursing with an equally unholy fury.

For instance, it seemed funny when Carson Williams, a range Lothario then, invited the good-looking actress in a traveling company playing at Pierre to take a ride with him, and the invitation was accepted. Carson made no effort at concealment of his conquest of the stage lady, and when he drove down to the Locke Hotel with his cracking fine team to get his actress, some of his friends were on hand and not solely in admiration. Just as the young woman was seated in the buggy and Carson was picking up his lines to move out, some one in the group, supposedly Manuel Sylva, quickly tied a long string of cowbells to the rear.[1]

When those spirited horses heard the jangle of those bells, they started down the rough uneven streets of Pierre, thereby adding to the music of the bells. Of course Carson had no time for admiration of his feminine captive. Indeed the most he could do was to keep that mad runaway

team pointing in some direction calculated to give him some chance for the survival of his girl and himself and do a minimum of property damage. He managed to keep the rig right side up and finally got his terror-stricken inamorata back to the Locke Hotel, where she promptly decided she had seen enough of Carson, and all things western, and all she wanted was the comfort of a right good cry. The danger to life and limb was wholly discounted by the practical jokers, and Carson's wrath put the cap sheaf on their mirth.

The Promissory Note

But this is not intended to discuss any more than a couple of good practical jokes from the nimble wit of Pat Oakes, who was married to your mother's aunt Alvira.[2] A fine, likeable fellow Pat was and filled

to the brim with energy. On one occasion Pat, who was usually hard up, was on a deal for a team, wagon and harness, which he was buying from Jim Cox. Jim, whose family lived in Pierre and whose ranch was up on the Cheyenne River where Elk Creek empties into it, and where his large herds of Spanish Five ⅄ cattle and horses had their main range, was a cowman of the old style. He had everything that went into the making of an old-timer and nothing about him that could be made into an approximation of the appearance of a newcomer.[3]

After no end of dickering on the price, they agreed on a figure of $150.00 for the outfit. Then it became a question of terms of payment, for Jim was not misled into believing that Pat could pay immediate cash. Jim insisted that payment must be made at the end of thirty days, while Pat, knowing that he could not pay in thirty days, tried hard for more time. Jim was adamant, and the note had to be for thirty days. Finally with a little show of irritation, Pat said, "All right. Let me have your damn note, and I'll make it out for thirty days."

A blank form of note was found in the little desk behind the bar, so Pat slipped back there, made out the note, signed it, and handed it to Jim, who put it in his pocket and set up the drinks. The next day when Jim handed in the note for discount at the First National Bank in Pierre, old C. C. ("Cash") Bennett noticed, and so informed Jim, the payee, that the bank did not want it because it was payable "thirty days after death."[4] Jim knew that, whatever the lawyers might say about it, under the law of the range he was stuck. But Pat got the team, the wagon and the harness.

About thirty years later when Pat died of cancer at Eagle Butte, where he was acting as janitor of the public schools and worked until the day before his death, his estate was not worth probating. I don't remember when Jim died, but it must have been along about the same time. They were two old-timers who knew the give and take of the law of the range. They knew that the fellow on the "give" end could chuckle, and the fellow on the "take" end could curse, but a deal was a deal and a note was a note.

Sherwood's Horse Hide

Religion, that appeal to unknown Power behind all the universe, is the common need of all mankind. No one can escape at all times the need to call for help. Some may need it all the time, while those at the other extreme may need it only rarely. Some may need it to sustain themselves, while others may need it only as a disposal plant for their enemies.

One of the cleanest-cut examples of a religious need that ever came across my line of vision had to do with Pat Oakes. The party of the second part was old man Sherwood, a really unique individual. He was a Civil War veteran, but in the dying days of the nineties, they were not necessarily so very old, but Sherwood was quite elderly.[5] He was harelipped, very much the victim of a cleft palate with an extraordinary nasal twang. Occasionally he would go out with the boys and get a few drinks too many. On such occasions he would sing lustily, and he really did a better job singing than he did speaking. He was a very well informed man and argumentative beyond expression. To cap it all, he was a profound and died-in-the-wool atheist. He knew all the answers and could confound any and all who chose to champion the cause of a religion, or the existence of a deity, or a hereafter.

It was no uncommon sight to see old Sherwood of an evening, seated on a beer case against the back wall of a saloon, arguing down a group of cattle men, cowboys, gamblers, and the like, who still wanted to believe that there was something stronger and more dependable in the universe than even a good cowpony and a strong rope. But Sherwood's thrusts were hard, and he had plenty arguments left when all the rest were silenced.

I have mentioned the saloon. Let me set you right. In the frontier town the saloon was the man's club, where he would be sure to meet all his friends who were in town; where he could sit down and enjoy a game of cards, for fun or for money as he wished; where he could engage in discussion of the topics of the day and hear all the news of interest; and where he could quench a thirst if so inclined. In a town like Fort Pierre was in those days, on nights when there was no Masonic Lodge, there was no other place than the saloon for the men to congregate. It was not chosen by Sherwood for his forum for discussion. There just was no other place.

One winter, when Sherwood was running a meat market in addition to his hotel on Main Street, with its little candy and tobacco store, all since long vanished into that fibreless land of dreams, dreadful storms caused the death of great numbers of cattle on the range. There was nothing the big operators could do about it with their widespread, roving cattle; but the nester, the fellow with a small bunch of one or two hundred, who aimed to keep his cattle fairly close within an area, could skin out some of his dead cattle and salvage the value of the hides.

Pat was a small cattle operator that winter, and he lost a high percentage of his cattle. To save what he could from the wreck, and having no bent for laziness nor for taking it easy, Pat went out into the winter and skinned such of his dead cattle as he could find. One day he brought in a large bundle of hides, frozen solid and tightly wrapped with bailing wire. Old man Sherwood was buying hides and shipping them to Sioux City, so Pat drove his team up to Sherwood's market with his hides. They were thrown off the wagon, put on the scales and weighed, and Sherwood gave Pat Oakes his check for the full Fort Pierre market price of cowhides.

In a week or so Sherwood got his returns from Sioux City, and it is hard to imagine his indignant horror at learning that a practical joke had crept into the deal. The returns from the Sioux City firm showed so many cowhides, so much, and one horse hide, so much. Of course a horse hide sold for about twenty-five percent of what a cowhide would bring by the pound. Pat Oakes had slipped one over on Sherwood, and the old man's abounding wrath was limited only by his belief in the principles of his atheism. He started out to look for Pat, who, in all his succeeding years, never failed to raise a laugh by telling about their meeting soon after.

Of course it was a small task to find Pat. A few steps took the old man, with the remittance slip in his hand and trembling with indignation, to the baseburner coziness of Gordon and Bradshaw's saloon. There, to be sure, was Pat discussing the news of the day and the state of the world with his companions. In unfeigned anger, the old atheist, now turned true believer, walked up to Pat and shook the incriminating paper under his nose as he said, in ringing tones, "Pat Oakes, you G____ D____ son of a _____, if there is a hell; and, by God, there is a hell; you'll be there, and I'll be there, and that G____ D____ horse hide will be there."

His atheistic philosophy had played him false. Without a religious belief, he had no proper place to put Pat. So he became a religious believer and consigned Pat to what in his mind was a very proper destination. In order to be sure that Pat did not escape unwhipped of measureless justice, he similarly consigned himself so that, with the offending horse hide, he could taunt Pat through an endless eternity.

Do not take your religion too lightly, for, seriously, you never can tell when you may need it.

Affectionately,

Dad

CHAPTER 11

You Know What That
Game of Poker Is

August 1, 1940

My dear Geordie, Jean, and Bob:

Many a lawyer has set out to acquaint himself with a multitude of legal rules only to find that a code commission or a legislative session has sat in on what he thought he knew, and he wakes up at some cold gray dawn to find out that about everything he knew has been repealed. A whole new set of rules is set up in place of what he knew, and he may be left without even the directing influence of an index. The mania for fast and still faster changes in a swiftly changing world may even invade man's sanctum and change the values of his cards and what constitutes a hand, depending on the mental agility of the dealer. With everything wild but the one-eyed jacks and the ladies sitting in a game where they do not belong, the wildest of all, one who made some investment in order to learn something about the game, is likely to find that the information he bought and paid for has been made wholly nugatory, if not wholly repealed, by the baleful influence of dealer's choice.

Some time in the first two or three years of this century, it was my fortune to be working with a roundup outfit that was gathering beef to be shipped from Fort Pierre. I do not remember just what outfit it was, but I am sure that Harry Briggs and Charlie Butts were riding with it, and, if memory serves me right, so was Eddie McIntire.[1] Having quit rounding up, the outfit was proceeding to the railroad with its beef herd. Ordinarily that was pleasant and leisurely work for the cowpunchers. While one part of the men was on herd from noon until suppertime and from breakfast until noon next day, the others moved camp and loafed.

In good weather that was the life of Riley. Although some of the outfits prohibited gambling because of the time it took, most of the bosses did not care and quite often were willing to match wits with the monte dealer.

In order to facilitate the movement of large herds to the railheads, the railway companies often constructed large dams for the storage of water for the herds, to their own advantage and likewise to the advantage of the cattlemen. The Chicago & Northwestern Railroad constructed two large dams along the beef trails into Fort Pierre, one on Frozenman Creek where Hayes now is and a large one on Willow Creek about eighteen miles west of Fort Pierre. . . . Large herds of horses, cattle, and sheep watered at these dams; some as they were on their way through to market, and some as livestock on the range. When we got into Willow Creek Dam and made a camp on this particular afternoon, we knew we would not move camp until next morning. Those of us who were not on herd set up our tepees, and soon a poker game was proposed.

My tepee was chosen as the place, my bed was rolled out to furnish a typical range gaming table, and with Harry Briggs agreeing to bank the games, the players sat down in cross-legged cowboy fashion around the bed. The chips were coffee beans at ten cents apiece. The afternoon wore on till suppertime, with the fellows enjoying the fluctuating fortunes of a poker game. For coffee beans, like regulation poker chips, have no home in a game. It was in the fall of the year, and it was beginning to show a poor state of lighting in that tepee by reason of descending dusk as the cook's stentorian challenge rang forth, "Come and get it, or I'll throw it out."

It should not be forgotten that cattle, horses, and sheep had been watering at that dam in great numbers. Also it should be remembered that we were playing with coffee beans and that it was getting dusk. Just as the cook called, a new hand had been dealt, and of course it was instantly agreed, and the information was shouted back to the cook, that this was the last hand. It so happened that several of the players, including me, held good hands on the deal. There was some play before the draw and a lot of it afterward, with calls and raises back and forth until none were left in the betting but Harry Briggs and me. In order to stop the game, which was going along with us raising each other's bets, I called Harry, and I had far the better hand. In fact it made me wonder why Harry was so desperately pressing his luck. Exultantly I raked in all

MICK
B.
HARRISON

the chips (coffee beans) on the bed, for I had just about cleaned up the game.

On making a collection of my winnings to present them to Harry Briggs, the banker, to be cashed, the state of my feelings can best be understood by my remarks when I said sternly, "There's some son of a _____ in this game playing sheep turds."

All I could cash was my coffee beans, and each fellow in the game denied my soft impeachment. I shall not hear the last word about that particular poker game until I am the sole survivor. It was years afterwards before Harry Briggs (and I love him in spite of it) admitted to me that he would not have done it except for the fact that he thought he could run me out, and he would never be called on to cash them. I would like to sit down with the same fellows now and play a game of poker with anything for money. We used no wild cards then, and in that afternoon's game there was nothing wild but me.

Years passed on, as they have a habit of doing, and unbelievable changes took place from the afternoon of that poker game on the bank of Willow Creek until the fall of 1910. In that time I had changed from a sunburned cowpuncher into a sore-eyed, headachy lawyer. Two railroads had built across the ranges from Chamberlain and Fort Pierre on the Missouri River to Rapid City in the Black Hills. The town of Stamford, about which I told you in my letter on the grave robbing, had been built on the Milwaukee. Stamford had a saloon, which was run by a man named Henry Walcott. Thinking that he would be safe from the prying eyes of the law abiding, Henry made no effort to observe the rules that had been laid down for the government of South Dakotans by the legislature. But Henry reckoned without his host, for Julius H. Johnson was the states attorney of Stanley County, a righteous man who had no fear of saloonkeepers, or railroads, or anything evil.[2]

On the 21st day of September 1910, the states attorney caused the arrest of Henry Walcott and charged him with keeping his saloon open in violation of law on Sunday, three days before. He was dragged by George S. Huston, the sheriff, before Hugh C. McGuire, a justice of the peace at Fort Pierre, who knew a lot about the law, the lawyers, and the dignity of the courts.[3] Poor Henry had no friend in that place but me, and the overwhelming volume of evidence of his guilt on that preliminary examination caused him to be bound over to the circuit court for trial.

As counsel for the defense, I thought it proper for me to tell Henry that he was in danger with no chance of escape and that he had better let me tell the states attorney he wanted some mercy. I also told him that the circuit judge, Hon. Lyman T. Boucher, was a real fellow with a lot of human attributes and some failings, and consequently he might be expected to have some common senses as well as kindness. But Henry scorned the thought of pleading guilty and would not have it. I then played my trump card and told him that he was guilty, not only of keeping his saloon open on Sundays, but also that he was guilty of every other possible violation of the saloon law, that I would not permit him to present any perjured testimony nor permit him to go on the stand to testify in his own behalf. Calmly and blandly Henry accepted that ultimatum, but he would not plead guilty.

On October 18th, 1910, when Julius H. Johnson filed his information, and arraigned my client on the charge of keeping his saloon open on Sundays, Henry entered a rather bored "Not guilty," and the case was on the trial calendars, and there were such things in those days, for the lawyers tried their cases. A few days later the case was reached for trial, and I sat down in front of him to await my defendant's doom, for we had nothing. Of course, not guilty is a splendid defense if you can only establish it. Indeed it can often be well worthwhile if you can hinder the other side from proving the contrary. We were not in position to do even that, but we could sit down at the counsel table.

Almost immediately began the task of calling a jury, and twelve good men and true, on being called by name, arose from their seats in the courtroom and took their places in the jury box. They were of the cattle-man and cowboy stripe, and to most of them a little thing like the unlawful method of furnishing a thirsty man a drink was not necessarily ignoble, nor was its punishment of paramount importance, for it did not infringe the cowman's code.

Julius poured on our unprotected heads the vials of society's wrath in the form of testimony, which we were not in position to dispute. It was just like being scolded over and over for something we were caught doing, and you have no adequate idea of how tiresome that can become in a jury trial. (But all bad things must come to an end, and that gives me some comfort in thinking about Hitler). After the by-play of objections and motions, wherever one seemed possible on our part, the states attorney finally got in all his evidence and rested. On that, and without giving it even the dignity of a pause, the defense rested. There we were, ready to go to the jury.

The judge, Old Bouch, who had done me the honor previously of saying that there was some promise of being a lawyer in me, looked at me disapprovingly from the bench, with a look that said plainly, "Well, you are not doing a good job this time." Of that I was more painfully aware than the judge, but there was little to do. Of course there was always the chance that Julius might misconstrue the evidence or the circumstances. He had been known to do that, so there was that much chance of a weak link in the chains that bound us.

The states attorney commenced his opening argument, and in distressing discussion he set forth the details of the proof that Henry had kept his saloon open on Sunday, while I hoped against hope that his mistake would come in the opening argument, so that there would be a chance to answer it. When the states attorney had discussed the actual evidence in all its fullness, he could scarcely believe that he had talked long enough. He then began to discuss the general evils of the saloon as an instrumentality of wrong and about things he had heard about Henry, which were true, but which were not in the evidence. I could have stopped that, and Bouch looked at me in disgust, but a lawyer can try his case too well. No objection came from us on Johnson's ramblings in the realm of fact beyond the proof, and soon came the reward of patience.

Waxing eloquent, and in tones stentorian, the states attorney said, "and gentlemen of the jury, not only did this man Walcott keep his saloon open on Sundays and on holidays, before hours and after hours, and sell to Indians and to minors, but he ran a gambling hall in connection with this saloon."

There was not a word of truth in that, but it was a fact that there was a door between Walcott's saloon and Ressigue's pool hall, which also was a violation, and in that gambling hall, they played poker.

"And you gentlemen of the jury know what that game of poker is," he continued.

Well did I know they knew the game.

"That is the game you play on a green cloth-covered table," Johnson said, "with a stick and balls, and you take the stick and poke the balls around and 'round."

At that Judge Boucher, who liked a little game of poker with the frills, swung his swivel chair to get his back to the audience, and the shaking of his shoulders and head showed that he was not a serious judge at the moment. The courtroom crowd took advantage of the situation and let go its mirth to the perplexity of the prosecutor. Slowly I turned seriously toward the jury to see how the ex-cowboys liked the innovation in the game of poker. Each one, with a face like a graven image, had turned in his seat and was surveying me.

Soon the prosecutor sat down, and it became my turn to discuss the case but not the evidence. Having made it competent by his discussion, I gave some attention to the game of poker, and the states attorney was in no position to stop me. Having then, as now, serious objection to too many "wild" novelties being permitted to spoil a noble game, I expressed objections to playing the game with sticks. A six-shooter, yes, but a billiard cue, never. There sat those stony-eyed jurors, listening to my tirade as though it were wisdom. After my finish the states attorney had very little to say because I had not discussed the evidence, and he had no argument to rebut, except on poker, and there he had my consent to go the limit.

After getting the instructions of the judge, the jury went out and decided that Henry Walcott had not been playing poker after all. They returned a verdict of not guilty, so it seems that Sunday and the saloon were lost in the poker game. It always seemed queer to me that Henry did not pay me for my work.

Affectionately,
Dad

CHAPTER 12

Plenty O' Nuttin'

August 14, 1940

My dear Geordie, Jean, and Bob:

Some of the greatest injustices are done to our successors by failing to recount our experiences so that they may be known, and the converse of that may be equally true. That gives us a lot of discretion, but with responsibility for making our discretion discreet. It resolves itself back into the field of good judgment. In my efforts to evade thoughts of this unholy war now going on, and which may spread, and likewise the consequences of political interference or worry over politics, there has come my age of personal experiences, or whatever it is that makes converts come down the sawdust trail in the evangelist's tent and give boastful testimony of their misdeeds.

It may not be amiss for me to recount one of quite a few trips taken in the company of the late Mr. Charles J. Buell, his son William, and his jack-of-all-trades, with special emphasis on the cooking, Bill Dilger.[1] Each of you was acquainted with each of them in practically all your recollection, and you will understand what imagination must fill in to add to the dry recital of the facts. This trip should be called the "great negation" because it was a succession of superlative negatives.

You know that when C. J. Buell ("Judge," as he was usually called, although he never was a judge) started out on a trip of only a few miles, he was likely to load the vehicle with enough food, drink, and other equipment to furnish a fair-sized party on a trip to Canada's Barren Lands.[2] On a party or on a trip, he was a great provider. Of course William Buell was a big, powerful fellow, and he could always be counted on to do his full part of any physical requirements on the trip. Bill Dilger, who was partly maintained by Judge Buell and who was almost an invariable member of Judge's parties (Colonel Dilger, as Buell frequently called him), was a handy mechanic, particularly with an automobile, a good game shot, an expert trout fisherman, a superb cook, and a handy man in almost every way.

In 1924 and 1925 the law firm of Buell, Denu and Philip represented Ed Saunders of Interior in a law suit that had been brought against him by Millay, as receiver of the First National Bank of Winner, to recover on a note that Saunders had given to his brother-in-law, Mitchell, for some stock in the bank while it was a going concern and while Mitchell was its president.[3] The deal was so saturated with fraud on the part of Mitchell that we were able to win the case for Saunders in federal court at Deadwood before Judge Elliott, but that has nothing to do with my story, except that it was the peg on which it hung.

Although it cannot be said that he was always in a happy frame of mind, the Judge was inclined to be that way in the company of a group of men companions of his choice. Many a hearty laugh I have heard from him in the convivial atmosphere of good fellowship, when some attempted the song immortalized by Harry Lauder when he sang:

"I'm a miserable devil when I'm sober
But I'm very, very happy when I'm fou!"[4]

Buell was an advocate of the philosophy of John Wolcot, often stated on the spur of the moment by Chambers Kellar, who believes that life should be lived without too much agony, or even annoyance, for others—

"Care to our coffin adds a nail, no doubt;
But every grin so merry draws one out."[5]

Although not a noticeably good trout fisherman, Buell was an excellent hunter to whom hardships offered no odds, and he was a boon companion on either a hunting or a fishing trip. He was prodigal of provisions for any trip, always far too much to eat and sometimes a little too much to drink. It was not unusual for the passengers in the back seat of the automobile, of whom he was frequently one, to be compelled to stow themselves wherever and however they could among the guns, shell boxes, duffle, and food and drink enough to last the size of the party for ten times as long as they expected to be out. Almost invariably, too, Buell selected, bought and paid for all the eatables and potables taken along.

As near as memory can place the time, it was in August of 1924 that Buell came into my room at the office one forenoon and said, "Don't you think we should be looking into those records at Winner to see what is in that Saunders case?"

I said, "Yes, and I plan to go down there within the week to look into it."

In a few minutes he was back, and it was plain that, like an old stage horse, he had the smell of the trail in his nostrils. He said, "What's the matter with you and me going down together on the Saunders case?"

I said, "That will be just fine."

He left and in a few minutes was back with the inquiry, "Are you working on something that you cannot leave?"

On my negative answer, he said, "Well, when can you go to Winner?"

I answered, "I can go this afternoon, but you will have to furnish the car because mine is being worked on."

He said, "I can't go until morning, but in the morning we will go, and we will take Alecia's car."

That arrangement seemed satisfactory to me, and I concurred in it entirely. Leaving my room he was back in a few minutes with the anxious inquiry, "Do you know how to drive Alecia's Elgin car?"

He knew that he and I had made trips in Alecia's car. She, like a dutiful daughter, was not hard to coerce into giving up her car.[6] I said, "Sure, I can drive her car."

He said, "You and I never did hurt Alecia's car."

I said, "No, and we're not going to this time."

It was not known to me at the moment that he and some other companion had, shortly before that, borrowed Alecia's Elgin car and had sent it to the garage for extensive repairs. Evidently he thought that I, as the proposed driver on this trip of about one hundred eighty miles each way, would make some appeal to Alecia. Maybe it did, but not enough.

Soon he was back in my room, and, chuckling at the memory of the good time he had wrecking it in his recent trip, he said, "Alecia says I just can't have her car." To my inquiry as to what had gone wrong, he said, "Well, I guess we must have done some little damage to it on some other trip."

Who "we" were I never tried to find out because it was an exceedingly difficult matter to pin him down to definite information or commitment. Thinking the trip was off for the next day, I said, "We will just have to wait until my Hudson is fixed up, and then we will go, if you still want to. If not I can run down by myself."

With a chuckle that could be a forecast of anything, he left my room, saying, "Well, we'll see."

Shortly he was back with the question, "Do you especially care what kind of a car you ride in?"

I said, "Beyond wanting one that will run, I have little preference." Away he went seeming content with his progress, which was not noticeable to me.

Soon he was back with, "How do you like the Ford car?"

I said, "All right."

He said, "Do you know how to drive one?" At that I merely laughed, for each of us knew that we had ridden many miles together, with me driving a Ford car (Henry had not progressed beyond his Model T at that time). Gone again.

Next time, and it surely must have been before five minutes had passed, came the question, "What do you think about going down in a fine Ford car?" Knowing that he did not own or have any interest in a Ford car, fine or otherwise, that was a bit of a poser, but a Ford car was perfectly acceptable to me for the trip.

All this time, and through these interruptions, I was trying to dispose of legal business that was on my desk, very likely there via Judge's desk. He rarely worried about getting legal business done, that being merely an annoying detail which he left to the more prosaic heads and hands of his associates, as can be vouched for by Judge A. K. Gardner of Huron, judge of the United States Circuit Court of Appeals for the Eighth Circuit; by Judge Albert R. Denu, judge of the Seventh Judicial Circuit of South Dakota; and even by myself.[7] We were all associates of Judge Buell for years, for differing times and periods. Not one of the three, I feel sure, would fail to admit many pleasant experiences with Judge Buell. But all that is only incidental to the trip that was brewing in Judge's mind, and when he once got the idea of a trip in his head, he was agitated as an electric vibrator until it was on the way. Denu, who did not like hunting, fishing, or trips of any sort by auto, was denied the finest side of Buell, which was freely given to me because I liked all those things to the limit.

The trips into my room in the office were becoming much closer spaced in point of time. On the next one he said, "I don't suppose you know it, but Colonel Dilger has traded Father _____ (I have forgotten the name) of Piedmont[8] out of one of the finest Ford cars anybody ever saw." To my inquiry whether we could borrow it, he said, "You know how handy Colonel Dilger is around a car, and he is one of the very finest Ford drivers in the world. I was thinking it would be a good idea to borrow his car and have him drive it." All that indicated that the trip was developing in typical Buell style, and as that almost invariably suited me, my approval was quickly expressed.

There was one thing about Judge: although he loved to plan a trip, and could get just as excited over it as a bride with her hope chest, if any member of the party made serious objection to any special detail of the plan, he was always willing to yield the point and go right on planning the other items and details. On his next return came the first intimation of some of the things we might have to get along without. I was like the half-witted dolt of a boy who walked in and sat down at the soda fountain. The equally half-witted young soda jerker said, "What do you want?"

The customer said, "I want some soda water without."

That gave the vender as much as he could think about at one time, but he finally said, "Without what?"

The customer thought a while and said, "No flavor."

That was a bit of a poser, but finally the clerk said, "What flavor do you want it without?"

That one really puzzled the customer, but finally he determined his course and said, "I guess I'll have it without chocolate flavor."

The clerk now was seriously at a loss, but he finally analyzed his situation and said, "We ain't got none without chocolate flavor. I guess you'll have to take it without vanilla."

Judge asked, "Are you dead sure you don't mind riding down there in a Ford?" On my assurance that such was the case, he then asked, "Well, what if the Ford shouldn't have a top on it?"

Realizing that this was becoming more and more of an adventure with Judge and less and less of a business trip, I said, "That will be plumb all right with me, but are you sure there is an engine in this car of Bill Dilger's?"

With a look almost devotional, Judge said, "Oh, Colonel Dilger tells me that that car has the finest Ford engine in it that he ever handled. It is just a perfect engine."

I then said, "Has it any tires on it?"

"Oh yes," Buell said, "it has just the finest kind of tires on it. But say, by gad, I think we'll have William go along too, he and the Colonel can fix them, and you and I won't need to."

That now made four of us in the car, and one of those three weighed well over two hundred pounds, while I was on the altar to contribute my hundred seventy-five.

We were rapidly reaching the focus. Judge was now hot on the trail of that trip. Almost at once he was back and said, "Now just when do you think you can get away?"

I said, "Any time you say, but knowing something about these trips, I want to go home to change clothes and put on my hunting togs."

He said, "All right. That is just fine. We will have the car all ready to go in front of the Basket Grocery at two o'clock."

There was one thing about Judge on a trip, he was punctuality personified. A little before two I was at the Basket Grocery, with nothing but my brief case containing the papers in the Saunders case and whatever else I considered it necessary to take along on such a trip. There were the three of them loading that car to the place where the top would have fashioned on, had there been a top, with more food than we could eat in two weeks and a case of near beer. Not only was there not a sign of a top, but the fine "Ford" was devoid of windshield, and even a novice could know that, no matter what he got in exchange, the Reverend Father at Piedmont, if indeed there was such a person, had not been worsted in the trade.

The loading done, on the tick of two, Judge said, "All right, let's get in and get going. Bill, you drive, William you get up in front. George and I will ride in the back seat. We may want to talk about this case."

There was no thought in my mind that he would bother me with any discussion of the case. As I looked dubiously at the back seat and asked where we were expected to ride, he said, "Lots of room, lots of room."

With that he perched up on top of the load and hung his feet over the right side of the fine Ford, while I did likewise on the left side. Bill Dilger twisted the crank, got in, backed out from the curb, and it was "Anchors aweigh." Each one of us, in preparation for what might come, had dressed in hunting boots and clothes. It was well we did so.

At that time the streets of Rapid City were dirt—not even graveled. Almost at the instant of backing away from the curb, the heavens opened, and rain fell in torrents. Such a thing as that was never a deterrent to the judge. As we turned north from St. Joe Street, around the corner of the Buell Building,[9] Judge began to fumble vigorously among the excess of furnishings in the back end of that car, and about the time we turned east on Main Street, around the First National Bank corner, he delivered an umbrella, which he promptly opened and held up over him and me. We were somewhat protected from the front wheels by the remnants of the front fenders, but the rear fenders were missing, and the mud flew in every direction.

Along Main Street under the wooden awnings, and there were still such things there then, people were standing on the sidewalks watching the downpour, when this marvelous caravan composed of us imposed itself on their view. Each one of them cheered and shouted some little word of encouragement to us, to which Judge graciously bowed a solemn response from under the passing umbrella. That slipping, sliding, bouncing, jumping car went along the street to the edge of town on what are now Highways 14 and 16, but it was a dirt road then. As soon as we were beyond the vision of cheering spectators, the vigorous downpour was modified into a steady rain.

As we were about ready to go over the hill to the east of Rapid City, we got into the ruts of a truck that was plowing its uneven and uneasy way ahead of us on the highway. That "finest Ford engine" that was pulling us along the road quickly got us up right behind that truck, but Henry Ford had not devised any plan, nor had Bill Dilger thought of one, for climbing out of that deep mud rut. Although he had owned more cars than any other man in the community, and had ridden thousands on thousands of miles in all sorts of road and weather conditions, Judge Buell had never learned to operate one, nor did he have any idea what could or could not be done with one. He was always giving directions on what to do in the operation of a car, which never irritated me in the very slightest degree when I happened to be driving, although I have seen others, including Bill Dilger and William Buell, both of whom were fine drivers, get well out of patience at some of the judge's unbelievable backseat driving suggestions.

Fretting at our slow progress, as we jerked along in the rut behind that truck, Judge said, "Bill, don't monkey along in that rut. Get out of it and go around him."

I explained to the judge how it was impossible for Bill to get out of the rut. Then he substituted ideas and said, "Bill, make him get out of the way."

Bill asked how the judge figured he could make that truck get out of the way, and of course there was no adequate explanation of that. After a restless minute Judge said, "Bill, honk him anyway."

To that little bit of driving advice, which even Judge Buell knew could almost always be followed, Bill answered, "Hell, we ain't got no horn."

After a time we did manage to pass that truck on the railway viaduct, and we went on through mud for about thirty miles east from Rapid City. When we got to a point about north of Owanka, we ran out of the mud and rain, and from there on Bill seemed almost able to make that engine live up to the recommendation of perfection that Buell had given it. We passed Wasta, crossed the Cheyenne River, and on by Wall and Quinn with that engine doing its stuff to the tinny trumpetings of the loose-jointed car.

After we had gone beyond Quinn, Buell said, "Isn't there a road here somewhere that goes down to Interior?"

I said, "Yes, a mile or so farther on there's a road that goes south, over the Wall of the Badlands, and down the Big Foot Pass."[10]

He said, "That's the way we want to go. I have to go to Interior to see Harlan Snodgrass."[11]

I knew very well he did not need to see Harlan Snodgrass, who was then the banker at Interior and a client of our office. I wanted to keep right on the regular road to Kadoka, where we expected to stay for the night. But Buell insisted that he must see Harlan Snodgrass, and then he added the information that was of no interest to me: "This is the closing night of the Interior Roundup, and they are having a big bowery dance there tonight." I looked with relief at my hunting boots, knowing that they would furnish me adequate excuse for not dancing. Judge had recently become rejuvenated into an enthusiastic dancer, after he had ceased the sport for twenty years.

We all knew that there was not the faintest chance of talking Buell out of the side trip to Interior, so, when we struck that road, we turned south toward the Big Foot Pass. That road in those days, riding the rims of Badlands erosions, diving into canyons, and swinging around the curves, was not in any sense to be compared with the turnpike highway from which the tourists of today view the Wall of the Badlands. We reached the top of the wall and started down just as it was getting dusk. When we had gone far enough to be definitely committed to the descent, Buell said, "Bill, it's rather dark. You better turn on your lights."

Bill gave the none too satisfying answer, "Hell, we ain't got no lights."

MICK
B.
HARRISON

About that time we were accumulating speed so rapidly as to under-mine our confidence in Bill as a cautious driver. We fairly whistled as we swung madly down the Big Foot Pass. William Buell and I sat in silence, both of us perhaps suspecting the reason for Bill's unseemly burst of speed. But Judge, with unfeigned concern, said, "My God, Bill, you're going to kill us at this rate. Put on your brakes."

Sternly facing the realities of the situation, Bill answered and left none of us in doubt when he said, "Hell, we ain't got no brakes."

But somehow our ticket was not up, and we sizzled to the foot of the pass right side up and going fine. There had been a rain some days before, and a deep ditch had been washed across the road. We hit that ditch, about a foot deep and about a foot wide, so hard that we literally jumped it, but no one could say that the car suffered in silence, for it made every kind of noise at once when it was bouncing over that ditch. As we rolled to a stop on that flat stretch of Badland road, beyond the foot of the pass, Bill got out and surveyed the situation. After a brief inspection he got in the car and gave us the cheering verdict, "Hell, we ain't hurt nothin'."

From there we staggered along in the increasing darkness until we got to Interior, gaily lighted with many extra electric lights to cheer the milling hundreds who were doing their last job of celebrating the roundup. As we got in there Buell had Bill Dilger drive the car up to the bowery dance. There Bill announced that he was going to fix the lights on his car. Buell and William, boots and all, got their partners and swung 'em around. While they were dancing, I sat around on the sidelines visiting with some friends. My memory does not serve to tell me that Buell interviewed Harlan Snodgrass that night, but no one expected that he would.

As the dance went on, soon I saw Bill Dilger working towards me in the company of a very tall, powerful gentleman with a star on him. Here it was my old cowboy friend Jet Calhoon, the same chap who had made the long ride for Dr. Lavery the time I have told you about when Terry (Thierry) Singleton was so badly injured by a horse. Sensing that there was something wrong, and not wanting to be at odds with the policeman even if he should happen to be my personal friend, I rushed forward and greeted Jet heartily. Jet, as deputy sheriff and town marshal of Interior, had too much business on his hands to waste much time with me. After shaking hands he said, "George, this fellow says he knows you. Do you know him?"

I said, "Certainly, he is Bill Dilger. He is in our party. What's the matter?"

Out of Bill's face, which was a picture of agony, came the words, "Hell, we ain't got no license plates on that car."

I said, "Good Heavens, Bill, you didn't forget to put on those plates we got this morning before you left Rapid City, did you?"

Bill looked as though he were about to say something, and might even tell the truth, so Jet, looking at me, stern as any policeman, winked and said, "George, you're still good," and hurried away leaving Bill with me.

Bill then went away to finish fixing the lights and soon was back announcing them functioning perfectly. It then became my job to convince the judge and William that the girls could have a good time even after they left town, and about then force was given to my argument by the commencement of a shower. Just as we were all of one mind about leaving Interior for Kadoka, along came A. G. Granger who wanted to get back there.[12] I knew Granger longer than anyone else in South Dakota had known him, and I knew that he would take no offense if the truth were told. I was about to tell him that we could not take as much as another sandwich into that car, far less another man weighing over two hundred pounds.

Before I could get started on it, Judge cut in with, "We're going to Kadoka. Sure. Get in with us. Plenty of room. Plenty of room." That is how we came to add A. G. Granger to our load.

Well, we loaded up; Bill twisted his crank; the engine started; and we were off on another lap of our trail. It was pitch dark and raining. With our lights trimmed and burning, we were away. So long as we were within the electrically lighted area, our lights seemed to function perfectly, but when we got out on civilization's fringe we found our lights had a bad case of diplopia, for the right light was so set that it cast its beneficent rays, not down the road, but off to the left and out into the country. The other one, having a modest and downcast look, was pointed directly at the road just in front of the left wheel. But they shone.

Slipping and sliding in that soapy Badlands mud, sometimes in the road and sometimes in the ditch, occasionally with all of us pushing, except the driver, we finally ran out of the mud about the top of the Badlands Wall at the head of the Chamberlain Pass, west of Kadoka. From there on into town, Bill rattled that splendid Ford along, while Buell, Granger and I hung to our precarious perches atop the dunnage. Soon we drove up in front of Frank Hafner's hotel,[13] and no one but Buell was regretting that there was no more fun to be had on that trip that day. Bidding Granger adieu, and I, at least, thankful that he would not be with us on the morrow, we retired.

Whatever may have been his hours in town, Buell was never the least energetic member of a traveling or hunting party, so we were breakfasted and gone in good season in the morning. Our plan was to go as far as Belvidere and there turn south on the Cedar Butte–White River road to Winner, that being shorter and an acceptable road. It is about thirteen miles from Kadoka to Belvidere, and we were scarcely well started when down went a tire due to a puncture. Buell, who had been doing a lot of his riding around home in his twelve-cylinder Packard, got out with the rest of us and said, "Bill, get the spare and put it on, and we'll be out of here in jig time."

For a moment Bill was slightly fuddled at this, but recovered himself to say, "Hell, we ain't got no spare."

That meant getting the tire off, patching the tube, pumping it up, and all the rest of the archaic form of motoring. The pilot and the co-pilot did most of the work. It is almost unbelievable, but between Kadoka and Belvidere we had thirteen flats by actual count. My indignation rose in corresponding proportion to Judge's effervescent good humor. At last, in complete exasperation, I said, "By God, we will stop in Belvidere long enough to put new tires on this damned fake of a thing, or else I will stay there and go west on the passenger train tonight, get my own car, drive to Winner alone and get this evidence."

Of course, it was just impossible to stay out of sorts long on a trip with Buell, but flats at the rate of better than one to the mile was far too great a tax on my patience. We stopped in Belvidere, got five brand new tubes and one new casing so that we were well shod and had a spare.

We went south from Belvidere to Cedar Butte and then east on the road to the town of White River. The dirt road was dry and smooth, and the "perfect engine" was doing all that anyone could ask of it. Amid the din created by the rest of the car, the engine's noise seemed unobtrusive. We were going along in splendid fashion, but suddenly the car seemed to put more enthusiasm into its noise making. Buell leaned over to me and said, with all the dignity and assurance of a master mechanic, "George, there's a knock in that engine."

I said, "Maybe there is. There's so much noise I can't hear it. There's something wrong here, but the engine seems to be doing all right."

Buell was determined that there was something wrong with the engine, and soon he addressed the driver, "Bill, I think there's a knock in that engine."

Bill shouted back, "No. The engine's all right. Take a look and see how the tires are."

I looked over my side and reported that the front and rear tires on the left side were standing up beautifully. Buell took a good, long look at his side and came up choking with laughter. Finally, through his mirth, he was able to say to Bill, in paraphrase of Bill's own inimitable style of negation, "Hell, we ain't got no tire on the right hind wheel."

Bill, mistaking the significance of the judge's remark, said he would stop the car and we could pump it up. Buell suggested that we would have to find it first.

When the car was brought to a stop, which was not an especially prompt measure because we had no brakes, we got out to survey the situation. It struck me just as funny as it did the judge to observe that all we had left of that tire and tube was the valve stem stuck in the rim of the wheel. While Bill and William prepared to put on the spare tire, Buell and I walked back along the road to find the tire that had been thrown off the wheel. The double rim track in the dirt road was plainly visible for about three-quarters of a mile, and then it disappeared. That showed us where the tire had come off, so we commenced to hunt the surrounding area to find the lost tire. Soon William and Bill came with the car, once again running on four tires. They joined in the search, but our efforts were fruitless. So far as we ever knew, that tire is still lost.

Finally giving it up, we drove into the town of White River. Buell, who was decidedly in a kidding mood, insisted that we stop at a garage there because he had to see the proprietor. The fact that we all thought, and correctly, that he had never heard of the proprietor made no difference. Stop we must, and stop we did. The proprietor was easily and quickly available. In an attitude of serious concern, Judge asked him if people ever left things at his garage that had been lost by other motorists. The man said that occasionally happened. Naturally, we thought he was going to leave word of the missing tire, but that would have been much too orthodox for the judge on a trip. Instead of that, we were quite surprised to hear him announce, "Well, sir, we were going along and somewhere we lost our top. We didn't notice it at all until one of the fellows later discovered that the top was missing. We were wondering if anybody happened to bring it in and leave it."

The garage man was at a loss for a moment and said, somewhat vaguely, "No, nobody brought in a top." Seeming to sense the situation, he looked from one to the other of us and then directed his remark to me, "Say, what the hell is this? Are you fellows crazy? Or are you drunk?"

Some explanation, that did not explain, was made, and we drove on toward Winner. In justice it should be said that there was not a drop of intoxicating drink on the whole trip. When we got down near Witten, we stopped and had a lunch, the first and, as it proved, the last inroad into our commissary. Arriving at Winner, we quickly examined the pertinent records of the defunct First National Bank and found them perfectly satisfactory to our view of Ed Saunders's defense and just as he had told us.

We had several flats on the way back between Winner and White River, but we were making the best time we could because we wanted to stay that night in Kadoka. At White River Buell insisted on stopping long enough to inquire of the garage man if our top had been brought in. The man had recovered, so he told us it had not.

"All right then," Buell said, "Let's go."

So Judge and I crawled into such seats as we had in the car, while Bill stepped up in front to do his cranking. We were shocked to see him come up quickly, raise his hands above his head, and say, not profanely but appealingly, "Jesus Christ, I lost my crank."

At that, I could not help feeling a bit thankful that the engine was not lost. Now we were really in the mood to transact some business with that garage man. But not in his place, nor in White River, nor anywhere on the way home could we secure a crank for a Ford car. That necessitated reversed procedure, so now Bill would get in the driver's seat and handle the clutch, while Judge, William and I would get out and push until the engine took hold. Then we would scramble in, and away we would go.

We had not gone very far on our way from White River to Belvidere when the perfect engine, which had played us so faithfully before Bill lost his crank, began to buck. Several times it stopped on the hills, and then we would have to turn the car by manpower until it pointed down hill, when we could push it until it started. No one got any fun out of that except Buell, but we finally got back to Belvidere, where we stopped long enough for Bill to do some tinkering on the engine, while the rest of us made unavailing efforts to buy or find a crank. We got Bill in the driver's seat while the rest of us pushed the car along the street in Belvidere until the engine started, when we scrambled in and came to no more stops until we halted in front of the hotel in Kadoka just at dusk.

We had not yet settled down for the night when the weather settled down to the business of giving the Kadoka neighborhood a good rain. When we got up in the morning, we found the country soaked and the roads the very embodiment of poor driving conditions. To add to our consternation, Judge insisted that we had to go back by way of Interior, which would take us through the full east and west width of the Badlands. To our protestations that the road that way would be terrible, the judge expressed good-natured regrets but said that it was very imperative that he see Harlan Snodgrass. My own belief is that Buell got deep delight out of a lot of trouble on an automobile trip when there were only fellows of his choosing in the party. He was always in excited transports of delight on such occasions. So the rest of us lost the argument, and we staggered our unsteady way over those ups and downs and roundabouts of Badland way to Interior, raining all the way, with Buell and me sitting up on the property pile where the hind seat should be and shielding ourselves from some part of the storm under the kindly shelter of Judge's umbrella.

When we got to Interior we found the gala-decorated city of a few days before now metamorphosed into a drab, water-soaked, muddy little Badlands town. We found more than that, for there standing under the wooden awning of the little building that housed the State Bank of Interior stood Harlan Snodgrass. We stopped the car and got off, wading through the deep, slippery white mud to the sidewalk where Snodgrass stood. By this time, with the mud thrown from the unprotected hind wheels, we were all as fully covered with that white as if we had been carefully plastered by experts with trowels. Along came Ed Saunders and I told him we were on our way home from Winner, and that it now seemed to me we might win his lawsuit. The interview with Harlan Snodgrass consisted only of laughing and joking on the part of Buell, lasting about five minutes and terminating with a sudden good-natured, "Well, let's get going," from him.

Acting on that impulse, Bill got in under the steering wheel, while the three of us pushed the car along the muddy Interior street until the engine started, much to the amusement of the few people standing on the sidewalks under the wooden awning. We had gone only a few miles west of Interior when we got completely beyond the area of the rain of the night before. When we were about halfway between Interior and Conata, and running on a perfectly dry dirt road with no sign of human habitation in sight, the road turned an abrupt square corner.

As we approached this corner from the east, an eastbound car was approaching it from the south. To the surprise of all of us, Bill, who was a really good driver, did not notice the car coming to meet us. The result was that we met squarely at the corner with Bill taking the inside of the curve, or the lefthand side of the road. Sensing the situation, the driver of the other car took the left side of the road, on the outside of the curve, and went on toward Interior. Unfortunately for our progress, on the inside of the curve was a mud puddle, just a lob-lolly that had been left from a previous rain, and when the Ford struck that, down it went to the body, stopped dead, stuck in the mud. For about the only time in all the multitude of misadventures in car trips with Buell, I heard him then speak in criticism of an unfortunate error.

Unwinding his long legs from among the plunder in the back end of the car and swinging them out to the ground as he stepped out, he looked with some reproach at the driver and said, "Oh, hell now, Bill."

When we surveyed our predicament, I said, "The four of us could lift that car out of there if necessary, and we can easily push it out."

In an amazing show of surrender, for he never was willing to do that on a motor trip, Judge said, "No. We are just stuck, and we will have to stay there until we are pulled out."

I said, "Judge, you are now thinking about a twelve-cylinder Packard, but you want to remember that this is a Ford with nothing in it but an engine and a little stuff to eat. A big, powerful fellow like William could push this out by himself."

At that I got my shoulder against the front of the car and pushed, which caused the car to move backward through the lob-lolly. Always quick to see an advantage, with a giggling chuckle that his companions knew and enjoyed, Judge said, "Grab on. Grab on. It's moving."

Everyone grabbed on, and in less than five seconds we had our car back on the perfectly dry road. Bill got in, the three of us pushed, and again we were westward ho. After we passed Conata, the judge proceeded to spur our appetites by telling about a wonderful dinner he would have Clem Coverston get for us at Imlay. Although William, Bill and I were for eating some of the food we had with us, the judge was purposeful to get filled up on the wonderful chicken dinner at Clem's with all the trimmings, with which even Henrici could not compete.

Overruled again, we drifted into Imlay, the town where Clem, and Clem alone, lived.[14] He was there, and, as soon as formal greetings were exchanged, the judge ordered the dinner. Even before then, we realized the futility of the order, for it was plain to the most casual observer that there was not a chicken, alive or dead, within miles of Imlay. Clem did say he could get substitution in the form of some chili con carne and crackers, to which Buell responded that the substitute was much better than the chicken dinner he had been considering. So it was canned chili instead of chicken.

Alive to almost any situation, Buell reminded us that we were in the midst of the famous Badlands melon country. Of course we all knew about the character of melons raised there and that they are the best. Clem said he had some watermelons but no cantaloupes, so, as soon as we had become saturated with chili, we went out to view the melons. Sure enough, there they were in a lean-to shed, nineteen big, beautiful watermelons. Clem stated his price, and Judge announced he was taking all of them.

I saw all possible chance of comfort on the trip leaving by the watermelon way and asked, "How the hell do you think you are going to transport nineteen melons to Rapid City in this rig?"

Judge laughed and surveyed me with a look of almost beatific assurance, as he said, "Oh, lots of room, George, lots of room."

In dismay and defeat, I sat down to watch Clem and the rest of them place those nineteen watermelons. On a higher perch than before, we mounted after we had pushed the car far enough to start the engine and headed for Rapid City.

No event of note disturbed our peace until after we came up over the Wall and on to the flat northwest of Scenic. There we were struck by the full force of a strong wind, accompanied by a dashing rain. Somehow, Buell was able to dig down through a wealth of watermelons and again produce his umbrella. He quickly got it up to protect us, and as quickly that wind turned it inside out, thereby fixing one umbrella so that it would be valueless on a trip to Munich. Almost instantaneously all of us were soaked to the skin, and the umbrella was thrown aside, making that much more room in the car. Of course a storm of that intensity cannot last long, and before we reached the Cheyenne River it was all over, although it had rained there and on beyond.

When we got to the steep hill on the old highway west of the Pete Lemley ranch, we got about halfway up when the gumbo mud became too much for the engine, and it stalled.[15] There we had to disembark and turn that car around so as to point it down hill, where we could push it until the engine started. After getting it going Bill went down the hill and back along the road to a point where he could try to turn around and face the hill. Then giving it the gun for all that was in it, he thundered past us on the hill and reached the top. We negotiated the hill afoot and caught up with Bill, whose engine was still running.

Just at sundown we entered Rapid City and drove up to the Buell home. There was Mrs. Maude Buell, that wonderful little lady, waiting on the porch.[16] As she surveyed the quartet of water-soaked, mud-plastered derelicts who got out of the car, her hearty, ringing laugh broke out as she asked, "Which one of these is my Charlie?" Either her knowledge or her intuition guided her, for she kissed the right one.

Buell then decided that we should do something to distribute the assets of the trip, and he said, "We'll take in a melon apiece into our house, then we'll leave some at George's and some at William's, and we'll take the rest down to the Black Diamond." That was Bill's bachelor quarters, where, in a hopeless disorder of housekeeping, Bill prepared those marvelous meals to which senators and governors had been pleased to sit down.

We each took in one of those big melons to the Buell kitchen, where each one in turn was cut open. Then with repeated trips, we took all of them into that kitchen, only to find, as each in turn was cut open, that we had carried to Rapid City nineteen watermelons each as green as a gourd, if a gourd can be that green. Taking my brief case, I decided to go to my own home and ruminate in silent thought on that trip, that carnival of negation, in which the only affirmative, positive things were a "perfect engine" that did not always work and Judge's "plenty of room," which was not there.

But for two reasons, (1) I did not know the song and (2) I could not sing it if I did know it, I could have lilted to the moon that night in the words that George Gershwin put into the mouth of the poverty-stricken, contented, religious old darky, "I got plenty o' nuttin'!"[17]

Affectionately,

Dad

CHAPTER 13

Rough Play

My dear Geordie, Jean, and Bob:

Although it now seems to be a part of the blood lust of the spectators in their demands on the performers at the rodeos, it was no part of a cowhand's business to ride cattle of any sort. Cattle were supposed to grow into money-making property for the owner, and the waddies who rode for them in roundups and elsewhere were fully expected to see to it that their care was directed to that end. That there were occasional transgressions from that rule was borne in on me at a meeting of the directors of the First National Bank of the Black Hills two weeks ago in Lead. G. A. McGarraugh, as a follow-up to something that was said about the rodeo held in connection with the Days of '76 at Deadwood,[1] looked over at me with a grin and asked me if I remembered a day in the long ago when he, Ort Nordvold, Eddie McIntire, and I were on day herd up on Minneconjou Creek.

It seems that time got to hanging heavy on our hands, and the sum total of the effect of all discussion was that we fell to roping some of the cattle and taking our turns trying to ride them. We were out on the wide-open range and had no corrals or chutes in which to mount them. All we could do was for one of the fellows to rope a steer around the head, while another put a rope on his hind feet and stretched him out. Then the prospective rider would release the head rope, and the steer would release the foot rope as soon as he stood up and spread his feet. The rider would then get on the steer so that he would be on its back when it got to its feet.

Although we were accustomed to lots of riding, and sometimes to riding bucking horses, we were ignominiously worsted in our efforts to ride those range steers. Neither Gib McGarraugh nor I could recall any ride made that afternoon when the rider was not involuntarily thrown by the steer. No doubt it all seemed a fitting way at the moment to blow off steam, but nearly forty years later it must seem quite incredible to Ort Nordvold, a serious farmer at McLaughlin; to Eddie McIntire, a retired cattleman at Fort Pierre; to G. A. McGarraugh, a vice-president of the First National Bank of the Black Hills and the executive officer of its branch office in Sturgis; and to a certain United States attorney that they could be the same fellows whose idea of fun on that afternoon was to catch and try to ride wild range steers. The chances are that not any one of the four would now care to get on the gentlest sort of a horse and shoo the gentlest sort of a cow down a fenced lane. But this is a changing world, and we change most of all. No matter how foolish it may all seem now, it is not without its pleasure to know that the time was when it was not considered beneath one's dignity, nor beyond his inclinations and abilities, to indulge on occasion in a bit of rough play.

Scotty Philip, after I was practicing law in Fort Pierre, often came to me on a Saturday afternoon in a state of worry over my health. On such occasions, and they were frequent, he would point out the bad effects of confining indoor work on a fellow whose life should really be lived in the open. My failing health was indicated by paleness, lassitude and other evidences. For a man of his profound taciturnity, he could on occasion find more to say about my health than one could reasonably expect, especially when my health was perfect at the time, as he knew.

He knew I kept a good horse in town, a fine, rangy, gray horse that Mike Dunn had given to me.[2] Such Saturday afternoon discussions would result in Scotty's suggestion that I saddle up and gallop out to the ranch, where I could get a little exercise and a little sun. There never was any question in my mind on such occasions that the exercise in the sun would be forthcoming in no uncertain quantity on the morrow. It never seemed to strike him as fitting that the condition of my health on Saturday called for greater and more tender care of me on Sunday than was provided. Perhaps there seemed to be an amazing recovery over night. Whatever it was, I always had enough exercise and sun to insure a fair degree of health until along about the next Saturday. There was never any thought in my mind of denying any wish of Scotty's if he just made it known and if it was possible to comply. One such accepted invitation out to the Buffalo Ranch should not be forgotten, nor its results allowed to go unrecorded.

After getting up on Sunday morning, we fooled around in rather aim-less fashion until about eight or half past, when Scotty said to Bunk White, who was working there at the time, "Bunk, what do you say if you run in the horses, and you and George and I take a ride out in the pas-ture?" This was about an eleven-thousand-acre pasture including a con-siderable quantity of rough government land along the Missouri River and leased by special Act of Congress for the grazing of native buffalo.[3]

Bunk got on the saddle horse, which was kept in the corral or the barn for such purpose, and quickly had a bunch of saddle horses in the corral at the ranch house. Scotty caught his big black horse, old Coaly; Bunk caught a good horse, called Flaxy; and I caught my own horse, Mike. Hugh Schultz was working at the ranch at the time, and he caught a horse, Six-shooter. We all saddled up and went out into the buffalo pasture. At that time the buffalo herd consisted of close to nine hundred head, roaming at will in the large pasture, unmolested and by them-selves.

As we got back into the brakes and up towards the Giddings Flat, we ran on to a very large part of the herd, grazing along quietly together. Without communicating to us by word or sign what he had in mind, Scotty rode around among the quietly grazing buffalo, and we rode with him. After a time Scotty said, pointing at a big bull about four or five years old, "Catch that one."

It seemed to me that my ears must be playing tricks on me, and a quick look at Bunk convinced me that he, too, doubted the service being rendered to him by a pair of ears heretofore quite reliable. Of course, that black man was a top hand in every department of the cowboy's work and could take it in his stride with a smile. Of him it could almost be asked, "What dam of lances brought thee forth to jest at the dawn with death?"[4] But even Bunk did not like to listen to what he was hearing.

To make sure, I looked at Scotty to see if he was serious, and his appearance gave every evidence of that. I said, "Do you mean to rope him?"

He said, "Yeah."

Not relishing any part of the job, I asked, "Why in the name of Heaven do you want him roped?"

He said, "I want to castrate him."

It was a known certainty that he could exercise no such beneficence to that buffalo bull unless somebody roped him, so we all rode off to one side to tighten our cinches, for that was no place to get a saddle pulled off your horse. We got off and tightened up, and Hugh Schultz announced that his cinch was too weak to justify him in attempting any part in it. I certainly would have been glad to have found something the matter with some part of my outfit, but mine was a good, strong rig in which it would take a vigorous imagination to find a serious fault. Bunk always needed a good outfit, and he had one. Scotty was not going to do any of the roping anyway, so he was all set.

As soon as we mounted, Hugh's horse ran away in vigorous fashion toward the ranch, but when he got about a half mile away he overcame his fear. It always seemed to me a strategic runaway effort, although quite unnecessary in view of the cinch that was too weak to allow him to tie on. I wanted my horse to run away with me but could hardly see my way clear to arrange it. My belief is that Bunk, even, would have been glad to have had his horse become unmanageable, although it is hard for one who had seen him perform in other days to conceive just what that conduct would be which would make him wholly unmanageable for the old cow hand.

Anyway, Bunk and I rode in the direction of the bull Scotty wanted caught, with our ropes down and loops made to try our luck. Now it is not the easiest thing in the world to get a loop on the front end of an animal, and it is not done every throw, but putting it on an ordinary cow critter is simplicity itself as compared to putting it on a buffalo. The perfect head throw, so far as ability to handle the animal on the rope is concerned, is when the loop settled around the horns. You there have the foremost point of purchase, the greatest leverage. The head of the ordinary cattle animal is in the right line from the body to make roping an efficient method of capture, but that is far from being true of the buffalo. To lay a horse up alongside a buffalo to catch him, one is confronted with that towering hump, which conceals the low-swung head and horns from the roper. The rope is almost certain to hit and be deflected by that high hump. In addition to all other difficulties, horses are justifiably afraid of those shaggy monsters, which in spite of their clumsy appearance can run so fast that only a splendid cow pony can lay up to one. Consequently, it takes a speedy and courageous horse to get a rider in position where he can attempt the throw. The horse must have as much confidence in his rider as the rider has in his horse.

Catching the animal by the head, it becomes the duty of the horse and rider to have him come to the end of the rope so hard that the animal is jerked in such fashion that his hind feet are swung to the farthest point from the pony. At that point the other roper must make his attempt to catch the hind feet. If the hind feet are then caught and the rope is tightened on them by the pony going quickly to the end of the rope, and that means tightening both ropes as tight as a fiddle string, there is not much for that animal to do except to go down. In fact there is nothing else he can do. When in that position, the knife man can work his will on him because two well-trained, straining rope horses will keep him just about as tightly stretched as the ropes themselves.

Quickly Bunk shot his horse alongside of this buffalo bull, and with the first throw his rope settled nicely around the animal's horns. It could not have been a more perfect throw, nor could it have been a luckier one. Bunk's horse turned quartering away from the animal, and when he came to the end of that rope, tied hard and fast to the saddle horn, it was a tremendous jerk on the horse and his rider, and a worse one on the buffalo. The bull's feet just flew out behind him like a whip cracker, offering the best kind of a target for getting a rope on the hind feet. Just as he popped, I let go my loop, and, as luck would have it, I caught him with the rope making a figure 8 around both hind feet. Bunk's throw had been perfect, he had made that animal come to the end of that rope perfectly, and I, not much of a roper, had caught the hind feet perfectly. Instantly my horse was at the end of that rope.

We often hear of the squeeze play, but that animal felt the stretch play being put on him in no uncertain way. Down he went, Scotty dismounted from old Coaly and, knife in hand, ran up to the prostrate and helpless animal. Having inducted him into the ignoble order of steerhood, an unknown status for a buffalo in those days, Bunk eased up on his rope, while I laid into the foot rope all the harder, and Scotty slipped the head rope off the bull's horns and made for his horse. As soon as he was on his horse, I eased up on my rope, and the buffalo got up, freeing himself from the loop when he spread his feet, and he was loose again. Everything worked with such precision that it seemed nothing had been done. A buffalo bull that weighed about a ton had been roped, thrown, altered and turned loose in less time than it takes to tell it.

Just why this adventure, or indulgence in curiosity, had ever been embarked upon I did not then know, and do not know now. It has always seemed to me that, in some of his soliloquizing, Scotty had gone to wondering just how a big buffalo bull would act on the loop end of a rope, and he just set about it to satisfy his curiosity. Well, the anticipation had changed into experience, and it all was so expeditiously and so perfectly

done that he must have thought it was worth repeating. The animals by this time were becoming excited, smelling the blood on the mutilated member of the herd, running around, emitting their rumbling, grunting bellow, hooking each other, and giving no small evidence of their willingness and ability to hook anything else in range.

About half a mile away Hugh's horse showed sporadic runaway activities. Scotty now seemed to me in his element, enjoying himself. Suddenly he pointed out a big one that was showing some activity out of the ordinary and said, "Catch that one."

Bunk, filled with the memory of the magnificent throw he had made in making his catch of the first one, tried to slip up alongside this one, and I was right close behind him, each with a well-fashioned loop. This excited animal was not to be so easily caught and made off at great speed through the herd. Soon Bunk cut in alongside and let fly his rope, only to have it hit the hump and fall, a harmless miss. On the instant he veered away, I was in his place, swinging my rope vigorously, which was done for the double purpose of gaining energy and speed for the throw and of keeping the loop wide open until the throw was completed. The swinging of the rope by a roper on a fast-moving horse and in pursuit of a fast-moving target was not for show but for a very practical purpose in the handling of the rope. Soon my position seemed right and my rope flew out, only to be deflected by the hump and to fall without making a catch. Quickly I got away from him, and Bunk was in my place with a new loop, all hungry for the catch. Even I was now imbued with the spirit of the chase, excitement having blanketed my fears, and it is almost a certainty that Bunk's fears were less than mine at all stages. As soon as Bunk got in close enough to his quarry, out flew his rope, only to hit the hump again and miss. Instantly I took his place and soon let fly, catching that buffalo, not around the horns, but around his big neck.

Many years later, when I was trout fishing up on Rapid Creek on a fishing party organized by Judge Buell, he gave me a pint of whiskey of which I was to be custodian. After carrying it in my creel for a time and seeing no further use in that, I slipped the bottle into what seemed a safe place in the creek, putting it among some rocks so that it could not get away. Along later in the day, the judge caught up with me on the creek and said that all was gone but my bottle. I told him it was hidden in the creek where it would be nice and cool. Immediately we went to the point of deposit, but, search as we would, we could find no trace of the bottle, which, by some freak action of the water, had been washed away. When we were finally confronted with the certain knowledge that the loss was irreparable, the judge looked at me and said in tones of finality, "George, that was a damn careless thing for you to do."

Long before that time, I was already in no position to deny the judge's accusation of my carelessness. Just as that loop in my lasso (as some of the fantastic writers would have it) settled around the big, hairy, woolly neck of that buffalo, my own thought was, "George, that was a damn careless thing for you to do." But there it was done, and there is no point of repentance or turning back when you catch something on a rope. I would gladly have exchanged places with Hugh and agree to give his horse a good dose of steel rowels if he showed any desire to quit running away, just as I suspected Hugh was doing.

The shape of a buffalo should be remembered. That short neck comes right back against the high hump, and right under that hump is the shoulder, the center of gravity, of weight, of strength, and of activity in the animal. That was where one end of my rope was, and the other was tied hard and fast to the horn of my saddle. Instantly that rope stretched as tight as the string on a present-day cowboy's guitar, the most hazardous instrument of his trade. Never having tied on to a speeding locomotive, and knowing perfectly well that none of you ever will, I can assure you that it seemed exactly like that. The full folly of Scotty's idea was now apparent, but Mike and I had to do what we could to handle that critter on the rope. Mike, being a good horse, was doing his best to hold that big, powerful thing to which he was tied, and his rider was offering every assistance within his knowledge so that with their combined efforts they could swing that buffalo around with his heels toward Bunk. After several efforts and several ineffectual throws by Bunk, he finally got a rope on one hind foot.

Things were not clicking so well on this effort as they did on the accidental display of roping skill on the first one. Here was Mike straining at the rope around the neck and Flaxy doing his best on the one around the hind foot, each pulling against the other in the vain hope of pulling that jerking, jumping buffalo apart. He would not even go down, and that checked the bet squarely up to Scotty. Realizing that he got everybody into this crazy mess and not being lacking in personal courage, Scotty got off his horse and ran over to the buffalo on the right side, Bunk having the right hind foot disabled by the rope. By concerted action of the two rope horses putting extra emphasis into their pulls in collaboration with Scotty's lusty pulls on the tail toward the animal's right side, where there was no hind leg to support him, down went the buffalo on his right side.

Then began the job of adjusting the ropes, which Scotty had to do, and here was where Bunk and I dared make no mistake. Tightening and easing up on the ropes as occasion demanded, we finally got my rope off the neck and put it around the horns and got Bunk's rope around both hind legs. That was more of a job than it sounds at this distance. I did not envy Scotty his job and, in fact, did not appreciate my own. Of course, when we got that buffalo around the horns and the heels, we could make him say "Uncle," for a good rope horse could exert a powerful pull from the saddle horn. Getting out his knife, Scotty quickly brought another steer into being. Then he slipped my rope off the horns, ran to old Coaly and mounted him, while Bunk was putting some pressure on those hind legs. Up got the buffalo, and turned himself loose by spreading his hind feet.

My hope was that Scotty would say "Selah," or whatever it is folks say when they are through.[5] That experience was much too recent to be pleasant and a bit too soul-searching to cause any desire to repeat. By this time the buffaloes were certainly in a state of agitation—running, fighting, smelling the two victims, and generally raising particular hell. We had to be decidedly on the alert to keep from getting our horses hooked. How I longed to be half a mile away from there with Hugh, having a comfortable runaway, and still be able to watch the whole performance with the buffaloes. I was just getting ready to encourage Mike to stage a runaway in competition with old Six-shooter, ridden by Hugh, when I heard what sounded like a soft-spoken pronouncement of doom from Scotty, "Catch that one, I want to cut him, too."

That really looked to me like biting the cherry a little too hard, but we were there, our ropes were down, our horses were in a lather, and we were soaked in sweat ourselves, so perhaps that was the best time to do it after all. Anyway, Bunk and I took in after him. He quit the bunch and went, uphill and down, across the brakes. Now the catching was difficult. After many wasted throws by each of us, Bunk's loop finally connected in terrible fashion. It went over the buffalo's head, neck, and one front foot, and he had him around the hump. That big brute scarcely slackened his pace as he started off, just a general westerly direction, with Bunk and Flaxy. It became my job to stop them somewhere short of the Big Horn Mountains. That called for running in ahead of the buffalo to give Bunk a chance to harass him with the rope and, as soon as could be, to get a chance at his hind feet.

After almost surrendering completely to despair and deciding that Bunk and the buffalo had better decide to get along together from then on as best they could, I managed to get a rope on one hind foot. That came nearer equalizing the tug-of-war, but it was not plain that the rope horses had much advantage. However, we were now in a position to stop any rapid forward progress. Scotty, who was riding close behind us all the time, was now on hand to do whatever was required of him. Six-shooter was still intermittently running away with Hugh, but in plain sight.

Scotty now had a real job on his hands. Here was a large buffalo bull on which he had designs, roped around the neck, shoulder, and one front leg at one end, and by one hind leg at the other. It was only by the utmost of effort that he could be kept from cross-country running, and yet he had to be put down. I had him by the left hind foot, so Scotty slipped up on his left side and grabbed the tail, while Bunk and I tried to apply additional pressure on the ropes. Finally Scotty pulled him over, and then came the battle, and what a battle it was, to get the ropes on him properly. By the continued application of everything we knew how to do, we finally got the ropes on the two hind feet. That reduced the annoyance of the situation and greatly increased the potency of the two men on horseback.

We were now able to hold that monarch of the plains in a state of nothing doing now, and Scotty was able quickly to put him in a state of nothing doing from now on. Then he slipped the head rope off the horns and started for his horse. Quickly, and with a struggle that would not be denied in spite of my best efforts to the contrary, that animal got to his feet and released himself from the footrope, making for Scotty, who was not yet on his horse. It took the quickest efforts Bunk and I could make to get his attention away from Scotty and on us, but we managed, and soon the buffalo mixed in with the herd, only to add more blood and more confusion to an already badly overstrained situation.

To sum it all up to a total of complete nonsense, Scotty began to look a bit longingly at some of the others. Realizing that the animals were getting more and more disturbed and difficult and that our technique was getting poorer instead of better, I began to coil my rope preparatory to hanging it on the pommel of my saddle. Scotty noticed that and then took another look in the direction of the now-frantic buffalo herd. Before he got a chance to indicate a fourth selection, I said with no lack of certainty, "By God, if you fellows want to alter every bull in that bunch it will be all right with me, but, as for me, I'm going to the ranch."

I knew I was out of courage, that Bunk was about in my frame of mind, and that Scotty would just as soon quit, but he wanted the suggestion to come from someone else. He said, "Well, maybe it would be just as well if we'd all go in to the ranch. It must be getting near dinner time."

The proximity to noon was a matter of no concern to me at the moment, but the proximity to those buffaloes was becoming utterly obnoxious. We turned to ride away from them, and that seemed to have a very quieting effect on old Six-shooter, for he, carrying Hugh, came trotting quietly to intersect our line of travel. As he came up to us, Hugh said, "I surely had a hell of a time with old Six-shooter. He wanted to run away all the time."

No comment was made except by me, and I said, "Six-shooter is pretty smart. He did exactly what I wanted to do."

Not a single comment was made about that unique experience on the way back to the ranch, nor was it ever mentioned by Scotty at any later time in his life time so far as I know. His curiosity seemed to have been fully satisfied. Bunk and I discussed the matter afterward, and our only conclusion was that Scotty wanted to see whether a grown buffalo bull could be handled by two ropers.

My having had enough sun for a day, and enough exercise for at least one week, Scotty's worry over the state of my health seemed to disappear. I knew that never again would I engage in similar exercise on this side of the happy hunting grounds, and the fact is that I never again threw a rope at any living thing from the back of a horse. Nothing could hire me completely to erase that incident from my memory, and at no time could a bribe have been made sufficiently large to tempt me to repeat it.

Affectionately,

Dad

CHAPTER 14

Old Dishrag
September 1, 1940

My dear Geordie, Jean, and Bob:

Although it was never my privilege to ride much on a horse roundup, therein were really some of the fastest-moving scenes of range activity. The speed of the range horses and their willingness to demonstrate it when pursued, and often when there were no pursuers, made the handling of range horses and the rounding up, branding, etc., of them an entirely different line of work than the handling of cattle for the same purposes. The horseman and the cowman were men engaged in different lines of work, although many riders rode on the horse roundups as well as working with the cows. By the way, "cows" was a generic term on the range, which was the cow country peopled by cowmen and cowboys riding on cow horses, and it did not necessarily indicate the sex of the cattle. The horse roundups usually were made before the cattle roundups commenced, and quite frequently the big outfits would send a rep (representative) to collect the saddle horses that had not been picked up already by individual riding and also to gather in the broncs (usually four-year-old geldings) that were to be broken that spring.

In the spring of 1902, the boss sent me to the horse roundup of Dan Powell (D P brand) to pick up whatever saddle horses and broncs of the L-7 outfit had already been collected and to take them all to Fort Pierre. There the saddle horses would be put in the saddle bunch, and the broncs were to be turned over to a man hired to break horses. He was the broncobuster, the bronc peeler, the horse breaker, or whatever other name indicated the character of the employment. The only qualifications ascribed by the cowpunchers to any one of their number who hired out to break horses were that he must have a strong back and a weak head.

That spring John Slaughter, a sort of renegade member from the great Slaughter family of Texas cowmen, hired out to break saddle horses for Scotty at the buffalo pasture near Fort Pierre.[1]

Knowing that Dan Powell's roundup was working somewhere above the Wall of the Badlands, which meant in general language anywhere between the place where the town of Belvidere now is to a point southwest of the present town of Wall, my job was to start out on horseback to find it. It was amazing how accurately a range man could locate in his mind the probable present location of a roundup outfit, especially if he knew the country. It was equally amazing how accurate a knowledge of a tremendously large area a fellow came to have, especially those who were usually employed as reps, representatives riding with other outfits. From the crack of dawn until the shades of evening, a fellow riding alone on horseback had plenty of time to think, and by thinking accurately on the probable moves of the roundup wagon of his search, he could save himself many miles of riding. My course was laid directly up Bad River. When a fellow was on his way with no horses but the one he was riding and no bed or pack, he had to get along with the horse that was under him and the clothes he had on, plus the slicker that was tied to his saddle except when it was raining. There were enough ranches along Bad River to furnish places to eat, and a rider just about had to know them all and all their brands so that there was no particular difficulty in going.

In good season on the second day, I came to the Forks of Bad River, exactly where the city of Philip was to stand five or six years later. Inquiring of Humpy Morrison, who had a place right at the forks, where the Dan Powell outfit was working brought no enlightenment, although he agreed with my conjecture that they should just about have reached Big Buffalo Creek. As I was resting my horse and letting him eat a bit of grass while visiting with Humpy, Johnnie Curington came riding along, and he had eaten at the horse roundup the noon before up towards the head of White Willow Creek, so now we were all in fair accord that a ride up Big Buffalo Creek would just about catch the outfit.[2]

Soon I called a halt on my horse's lunch and got on him. Riding up the South Fork of Bad River to the mouth of Big Buffalo and then up the latter creek brought me before sundown to the horse roundup. My memory is that young Dan Powell was acting as the boss under the supervision of his father, who was with the outfit but did not do any riding. Old Dan passed away some years ago, and young Dan (no matter how old he gets, and he is now nearing sixty, he will be young Dan to the fellows who knew him then) now lives at Eagle Butte. His younger brother, Billy, was also on the roundup. They were mixed-blood Indians, old Dan's wife being a Sioux and a fine woman. Billy is now the sheriff of Stanley County and lives at Fort Pierre. I think Fred Ervin was riding with this horse roundup, repping for Scotty. . . . It seems to me that my good friend Bret Douglass, who for years has lived at La Jolla, California, was riding there for some outfit. Of course, memory dims as to the details of long ago. . . . My horse was turned loose with the saddle bunch, and with a supper inside me, the pleasure of the day was complete on finding some chap who was willing to widen his roundup bed and let me sleep with him, which was always a more comfortable arrangement than rolling up in your slicker.

In the morning Dan agreed to work the herd so that I could get such L-7 horses, broken and unbroken, as had already been collected. When we finished, I had about thirty head of saddle horses and about twenty head of broncs, and away I went for Fort Pierre, well over a hundred miles away. Anyone who has never gone across country driving a bunch of saddle horses, some gentle, some wild, some slow, some fast, and all smart, does not know real trouble. Add to that a bunch of wholly wild and untrained broncs, which have neither knowledge of what to do in a driven bunch nor the inclination to do it, and the person without that experience cannot possibly have the requisite amount of charity and understanding for the rider who might throw away all his chances of salvation for the privilege of expressing his honest opinion of those infernal horses.

I was now on a different horse from my mount of the day before, but I had about thirty horses that had not been ridden since the fall before from which to choose. One did not make slow time with such a bunch of horses, and quite a long while before noon I drove all of them into the round corral at Dick Mathieson's ranch on Bad River, below the mouth of Grindstone Creek about seven miles east of Philip, for the purpose of catching another horse and turning loose in the bunch the one that I had been riding. While I was roping out a fresh horse and saddling him, a fellow at the ranch had made some coffee and set out some grub, so I partook of that typical hospitality. A cowpuncher took food on every available chance and in a manner that did violence to all the rules of dieticians. When in a hurry, he could practically inhale a considerable quantity of food and away to his horse. Such was my conduct on that occasion.

. . . . As I got on my horse in the corral, Kenneth Mathieson, then just a boy, opened the gate to allow me to drive out the horses.[3] Realizing that he had to do something more vigorous than passive resistance if he were to be as free on the next section of that journey as he was on the first, that horse set to with right good will (or was it good will?) to slip his pack—me. Failing to buck me off, we were soon on our way down Bad River and making the best time we could. What was said by me to any one of those horses on the way from Mathieson's ranch to Dan Bastion's,[4] about twenty-five miles further on, must be considered in the nature of a privileged communication, although it could hardly be said to be confidential, for anyone within four miles could have heard it if sulphur and brimstone did not affect his hearing. Scurrying along down Bad River until we passed where the town of Midland now is and reached the Dan Bastion ranch just below the mouth of Mitchell Creek, I put the horses in the round corral there and caught myself a new saddle horse to replace the one caught at Dick Mathieson's ranch. After the hard ride he had had from Mathieson's to Bastion's, a great deal of the time on a high gallop in an effort to bring some form of cohesion, coupled with forward movement, into that incompatible group, he was glad of my change of horses.

From Midland to Fort Pierre down Bad River was considered then to be about sixty miles, although the railroad afterwards built reduced that mileage to about fifty. Soon we were away again, and when we got down to about the place where the town of Capa now stands, it seemed that demons more potent than any which housed themselves in the Gadarene swine took possession of those driven horses.[5] The broncs insisted on scattering and running in every direction, while the saddle horses, being smarter, knew what was the matter with them, and they insisted on stopping to graze. There may at that moment have been an angrier man in South Dakota than the driver of those horses. There may even have been someone who was swearing more earnestly and more loudly, but that is subject to doubt. It seems to me that the reverberating echoes of my comments on those horses, individually and collectively, must still be bounding back and forth along those brakes of Bad River. Surely they could not have died down completely in the short space of just a little over thirty-eight years.

Just about sundown I was passing on the road by the ranch of Tom Hill, whom I know very well indeed. He lived there with his wife, the former Julia Ducheneaux, a mixed-blood Indian woman and a queen at that, with their children. Their little boy, Frankie, about eleven years old came riding out to me on horseback and said that his dad thought I was the one riding after those horses and for me to come into the ranch and get some supper.[6] My hunger overcame my reluctance and my anger at those horses, and Frankie and I turned the horses in toward the ranch. While I said hello to Tom and his wife, Frankie turned the horses into the pasture. When Tom asked me what I was driving and was told that it was broncs and saddle horses, which I had taken that day from Big Buffalo and intended to take on to Fort Pierre and the Buffalo Ranch, six miles beyond, he knew it all, including my feelings.

He asked, "When do you expect to get there?"

I said, "Sometime before morning."

He said with an amused grin, "You can drive them so much easier in the night." None of his good-natured sarcasm was lost on me, but Mrs. Hill was there, and my comments had to be more restrained than they had been at any time before that day. Then he added, "And I suppose as soon as you turn over the horses you'll quit."

I said, "Yes, sir, I'll turn those horses in by daylight in the morning. Then I'll quit, and I'll never ride again."

Tom, from long personal experience, knew it all by heart. He knew what a hard day's riding after that sort of aggregation of horses did to the nerves and the temper of a rider. He knew how certain he would be to determine under those circumstances to choose some other form of life endeavor, if indeed he had any inclination to continue life itself, so he said, "Well, it is over forty miles into that buffalo pasture, so you'd better have a bite to eat."

The meal was soon prepared and served by that lovely lady, Mrs. Hill, who was herself a product of the range, and who knew exactly what to do and say to a range man to appease his anger and quiet his nerves after a heart-rending day with his work. After supper, Tom, Frankie and I went out to the corral and sat cross-legged on the ground, while I made and smoked a couple of handmade Bull Durham cigarettes to top off a fine meal. That was long before the day of the grossly bad social manners that call for smoking at the table and poisoning the air for those who prefer it fresh. Of course, Mrs. Hill, like all the decent ladies of her day, did not smoke. She was not like a sweet young matron of society's elite who recently remarked to me without any thought that she would shock me to my boot soles, "I seem to smoke more when I am drinking."

My nerves were in repose, my good nature was restored, and a sense of well-being from the meal and the surroundings enveloped me, so when Tom with a grin said to me, "George, don't you think it's about time for you to get going if you plan to get to the buffalo pasture by daybreak?" I merely said, "Oh, you go to hell." After a good night's rest in a good bed at Tom's house, a good breakfast in the morning, and a fresh horse, I was all set for the rest of the trip. After changing horses again at Harry Brigg's ranch, the saddle horses and the broncs were turned in by me at the Buffalo Ranch in good season and in good shape that afternoon, and with no thought of quitting. . . .

The horses were turned over—the saddle horses to the horse wrangler, and the broncs to John Slaughter, the bronco peeler. In the bunch of unbroken horses taken down Bad River by me, without specially calling my attention to him by his bad behavior, was a tall, rangy, well-set-up bay four-year-old gelding (nothing but geldings were ever ridden or worked on the range) that was afterwards to travel the highways and byways of life under the none-too-euphonious name of "Old Dishrag." Horses were usually named on the range because of a characteristic, or a brand, or the name of a former owner, or some item of appearance. This bay horse had no name when I turned him over, but he did a few days later after he threw John Slaughter off.

John, in explanation of the incident said, "Riding that horse is just like riding an old dishrag on a clothes line in a high wind." What John meant was that the horse pitched (bucked) so limber and so hard that this made him very difficult to ride, and so Old Dishrag became his name, and Old Dishrag he remained.

It may not be too much out of place to interpolate a little explanation about the way horses were broken for the big cow outfits. Usually one man was hired to break a bunch of horses to ride. He would be given about twenty or twenty-five head to break at five dollars a head. He would live at the headquarters ranch during that employment. He was supposed to break each one so that he could be led and would not run on the rope. Also he had to ride each one of them ten times.

He soon broke them of running on the rope. Naturally, a completely wild horse, which had never had a human hand on him except at the time he was branded and had never seen a human being except men on horseback on the range, would have little thought of doing anything but running away as soon as he felt the loop of a hard-twist rope settling on his neck in the round corral. Then the man with the rope would see to it that he got a good turn of the rope around a firmly set snubbing post in the center of the corral. The horse would take a few hard runs on the snubbing post and would get stopped terrifically, and sometimes he would choke himself down by suddenly pulling back on the rope. His breath would come harder and harder, and his eyes would roll until soon he would fall over choked down.

Then the man would be on him with a hackamore, which that horse would be wearing when he came to. The hackamore was really a halter, usually made of hard three-eighths-inch rope, with another rope, usually a thick, soft one, fastened under the jaw, and that he continued to wear until he was "broke to ride." To the hackamore rope could be attached another rope fastened to a loose log lying on the ground outside the corral. As soon as the rope attached to the log was properly in place so that it would not get caught in the gate or in the corral, the gate would be thrown open (or the gate poles removed as the case required), and the horse, thinking he saw a sure way to freedom, would run out of the gate and away. Never realizing his danger until reaching the end of the rope, he would almost certainly be thrown with terrific force to the ground.

The purpose of the loose log was to keep the horse from breaking either his neck or the rope as he came to the end, because it would always give enough to avoid a solid jerk. It usually took a good many runs on that rope to convince that horse that no matter what was there to bother him, it was safer and more comfortable for him to remain safely within the radius of that rope than to attempt to get beyond it. After a time, with his head bruised and skinned and battered by running on the rope, he would realize the futility of such conduct, and in nearly all instances, he would remain from then on a horse that would not fight or stretch a rope unless it happened to be fastened to the saddle on his back in later days, but that was another part of his education. In case there were two men in the corral at the time the horse was ready to be caught, one would rope him by the front feet and throw him, holding him down while the other man put on the hackamore. From there on the process was the same.

After being tethered to the log for about a day, the horse would then be saddled, which was frequently accomplished by tying up a hind leg and blindfolding him. All this resulted in fresh and additional rope burns on the legs and body of the horse, thereby greatly enhancing his respect for this new thing to him—a rope. Also, while his head was sore, he would be taught to lead, because a cowboy's horse must lead well, and he must not run on a rope.

I knew two powerful young men who had a way of their own in letting a bronc first come to the end of the rope. One was Bill Carroll (who moved out to Wyoming with a new wife), old in experience, and the other was Sam Baker, a colored Texas boy. Either of those men would tie his rope hard and fast around his hips, open the corral gate, and throw his loop around a bronc's neck as he would dash through the gate to supposed freedom. Then by split-second timing, he would see to it that the bronc came full force to the end of that rope as his feet were off the ground. The consequent fall he would get, throwing him flat on his side, would simply knock all the wind out of the horse. A few such falls and that horse would be willing to indulge his shyness and wildness in other ways than by running on the rope. Those two fellows were certainly welcome to any glory they got out of their method, but it worked for them. John Slaughter did not use it.

A bronc was supposed to be ridden ten times by the broncobuster, the last two times with a bridle instead of a hackamore to accustom him to the bit—there being no bit in a hackamore. When he was able to lead the horse up to the saddle lying on the ground, put a bridle on him, then the blanket, then the saddle, and get on him, after having ridden him ten times, the broncobuster turned him over to some cowpuncher as a "broke" horse, and the cowboy was supposed to do his work with him. Looking back over a long series of years, to call such an animal a broke horse was the ultimate in freedom of expression, poetic license.

According to the broncobuster, Old Dishrag was not a mean horse to handle. He quickly quit fighting the rope and did not long worry over having a saddle put on him. He was just a smart horse by nature and made the best of his circumstances without too much fuss. But he could buck in a fashion that would put the Strawberry Roan of the radio-yodeling cowboys out of competition.[7] Horses bucked in many ways. Some jumped high and straight ahead; some bucked low and fast and straight ahead; some sunfished, which meant jumping crooked and turning the sides of the belly alternately to the sun; some whirled, which meant bucking in a whirling motion; some swapped ends, meaning that where his tail is this jump his head will be next; some seemed to be able to roll their skins, which made the saddle seem loose fitting, first appearing to be down on one side and then on the other. The first two types mentioned were the least difficult to ride. In spite of his good behavior, nice manner and kindly attitude, Dishrag seemed to be able to combine all types in each jump. He was the only one of the bunch of broncs I turned over to him, and others that were turned over later, that threw John Slaughter or came near doing it. . . .

Old Dishrag was turned over with a bunch of so-called broke horses and was assigned to the string of Pete Ashley, while the rest of the riders were assigned the others. Each year, time-worn horses were going out, and young horses were coming in. Pete Ashley and I were just about on a par as cowhands. Although he was an expert horseman with a good, gentle horse, he was not a good bronco rider, but he planned to stay on when occasion demanded. He could catch animals with a rope, although he was far from expert. He could get the maximum of needed effort out of his string of horses and yet could keep them in good shape and without saddle and cinch sores. He had a good eye for reading brands and a good memory for owners and locations on the range. He had a pleasant disposition, was a fine hand who was never afraid of work, but a poor one for showoff. With these qualifications, he soon became a rider with outside outfits—a rep. After all, they were classed as the top hands. That is the type of man who drew Old Dishrag.

Although we both worked for the same outfit that summer, it was fall before he and I met up with each other again, and he laughingly told me of his experience. He had ridden Old Dishrag as a member of his string with an outfit working on the Moreau River and was coming back up Green Grass Creek, which runs north into the Moreau River from Eagle Butte, riding this horse and driving the cattle he had picked up with this roundup and also his string. In his everyday life Old Dishrag was a well-behaved horse, except that he would buck once in a while, but without malice, just as a game of skill. Pete had been able to ride him each time he had bucked, but with no glory. On this occasion, the tall, bay beauty decided it was too nice a day to waste with no sport at all, so he downed his head with no apparent reason and in most enthusiastic fashion made Pete wish that he had picked some other line of work than punching cows. Pete hung on to everything he could see or feel and with all he had, but one time he came down and Old Dishrag was not under him. A few more jumps and off went the saddle and blanket, taking with them the bridle as they went over the horse's head. After having done this perfect Houdini escape, Dishrag was as free as the wind. Instead of going into the string of horses, as an orthodox horse would have done, this one made a bee-line for the distant horizon, leaving Pete afoot many miles from everywhere.

You were told in another letter that it took the combination of a horse, with a saddle, blanket and bridle on him, and a rider in the saddle to make a cowboy.[8] Here was Pete, without a horse under him, alone and out on the wide prairie, so he was just that meaningless and valueless thing, a man afoot. Gathering his saddle, blanket and bridle into one place, getting his rope off his saddle, he decided to exercise all the ingenuity he had in getting his rope on one of his loose saddle horses. That was no easy task because those horses were just as prairie-wise as their riders. With skill born of desperation, Pete got his rope on one of his horses, saddled and mounted him—all right again. But Dishrag was gone, never to return so far as Pete was concerned.

Time passed on until the next spring, and it was my bad luck to go as a rep with a roundup wagon working up the Missouri River from Fort Pierre, then up the Cheyenne River to a point a little beyond Leslie (a small settlement and post office on the south bank of the Cheyenne, opposite Cherry Creek, and now completely obliterated; it was quite a center when Jim Benthine held sway), and then down the divide to the Willow Creek dam west of Fort Pierre, which would work out all that large area. The reason that was classed as my bad luck is that none of the saddle ponies in my regular string had been picked up by any of those riding after horses, of whom I was one. That left me to get along with about half a dozen horses that were not wanted by any rider. Even a poor guesser could know that they were of very limited value and maybe none too gentle. That was the reason of making the intimate personal acquaintance of Old Dishrag a few days later.

About the time the roundup started, my old friend, Henry Livermont,[9] a mixed-blood Indian rancher who had a place on Bad River just below where Van Metre is, came to me and said, "George, I see you are short of saddle horses and have none of your regular string. I have a dandy young horse that has the making of a fine cutting horse, but I don't have enough extra work of that sort for him. You are going to have more than you can do on those plug horses you have, and I wish you would ride him."

The offer was accepted, and I rode Henry's horse, Watcheye, so called from a white or glass eye, a great deal and altogether as a cow horse, a cutting horse, giving him about all he could stand of the kind of work Henry said he wanted him to have. He was a good horse, and I got a lot of service out of him on that roundup not then realizing that there was a barb in the bait Henry threw to me.[10]

We had been working for two or three days and had reached the head of Chantier Creek, when one of the riders came to me and said that on circle he had found a fine-looking, bay, L-7 saddle horse with a bunch of range horses and had run him into the saddle bunch. The first time our saddle horses were brought in to the wagon, I looked this quiet-looking, handsome bay horse over and realized that, although I did not recognize him at all, he must be one of those broken the year before, and that left Dishrag because I knew all the others. I told some of the fellows that he had been in the habit of throwing off his riders, although from reports he was not otherwise a bad horse. I was frankly afraid of getting thrown by him but decided to ride him next morning. Remember, the last man who had put a hand, or anything else, on him was Pete Ashley in the summer before, and the manner of his leave-taking of Pete was not calculated to discourage him now.

Happy Jack, who was riding a string of John Hayes horses in this roundup, was a very good rider, and he rather enjoyed the show of doing it (a couple of years afterward the poor fellow was killed by a wild horse on Deadwood Street in Fort Pierre).[11] In the morning, when I caught this bay horse, I asked Jack to top him off for me. That meant to get on him and ride him so that he could get the bucking out of his system. Jack agreed, and we put Jack's saddle on him, which was not at all hard to do, for Dishrag was not the type of horse that wore himself out with wild demonstrations. Jack got on him, and he bucked, but not as I saw him do on a number of occasions afterwards. After Jack had run him around for a while with the idea of taking it out of him, he took off his saddle and I put mine on, and he caught one of his own horses.

By that time all the fellows were ready to go on circle, and Dishrag bucked two or three times on that circle with me. Of course I was very much alert because of my fear of the horse. Because of that and of the fact that my saddle had a good, solid horn, which I could not pull out, I came in off circle along toward noon, still on that horse's back. That was ride number one on him, to be followed by many another, and it is a strange commentary on riders that except for Happy Jack, who rode him for a few minutes that one morning, I was the only rider ever on that horse who did not get thrown by him. That was true before my day with him and also afterward, and, with no show of false modesty, it can be said that I was the least-expert bucking-horse rider that was ever on his back, which is probably true as to Pete Ashley and certainly true as to the others.

One day, up towards the head of Deep Creek, a group of us were riding out on circle at a stiff gallop. Suddenly Harry Briggs, who was riding close to me, said, "George, your latigo is dragging."

Without thinking of what was under me, I swung down on the left side of my galloping horse to pick up the dragging latigo. Sensing a splendid chance, Old Dishrag laid himself into the job of sending me far, and he did everything in his repertoire of tricks. Like the concentrated ghost of a cyclone, he hammered me and tossed me about. He was just like an infuriated dynamo and paid not the slightest attention to the quirt whipping he was getting from the other riders, to the accompaniment of yells, in an effort to make him break into a run, while they shouted in frantic encouragement to me to "stay with him."

Stay with him I did with no credit to me for the result because, if there was any part of that horse and saddle and of the surrounding atmosphere for that matter where I did not appear and suffer, the fault was not mine, but Dishrag's, for he was wholly in charge of the situation. It began to appear to me that, instead of trying to throw me off, he was just playing a rough game of catch and doing anything to frustrate my single wish at the moment, and that was to hit the ground, which would be comfortably still if nothing else. But after making his final catch and leaving me sitting in the saddle, the horse quit as quickly as he had begun. Without any pride of calling as a bronco rider, but still on top of the horse, I hastened to dismount and, getting down on my hands and knees, to feed my breakfast to the ants. It was not so especially unusual to see a fellow so shaken up by a bucking horse that he would spring a nosebleed or get nauseated and throw up, so all the fellows stuck around for me to finish that job, after which I got on my horse, and we all went about our business. It was all just a part of the game and not worthy of comment.

A little later in the summer when I was back with the home wagon, riding my own string of which Dishrag was now a member, and we were working down the north side of the Cheyenne River. Scotty came out to the outfit with a team and buggy, and with him was my cousin, George Philip, from Hays, Kansas. Next morning, as we were getting ready for a long circle, George decided that he would ride with us, so he was furnished a horse, and he saddled him up with Scotty's saddle, which was in the buggy. Inasmuch as we were going to make a long ride, and as he had been behaving like a perfect gentleman for a pretty long time, I caught and saddled Dishrag.

Treatment of saddle horses on the range was anything but uniform. Most of the men never petted their horses at all, nor used any particular

terms of endearment to them. They handled and used them imperson-
ally, about as a modern motor patrolman would his motorcycle. Some
men, and they were seldom with their jobs long, were inordinately cruel
to their horses, using fierce spade bits in their bridles, which would
cut a horse's mouth and tongue pitifully, and being unnecessarily free
with their spurs and quirts. Some petted and fussed over their horses,
although when occasion demanded they would give them a good roweling or sharp cuts with a quirt. As a result of the varying attitudes of the
men, very few of those horses became what would be considered gentle
by the standards of today. They were merely well trained to do the things
required of them.

I was always a petter of my horses, teaching them to do some minor
tricks. The first requirement of that was to get them to allow me to
scratch their itching ears, eyes and corners of the mouth, all of which
was no small task in itself because their naturally suspicious nature was
made more alert by the treatment they had received from men. Once in
a while there was a horse so much like some humans that nobody could
like it, and those were simply never petted by anybody; they were just
used. Most of my saddle horses soon got to demand that their heads be
scratched and rubbed, and if I appeared dilatory in doing it, they would
rub themselves against me so vigorously as almost to knock me down.
By that time you are on sufficiently friendly terms with that horse to
teach him to kiss you, shake hands, and other such things. One thing
that I would practice by the hour on day herd was to run at the horse in
all manner of grotesque ways, jumping, yelling, etc., and get on him. It
usually took a lot of patience to acquaint him with the fact that this was
a game, in which he was supposed to stand still. After a time he would
learn it and seemed to enjoy playing it, a handy frame of mind in which
to have a saddle horse, for one could never be sure that he might not,
sometime, have to make just that kind of a run and mount his horse.

Dishrag was one of my pets, and he was always willing to love and
caress me when I was with him and afoot. Moreover, he was one of the
very few horses I ever knew on the range that did not have to be caught by
a rope. I could take my bridle and catch him in the rope corral and even
loose on the prairie. He was a queer combination, but I loved him, and
he loved me, even though he made atrocious efforts at times to throw
me off for no good reason at all, for he would have made no objections
at all to my getting right back on, I feel sure. Maybe he had dreams of

repeating his miracle of Green Grass Creek, when he dumped his whole pack, rider, saddle, blanket, and bridle.

Anyway, this morning on Rudy Creek, I caught Dishrag under the confident expectation that he would be well behaved. It so happened that Bill Kleinsmith decided to take the long ride we expected on a young horse in his string, which everyone expected to buck. Cousin George, who was quite a camera enthusiast in those days, got off to one side so that he could get a good picture of Bill on the bucking horse. All the rest of us were sitting more or less at ease on our horses, waiting for Bill to get on. Then Bill swung onto his horse, which made one big, lunging buck jump and hit Dishrag with his head, right smack in the side, just back of my left leg. It was well that the impact set me squarely in the saddle and on balance because, contemptuous of such efforts as Bill's horse could make, Dishrag decided to put on the show himself.

It would be an improper withholding of credit to deny, or to fail to assert, that he did put on a show, and by some freak of fortune, I held throughout the state of balance with which the performance commenced. To my own surprise, and perhaps to Dishrag's utter amazement, I was making a good ride. As he performed, close in front of him loomed a cut bank of Rudy Creek, about twelve feet high. Being always so coldly calculating in his efforts, my flash was that he would buck up to it and then turn quickly, intending to throw me on the turn. Instead, he bucked up to the bank and straight over, landing in the dry bottom of Rudy Creek still bucking and, strangely, with me still riding him in approved fashion. A few more jumps and it was all over.

Then he trotted quietly and unconcernedly to the place indicated by me where we could best and most quickly go up the bank. Joining the others, we went on with our ride. Incidentally, George looked on at my ride with open-mouthed interest and forgot to snap a picture of anything. A picture would have meant little then, but it would be nice to have it now. Memory does not serve to remind me that that horse ever bucked with me again. Months later he was turned in with the rest of my string on the first of November that year as I was getting ready to go to law school. I never rode him, nor any of the others, again.

According to authentic information, when the horses were assigned next spring, Pat Gallagher wanted Old Dishrag.[12] The boss told him if he really wanted him he could have him, but he added, "He is a bad horse, and you may have trouble riding him."

MICK
B.
HARRISON

Knowing that he was a good bronco rider, and that I was not, and perhaps with his pride touched a bit, Pat said, "I understand George rode him all last summer and never got thrown. If he could ride him, it's a damn cinch I can."

. . . Pat got Dishrag, and a few minutes later the horse undertook to throw him and accomplished his purpose. A little later on the same ride, he repeated the performance, and in Pat's own language, "That time my body just flew in an arc at the full length of the bridle reins."[13]

That determined the boss to turn him and another tall, rangy bay, called "Glassy" from one white eye he had, and that I used to ride, over to Scotty for a buggy team. Glassy was just a good long-distance horse and nothing more, but I somehow flatter myself to believe that if the open range had done a better job of surviving, and if Dishrag and I had stayed together, he would have shown himself a good horse for me.

Years rolled on. My law school days were over, and my law practice was interrupted by two or three trips each year for a week each time to attend Scottish Rite (Masonic) reunions in Yankton. On one such occasion, as I was walking down the street from the Masonic Temple to the Portland Hotel in Yankton in the company of my good friend Hite Brisbine,[14] I noticed a buggy team tied to a hitching rack. Glassy was not there, but the off horse (right hand) in that team evoked from me the surprised ejaculation, "My God, Old Dishrag."

Instantly that horse's ears snapped forward, and he was all alert as he tried to shove himself over the hitching rack to get to me. I got to him and took his head in my arms, rubbing his ears, his eyes, the corners of his mouth, and under his chin. In turn he rubbed his head against me and, with his long strong lips, he nibbled his caresses on my ear, neck, and cheek. Changed as conditions were for both of us, we were glad to see each other. Maybe we were both thinking of a world long gone and that could never come back. Maybe he was thinking of a world where a free-swinging horse, with a free-swinging rider, was as free as the winds of their prairie, unhampered by fences or buggy harness. To the paleontologist the glory that was Anuradhapura may be conjured up from under its forested jungle.[15] Maybe to Dishrag on that occasion, and to his former rider as well, the glory that was the cow country, the open range was forever buried in a jungle of barbed wire, plow dust, and real-estate mortgages.

As I finally pulled away from that horse that day, Hite Brisbine, who had been intensely interested in the exchange of greetings over that hitching rack, said, "Well, by gracious, I don't know where you fellows met, but you are certainly acquainted." We were, we had met again, and we had parted forever.

The cowboy, just like his horse (no particular cowboy and no particular horse), may have had his faults of conduct and of expression, measured by counsel of perfection. Each lived his life on the outer fringe of society. He, like his horse, may have been a bit snorty in the silky haired crowd, but each could be relied on when reliance was a definite need. Each may have lacked the polish, but each was of intrinsic value. The authoress of the "Lost Chord," speaking through another poem, may have had some such example in mind when she said:

> Judge not; the workings of his brain
> And of his heart thou canst not see;
> What looks to thy dim eyes a stain,
> In God's pure light may only be
> A scar, brought from some well-fought field,
> Where thou wouldst only faint and yield.[16]

Affectionately,
Dad

CHAPTER 15

An Indian Roundup

September 30, 1940

My dear Geordie, Jean, and Bob:

In a letter to you on September 1, giving you a brief outline of the life of a range horse in the story of Old Dishrag, it can be remembered without too specific restatement that my old friend, Henry Livermont, offered me the use of his gray horse Watcheye or Watchey. Henry knew that my regular string of horses had not been gathered yet that spring, and as a consequence I was compelled to ride horses that were in nobody's string, therefore of little value. Henry suggested that, as I was short-mounted and on inferior horses, he would lend me a young horse of his, which he wanted to be educated into the cutting-horse class. According to Henry, the horse was gentle and intelligent, in addition to being a good physical animal, and had an aptitude for the work in which Henry wanted him trained. Not all horses had aptitude for that line of work, and when evidence of being able to follow a particular cow critter through hell and high water was detected in a horse, an effort was made to develop it. So when Henry offered me the makings of a good cow horse to ride during that spring roundup, the offer was accepted.

After the five or six weeks that the roundup lasted, Henry was willing to admit that his horse had more experience in that time than he might have in all the rest of his life, for he was ridden a great deal and in no other work than what Henry wanted him to have. On my side was good satisfaction with the performance and prospect of the tall, gray, watch-eyed horse. A watcheye or a glass eye, which was really a natural white eye, was very likely to be the cause for the name of such a horse, and so it was with Henry's. Henry had not greatly misrepresented the potentiality of Watcheye as a good cow horse, and he benefited under the amount of work he received from me about every other day, and sometimes more often, during that roundup.

As soon as it was over, Henry took his horses, including Watcheye and what cattle there had been collected belonging to him and neighboring ranchers, and went home to his place on Bad River, while I took my collected cattle and saddle horses and worked them up toward the Cheyenne River, where Scotty's outfit would soon be working. It gave me no small pleasure to get back to the home outfit, get my own regular saddle ponies, and get rid of the plugs that had to be used as substitutes for what, according to my ideas, was as good a string of saddle horses as there was on the range. Sure enough they had been picked up, to my delight, and with Dishrag added, I was on my own horses (not in ownership but in assignment).

You were told in the letter about Old Dishrag about the time my cousin George failed to snap the camera. Well, a few days after that incident when we were down about the head of Abare (spelled *Herbert*, French) Creek, the boss told me to cut my string and go down and work with Johnnie Burnett's[1] Indian roundup, which was to work down the Niobrara River in northern Nebraska, then up the Keyapaha, and on through the Rosebud Indian Reservation to a point on White River where the Rosebud and Pine Ridge Indian reservations joined. He did not know, nor did I, where the outfit would commence nor whether it had already commenced. It did not take more than a few minutes to prepare my bed for packing, get it on a horse, rope out the other members of my string, and get going, without knowing anything more about the location of that roundup outfit than that it was south of there, a hundred twenty-five miles or more, but that was a matter of small concern to anyone but me, and for me just a problem to be solved in the next few days.

Hitting straight across country for the Rosebud Agency took me directly past old Henry Livermont's ranch on Bad River, where a welcome was sure to await the cowboy traveling across country with a string of horses. On arriving at Henry's place, my horses were run into the corral, and the packhorse roped. About that time Henry and the boys, Jack and young Henry, came out to the corral where greetings were exchanged and a welcome extended. It was a certainty that Mrs. Livermont was even then getting supper for the fellow who had ridden up, with no inquiry at that stage as to who he was. The horses were turned into Henry's horse pasture; my bed was rearranged from the pack and made up out by the corral. Then we all went to the house.

It so happened that more information than was available at the time of riding him in the spring roundup was now known to me about Watcheye. Jack Mathieson, who lived with and worked for his father, George D. Mathieson,[2] on Bad River a few miles below Henry's and about where the railroad town of Wendte now is, met up with me on the Cheyenne River a short time before, and he then asked me about this horse of Henry's, saying, "I heard you rode Henry Livermont's Watcheye with Ed Delehan's wagon this spring. How did you get along with him?"

My answer was, "Fine. He is a good horse and has promise of making a good cow horse."

Jack asked, "Didn't you have any trouble with him at all?"

I said, "Not a bit. What sort of trouble would you expect a fellow to have with him?"

Jack laughed and said, "You were plumb lucky. That horse threw off everybody around Henry's place, and he took him to the spring roundup just to get someone to ride him and take it out of him. It was quite a joke that you rode him all through that roundup as a cutting horse."

There was a lot more of the same kind of conversation with appropriate comments by me on the general attributes of fellows who would do what Henry did, very much enfeebled, of course, by the fact that Watcheye had done nothing but work and had behaved himself in most-approved fashion in doing so.

It was clearly the law of the range that, if one man asked another to ride a horse for him, he was supposed to tell just what sort that horse was and what he might be expected to do. If a man borrowed a horse from another, no duty devolved upon the lender to tell the borrower anything, but whatever he did tell him was supposed to be the truth. You did not need to inform him, but you must not mislead him under the best traditions of the range. That rule was not completely rigid because any fellow who claimed to be "Bronco Bill from Busterville" was not unlikely to find himself with a first-class private rodeo between his knees in the form of a borrowed horse that was likely to test his powers.

Henry was clearly wrong in telling me that the horse he wanted me to ride was gentle and that what he wanted was to have him worked as a cutting horse. But I pardoned Henry, knowing that he did not want the horse to buck with me and that he did want him to get some real experience calculated to make a good cow horse out of him. Besides, the horse had played his part, and there was always the chance that Jack, who frequently acted more like a descendent of Ananias than of George

Washington, was not concerned with reliability of statement at the moment.³ Be that as it might, he had given me full warning of Watcheye, and I would get on him next time on my own responsibility, without any right to charge Henry with bad faith.

At the house we indulged ourselves in the comfort of a good visit, for in that life a large part of one's information, outside of what he personally experienced or saw, came through the medium of conversation in visits with friends. In that way one kept quite accurate track of what was happening throughout the length and breadth of the range country. Besides the splendid art of conversation was still in vogue. It had not been supplanted by the enthusiastic and forceful mendacity of soap and coffee peddlers on the radio, nor interrupted by the women of the party having to get up and go search for a match. When we had spread our information and had answered all questions back and forth, I asked Henry how his horse Watcheye was getting along. He said he was just fine, could not be better, and was big and fat. A few careful questions brought the information that he had not been ridden since the spring roundup, and that I was the last person who had been on his back.

Henry then said, "You're going to have lots of work for your horses riding down in that Rosebud country. You know Watcheye as well as anybody, and you can work him. Why don't you just take him along and give him some more work?"

To my expression of fear that he might buck with me came the assurance that, although he might do that, I could ride him all right. Henry was now on safe and proper ground when he put the responsibility squarely on the fellow who was expected to ride the horse. It was soon agreed that Watcheye would be a temporary member of my string when I left in the morning. Soon after I went out to my bed at the corral and turned in for the night.

On awakening in the morning, a phenomenon that was quite occasional in those days had occurred, was in fact occurring, — it was raining. Quickly getting dressed, I prepared my bed for the pack, and one of the Livermont boys ran in the horses. Breakfast over and my bed on a packhorse, my string was cut out, including Watcheye, but he refused to leave the place, although mine, well-trained ponies that they were for that sort of thing, had no objection. That left the alternative of leaving Watcheye or riding him. I told Henry that it was going to be more trouble than it was worth to try to drive him away with my horses and I would have to leave him unless I rode him.

On Henry's earnest solicitation that he be ridden, and it was plain that he wanted somebody to be riding that horse, they were all put back in the corral. My horse was unsaddled, Watcheye was caught and saddled, and we were ready to be off. Watcheye made objection to my getting on him with a slicker on, and it was plain that he never before had been ridden with a slicker, but a man in that business dared not cater too much to the idiosyncrasies of a horse. Some one had to be boss and it better not be the horse. So waiving further ceremony, I jammed Watcheye up against the side of the corral and swung on, slicker and all. Although Watcheye tried to throw me off, the ground was much too slippery for a good job of bucking in that gumbo mud, and I had no great difficulty in overcoming his scruples against leaving his home. Giving him a good roweling just to convince him that my plans were seriously intended, we got on our way, and those horses of mine just got along in the right direction as soon as that was indicated to them.

On and on to the south we went, after a while running out of the mud, over the White Clay Buttes and beyond to old Pat McGrath's little store on Big White River above the forks.[4] That was about forty miles, and it was getting well along toward the latter part of the day, so I just unpacked, picketed one horse and put the others into a little pasture of Pat's, and stayed for the night. After sharing old Pat's hospitality for supper and breakfast, and paying for it because he was a storekeeper, I was on my way down the river to the reservation gate just below the confluence of the Big and Little White rivers. The Rosebud reservation had just been enclosed, and it was necessary to go through the gate, which was just about where the highway now crosses White River south of Murdo.[5]

That morning I was riding one of my own horses, and a dandy. On arriving at the gate, fortunately and by mistake, it was not locked as it was supposed to be, nor was the Indian policeman who was supposed to be on duty there anywhere in sight. Accordingly I opened the gate, ran my string of horses through, and closed it. Then I strung out along the trail that was expected to land me at the Rosebud Agency, about thirty-five or forty miles away, along toward evening. Although I had on previous occasions ridden with roundups on the Rosebud reservation, I had never before seen that newly constructed fence and had never been to the Rosebud Indian Agency. Of course that made no difference because I knew its direction, and that was about all we needed in a new part of the country in those days.

Before we get too far away from the Forks of White River and the little store of Pat McGrath there at Westover, let me set you right on that genial Irishman. He was never a cowpuncher, but he did own some cattle and horses, which were always turned in his proper direction by the cowboys whose friend he was. There are many phrases filled with friendly meaning: "He was in my class at school"; "I have often sat in lodge with him"; "We belong to the same fraternity"; and many others of like tenor, but it is doubtful, since it has passed completely out of existence, if there is any more potent phrase of friendship than to say, "He is all right. I knew him on the range." That is likely to forgive and gloss over errors of conduct in complicated society because of known value in a more fundamental social state. (Incidentally, it may be remarked that some time in 1934 it came to my attention from a file in the United States attorney's office that Pat McGrath was charged with the larceny of an Indian horse on the reservation. A close inspection of the file convinced me that no horse had been stolen by old Pat, who was now really an old man, and the case was dismissed without any effort of prosecution. Just how much recollection of former sterling qualities may have entered into the analysis of present official reports may properly rest within the field of psychiatry, but certain it is that old Pat neither deserved, nor experienced, a criminal prosecution.)

About the time I got the gate closed behind me and got strung out to pursue my way up the east side of the Little White River, the long-haired Sioux Indian policeman, whose job it was to guard the gate to see that it was kept locked and that no alien hoof prints were permitted on the reservation, came dashing in from the west, kicking the ribs of his white horse in well-defined purpose. Instead of attempting any form of parley, he headed off my horses and tried to drive them and me off the precincts that should have been considered sacred to the use of the Indians, but were not. His understanding of the particular traits of that string of horses nowhere near approached mine, their steady rider and their frequent driver on long cross-country trips. Also the horse he was riding was not even a counterfeit of the animal that was my mount that morning, for that Indian pony did not look like the real thing. The unequal struggle for that string of horses would have been a laughable contest to any witnesses, but, like all too many instances of range life, there was no gallery to cheer the contestants.

After many faithful efforts to get those horses started north toward the closed gate, only to find them being steadily forced farther to the south, and after finding himself and his horse actually forced away from interference by a horse and rider that relentlessly seemed to interfere with his steadfast purpose to do his duty, the Indian called for a parley. He could talk no English, but I knew a very little Sioux as almost all of the cowhands did. However, the Indians are expert in communicating their thoughts by signs. The cowboys were not above the use of explanatory gestures on their own account, but the Indian is a master of the sign.

The first signs merely confirmed what I already knew, that the reservation had been recently fenced, that none but Indians had a right to be on there without official permission, that the gate was supposed to be locked and watched by him to the end that none but authorized persons should enter, that I was not an authorized person, and therefore must depart. I told him that I was going to the roundup run by Johnnie Burnett, whom we both knew well, and that I would not go out through the gate, nor any other way except to that roundup. He realized his inability to put me and my horses out, and so he placed me under arrest, to which there was perfect submission on my part, knowing that it was easy for him to place me under a technical arrest but more difficult for him to figure out how to dispose of his prisoner. Having arrested me, it now became his duty to take me to Rosebud Agency. As that was my prospective destination for that night, I submitted to his official announcement with a disappointing meekness.

Our discussion now resolved itself into ways and means of getting the prisoner into the agency jail. His job was to tend that gate, and he could not do that very well if he was taking my horses and me to the agency. Fortunately for all of us, at that time I had not wholly reformed, and the Indian policeman spied a long plug of Horseshoe chewing tobacco in my saddle pocket. Under the skin most men, and even most policemen, are alike, and he informed me that I could go on with my string on condition that I would go on to the agency and report myself under arrest, but that plug of tobacco would have to be left with him. We finally compromised on four-fifths of the plug for him and one-fifth for me and my promise to report myself under arrest at the agency.

He went his way and I went mine to the Rosebud Agency, which I reached about sundown, and reported myself to the agent, Major McChesney, in accordance with the promise to "the law." Immediately on arriving at the agency, my horses were put in a livery barn, after which I went to the store of Charlie Jordan of Rosebud reservation fame, where a supper was made from foodstuffs from the shelves. Riding from early morning until nightfall is not a way of life that leaves one in a grumbling mood over the food. While eating in the store and conversing with Charlie Jordan and Mark Marston, two new-found friends, along came Major McChesney, to whom Jordan introduced me.[6] Early in our conversation I reported to the major that he was looking squarely at his prisoner. When the whole circumstances were explained to him, he suggested the jail was probably lousy, and, if I had any contrariwise assurance of my own bed, I would be better in it on the ground down by the livery barn corral. That ended the state of arrest.

In the morning, after making inquiries without getting much information on Johnnie Burnett's movements, the course lay south from the agency toward Nebraska. I crossed into our neighbor state to the south close to a country post office named Britt, and as I was getting ready to make inquiry at this outpost of Uncle Sam's Post Office Department, two riders were seen galloping in. My hopes were confirmed, for they were on circle from the roundup of my search, and one of them was George Bowley, who was riding for Rea and Bunker from the Bad River country.[7] They told where the wagon was to camp for noon, and it was now no problem to get there, unpack my bed, and turn loose all my horses, including the one I had ridden that morning, into the saddle bunch. Immediately making over my bed from a pack to a roll, it was laid by the bed wagon, and thus was an L-7 rep duly installed as a member of Johnny Burnett's crew.

A motley crew that was, practically all of them full- or mixed-blood Indians. In fact Billy Pressler, George Bowley and I were the only white folks in the outfit, except the nighthawk. Although we looked little different than the others, we were better workers. At the very least that can be said, we took the job of gathering cattle and getting them back to their home range seriously. Realizing that it was out of the question for me to quit that roundup until it disbanded, and on my assurance of gathering all the cattle which he would be representing if present and getting them back on Bad River, George Bowley cut out his string, packed his bed, and left for home a couple of days after my arrival. That left Billy Pressler and me to carry the Caucasian banner.

There is probably no more agreeable or less controversial race than the Sioux Indians. They were willing in those days to ride horseback all day long, but whether they found or left cattle was a matter of indifference to them. Probably the Indian of today would prefer to use a gasoline-driven, rather than a grass-powered, vehicle, just like his white brother. It should not be forgotten that in western South Dakota in the early days of this century, except in the Black Hills where there were railroads, the fastest means of communication and of transportation were exactly what they were in the days of Alexander the Great, the four legs of a horse. In that form of transportation, the Indian could make good time, but it must be said, if one is to speak fairly, that the white rider was not nearly so likely to reach his destination on a played-out horse. He was a better horseman, as a rule, than the Indian. The metaphor "ride like an Indian!" was not taken seriously by the man of the range, who aimed to get all the ride that was necessary out of a horse without hurting him.

Ever since Pope wrote "Lo, the poor Indian! whose untutored mind," etc., cartoonists, columnists, and the erudite generally have taken no small pains to parade their learning by referring to the Indian as "Lo" or "Poor Lo." It is a God's mercy that Pope saved us from what he might have done if, when calling attention to the Indian, he had used the synonym for "Lo" and had said "Behold." In the event of that use of language, which would have done no violence to his rhyme, we would have had to suffer worse as the learned would show off their ignorance in referring to the Indian as "Poor Behold." That can take proper place beside their talk of a "vanishing race," which happens to be increasing in numbers as shown by genuine mathematics.[8]

While on the subject, let us pay a little attention to another learned inaccuracy and that is the common saying that you just must not let Indian and alcohol mix. It would be much better for the Indian, just as it is for the white man, the black man, the yellow man, not to get mixed up with alcohol, but I have seen drunken Indians and drunken white men in sufficient numbers to know that a city policeman or town marshal would have an easier time getting twenty drunken Indians, individually or collectively, into his jail house than he would one lively drunken Irishman. Another common mistake was, and is, that any and all Indians crave liquor, when the fact is that a large percentage of them are strictly teetotalers—a higher percent of them than their white neighbors can honestly boast. So much of what we know is not so. Unless we are especially careful in selection first and analysis and comparison later, our stock of ignorance is quite likely to be increased by voluminous reading. It is only the constantly discriminating reader who can be sure that his reading is adding to his fund of knowledge rather than to his margin of error. But, getting back to our subject, it was only in rare instances that the Sioux Indian in western South Dakota was as reliable a cowhand as the mine run of white fellows in that line of work.

There was another strange manifestation on this roundup in that almost all the fellows wore six-shooters at their work. Now, a 44 caliber, Frontier Colt, single-action six-shooter with a heavy belt loaded with cartridges is a heavy piece of equipment, and one which added nothing to the comfort of the wearer, especially in hot weather. Besides, on a fast-working horse, it was no easy task to keep that gun slung from your hip at the exact angle prescribed by picture makers. As a consequence, it was likely to flop in front of you or behind you, especially when on a cutting horse, with the consequence that the wearer would soon cease wearing it if he did that work for a steady diet. Practically every rider owned such a gun and carried it in his bed, where he could get it if he really wanted to wear it for any purpose. About the only occasion there was to wear one on the range in my day was when riding in an area frequented by a bad, or attacking, stallion. Then it was no show-off to carry a gun. Like most other fellows on the range, I never wore a gun unless it might be in the country of such a stallion and sometimes in going across country with a string of horses, in which case it was easier to strap it on and wear it than it was to pack it in the bed on the pack horse.

There is a good shooting story in connection with that roundup. After we had worked down the Niobrara River in Nebraska, back up the Keyapaha into the Rosebud Indian Reservation, and to a point about fifteen miles or so east of the Rosebud Agency, somebody made the suggestion that there should be no circle that afternoon and that we all ride in to the agency. That was agreeable all around because, even if there had been the counter suggestion that we should keep on working in order to get the country covered and the work behind us, it would have been so overwhelmingly overruled that there was no use to offer it. This was an Indian roundup; the boss, Johnny Burnett, was an Indian; an Indian cannot overlook a fair chance to go to the agency; and their attitude toward the serious business of a roundup was, "Aw, what the hell?" So we rode in to the agency, and every man in the outfit, except me, had his gun on. Even Billy Pressler was wearing his. In later years it has occurred to me that maybe my reason for not carrying one was fear, a fear that some ill-intentioned individual would take my gun away from me and do personal violence or indignity to me with it. No matter what the reason was, there was no gun strapped on me.

As we went towards the agency and were at a point about two or three miles away in the rolling sandhill country, up popped a jack rabbit in front of this cavalcade of about twenty riders. It should not be considered that cowboys were good pistol shots, for they were not. In fact most of them were like myself and could not hit a barn if they were shooting inside it with the door closed. In fact the only fancy shot of my acquaintance was Bob Adams, and he was really the kind you read about, but he went to the penitentiary for shooting Mexican Ed through the eye and out the back of his head.[9] But here was a jack rabbit tempting the fates, and the fates took action, for every man in the crowd, except the single unarmed individual, began banging away at him in a furious fusillade. There was so much shooting going on, and so many bullets hitting around him, that the jack rabbit got completely confused. He would run a few steps in one direction and then would stop and rub his whiskers with his front feet as perplexed jack rabbits do, but the barrage persisted.

I was riding a young horse, which was gentle and well broke but was wholly unaccustomed to such a display of pistol practice, and he was tempted to get out of there and leave me behind. Not being in accord with him on either of those desires, it became my chief aim at the moment to keep him in control. As my horse was jumping around, and the jack rabbit was struggling to overcome his confusion, seemingly wholly safe from any of the shots, I said to Nick Janis,[10] who was blasting away with the others, "Oh, for Heaven's sake, Nick, hand me that gun."

Not having the slightest thought that he would do it, imagine my chagrin when he took his pistol by the muzzle and handed it butt-first to me. There was nothing to do but to take it. There were probably several things I did not want at the moment, but the only one I could think of was a six-shooter. But there I was now with one in my hand and a crazed horse under me. There was nothing to do but to shoot once anyway, so I took a look in the direction of the jack rabbit, which had now recovered its sense of direction and had made up its mind to go far from there. He was going full speed ahead in the direction from which we had come, about a hundred yards away, and that is no time to lay any bets on the tortoise. As my horse made a wild jump away from the rabbit, I took one shot over his rump, really to save my face, and that clumsy jack rabbit got right square in the way.

As I got some small degree of composure into my horse, the reason for the profane ejaculations became apparent, for there stretched out on

MICK
B.
HARRISON

the prairie, with a bullet hole amidships in the side next to me and his insides blown out on the other, was the jack rabbit. There was unearned fame, so, just as soon as could be arranged, the gun was handed back to Nick Janis without comment or self-abnegation. Although Billy Pressler knew how completely accidental the result was, he neither said nor did anything to prevent me from wallowing in the luxury of a reputation as a pistol shot, which could not by any possibility have been maintained. More or less we are all the toys of fortune or misfortune.

Late that afternoon, after we had our visit at the agency and had returned to camp, prowess with the pistol in general, and mine in particular, was the central topic of conversation. . . . Of course Billy Pressler knew better and he smiled. I just looked serious, like a champion about to sign an endorsement of Cornies, and said nothing. My only untruth in the whole performance was the shot itself. Then some of the Indian boys fastened an empty tomato can on a plum bush close to the camp as a mark for proposed practice shooting. Their pressing invitation to me to join in the sport was not accepted, but I did observe their efforts and offer suggestions as to the proper way to hold the pistol, just how to bring it up or down to catch the target, how to press and not to pull the trigger. I was especially careful not to get a gun in my hand because thus there was no chance of shooting and exploding the myth. Reputations are not infrequently built up on situations just as accidental and just as impossible of repetition as that was.

Another instance of a reputation came to me during that roundup. All of a sudden around our camp buzzed discussion of an expected visit from Black Sam. Never having heard of this individual before, my interest was aroused. The stories told of him were enough to make fathers hunt the rough country, mothers to turn white with fright, and children to quake in their beds. Such a character is certain to intrigue any person, and so did he me. One night the nighthawk was talking to me before going out with the saddle horses for the night. He was a young man who had come into that country from Iowa during the preceding winter and got a job as a ranch hand from old Adam Smith, a squaw man and stepfather of Johnnie Burnett.[11]

Perhaps here should be drawn the distinction between a cowhand and a ranch hand. The cowhand was one hired to work on the roundups, to go repping, and to do any work that related to the handling of cattle and horses. A ranch hand was one hired to work around the ranch. He would put up some hay, feed any poor cattle taken in to the ranch, do whatever riding was needed to be done from the ranch, build and maintain a fence for a horse pasture, and do any of the thousand and one things that might show up to be done around the ranch. Such was the nighthawk who came to me for a little comfort for his thoughts on Black Sam. He assured me that this would be his last night with the horses because he did not propose to be in charge of them the night that Black Sam showed up, which could not now be long deferred.

Finally I said, "Well, who in the world is this Black Sam anyway? You fellows are all talking about his expected visit all the time. Who is he and why is he coming to this outfit?"

He expressed great surprise at my lack of acquaintance with the subject of our discussion and said, "I thought all you northern men would certainly know him. He is from up in that northern country, and he is bad."

To the people in the Rosebud country and along White River, northern outfits and northern men were those from Bad River north. I told him again that Black Sam was a stranger to me and asked him if he had ever heard the full name of this individual.

He said, "His name is Sam Dolphus."

I did not and could not restrain my laughter at this bit of information. I said, "Yea, I know Sammy Dolphus. He is a half-brother of Van Moore who is a bad man, now in the penitentiary.[12] He is a mixed-blood Indian, about a half-breed. He is a little bit of a wizened up Indian who couldn't whip a sick cat, and he wants to be considered bad. He hung around Fort Pierre most of last winter and was drunk every time he could get enough to drink. I think every young follow around Fort Pierre, except myself, licked him at one time or another during the winter. I never had reason or inclination to do it, but, if he comes to this outfit, for no reason at all except to dissipate this mystery about him, I will lick the hell out of him."

The nighthawk, still impressed with Black Sam, told me not to attempt any such thing, for I would surely get shot. I told him that Sam would not have a gun on him at the time, for I would see to that. The fact is I knew that Sammy Dolphus was so impressed with his own insignificance, and so disgusted with it, that he carried a gun, not only to impress people who did not know him, but also to overcome the handicap he felt in his relation to other fellows. I knew, too, that it would never be necessary to lay a hand on Sammy Dolphus, but merely to catch him away from his gun and threaten to do it, and Sammy would crawfish. He never came to the roundup, so there was no need for all the worry those fellows put in about nothing. That was just like nearly all of the things we worry about—it never happened. . . .

Fortunately for that nature of roundup or that character of crew, we were not finding many cattle until we got to working down Little White River and up the Big White. There we found many, and, as a consequence, we had plenty of work to do, including two brandings a day. We were nearing the end of the territory we were going to work, and so there was hope that all the riders would stay through to the end, which they did.

As we were working up Big White River, Johnnie Burnett's wife came out to the roundup, and it was announced that she would cook for the outfit the few remaining days. We were all of the opinion that she would prove a better cook than the Indian boy who had been holding down that job, but it was too much of an invasion of man's domain to bring any joy to the heart of the cowboys. We did not realize then how soon equal suffrage would be upon us, nor that the men would all too soon have difficulty finding room in the barber shops and bars by reason of the increasing number of feminine patrons. We live in a changing world, but it is sometimes a bit difficult to know why we need change it so much.

The first night that Mrs. Burnett was out with that roundup was a bad experience for me. I was put on last guard, supposed to be from two in the morning until relieved between four and five by the day herders. Two Indians were put on first guard, two Indians were put on second guard, two Indians were put on third guard, and I was put on last guard alone. There was a known piece of skullduggery on the range known as "working the watch," which merely meant putting the watch ahead and thereby shortening your guard. It was such extremely bad form that no regular cowhand would permit himself even to be tempted to indulge in it. Sometimes an irregular would do it, but not one who made his living as a rider. The other fellows' rights intervened to prevent that luxury, and of course the last guard was bound to be the victim. On this particular night the first guard went on, worked the watch and called second guard; that guard went on, worked the watch and called third guard; that guard went on, worked the watch and called me. The mathematics of the situation in the morning proved that all of them put together had stood less than one hour when they should have stood six. Of course no succeeding guard knew that its predecessor worked the watch, but I could tell in the morning that all of them did, and I certainly told it in the only two languages I knew, English and profane, without overworking the English.

Just as soon as I was called, as my old friend Hugh McGuire used to say, "I knew there was something dead in that bread," but there was nothing to do but to take over, even if it was not yet quite nine o'clock at night. Of course there was no suspicion in my mind that the watch had been worked quite as much as it had, but there were signs that told a cowhand the approximate time of night—the way the cattle acted and also the position of the Big Dipper in relation to the North Star. Still there was nothing to do but to hold those cattle throughout the whole blessed night.

The watch ticked away the hours that should have been occupied by the first, second and third guards, and when two o'clock in the morning came in fact, the time when my guard should have commenced, that guard watch was pointing to about seven o'clock in the morning. It seemed to be completely out of tune with nature, for there was no sign of sun or daylight. About four o'clock in the morning (in fact), it was enough daylight to let that herd begin to move off the bed ground. Knowing the direction in which we would move that day, I got the herd moving in the right direction because, no matter if the watch was worked on him, it was a cowpuncher's duty to do the best he knew for the cattle, and that was my purpose even then.

Each guard did not stand on the time told by the watch of any member of the guard. A watch was handed by the boss to the first guard. It was passed on by them to the second guard, and so on throughout the night, and in the morning someone on last guard handed the watch back to the boss. It would be quite improper at this late day to tell where I told Johnnie Burnett to put that watch as it was handed back to him that morning. Although that night looks funny at this distance, it was a series of tragedies at the time. Although I have always been a champion of the rights of the Indians, I would be more wholehearted in it if I had never been called upon to stand that particular guard.

Ordinarily it was the duty of one of the men on last guard to wake the cook about three-thirty, but Johnnie Burnett told me there would be no use to do that in the morning because his wife had brought an alarm clock out with her, and she would set it. That was another innovation on the range, and it did not work because they forgot to set the alarm. It was the job of the nighthawk to get the horses in about four o'clock in the morning, and this particular nighthawk had not failed in that duty until that morning. He had gone to sleep out on the prairie and was a long time late.

The camp was in plain view from where I was with the herd. Its inert appearance helped my temper not at all. Shakespeare would say that I was exceeding wroth, and indeed he would be remarkably accurate in such diagnosis. Mounting anger causes increase of the blood pressure, and it may be that mine has never been quite down to normal since that night. There lay the camp in peaceful slumber, and the nighthawk likewise somewhere in the brakes of White River. Along about six o'clock by real time, and about eleven in the forenoon by the guard watch, which I had grown to hate, came a madly active nighthawk driving in a bunch of saddle horses, whipping his charges furiously to hurry them along and get them to camp and into that rope corral. But he need have been in no such rush. There was no one awake to receive him, and I was the only onlooker from a distance. That stirred up the camp, and soon smoke was coming from the stovepipe in the roof of the cook tent, and men were seen getting up and making their beds. All this time I was drifting the cattle farther and farther along the course they were expected to take on that day. The cattle were being handled as they should be.

After what seemed an unusually leisurely breakfast for a cow outfit, three Indian day herders were seen to leave the camp to come out to relieve last guard and take over the herd. It was then about seven o'clock in the morning and about noon by that watch. To add a final crowning insult to the man who had been on last guard since about nine o'clock the night before, instead of coming out on a brisk gallop, as relieving day herders were always supposed to do, here came those three Indians, and visiting as they came, on a slow trot. But they finally got there, and I went to camp, but not on a slow trot.

By the time I got there they were breaking camp, and Johnnie Burnett said to me, "We're late. Hurry up and get a bite of breakfast and catch your horse."

What I said in reply is of small significance now, but it seemed appropriate at the moment. I handed him the guard watch. The night was over and the day was on. Wise Billy Pressler knew just what had happened, and he stood around with a smile on his face, but without risking comment. As I hurried through the job of getting breakfast and went out to the corral to catch my horses, my mind turned to Watcheye and to the fact that he had bucked with me on several rides during this roundup. Nothing could be more fitting than to ride Watcheye on circle that morning, so he was caught and saddled. Now the whole outfit seemed to be waiting for me, which appeared to me a further indignity. My picket rope, where my night horse should have been tethered until two o'clock in the morning instead of nine o'clock the night before, was about fifty yards away from the rope corral.

Now who was to blame for all this? I looked at Watcheye and must have decided that he was, so I cheeked him to get on. "Cheeking him" meant catching the side of the headstall of the bridle, pulling the horse's head around to his neck as you caught the saddle horn with the right hand, stuck your left toe in the stirrup, and swung on. Cheeking was used for horses that were likely to buck or create some other disturbance as you were getting on. The fact is Watcheye really did not need that, for he was not hard to mount nor difficult in any way except that once in a while he would buck. I think he was confused and maybe irritated by my precautions because the moment I was on him he showed an inclination to buck.

Under normal circumstances such an inclination would have been vigorously discouraged by me, but nothing was normal that morning, so instead of discouragement, Watcheye got a severe raking with the spurs. Then he bucked, and with the recklessness of rage, I rode him and abused him like the polished broncobuster. Understand, I was not a good bronco rider, but there was nothing in my attitude that morning to cause Watcheye to suspect that there was any inferiority complex in his rider. In fact on that particular morning, there was none. As Watcheye bucked, I spurred him unmercifully in the sides, flanks and shoulders. Most of the big outfits would not tolerate spurring a horse in the shoulder and would discharge a rider who would do it. Besides, it was no easy thing to do, but it seemed not so difficult to me that morning in my wish to get even with someone or something.

Watcheye got all that was coming to him by the time that we got out to the picket rope. I got off, pulled my picket pin, coiled up my picket rope, and got back on Watcheye. He was in no mood at the moment to be anything but a nice horse, but my heart was still bad, so I raised the picket rope and brought it down full force, pin and all, right between Watcheye's ears. That set him afire, and now he was determined to throw me off, but that was not the right morning, so the whole result was further abuse for him. When we got back to camp, still bucking, I yanked his head up as he was about ready to quit anyway, and the show was over. I got off and hung my picket rope on the bed wagon.

Then it was I noticed that Billy Pressler was convulsed with laughter. He could hold it no longer. He was a splendid rider of bucking horses, and he knew that I was not and did not aspire to be. Finally he said, "George, I've got it all figured out. Some morning when I've got to ride a hell of a hard bronc, I'll just see to it that you're put on last guard, with Injuns on the first three guards to work the watch. Then I'll have no one wake the cook and have the nighthawk go to sleep with the horses. Then I'll have the day herders go out on a slow trot to relieve you. Then I'll have the boss tell you to hurry up because we're late. Then I'll get you to ride that bronc."

My good humor was somewhat restored by that time, so I joined with Billy in the laugh on myself. But poor Watcheye was a sight. From shoulders to hips, his gray sides were bleeding from the spurring that had just been administered to him. As one who never approved of severe punishment to a horse, my sense of regret was now asserting itself. Really, he was just a vicarious sacrifice for the Indian guards and day herders whom I would gladly have gutted, even as late as the time Watcheye was bucking. I petted him a little, got on, and we went off on circle.

Two or three days later, as we were working in Redstone Basin, generally south of where Belvidere is now, we had made a big roundup in the area where J. E. ("Corny") Utterback's cattle ranged.[13] Corny had not been on that roundup, nor had he a man with it, but he was one of those who had financed it. He, his son Ben, then just a mere boy, and a ranch hand of his who knew nothing much about the business of a roundup outfit came out to help us work the roundup we had made. It so happened that I was riding a favorite horse, and one of my best, a horse named Greyhound. In turning a cow that seemed ambitious to be troublesome, I put on a real burst of speed and something happened.

A sure-footed horse on a perfectly level piece of ground, going full tilt, fell down so quickly that there was no way to get loose from him. He went over squarely, his face hit the ground, my head hit next, his hindquarters next, and he was back to his feet, but I remained. One's reactions must be fast with a falling horse, but sometimes they cannot be quite fast enough. In order to avoid being tangled up and dragged, my knees tightened their grip on the saddle, but, on getting to my feet on arising, all I had of my outfit was my rope, which my gripping knees had torn loose from the saddle, breaking the rope-strap. As was always the way with those horses after a fall, Greyhound was gone, running away with a couple of Indian riders in hot pursuit.

It so happened that Utterback's hired man was right close to me as the horse fell, and I shall always remember his look of openmouthed astonishment as I got to my feet, and he asked, "Good God, aren't you dead?"

I answered, "Not quite. Go get my horse."

Of course that was a useless request, for he was not enough of a rider for that. However, he had witnessed at close range the hardest fall I ever experienced, and, although I have seen fellows hurt worse, the hardest fall I ever saw. That was a case of a horse going directly over a rider who was sitting squarely in the saddle. They told me afterward, as they joshed me about my inability to keep my horse right side up, that, at the moment of the fall, Corny Utterback said to Billy Pressler, who was close by him, "George is hurt in that fall," and Billy, who saw me getting to my feet said, "No, he isn't hurt. He lit on his head."

But Billy was concerned enough to ride out to me to inquire about injuries. On getting word that there were none, he said, "Well, I see you are being independent about it. You kept your rope so you can catch him yourself." But Billy's joviality did not conceal his concern from me.

That night, instead of eating my supper, I went and laid down on my bed, seeking to get my badly swollen neck into what was then impossible—a comfortable situation. Billy Pressler knew that a neck, swelled up as that one was then, was not concealing any sensations of delight. That night Johnnie Burnett put me on third guard, so I had a cinch on not standing more than two hours, and that would have been long enough. The next morning when the cook announced that breakfast was ready, which is a lady's way of saying what, in man's language, would be that if you failed to come and got it immediately it would all be thrown out, I was awakened by the general bustle around there.

Realizing that my rest, such as it was, had not been interrupted during the night, I asked Billy Pressler, who was on second guard, "Why the _____ didn't you call me for third guard?"

As he walked away with a plate full of breakfast in one hand and a cup of steaming black coffee in the other, he said "_____ _____ you, I did call you and you fell back."

"Fell back" was a term of ignominy among the men who followed the cows. Technically it referred to the man who, being called for guard, put self-indulgence above his task and would lie down again for a few more winks and go back to sleep. It meant one who disregarded the rights of the other fellow, by failing to relieve him as was his due. Billy would never say, "George, I knew you were hurt, and I stood your guard as well as my own." But I know that Billy knew that I knew just what had happened. Each knew that the subject would never be referred to by either to the other so long as we rode after cattle, which each of us then thought would be from then on. Whatever might be his social errors in town, and Billy could commit them in amazing and startling fashion sometimes, he had a cooperative understanding of his fellow man in the country, and it was in the country only that a cowboy was a cowboy. You can't help loving a fellow like Billy.

The next day after the fall mentioned, the roundup was through. We worked the herd, and into my cut was put all the cattle belonging in the north country. It is a little tough to ride a dodging cow pony, cutting out as many cattle as had to be cut out that day, with a neck as sore as mine was that day, and a thousand other aching places that were now becoming manifest. But things can be done on a good horse. Kipling said:

> When Horse and Rider each can trust the other everywhere,
> It takes a fence and more than a fence to pound that happy pair;
> For the one will do what the other demands, although he is beaten and blown,
> And when it is done, they can live through a run that neither could face alone.[14]

As soon as all the cattle belonging in my cut were together, an Indian rider was put in charge while I went to camp, got my horses and packed my bed. Then taking my string and throwing them in with those cattle, we started off to a gate in the reservation fence, then northeast across country to Henry Livermont's, where Watcheye would be left at his home and all the cattle I had belonging in the Bad River country would be turned loose, and the others taken on toward the Cheyenne River country. It was fifty miles or more from where that roundup quit to Henry's place. Memory does not recall the details of that trip. Where night overtook me on the several nights, where meals were had, and when they were missed, what horses were ridden is all blotted out from the record of my mind. It is a dead certainly that Watcheye, or Dishrag, or any horse that could be suspected of a possible inclination to buck was given a complete holiday on that aching ride.

We nearly always have something to worry about, and the concern it gave me every time I saw the spur scabs, from shoulder to hip on each side of Watcheye, is still a clear memory. Here was the horse for which Henry had professed such favoritism, and from which he expected so much as a cow horse, all scratched up in most unseemly fashion. How could the matter be explained to Henry? How would he take the explanation? After trailing across country for several days alone, we got to Henry's place, care being taken to see that the cattle were turned loose in a convenient place where they would not be likely to scatter much and where they could be rounded up without too much trouble in the morning. Still greater care was taken to be sure that I got to Henry's ranch buildings just about dark, so that the horses could be turned loose in the horse pasture without too much notice being taken of the scratches on Watcheye's gray sides. Perhaps we could escape without any notice being taken that night, and we did, all the horses being turned loose in the horse pasture.

Mrs. Livermont quickly got supper for me, and then we settled down to a visit, particularly about this recent roundup, the persons I had seen, and all about it. Soon Henry said, "Did you ride Watcheye again?" I told him that I had ridden him a good many times. "Did he buck with you again?"

"Yes, he did several times."

"Did he throw off?"

"No, but the last time I rode him I scratched him up pretty badly."

That broke the news, but Henry only said, "That's fine."

I said, "Yes, but he is badly scratched."

"Oh," Henry said, "that is fine. It is probably just what he needed."

There seemed to be no way of acquainting Henry with my real transgression, so we must wait until morning. In the morning one of the boys ran in the horses, and the first thing that happened was that Henry, in a semi-crouching position, began looking over his prospective top cow horse, while I was vowing to myself that never again would anyone be able to lend or give me the use of any horse, except a bay, and a dark bay at that. After looking him over carefully, first on one side and then the other, and observing how far forward and how far backward went the scratches, Henry came up to me, patted me on the shoulder, and said, "Good. By God, I'm certainly glad you did that to that damn son of a gun. He threw everybody off around here."

There went all my wasted worry. Henry in fact had been looking for someone to take it out of that horse, and he slipped him on to me under the guise of wanting to make a cutting horse out of him. Well, he got him made into a better than fair cutting horse, and, although that was my last year on the range, Henry told me some years afterward in Fort Pierre that Watcheye never bucked again. The sequel to that long last guard seemed to reform him completely. It did not, however, give me the idea that I was a good bronco rider.

Henry and the boys saddled up, helped me quickly to round up the cattle turned loose the evening before. We soon got all the cattle belonging in that region cut out, and we shoved the ones that were to go farther north on to the north side of Bad River. Then we went to the ranch where I got my horses, packed my bed on one, waved a so-long to Henry and his family as we went north, leaving Watcheye at his home. It is doubtful if he was ever ridden on a roundup again, for the world of the cow country soon came to a sudden and complete end.

Billy Pressler, now seventy and living at Newcastle, Wyoming, was recently at our home with his bride of a few days for dinner. Having dinner at supper-time never did seem right to me, but so it is. We visited about many things, including the Indian roundup run by Johnnie Burnett, which was sufficiently unorthodox to justify comment from fellows who had been punching cows in regular fashion. My only desire in telling you about it is to give you a brief view from still another angle of the way some folks lived and made their living in those days, now gone. Maybe Robert V. Carr knew what he was talking about when he said in his poem "Sleeping Out":

Once let a feller git in tune
    With all outdoors, there hain't no use
Fer him to think he kin ferget,
    Or from the wild's big ways jar loose.
He's always thinkin' 'bout them nights—
    Jes' listen now, and hear him sigh,
A-dreamin' of an old tarp bed,
    And sleepin' out beneath the sky.[15]

Affectionately,
Dad

CHAPTER 16

The Swinging Cinch

November 27, 1940

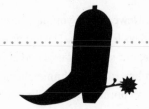

My dear Geordie, Jean, and Bob:

That great variant we call fashion controls our methods of life, of food, of clothing, of morals, of vacations, and even of our religious observances. What was style yesterday is bizarre today. . . . Many get hurt in fashion's swing. Some designer with a neck like a crane and as callous as the long shanks of a secretary-bird sets himself to the task of designing a collar and decrees that it must be worn by all, even by a person whose neck is a reproach to proper measurement and whose carotid arteries are as sensitive as a shop girl's corn. If one were to be garbed always in the latest style of everything, it would take a small army of the underprivileged to get the use out of what he is decreed to have. The 1941 automobile is out-moded before the end of 1940. So it is all along the way.

It was even so in those long gone days when men rode many horses. Although the main parts of his equipment remained fairly static, it should not be forgotten that the epoch known as the cow country and the individual whose life was cast in it, the cowboy, lasted only about forty, and at the most fifty, years from its beginning to its close. Of course there were some styles that were almost immutable: for instance, good, strong, high-heeled boots; a strong saddle, which might be a double-cinch rig, a three-quarters rig, a center-fire rig, or the like; a good Stetson hat; and all else was variable. One man might choose corduroy pants, another Californias, and another would ride in overalls. Changes were dictated by fancy or temporary affluence. But occasionally changes of fashion crept into that life, just as it will into any other, and the folks who lived in that atmosphere were not wholly free from the lure of the gadget.

Usually a cinch was fastened by taking the long, strong strap, called a latigo, fastened to a strong iron ring on the rigging of the saddle tree, putting it through the cinch ring, back through the ring on the saddle tree, through the cinch ring again, through the upper ring again, and then looped over itself. That made secure fastening of the saddle, so long as the cinch or cinches happened to be kept tight. It was the time honored and the safe way to fasten that sort of saddle on that sort of horse for that sort of work. Nevertheless the lure of the gadget, the novelties of fashion, crept into the life of the cowboy, and one that came along getting quite a play for part of a year was a patent cinch buckle, or fastener. Instead of running the latigo strap through the cinch ring, it was run through two slots on this patent fastener, which had a hook arrangement that caught and held the cinch ring. It was a quick way of cinching a saddle, and it was used only by those who used only the front cinch on a double-rigged saddle, which was the way most of the fellows rode in the summer time.

My patent cinch buckle, for at that time I had not overcome within my inclinations the lure of the gadget, which is no small curse, came very near causing me one of the most ludicrous of disasters. On a roundup that was breaking up after finishing working the country to the northwest of Fort Pierre, it became my misfortune to have my thoughts "lightly turn to thoughts of love," as Tennyson would explain the desire of a fellow to visit his girl.[1] To be in love is a great human delight, and it is far from wrong for a young person to flit from flower to flower in honorable admiration, provided a halt is called on the flitting "when you first kiss the last girl you love."[2] That was my fix as that roundup closed its work, with me in charge of a lot of cattle I had gathered on the roundup that had to be thrown back to the Cheyenne River and at the same time to be ardently wishing just to see Julia Sylva, the really beautiful daughter of Manuel Sylva, a rancher located near the mouth of Antelope Creek, which ran into the Missouri River about fifteen miles below Fort Pierre.

It was not hard to prevail on some of the fellows going to the Cheyenne River to take my cattle in with theirs, to be thrown back and turned loose, but of course there had to be a reason. Always a good reason was to lose a saddle horse, and that was not too difficult to arrange as the set-up was at the moment. On the theory that a good many things are fair in love and war that would not pass an inspection by a lie detector machine, I rode up to camp, where Harry Briggs had already cut his string and packed his bed, and asked him to steal one of my horses. He immediately asked if I wanted to go horse hunting down around the mouth of Antelope. My prompt admission won his approval of the deal, and he said, "All right, I'll take one and keep him in my pasture until you call for him." Harry's ranch was about twelve miles up Bad River from Fort Pierre.

I told him to take a young, gray horse by the name of Walker from my string. The name of that particular horse came from his ability to go along at higher speed on a flat-footed walk than any other horse of all my acquaintance. He wasn't much good for anything else. Really, the most valuable horse to work on the range was just the ordinary, three-gaited, walk, trot and gallop horse. The other gaits, such as single-foot, pace, fast walk, and the like, were nice to rest one with the change or to show off when there was good occasion, if indeed there can be good occasion for that.

Well, by the time I got through working the herd and getting the cut for the Cheyenne River country shaped up, imagine my consternation on finding that one of my saddle horses was missing. A cowboy was not supposed to lose any of his horses, and, when one turned up missing, he was frequently in for a lot of individual riding to find him. It was about as satisfying as an ace in the hole to know that, when my Walker horse was really wanted, he would be at Harry Brigg's ranch in the pasture. Fuming about the wrangler losing my horse, and arranging to have the Cheyenne River fellows take my cattle without me being along to help, left me with little to do but to cut out my string, pack my bed, and go towards Fort Pierre, about twenty miles away from the point on Willow Creek where we quit. Scotty had by this time established permanent headquarters at the Buffalo Ranch, about six miles up the Missouri River from Fort Pierre, so I went there, unpacked, and turned loose after catching a new horse for the ride down to Sylva's, another twenty miles away. With plenty of horses, one could make a good many miles in a day. Scotty saw me, and I always felt, and feel now, that he was wise to my game, but he knew that I knew that it was the law of the range that a cowpuncher was expected to ride for a lost saddle horse until he found him, and he knew that my story was almost sure to be too plausible for attack.

The horse that I caught and saddled for the ride to Sylva's ranch was a young, chunky sorrel. He was a good horse, broken to ride that spring, but far from gentle. Although he had never bucked hard with me, in fact was not a horse that knew how to do a hard job of pitching, he was certainly not too proud to try it. Also, he was a mean, skittish, unfriendly animal, and the result was that he and I were not on the best of terms. We had almost reached the stage that my old friend Judge Gaffy used to describe as "being warm personal enemies." It should be remembered that my saddle was being used then with only the front cinch, which was held in place by the patent cinch fastener.

It was small work to unroll the miles from there to the mouth of Antelope, and the sorrel pony, with his rider right side up, came drifting in to Sylva's about sundown. That called for a bite of supper under range law, which Julia quickly prepared, she being a genuine product of the cow country. It was no small delight for a hungry cowpuncher to get food from any source, but for a love-lorn swain, if a cowpuncher can properly be called a swain, to get good food direct from the hands of his one and only was almost more than the gods could have to offer. Feasting the appetite on the food and the eyes on the lady left little to be desired, especially when she was as good to look at as was Julia. Her father, mother, two brothers, and her younger sister were all at the ranch. It did not seem to be necessary in those days to get a girl away, fourteen miles from anywhere and in an automobile, in order to tell her that she stood ace high. (Although we both married others, we remained friends who continued to have high respect each for the other until her untimely death about ten years ago during a surgical operation out in San Francisco where her home was.) . . .

The next morning there was nothing to do but to ride away, and that meant following the Fort Pierre trail about halfway to town and then striking off across country toward the ranch of Harry Briggs, where I was sure to find my missing saddle horse. It took a lot of riding just to have a visit with that girl, but that added nothing to my burdens because I would have been riding all day anyway, and that made a pleasant interlude in the events of range life. As we, the sorrel pony and I, were swinging along on the trail and almost to the point where it would be advisable to go across country to my immediate goal, my thoughts were on anything but trouble, and I may have been singing as well as thinking about "The Girl I Left Behind Me."

Suddenly, the whole world seemed to be transformed into a fury of motion, and that saddle came into violent contact with me. One can do a great deal of fast thinking, if it can be called such, when a situation of that nature confronts him. Reduced to leisurely comment, my thought was, "Well now, surely a horse never jumped that high before," and so it was. In the twinkling of an eye, the leg grip on my saddle had clamped

down automatically with the thought of riding out the sudden and force-ful storm. Just as suddenly, I, still seated squarely in the saddle, was riding through space in an arc and at the end of my bridle reins. The next contact was when the top of my head met solid ground, and with me still seated squarely in the saddle. That brought the reaction, "Good Heavens, that horse jumped so high and so hard that he turned over in the air, and now he is landing on top of me, with me still straight in the saddle."

That thought was quickly dispelled by the reality of the situation, for I had been thrown off, my saddle had been thrown off with me, and my horse was running madly away with the bridle on him. There I was, one of the most abject and dejected things in all creation, a cowpuncher afoot and far from anywhere, with a forty-pound saddle as well as a

saddle blanket to carry to some place where a horse could be borrowed. King Richard had only a faint idea of the needs of such a situation when he offered to swap his kingdom for a horse, "even-Steven." If he had been a cowpuncher, afoot on the lone prairie, caught *flagrante delicto* in the web of circumstances, far away from anywhere that his duty called, subject to be the butt of country-wide jokes in which even his *enamorata* would join, the victim of cruel, cruel fate, he would have been more than willing to throw in with the kingdom a few African colonies and maybe Alsace-Lorraine for a horse with no registered pedigree.[3]

The place where this dreadful catastrophe had taken place was at the lowest point of a deep swale, and the reason it happened was that the patent cinch buckle had come undone, allowing the cinch to swing loose with nothing to keep the saddle on except gravity, an unavailing force against a bucking horse. As soon as that young horse saw that cinch swinging under him, he became frightened. His single refuge was to throw down his head and buck, and he sought refuge. The first jump sent me and the saddle sailing off in an arc through space. By the time I had disengaged myself from the saddle and got to my feet, that horse was about a hundred yards away and adding yards faster than Willie Heston or Tom Harmon ever hoped to do.[4]

The potent power of prayer should never be underestimated. It should always be invoked in time of real need, of dire necessity, and I was humble and of contrite heart. From that heart direct to that running horse went the ardent and earnest prayer, "Pony, pony, if you will only stop so that I can contrive in some way to catch you, I will never be severe with you again no matter what you do."

That inaudible, unspoken prayer was answered, amazingly, for, when he had run to a point about a hundred fifty yards away from me, he stopped short and faced about. There he stood, facing me, snorting as only a range horse can, and trembling in every fiber of his frame. It just seemed that he was overcome with the fear of being alone and was repentant over the rude interruption to the thoughts of a young man temporarily in love. Just what really possessed him is still a mystery, but he made no effort to escape me as I walked up to him and caught the bridle reins. Leading him back to that saddle was a triumphant march, let me assure you, and it would give me unending joy to be able some day to build a great arch at that place and have Hitler mixing the mortar, even though he be a poor workman.

Taking that cinch fastener off and putting it in a saddle pocket was a task quickly done. Then the saddle was put on and I mounted. Then I felt richer than King Dick and, at the moment, would not have traded that horse for any gift, mortal or divine. We veered off toward the Briggs ranch, and it can be set to my credit that never again was that horse severely treated or spoken to by me. My kindness to him was soon reciprocated by a decent attitude on his part toward me, and we became great friends. Not long afterward another fellow in the outfit wanted him so badly that we traded horses, as cowpunchers were permitted to do within their strings. Because of a very hard ride he had to give him, the sorrel horse became wind-broken and of little value. Anyway, on one occasion he was exceptionally nice to me.

About noon we came along to Harry's place. I immediately went out in the pasture and ran in some saddle horses, including my Walker horse. Taking the saddle off the sorrel, putting it on Walker, and turning the Briggs horses loose was a job of few minutes. Knowing that my friend Mamie, Harry's wife, would just about have dinner ready, I went over to the house, got fed, visited awhile, and, after proudly confessing to both of them that I had a nice visit with Julia the evening before, got on Walker and led the sorrel down Bad River to Fort Pierre and up the Missouri to the buffalo pasture where my string was. Next morning I was away with my string, heading for the outfit which was working on the Moreau River, many miles to the north. I had seen my girl, and that was just as compensating to a cowboy as to any other of God's creatures.

Shorty

Now that we are in confessional mood on the subject of being thrown off a horse, we may as well go the whole way and confess them all. The first fall I was in South Dakota and was riding with the 73, we were on our way into Fort Pierre with a big beef herd. After dinner several of us were going out to relieve the day herders for that afternoon and the next forenoon. I was riding a bay horse called Shorty and was galloping along out towards the beef herd.

Shorty, like some horses and most humans, had some unreasoning idiosyncrasies and was disposed to indulge them. He was a gentle horse, but he seemed to be pleased always with the trouble he caused himself by getting scared of his tail. It would seem that he should have been used to it, but he was not. As we hurried along toward the herd with a strong wind from behind, Shorty's tail suddenly hove in the line of his vision as it was blown back and forth by the wind. There was no suspicion in my mind that Shorty had any apprehensions of attack from that tail, but so it was. Suddenly and unexpectedly he commenced to buck, and with simultaneity worthy of a better cause, I began to leave him. Wherever I grabbed, the saddle was not there, and soon I was dumped "clean heels over body," and Shorty was gone with the saddle on him. It would never do to let him get near the beef herd because his madness would be communicated to them, and they would run, stampede.

Everybody knew in that life that a rudderless, saddled horse had no business running anyway, and Pecos Bill, who was also going out to relieve the day herders, took in after Shorty, riding a big gray horse called Gray Eagle. Just as he closed up the gap between him and Shorty and was reaching over to catch the bridle reins, Gray Eagle concluded that he had carried that southern gentleman far enough, and with two or three jumps, he put Pecos on equality with me. Pecos Bill was an old-time cowpuncher, and he did not like to be shown up, but it made little difference to me, just so somebody caught my horse.[5] Soon Cy Hiett came in from the chase leading Shorty, and Billy Pressler came leading Gray Eagle. Pecos was angry toward me for some days, apparently without realizing that he did not need to follow my example so closely.

Shorty was a nice horse, and we continued to be friends in spite of that misadventure. Also he got his tail trimmed to a shadow of its former abundance.

Cub

In the spring of 1900 after my friend, old Tom Beverly, was demoted from the position of foreman of the outfit, and my friend Ira Miller was put in his place,[6] he assigned to me a nice-looking, moderate-sized brown horse named Cub. We were then camped on the west bank of the Missouri River, about where the present grade of the Chicago & Northwestern crosses what was once the channel on the west side of Marion's Island, near Fort Pierre. . . . Going out on day herd one morning, Ira announced to me that Cub was mine to ride. He looked nice and had all the appearance of being gentle. In fact he was gentle. I put my rope on that Cub horse, led him out of the rope corral and saddled him. At the moment I had no fear of him, and there seemed to be no reason for having any. He was a strange horse to me. We soon became acquaintances, but not friends.

As I got on him, with no thought that there would be anything to the forenoon except the usual mixture of monotony and excitement of day herding southern cattle just unloaded from the cars, branded, and put into a herd. Cub seemed otherwise disposed, and he bucked with me. Although he made me pull leather, he failed to throw me. Not knowing him by reputation or otherwise, my conclusion was that he was such a horse as could be ridden by me. Less than an hour later a group of riders on circle with the Bad River Pool roundup wagon, with Bogus Mathieson the foreman in the group, came by where I was on day herd in the brakes of Dry Run. (Bogus, who was a stranger to me at the time, quit riding the range after that spring roundup was completed, and before long became postmaster at Fort Pierre, a position he held for years.)[7] With that pleasant smile of his, Bogus rode up to me in the company of a group of riders to take a look at the southern cattle we were just about ready to take out and turn loose on the range. Noticing my horse, which seemed to be no stranger to him, as the rider was at the time, he said, "Young fellow, have you had any trouble with Cub?"

I said, "No. I have had no trouble with him. He bucked with me this morning, but I rode him all right."

Bogus said, "Well, you better watch out for him, for he bucks like hell."

With an assurance born of my ignorance, and of remembrance of the fact that I had stayed on him that morning, I said, "Oh, I can ride him all right."

As he rode away with his group, Bogus smiled and said, "Well, anyway, I wish you good luck with him."

It seemed that Cub must have understood the conversation and that he wanted to set me right on some things. The men were scarcely out of sight when Cub commenced his forward passing attack. There could be no alibi of being taken unawares, for he was the central point of all my attention, but that made little difference in my behalf, for he quickly dislodged me from all pretensions to a hold on that saddle and sent me up and forward on what almost seemed an astral excursion. Perhaps it would have been such, except for the application of Isaac Newton's discovery, which seemed to attach itself to me somewhere off in space and started me in a wide arc on an earthbound journey. Contact with old Mother Earth in such circumstances gives one a clear idea of what is meant by terra firma, for it is nothing short of a model of understatement to say that it gives one a feeling of firmness at the end of a fall. Not being versed in the science of geology, it is difficult for me to say whether any faults occurred in the earth's crust as a result of that collision the first time Cub threw me off.

With his usual practice of adding insult to ignominy and injured pride, on my return to mundane surroundings there was Cub quietly grazing and waiting for me to try my luck again if so inclined. He was one of the few range horses I ever knew that would not run away when he dumped his man. There was nothing to do except to go up to him and get back on and that was done, but with greater caution and less confidence. None of the other fellows on herd with that feverish, restless herd of Texas yearlings, just come to the end of that long train ride from the

South and from the local branding pens, had seen Cub toying with me as a wild mid-Atlantic storm might play with a dory, for all were busy with difficult cattle in rough terrain.

It was not long until Cub decided that the listlessness of good behavior furnished too little excitement for a master of his art, and he proceeded to buck down the sharp slope of one of those black gumbo hills. With an earnestness born of desperation I clung to everything that seemed in the least substantial, but there was little stability in anything about him when Cub got to rolling his skin and dancing the rumba to the music of his rider's grunts, with the result that when he was through with his part of the show, although it was an ignoble exhibition of riding and somewhat accidental as well, I was still on Cub's back. In spite of sincere efforts at forgetfulness, that ride down that hill on that hard-hitting bucking horse is still a clear recollection.

A little while later, perhaps feeling the urge to nibble a little grass, Cub cut loose again on a level place atop one of those hills. He took no undue advantage that time, in fact he never needed to and seldom did, because I was watching for it, the ground was level, and everything was set for fair competition. For a couple of jumps the battle seemed to be on even terms, if that can be said of a fellow hanging on to everything in range. Then Cub, in addition to whirling, sunfishing, and all the other things that a broke horse like him should not do, began turning himself inside out twice each jump. At that my poise left, and so did I. Too crushed to curse, completely sapped of courage, and with no assurance of being able to ride a stick horse, I stepped up to where Cub was grazing a few feet away. Gathering up the reins I got back again on that unsure seat, only to be relieved in a little while by the next group of day herders. That meant going back to camp, to dinner for me and to a turn loose for Cub. That seemed to be entirely to his liking, and he galloped off like the well-broke horse he knew how to be, straight for camp. It was nice to get off Cub voluntarily. It may be, but it is no certainty, that in later years with much more experience I could have done a better job riding Cub. He was the victor from every angle that time.

A few days later as we were camped at the Willow Creek Dam, taking these cattle out on the range, it was Cub's turn for a ride. After catching, saddling, and mounting him, he just threw me off at the rope corral, which meant right in camp. Catching him again, which was no trick at all because there he stood with insulting indifference waiting for it, I got on and went out to the herd. Not long after being out with the herd, he threw down his head and went to it again. Maybe he was just being nice to me in giving me experience. If so, his kindness is not appreciated even yet. That time I stayed on somehow. Later in the forenoon, as we were working the herd in to water and were close to camp, Cub seemed to conclude that time was hanging heavy on our hands, and that he should shake me up a bit. He not only shook me up, but he must have shaken all the surrounding territory with the impact of my body hitting the ground. He did that so close to the cattle that they ran a little way because of the disturbance. Walking up to where Cub was quietly nibbling at the grass, I took the bridle reins and led him into camp, not over a hundred yards away. There he was unsaddled and turned loose. He was just too hard a horse to learn on.

Crushed and meditating on the disaster of complete defeat, I sat down on the ground alongside my saddle. My old friend, Tom Beverly, who had watched the whole performance from a little distance, came loping in to give me some encouragement about continuing to ride Cub. Realizing even then that a cowpuncher was of no value in handling cattle except when he was on his horse, and realizing, too, that there was no way of knowing just when I should be induced to make an involuntary dismount from the back of that horse, I merely told Tom that, when Cub was launched into eternity, it was my sincere hope that he would be in a part of that never-ending domain from which I should be spared. My recollection is that it was more tersely stated than that. Anyway, that was my last time on Cub's back. He bucked very little the rest of that summer, and it should be said to his credit that he never sought to hurt a thrown rider by kicking him or the like, as some of those horses seemed only too willing to do.

Soon after my relinquishment of the doubtful honor of riding him, Billy Hess confided to me that, as he was riding him alone one day, he came to an erosion ditch about a foot and a half or two feet across. As he jumped the little ditch, Cub lit on the other side bucking. In spite of Billy's best endeavors, he had to pick himself up from the ground. He soon evolved a good excuse for getting Cub out of his string.

About three years later, as I was repping for Scotty with the W M wagon (Dick Mathieson's outfit then being run by the super-cowman Tom Jones),[8] one morning on circle some of the fellows got to joshing me about Cub and asking why he was not in my string. In fact there was enough reason in that I had a string of good horses. Also there was the fact that Cub was on occasion hard to ride and, in cowboy parlance, "wasn't worth a damn after you got him rode." He was just like some people, so discontented that it showed right in his face. While it might be possible that I could ride him then, he was not worth riding as compared with the horses I already had.

As we were riding along on this circle on Whitcher Holes Creek, Bunk White, who had been listening to the group efforts on me, suddenly spoke up and said, "Well, George, it's all right if you don't want to ride Cub. I don't blame you. He bucks awful hard, and he isn't any good. I used to ride him before you did, and I know. I remember one time when he dealt me a lot of misery, and when that dad-blamed Cub got through pitching with me, I was as white as a sheet."

It was a relief to me to know that Cub had reduced my colored friend to such a blanched appearance, because it must have taken something unusual to do that. While it is hard for me to believe that Cub threw Bunk, who was a superb bucking-horse rider, Billy Hess insisted to me on the side that he believed exactly that thing had happened. I still doubt it.

After the midday meal on that very day at our camp on Whitcher Holes, some of the boys who were working for the W. I. Walker outfit 7, which was run in conjunction with the W M, were having trouble with their horses.[9] The Walker outfit did not have good cattle, and they had poorer horses. The result was that the better class of range hands did not seek employment there. We were going to make a long ride that afternoon without moving camp. Bunk White, not desiring to expend energy unnecessarily, had caught and saddled his horse for the afternoon ride and was sitting in his shade, watching the antics of the Walker horses and men. I had caught and saddled my horse, Dishrag, and was standing by him waiting for the excitement to subside.

Bunk apparently had not noticed what horse was under my saddle until I began to show signs of getting on him. As the safety point for a sailor is usually in the open sea, and for an aviator is high in the air, so for a cowpuncher his point was to be on top of his horse in time of trouble, and he was all right so long as he stayed there. Bunk's amused grin subsided as he jumped up and said, "Dad-blame, here where I gets on my horse. When that gen'man does things, he perfo'ms."

The gentleman to whom Bunk referred was Dishrag and not his rider. Bunk knew better than to make any such remark about the rider. As if to verify Bunk's assertion, Dishrag "perfo'med" to the satisfaction of every one but me, and, fortunately, I suffered no disadvantage. And Cub—well, wherever he is, I hope it is bad.

Dave

Dave was a tall, slim, gray, semi-stupid, crop-eared young horse. He had been raised on the horse ranch of Judge Gaffy on the east side of the Missouri River, up near Okobojo. After being broken to ride, he was sold by Judge Gaffy and got into the hands of old Dave Crippen, a livery-stable keeper in Fort Pierre. Dave Crippen was an ex-forty-niner who had gone west across the Plains and back around Cape Horn. Such was the man who sold that saddle horse to Scotty.[10] Except for the fiction in which range folks indulged (that a raw horse, which could be led from a corral, saddled, and ridden ten times, was a broke horse and ready for the rider who had to do his work on him), Dave was not much of a saddle horse. In my opinion he never could be much of a saddle horse. Clearly he came within the cowboys' none too complimentary classification of "knot-head," or "buzzard-head." . . .

Dave was turned over to me as a member of my string, and it was not long before I was cursing the luck that froze his ears as a young colt. It was a belated wish that his ears could have been frozen off at his shoulders instead of about two-thirds of their length, for then he would not need to be ridden. As we were working down the north side of the Cheyenne River, Dave bucked with me one day. He could buck fairly hard, but after several jumps while I seemed to be doing all right, he reared up on his hind legs and balanced indecisively between falling over backwards and coming down on his feet. At that stage the rider must be prepared to get out of the way if the horse falls backward in order to escape the likelihood of injury. The person who got hurt or sick was of no value around an outfit, unless he still remained on his own power and able to do his work. So he must not let himself get hurt if the horse falls over backward. Consequently, when the horse is straight up on his hind legs, the rider must be loose in the saddle. Then the difficulty is to recover a firm seat if he quickly comes back to his feet. That time Dave came back to his feet, having his rider out of balance. That was the chief reason for getting dumped.

A couple of days later near the old Mike Dunn ranch on the north bank of the Cheyenne River, Dave repeated his performance with like result.

The indignity of that occasion was increased by the fact that he chose a spot where the sand burrs were thick as a dumping ground for me. Stanley Philip, then a youngster of about eleven, and not the strapping physical specimen he afterwards turned out to be, was riding with the outfit, so I asked him to go down with me on the Cheyenne River sand bar, where it was my plan to take it all out of Dave for all time. He rode his horse, and I rode Dave down to the sand bar, and immediately on getting well set, I ran my thumbs up Dave's neck, which, of course, set him to bucking immediately. A jump or two in that loose sand showed Dave his handicap, so up he came on his hind legs. When he came down on all four feet, I was off balance, and a jump or two more and my hat was thrown off, followed by me the next jump. Although it is downright silly to say that an ostrich buries his head in the sand when danger threatens, because to do so would exterminate his species over night, it is no exaggeration to state that mine was practically buried in the Cheyenne River sand that day, as I lit in it straight head on. Stanley kids me yet about the difficulty of getting the sand out of my hair.

Mention was made of my hat being thrown off. Even as great an artist as the late Charles M. Russell, who is properly acknowledged as the Cowboy Artist, frequently makes the mistake of having his cowboys lose their hats, which in real life rarely happened. But we must not be hard on Russell for that one mistake in otherwise marvelous pictures. We should remember that even Michelangelo painted a navel on Adam.

Riding Dave was just a matter of catch-as-catch-can from then on, but somehow he threw me off no more. Not long after that I was with a roundup working in the Fort Bennett country.[11] Going along at a fair gallop and riding between Harry Briggs and Guy Moulton, as memory now serves, Dave suddenly commenced to buck without any known reason. A few jumps and up he came on his hind legs, but that time the balance was the other way, and he went over, landing squarely on his back. Fortunately, I was loose as he went over and got out of the way. Picking myself up sooner than he did, I held his head off the ground by the reins, thereby preventing him from getting up.

Harry Briggs shouted, "Are you hurt, Georgie?"

My answer was always to plague me on the range as I shouted back at him, "Hell, no. I lit on my head." The fact was that I lit partly on my feet, but the remark stuck.

Holding Dave's head off the ground, I gave him a boot-heel massage that completely disfigured him and necessitated letting out the bridle to the last notch by reason of the swelling of his head under that treatment. When he was finally permitted to get up to his feet and we all started again on our ride, Dave was groggy from his punishment, but, knothead that he was, he realized there was some danger in falling over backward. Of course a horse that has that trick in his repertoire is always dangerous, so Dave was soon sold to a horse buyer taking horses down into the farming country east of the Missouri River, where he likely would not be used as a saddle horse. He threw me those three times before he went.

Of course there were occasions when he did not throw me. He did not have a clean score, but it was good enough. He could reasonably enough have hurt somebody had he been continued as a saddle horse. He never hurt me, and no other L-7 man ever rode him. It was small loss when he left.

Mouse

Then there was Mouse. A small, mouse-colored horse he was, purchased from Dan Powell. But for his trim legs and slick coat, he could almost be considered an oversized Shetland pony. Mouse was a good pony, with lots of promise and a good deal of performance. As soon as he was purchased from Dan Powell, which was just after he was broken to ride, he was turned over to me as part of my string. He was a bit snuffy at first, but petting and fondling made him friendly, although on a few occasions his nervous and energetic attitude toward things prompted him to buck with me. He was a wiry and active little fellow, and it gave me neither physical nor mental comfort. I always managed to ride him, but in my own fashion, which would never win the silver-horned, full-stamped saddle at a rodeo contest. The rodeos of that day were serious, everyday business, without judges or prizes, just part of the day's work—a hard day's work.

I always managed to ride him until one day Mouse had his inning, and he scored. We were working up Bad River with George Jackson's pool wagon and were camped near the mouth of Plum Creek at the spot where, at a later time, Jimmie Schneider was thrown into the cactus patch.[12] Plum Creek was in flood, bank full. Some of us were sent out on circle down the river for a way, and we had to cross Plum Creek. That necessitated swimming the horses across. Having a disinclination to get wet all over, as soon as we got our horses into the stream I slipped up until my knees were in the seat of the saddle and then bragged about my foresight on the way over, as compared to the rest of the fellows who were taking it badly in that muddy stream. Just as his feet struck the steep bank and he had footing, Mouse, realizing that only "he that humbleth himself shall be exalted," gave me a lesson in humility.[13] Before I could slip back securely into the saddle, he was at it, bucking in a whirling motion so as not to get away from that water. In very few jumps he gave me a real lesson in humility, for he threw me splashing into the edge of the stream.

That was a case where, literally, pride went before a fall, and the lesson in humility was taught by a little range pony. It may be that the other fellows did not take full advantage of the situation, but my recollection quite clearly points that they did. Among those boys was a poor place to show your pride even when you got away with it, but Heaven help the poor cowboy who showed his pride and then was humbled. Anyway, it was such a good joke that even I enjoyed it, and when somebody caught Mouse and brought him back to me, I petted him and got on. . . .

In several letters you have been told about horses of mine failing to accomplish the purpose of their bucking with me. In order that you may get a clearer picture of that line of activity, and know the full extent of the times I took the count in my five seasons on the range, you are given the foregoing story of my shame. But the shame was not felt as much in my case as with some, for two reasons: (1) there were no grandiose opinions of my own ability, and (2) there was no ambition to be a great bronco rider. So the inconvenience of it annoyed, but the shame took no hold. But remember, it was hard work riding those horses for thirty-five or forty dollars a month. We did not see that life through the yellow backs of dime novels; we saw it through the sunshine and the storm, through the dust and the mud. Each man could see his fellows, and he knew that they were sweat streaked and dirty. The make-believe makes it silly. The reality made it superb.

Affectionately,

Dad

CHAPTER 17

Fixing the Wheel

My dear Geordie, Jean and Bob:

In the last letter you were told the incident of Pecos Bill getting thrown off Gray Eagle as he was seeking to catch the Shorty horse that had just thrown me and was running away with my saddle. . . . Probably as variegated a group as ever assembled with one main purpose were the cowpunchers. Big men and little men; good men and bad men; worthwhile men and worthless men; almost every variety and combination could be found. A man of the type of Pecos Bill furnished a good bit of variety in himself.

Pecos Bill, whose real name was William Broderick as I recall it, got his nickname from his recitals of experiences when he punched cows on the Pecos and Brazos rivers in Texas.[1] Few knew him except as Pecos Bill. Pecos was a sure-thing gambler, and he was fond of money. In the roundup months, from about May till along in November, he rode on the range, and in the wintertime, he gambled in town. He gambled for neither excitement nor fun. His sole purpose in it was to win money. He was the dealer, the banker, and his chief game was Mexican monte, a game in which the banker had a considerable percentage in his favor. It was almost always played with special monte cards with unusual figures on them, but it could be played with a deck of ordinary playing cards with the eights, nines, and tens removed. The monte deck was forty cards, and there was no joker. . . .

Part of Pecos's outfit on the range consisted of a long leather sack and a package, wrapped in oilskin, containing several decks of monte cards. Any time and any place, with any outfit that allowed gambling, and not all of them did, Pecos would open up a monte game. He would pull out the long leather sack that contained his money, get a deck of monte cards (both of which gambling conveniences he always had with him), and if in camp, he would unroll a roundup bed. Then the boys would gather around, fretting, talking, and cursing in their usual manner, not unlike a group of youngsters around a marble game, to buck Pecos's monte game. Sometimes they would flourish temporarily and leave the game to go on with their work, jingling a little of the banker's money. Sometimes Pecos's long leather sack took on an emaciated look, but it always seemed to reestablish itself and fatten on weakness—the weakness of cowpunchers to buck a monte game. If they happened to be out on a hillside, he would spread a slicker or maybe unsaddle his horse and spread the saddle blanket to be used as a gaming table. My early Presbyterian training taught me that gambling was wrong. As a consequence, I always regretted having engaged in it, when I lost. In my belongings is an old monte deck. Sometime when you feel cocky, I may deal you a game in the hope of making recoupment.

No small part of cowpuncher conversation consisted of discussion of systems to beat the monte game. They were serious discussions, too. On one occasion that dwells clearly in my memory, during the shipping season at Fort Pierre, Tom Beverly and I were back in the black gumbo hills, holding a bunch of beef cattle that would be shipped later in the day. On the flat below us were about half a dozen riders, who were with an outfit that had already shipped, and they were riding pell-mell into town.

Tom said to me, "Now, just take a good look at those gobblers. They're riding like hell into town, every one with his summer's wages and his system to beat the monte game. It may take a couple of days, but every one will come riding out slowly, and he'll still have his system."

Tom knew the breed of folks he was discussing. He did not play cards at all. Indeed, he was like the old Scotsman on the beach, who, when he was winked at and otherwise approached by the beauty in the bathing suit, said, "Run along now, lassie. Dinna mind me. Ma only failin' is whuskey." Although Tom did not save his money in very accomplished fashion, he wasted none of it in increment for the fellows like Pecos Bill.

Bill was no novelty. He was just a type among the men that followed the cows, but he was the most persistent man I ever knew in his refusal to buck any kind of a game. He would not even play poker, on the theory that was afterward given prominence on the stage when W. C. Fields promulgated the aphorism, "Never give a sucker an even break." Some of the fellows would win a little. Some would lose all their wages, private horse, saddle, and all their belongings. Because of the disturbance caused by that condition, and also because it sometimes would occupy the attention of the men when they should be attending to their work, many of the cow outfits prohibited monte games.

In the fall of 1901, after the escapade that made me the proud possessor of Jimmie Harrell's itch medicine and after the roundups had ceased, I was working for Bill Hayes at his ranch on Deep Creek. It was called Deep Creek, not because the water in it was deep, for it did not even run, but for the deep and rough canyon it had dug for itself through the ages. Before long out came Bill Hayes from Fort Pierre, bringing with him Pecos Bill, with whom I had previously worked a great deal. Pecos was a good hand and a willing worker, who always knew what to do and who was always in condition to do it. He never drank, nor did he use tobacco. The dancehall girls would starve to death if they depended on the patronage of Pecos Bill, but he was a sure-thing gambler.

He had not been out there long when he confided to me that he had a plan to beat the roulette wheel. Of course, groups, and even families when one of their number has learned three or four simple card tricks, will sit around and discuss as earnestly as if they were creating a new South Sea Bubble or a Credit Mobilier and plan the details of how that smart member will take in the big bank.[2] So long as that is confined to fireside discussion, no harm comes to the novice who aspires to best the professionals in their own game of cheating.

But this was Pecos Bill, who knew the way around the inside and was a sure-thing gambler. Consequently his words were entitled to a good job of listening. He informed me that he had written to Denver for a set of leaden frets and a diagram for the working of a roulette wheel. The frets on a roulette wheel are the shiny steel plates that form the numbered pockets on the wheel, into one of which the small ball spun by the operator of the wheel will drop. The numbers on the wheel correspond to the numbers on the betting table forming a part of the apparatus. The number into which the little ball drops is the winning number on the betting table. After a hard day of riding or doing whatever was necessary for the welfare of the cattle, Bill would get out his diagram as soon as we had cleaned and put away our supper dishes, and, by the glaring light of a tallow candle, we would pore over the diagrams to study out just where in the wheel to place the lead frets and on what numbers to bet when the frets were so placed. The idea was that the lead frets would deaden the ball and cause it to drop much earlier in its course than would be the case when it would strike the highly tempered, resilient steel frets normally in a wheel.

After learning the lesson figured out by the crooked gamblers of Denver, and to know that Denver was a hotbed for such things one has only to read Philip Van Cise's book *Fighting the Underworld* [1936]. Pecos outlined the rest of his plan to me. We knew that everybody else in the country knew, and the regular gamblers best of all, that Bill never bucked a gambling game. It was a certainty that the fixing of the wheel would soon become known, and that the operators would discover that about a third of the frets were deadening lead instead of sprightly steel. Then, if he had bucked the wheel and made a winning, he would be persona non grata with his own fraternity, the gamblers. Therefore, he was out as the man to buck the wheel.

Only a limited few dare be let in on a deal like that, so it was finally arranged that Bill would give notice to Bill Hayes that he was going to quit. That he did, and he quit and went away to Fort Pierre to fix some wheel in any one of the gambling houses. That in itself was not expected to be an easy task because the gambling apparatus in those border towns was closely guarded, not against cattlemen and cowpunchers, but against other members of the cut-throat brotherhood. After Pecos Bill had been in town for two weeks, I was to quit and go to Fort Pierre, for by that time he was expected to have enough time to fix the wheel. Although I was little of a gambler and no plunger at all, I was to buck the wheel by betting on the sacred numbers already committed to memory. It was dead easy to get up a play on the wheel in Fort Pierre in those days.

When Pecos had been gone about two weeks, I quit and went to town, all thrilled with the prospect of getting something for nothing. It is strange what a soul-pervading thrill comes to almost any member of the so-called human race in getting something for nothing. To find a dime on Broadway would thrill a financier more than a big deal with large profits, just as the ghetto-born boy rejoices in the unearned enrichment of a meal of Virginia ham when no one is looking. Even so, a young cowpuncher could almost travel on his own elation at the thought of being a party to the job of besting the gamblers. There was no question of morals involved, for the gamblers lived by their wits. They toiled not, neither did they spin. They never endured the hazards of the storm. They were always indoors in bad weather. They never had to eat soured beans nor drink vile water. They dressed well, lived on the fat of the land, and earned nothing. There was no harm in cheating them at their own game. Thus we rationalize to the conclusion at which we wish to arrive, or have already reached.

So on the way in from the Bill Hayes ranch, I stopped at the road ranch of Harry Hopkins, a former Fort Pierre gambler, about twenty or more miles west of Fort Pierre on the old Deadwood Trail. The idea was that, if the wheel came on bad luck the next day, Hop Lee, as Harry was usually called by his friends, and his wife, the former Dorothy Feezer, would know of my paid sojourn at their road ranch the night before and would know that I had not touched the wheel.[3] Of course there was nothing wrong, unless one accepts the wrong of gambling itself, in fixing up a game to take in the game of the gamesters. That was exactly what Pecos was doing. The comfortable accessory we call an elastic conscience kept me convinced that Pecos Bill should not have betrayed his fellow gamblers, but that my part in the plan was purity of conduct.

In the mid-forenoon of a day in late December, shortly before the Christmas holidays, I rode in to Fort Pierre and put my horse in the livery barn. Then came the pleasant job of passing the hellos to a lot of friends, some of whom had not been seen by me since the preceding winter. In Bradshaw's saloon I ran on to my friend, Pecos, and we got to visiting. When the coast was all clear for passing the information, I asked Pecos if he had everything fixed. He replied that he had. There had been a great deal of difficulty in getting at the wheel, but only the night before he had got old John Hack, the watchman in Billie Nichol's gambling hall, drunk and laid out.[4] Then he had removed the required number of hard steel frets from the wheel and had substituted the Denver lead frets in their place. It was all set, and there had been no play on the roulette wheel that morning, and it had not been uncovered since the job was done.

Billie Nichol's gambling hall was at the back end of Bradshaw's saloon. We soon separated, and Pecos sauntered back in the gambling hall. Before long I, too, went in to see what was going on. There was some minor play going on at some of the tables, but no excitement. Hugh Burgess, who had been riding all summer for Scotty, . . . had arranged for a job for himself that winter with Billy Nichols and was among the folks in there that day. It would never do for me to show much interest in the games if suspicion were to be averted later on. As Hugh and I were visiting, some one said, "Hughie, uncover the wheel and I'll give you a play."

Without any ado, Hugh uncovered the wheel, and got ready to spin it. He put his finger in one of the number squares of the wheel and gave it a

MICK
B.
HARRISON

vigorous spin. He did not know that Pecos Bill and I were more horrified than he when a lead fret came out of the wheel with his finger and struck the low ceiling of the room. There may have been "racing and chasing on Lockerby Lea" when Lochinvar was making good his getaway with the lost bride of Netherby,[5] but it was no more excited, or exciting, than the cattlemen, cowboys, and gamblers who gathered around to see and to discuss the invasion of the wheel.

Of course all play was called off before a single bet had been laid. It was love's labor lost for Pecos, and the chance for excitement had vanished for me. We could take pity on the field mouse for the failure of her well-laid schemes.[6] Pecos quickly drifted out, but I stayed to see the show. They all knew that it was less than an hour before that I had come into town. A close examination of the wheel disclosed that about a third of its frets, properly distributed to play the sacred numbers Pecos Bill had taught me to commit to memory, were of the lead that would deaden the ball and not of the steel that would give it life. Not a single fret could be removed by any set of fingers in the room, except the one Hughie Burgess happened to press as he spun the wheel. That ended our adventure, and that was the nearest I ever came to being "the man that broke the bank at Monte Carlo."[7]

Smoky Tom was a fellow who divided his time between the range and town. The gamblers called him a cowpuncher, and the cowpunchers called him a gambler. There really was no reason for me to share any of the blame that the gambling fraternity heaped on Smoky for sneaking in and working Billie Nichols's wheel. If he could not stand the criticism, he had no business earning the reputation that brought it to him so readily.

A little later that winter Hugh Burgess went to Huron and got a job firing a locomotive on the Chicago & Northwestern Railway, setting the range and the gambling halls behind him forever. A couple of years ago one day, Hugh and I were visiting in the First National Bank at Rapid City. When this deal popped into my head, I asked him if he remembered it. He certainly did remember it, and then he told me all about how he accidentally caught with his finger the only fret that was loose, and how it flew to the ceiling. He had forgotten all about my presence on the occasion. When I asked him if he knew who did it, he said, "Oh sure. We knew who did it."

I asked him who it was, and he said, "It was that _____ son of _____, Smoky Tom."

I said, "How do you know it was Smoky Tom?"

"Oh," he said, "We went right into it, and we pinned it right onto Smoky."

I said, "It will surprise you to know that I know exactly who it was, and it was not Smoky." Then I told him the whole story. He did not like to reverse his conviction of Smoky Tom, but we had a good laugh over that long gone incident.

The range is gone, the cowpunchers are gone, and the old-time gamblers are no more. No longer do booted men play the games. Now polite gamblers spin the wheels and deal the cards so the ladies can try their luck as they sip their highballs, while the men sit out in their automobiles, or wherever else they can be comfortable, waiting for the gaming to end so they can go to their homes and to rest. Only the world has changed.

Affectionately,

Dad

CHAPTER 18

Mostly 'Cross Country

December 30, 1940

My dear Geordie, Jean and Bob:

One who had more of perception in his head than he had poesy in his heart wrote:

> King David and King Solomon
> Lived merry, merry lives,
> With many, many concubines,
> And many, many wives;
> But when old age came creeping on,
> With all its aches and qualms,
> King Solomon wrote the Proverbs,
> And King David wrote the Psalms.[1]

Do not infer that old age is causing aches to me as it is creeping on. Above all, do not get the idea that there are any qualms. The case is too far along in the trial for any decent attempt now to mend the record. It is so far written that it will just have to go on, without apology or offer of amendment, catch-as-catch-can to the end. My efforts are not to harbor within myself any aches or qualms, nor to produce in expiation of them anything in the nature of the latter-day works of King David or his wise son, who in an earlier day so dearly loved the lasses. Those two men were great press agents of an insignificant kingdom, who kept it alive to the ages, while much greater contemporary ones are buried deep beneath the cobwebs in the land of Forgot. My hope is to chronicle for your benefit, if not for others, a few simple truths of a now-dead epoch, which is becoming a fairyland.

If that epoch was romantic, it did not seem so at the time, as one can readily perceive by a careful inspection of Charlie Russell's picture—*A Rainy Morning in a Cow Camp.* If it was romantic (to me it seemed realistic to the limit of endurance), then one can do a service by bringing the romance of a youthful America firsthand, and correctly, to the romantic youth of an older America. You already have one incident of a swinging cinch, due to a slavery to novel fashion, and, if this chronicle is pursued to its prospective close, a similar experience in part will get into this letter.

In my last summer regularly on the range, I was with the home outfit working down through the creeks on the south side of the Cheyenne River, after being actively and fitfully repping all spring and most of the summer with other outfits here and there. One day in August a rider came out from Fort Pierre to where we were on Sansarc Creek with a letter to Jesse Knight, the foreman, from the Stock Growers Bank.[2] It contained the information that Frank Porter had bought the Bar Bell horse outfit ☨ from Aukerman brothers, and Scotty Philip, who was then heavily interested in the bank, had agreed to furnish a rider to help Porter round up and check out the horses. Scotty's man was really to be a checker for the bank, and the letter suggested that I should be sent if I was with the outfit, and, if not, someone else should go.

The rider happened along just about noon as we were eating our dinner. The boss read me the letter, which contained only the bare skeleton instructions given above. Specified and detailed instructions were not for that life. When the task was assigned, the job of carrying it out was entirely up to the assignee. The location of the Bar Bell Ranch was, at the moment, as unknown to me as is now the present exact location of Halley's Comet. Inquiry brought the information from some fellow with the outfit, who had been there, that it was on the right bank of the Cheyenne River, below the mouth of Bull Creek and a few miles above Frank Cottle's store at the mouth of Elk Creek.[3] It was only about a hundred miles away and to the west, so, with neither roads nor fences to divert one from his path, the route was easy, so easy, in fact, that all recollection of it has vanished, except that on the late afternoon of the second day I came drifting in with my string of horses to the Bar Bell Ranch. The entire crew at the ranch consisted of Frank Porter and Rex Terry of Fort Pierre, going on fifteen years of age. Rex still lives in Fort Pierre, where he is the community's leading banker, leading Mason and leading citizen.[4] At that time he was probably imbued with the idea of becoming a range rider, and they started young in that line of hard labor. Rex was soon to be initiated into the mysteries of hard riding and hard work, and he qualified in both.

Mention was made of Bull Creek. To the passenger on a Northwestern train going from Wall to Wasta, or vice versa, the trip up or down Bull Creek is just as easy as is the automobile trip over the finely engineered highway. To the horseback rider in pursuit of horses or even of slower moving cattle, a much lower degree of ease and comfort was presented. All the rivers that drained the part of South Dakota west of the Missouri River, the main ones being Grand River, Moreau River, Cheyenne River, Bad River, and White River, had by erosion through the ages worn rough brakes for their adjoining country. The Cheyenne, perhaps because it was the largest of them and drained a larger territory, including the entire Black Hills and Bear Lodge Mountain uplifts, or uplift, had worn for itself the roughest surrounding terrain.[5] There was no part of it rougher than the Bull Creek country.

Frank Porter was a tall, lanky fellow who had something of a reputation. I knew him well and liked him. It was reported of him that on one occasion, after he had put in a spell of gambling in Fort Pierre, he went out on the range, rounded up a bunch of horses, and took them to the north bank of the Cheyenne River. The river was in high flood, and it is a wild river on those occasions. At dusk Frank drove that bunch of range horses into the Cheyenne River, then all swollen out of shape. Then he rode his own horse in after them. The last that was known of him on that occasion was when he was sweeping down that terrible torrent in a bunch of struggling, swimming wild horses. Frank was given up for lost, and no one knew, nor could identify the ownership of, any of the horses shoved off into the river. Of course, no one claimed that they were owned by Frank. After a long period of time Frank came in to Pierre on the train and then over to Fort Pierre. His quizzical smile was the only reward of questioners, but, at this late day, I can tell you that the horses were sold in Nebraska. "I know not what the truth may be;/I tell the tale as 'twas told to me," by none other than Frank himself.[6] Now he was the real owner of a real bunch of real horses, the Bar Bell outfit.

The next day after my arrival, under the guise of giving my horses a day of rest, we did not commence gathering horses, but we did ride down to Frank Cottle's store to buy some grub in a form that would be easy to carry on a packhorse. The next morning we got ready to go. Getting ready meant running in the saddle horses, which included my string and enough Bar Bell horses to mount Frank and Rex. Then I put my bed on my own packhorse, and Frank put a bed for him and Rex on another. Our cooking outfit and grub, surely a modest enough lay-out was out on another horse; our mounts for the morning were already saddled and we were away.

On the way over, a couple of days before, the mosquitoes were in swarms and clouds on Lake Flat, a large tract of territory generally north of where the town of Wall now is, covered with lake beds, which then contained water. That prompted me to conclude, and to state to Frank, that we would not be able to find many horses, perhaps not any, on Lake Flat, their usual range. Although range horses and cattle are disposed to be a bit more stoical about mosquitoes than are the thinner-skinned and fussier human animals, they can be driven off when the mosquito pest becomes altogether too obnoxious.

Of late the Nazi war has caused us to revise our ideas of geography and of human residence. The wholly unwarranted invasion of peaceful Norway has caused us to remember anew that one of the well-known towns of that northern country is Hell, Norway.[7] Some of the natives of that notable town must have been active and prominent members of the cowboy fraternity in earlier days because the amount of attention it got from the cowboys, and the frequency with which it was referred to by them in everyday speech, would bring delight to the soul of the secretary of the Chamber of Commerce of Rapid City, or of Sioux Falls, or of Minneapolis, if only he could find his own pet town so frequently referred to. Innumerable persons, countless horses, and no end of recalcitrant cattle have been invited and consigned to that well-known place. Moreover, it was used as a measuring stick for everything. The weather was either hotter, or colder, or wetter, or drier than Hell. Horses bucked higher and harder than Hell. Cattle were meaner than Hell. It must have been a most competitive sort of place because nearly everything was done in the spirit of doing it "to beat Hell!" A thousand other examples could be given to show that this somewhat insignificant Norwegian town was the most popular yardstick for measurements of all sorts of values in the whole lexicon of geography. It surpasses fiction the widespread publicity given to that place. It is very probable that, in my explanation of the whereabouts of the horses normally to be found on Lake Flat, some reference may have been made to it; and it is almost a dead certainty that the wish was expressed that all the mosquitoes could be transported for permanent residence in that town in the land of the fjords. Oh well, there is nothing better than being able to boost the other fellow's community part of the time, to play the good neighbor.

Frank expressed the purpose of rounding up as many of the horses as he could, taking them down among the farmers for sale, and applying the proceeds on his indebtedness to the Stock Growers Bank. That was fine with me because I was sure to be riding anyway, and it might just as well be after Bar Bell horses. True to our calculations there was no live-stock on Lake Flat, but plenty of mosquitoes. The prevailing winds had been from the south, and the horses, seeking relief from the mosquitoes that had hatched and become virile on the Lake Flat, had gone against that wind for such relief as it might offer. That should put them along the Wall of the Bad Lands, south of where the towns of Wall, Quinn, and Cottonwood for thirty-five years have sought to survive. Our conclusion, if correct, would not make our problem too difficult.

Accordingly, we went directly to the ranch of old Mike Quinn on Cottonwood Creek, close to where the town of Quinn now is.[8] There we unpacked our bed horses and the other packhorse and turned our little saddle bunch loose. One of the advantages of that place was that we had a good round corral in which to pen any Bar Bell horses we should gather. Mike Quinn, who died wealthy a few years ago in Rapid City, had many cattle and horses on the range, but his ranch consisted of a small, one-room log house with dirt floor, a small log barn and a round, pole corral. He did not believe in owning, or improving, real estate on the range.

Leaving Rex in charge of the saddle horses, Frank and I made a long ride that afternoon down towards the Wall of the Bad Lands and found a good many bunches of horses, each containing horses bearing the Bar Bell brand. Assembling them into one large bunch, we ran them up to the corral at Mike's place. There we cut loose the ones we did not want, retaining only those that Frank considered fit for sale. The turn loose was given a good, hurried run for a couple of miles off to the south until they developed the mood to go on some more miles on the dead run. Then the ones that were kept were turned in with the saddle horses, and from then on until they were penned at Fort Pierre about ten days later, preparatory to taking the horses we gathered into the farming country, they were herded day and night. Porter and I did most of the riding after range horses, picking up considerable numbers each day, thereby increasing our herd considerably. Memory does not serve to remind me now how many horses we took to Fort Pierre, but it probably was about a hundred head, including our saddle horses.

After we got enough gathered to suit Frank, we started for Fort Pierre, roughly about a hundred twenty-five miles away. On the way we did not unpack at noon, so we cooked nothing, and, of course, for that meal we ate nothing unless we happened to think to slip something in the morning into a saddle pocket. Only a confirmed optimist would recommend that line of work with its accompanying dietetics as a means of restoring lost weight. No matter how long he kept at it, the patient would not be likely to discover abdominal obtrusion. I don't recall that Frank rode any young horses on the way to the Missouri, but Rex and I each took a whirl at it. Just why has escaped me, but it certainly could not be for lack of other exercise. We got plenty of that driving that conglomeration of horses along in the daytime, without taking into account the three-hour guard each of us stood to see that none of those horses were missing in the morning. Range horses are notorious for going back to their home range if given half a chance, and not infrequently that chance came at night. However, we held all of ours and got them in the railroad pens in due time. When that was accomplished, we cut out all the saddle horses.

I do not recollect whether Rex went east of the river with Frank and the horses, but it is certain that Scotty agreed that Frank could have me and my string for the purpose of rounding up at least one more bunch of the Bar Bell horses. As a matter of fact, Scotty was very fond of Frank Porter, and I liked him, too, much better than the immediate type of work he had for me to do. Anyway, Frank went east of the river to peddle his horses, and I started back for the Bar Bell ranch the next morning, driving my own string of horses, most of those that Frank had been riding and, as I remember it, all of those in Rex's string. I never saw Frank again. We missed each other when he got back, and he died of pneumonia in Rapid City that fall. I was to ride for more Bell horses and have enough on hand, or easily available, to allow Frank to start away without delay to peddle them. The affairs of both of us were in the laps of the gods, soon terminating in death for him and in injury for me.

The day of leaving Fort Pierre was an easy one because all it meant was riding along the old Deadwood Trail, driving about twenty head of saddle horses. On reaching Will Hopkin's place on Frozenman Creek, just a little below where Hayes now is, the horses were out in a small pasture he had, and I sat down to a sumptuous supper at his place, prepared and served by his widowed sister, Mrs. Porterfield, who served meals for pay to passers by.[9] The fellows who rode were not of the type one sees so often today, and perhaps could see then if he were properly placed. They did not approach the table like a grand dame of either sex, with a countenance exuding discontent, order a meal the like of which they never suspected until after, maybe long after, their maturity, and then show off an attitude of mind that should be eternally concealed as they growl about the quantity, the quality and the constituency of the food. No. Cowboys were not like that, so I had a fine supper and a fine breakfast the next morning at Mrs. Porterfield's.

There was no hurry on me now, and so the world was taken without too much fret as we went along in fair leisure, across the watershed of creek after creek, tributaries from the north of Bad River, and every inch of the country known intimately to me. It was not such an easy-going journey retracing it the next day, but, fortunately for our peace of mind, coming events do not cast their shadows before.

Without any particular thoughts of where or how to spend the night, and no worry at all over it, I was delighted to find a hay camp, where Dan and Billy Powell were cutting up hay, at the Deadwood Trail crossing on Big Buzzard Creek. There was food and a small pasture, luxury supreme, for nothing more was needed by a young cowpuncher traveling across country with some saddle horses. My own bed would furnish ample accommodations for the night, and food, pasture and a chance to visit with a couple of friends gave all that was needed. Immediately on getting my bed horse unpacked and the horses turned into the pasture, I rode out to where the Powell boys were at work. Incidentally, I was riding a freshly caught young horse of Frank Porter's at the time, which proved disadvantageous later, for young horses were not as smart as their older brothers under the saddle.

On reaching the Powell boys, we halted for the inevitable visit because that was the main way, and almost the only way, of spreading range information. Telling where been, where going, etc., the boys were not at all surprised to learn of my decision to stay with them for the night. That was always all right on the range. However, Dan spoke up and said, "The L-7 outfit is camped about seven miles down Buzzard and not doing anything right now. I thought maybe you would like to see them."

Of course that was certain, so my reaction was set forth in my remark, "Fine. I'll go down and see the fellows. I will leave my bed and horses at your place and pick them up in the morning."

With no more ado, I turned and rode down toward the south and soon came in sight of the L-7 saddle bunch and, very little later, the camp. The boys were there, "in leisure postures on the ground." A gab-fest, supper, some more gab, and an invitation to one of the fellows to spread out his bed wide enough for two, made a pleasant evening merge into Morpheus.

In the morning, before daylight, the nighthawk came in with the horses. Cliff Ricker, the roundup cook, had breakfast ready and was shouting his reproachful challenge that unless it was quickly acquired by each man it would be as quickly thrown away. Everybody in a cow camp always bustled into extreme activity when the cook roared out, "Come and get it or I'll throw it out." No one in the history of the range ever called the cook's bluff. Perhaps that was due to the fact that they were always in the mood for food. Just why in the name of one and all Norwegian towns it was deemed necessary to get in the horses, and to have breakfast eaten in the dark of the morning in a cow camp that for a few days was doing absolutely nothing, still remains a mystery to me, but so it was. Of course, it was easy to see the nighthawk's point of view.

However, all that may be explained or left unexplained; my horse was caught and saddled, and I was on my way to the Powell boys' camp in the dark of the morning. Man's accursed inclination for alleged improvements that deface the open beauty of nature had interfered on Buzzard Creek. Ed Olney had built a barbed-wire pasture fence, which had not been observed by me on my way down the previous afternoon because my route then was not so direct as the one taken in the morning, somewhat to the west of the afternoon course.[10] Here is where the young horse feature came in. Riding along in that darkest hour just before the dawn, my horse ran slanting sidewise into Ed Olney's fence, and before I could jerk him out of it, the evidence seemed clear that my left boot had been caught and maybe damaged in the fence. An old saddle horse would have seen, or felt, the fence and would have shied away. He might get spurred for his pains, because no rider liked to have a horse shying under him (although I never heard of a cowpuncher being unseated by a shying horse), but he would save himself and his rider from injury in the fence.

The complete absence of pain convinced me that my foot and leg were wholly unharmed, but the dragging effect was equally convincing that the boot did not entirely escape. To damage a cowboy's boots was a great calamity to him, for those boots, usually expensive ones, were necessary to him. The darkness incident to the gray of the dawn soon yielded to the red of the rising sun, and in a few minutes it was light enough to make inspection. When the left foot was put up in front of the saddle horn on the horse's neck, it was plain the boot was badly torn. What seemed a piece of boot was hanging from the ragged tear, and I caught hold of that with the idea of tearing it away, but I relinquished that idea when it developed to be a rag from my foot instead of my boot. That pull seemed to awaken that foot, and it is a modest enough declaration to say that the foot really commenced to hurt. Needless to say, the builder of that fence, whoever he might be, was heartily recommended by me as an immediate deportee to Norway.

Cowpunchers, as horseback riders, were the despair of the authorities on equitation. They sat this way and that way in their saddles, chiefly to keep the skin from wearing through in any one particular spot on themselves, and that in turn served to change the distribution of weight on the horse, thereby keeping his skin from wearing through too much in one spot. If the equitation expert were to follow a spring roundup, riding every kind of a horse that the boss of an outfit saw fit to assign to him, and on that horse doing every kind of work that came to hand, and doing it for eighteen or twenty hours out of the twenty four, he would discard his principles of scientific equitation and adopt the jaunty slouchiness of the cowboy, or he would be so completely worn out that he could no longer follow the roundup.

That principle was what saved my foot in part, for I was unconsciously riding along with my left foot tilted with the outer side upward. Thus, although it developed that the boot was cut to the iron stirrup on the outside, and the foot likewise, the downward tilt of big-toe side of the foot, next to the horse, saved that side from any great damage. Now it was hurting and known to be bleeding, so the strategy of the situation called for quick time to the hay camp. There seemed to be no thought of going back to the cow outfit but, instead, to go on to the hay camp, get fixed up, pack my bed, get my horses, and go on about my work. Let there be no mistake about it, punching cows was work with few, if any, of the type of romances and thrills thrown into their lives in books, magazines, screen and stage. If these letters do not acquaint you in some measure with the type of work they had to do, then they have failed in their purpose.

A little hurry and the hay camp was reached as the Powell boys were getting breakfast. I rode up to the flap of their tent and got off my horse, only to find that my left foot would not support me, and at the first attempted step on it, I was unceremoniously tumbled to the ground. I got up and hopped into the tent on my right foot. The boys quickly saw I was hurt, and they got me seated on a bedroll. By this time it was complete daylight, and an examination of the situation by the three of us quickly disclosed that the boot and the sock must be cut off. That was long before the days of silk socks but, oh, ye gods, my good kangaroo-skin Olathe boot. But it had to be. Execution of a decision was never postponed in that life, so, as Dan's knife came out, and a range man was never without a pocketknife, Billy took hold of the leg.[11] Almost instantly that boot and sock were off, and a badly mutilated foot, with pieces of sock and of boot worked into its construction, was brought to full view. . . . Efforts of the Powell boys were availing nothing to stop the flow of blood, and suddenly I passed out.

On my recovering consciousness a few minutes later, the blood flow had been stopped by an ingenious arrangement of the Powells. Taking the ordinary flour they had in camp, they filled the wound with it. That retarded the flow. If a little was good, more must be better, and so it proved. They took a lot of flour and built it up around the foot, then a flour sack was wrapped around it to keep the flour in place. Then a gunnysack was tightly wrapped around that to hold everything in place. On my return to consciousness, my left foot resembled a large-sized, well-wrapped ham.

Now began a council of strategy. Dan and Billy convinced me that it would be utter folly to attempt to go on to the Bar Bell, because I "would not be worth a damn" if I got there. They had carefully surveyed the foot, and it should be doctored. The nearest doctor was in Fort Pierre, about seventy-five miles away. My decision was quickly made to go down to the L-7 outfit, get a good and gentle horse fitted for that sort of a ride. So while Billy went out and brought my saddle horse up to the tent, Dan helped me to get out there. Putting weight on that foot was now out of the question, and there was not a stirrup on earth large enough to accommodate it.

Those horses permitted themselves to be mounted only from the left side. I could not put that left foot in the stirrup and, consequently, could not mount in orthodox style. Also there was not enough spring in me at the moment to swing on without using the stirrup, which could have been done under more favorable circumstances. There was simply nothing to do but to bundle me on, and this was done by Billy hanging on to the horse's head and Dan shoving me up on him, while I rendered all available assistance by pulling on the saddle horn and the cantle. It took less time to do it than to write about it. As soon as I was seated on the young horse, with my right foot in the stirrup and my left one swinging, or hanging, free, the boys said "Good luck" as I turned my horse in the direction of the L-7 outfit and waved them goodbye. It must be remembered that this accident occurred before Mercurochrome and germs were invented. While pain was not unknown, it was not considered good manners to give it undue prominence.

It took but a short time to gallop down to the L-7 and explain the situation. On the way there my thoughts had turned to old Blue Dog, a gentle, easy-gaited horse that was a gift from the gods. Blue Dog was smart, too. While the wrangler was running in the horses, I asked Jesse Knight, the boss, who was riding Blue Dog. He was not then assigned to anybody, and I could have him. As soon as the horses were run in, one of the fellows caught Blue Dog, put my saddle on him, and then put me on. It seemed as though Blue Dog sensed the situation, and, with a cowboy and Blue Dog helping me on, it was not so much of a task. I don't remember who that was, but it seems to me it was Bob Withers. At any rate, it was quick work to get on, wave goodbye as my horse was pointed toward Fort Pierre, and hear their good-luck expressions. It seems a bit queer at this distance in time that no one thought it would be all right to have some one go with me, but it never occurred to any one, and certainly not to me. My only request before leaving the outfit brought from the boss the assurance that he would send one of the boys up to the Powell hay camp to get my bed and string of horses and the Porter horses, my horses to be carried along in the saddle bunch until I was ready to rejoin the outfit, and Porter's horses to be carried along until some one from him came after them.

It was a good long way from there to Fort Pierre, in fact, a little further than it was from the trail crossing on Buzzard Creek to that Missouri River western metropolis. The way was long for an injured rider, and an equally long way for the horse under him. Good old Blue Dog. There was no chance at all to hurry, and none to loiter. The strength of the horse must be conserved to make that continuous trip. There was no way to give him any rest because there was no way for the rider to dismount and mount again. Functions usually attended to on the ground had to be executed from the saddle, and of course they were, because necessity is a great spur to originality. Those long miles across Whitcher Holes

Creek, Mule Creek, Mitchell Creek, Burnt Creek, Little Prairie Dog, and Big Prairie Dog seemed endless, but they were steadily unwinding behind us.

You will recall my unfortunate experience in getting thrown off the young sorrel horse when my cinch swung loose under him.[12] That should be an adequate lesson, but it wasn't, for here I was again riding with the patent cinch buckle. At the road crossing on Cottonwood Creek at that time lived Bob Gray and his widowed sister, Mary. They were elderly people then, but typical western range folks in their hospitality. I knew them both very well. About twelve miles west of their place, imagine my horror to realize that my loosened cinch had come undone and was swinging loose. Blue Dog saw it, too, and did his best to avoid any trouble incident to that situation. It was my job to balance that wholly loose saddle, to keep it on the right part of the horse, and to keep the saddle blanket from slipping away. With the full cooperation of that truly noble horse, we finally reached the front of Bob Gray's house and stopped there all intact. A loud "Hello" brought Mary to the door.

Noticing me she said, "Well, get off, Georgie, and I'll make you a cup of coffee."

I said, "No, Mary, I got hurt this morning, and I am heading for Fort Pierre to see Doc Lavery, but I wish you'd fix my cinch."

Although she realized the seriousness of my predicament, she laughed and said, "Yes. You fellows will ride with these fancy dew-dads. They're no good." With that she fastened my cinch and wished me luck as I went on.

Plum Creek, Telegraph Creek, two branches of Broken Wagon-Hound and then Frozenman Creek. At Will Hopkin's place were Will and his brother, with two other men whom I knew, but memory does not now serve to identify them. Their invitation to get off and take a smoke, which really meant having a visit, and Will's inquiry as to why I was going back so soon, having just gone west the morning before, evoked the information that I was heading for Doc Lavery, whom we all knew. They said, "Well, good luck," and I left them.

Brush Creek, Lance Creek Holes, Lance Creek, Government Holes Creek, up and down, up and down. Would it ever end? The wide stretch of the brakes of Willow Creek, followed by the Giddings Flat made Fort Pierre more and more a possibility. A weary horse was carrying a weary rider, sick by now, and who that morning had swooned from loss of blood. It was a hard day.

Just a few miles out of Fort Pierre, who should came along and catch up with us in a buggy, with a good fresh team, but Ed Morgan, himself a cowpuncher but then a local representative of the Rosenbaum Brothers Cattle Commission Company.[13] His invitation to ride the remaining few miles in the buggy was accepted as avidly as a young man as tired as I was at the moment could accept. Ed got out of his buggy and helped lift me off old Blue Dog and into the buggy. Then he unsaddled my horse and put the saddle in the back end of the buggy. It is amazing how comfortable a buggy can seem under some circumstances. My horse may have been equally amazed at the forgotten comfort of a bare back. He was tired, but not hurt. As one looks at a cowboy screen play these days, he realizes that, if a cowpuncher on a real ride used his horse as those celluloid heroes do, at the end of seven and a half miles his horse would have to be hauled back on a stone boat, but Blue Dog, with all the handicaps of the day, had come more than seventy-five and was good for some more. I never was on his back again. God bless and keep Blue Dog forever in the most luscious grassed corner of horse heaven, assigned to a gentle rider, with a kindly bridle bit.

Just at sundown, Ed drove his team up to Fletcher's drug store, in adjoining rooms to which Dr. C. J. Lavery had his office. Dr. Lavery was a man of fine intellectual and medical attainments. He had the five usual human senses, unimpaired, and common sense enough to use each and all of them. He could diagnose and he could cure by treatment. If surgical treatment was indicated, he could use that method with proficiency. Fortunate was the frontier community that had for its medical aid a man of the qualifications of Doc Lavery. Aside from his medical attainments, I greatly admired him and was fond of him as a personal friend. He was not a medical machinist. He did not have to rely on some gadget to tell him what was the matter and what to do about it. Such was the man in front of whose office Ed Morgan stopped his team.

The doctor happened to be in his office at the time, just at sundown. After unwrapping the left foot, washing the flour and all other foreign substances away, he got down to the business of estimating the damage. Skin and flesh had been torn; blood vessels and sinews had been cut and mangled. Realizing that harmful germs were a reality, the doctor said he would have to burn it out if I could stand it. My rashness in saying that would be easy was soon regretted, for, taking me at my word, the doctor poured something on that wound that caused it literally to smoke. His question as to whether it hurt, when he knew the answer perfectly, aroused me sufficiently to consign him to go with Ed Olney.

Doc threw his head back and laughed heartily. After some more swabbing out, he said, "Now we've got to do some tailoring on this. Can you stand it without giving you something?"

My being sure that it could not be worse than the conflagration he had produced there a little while before, he had my assurance of being able to stand it. However much I would have welcomed the courage to tell him to the contrary, it was not there, so the doctor went to work doing things to my temporary discomfort. He seemed to sew things together, and before long he said, "Well, that's all we can do today. Now we'll wrap it up, and you come in tomorrow."

Soon he had that done and called Daddy Fletcher to find out if he had a pair of crutches in the drugstore. He did, my size or length. It was not a wholly unheard of thing to have cowpunchers going about on crutches, so I immediately toddled off to a restaurant to get me a little something to eat, the first since before dawn that morning at the L-7 wagon. It took several months for the foot to get entirely well, but, except for scars, and those smooth, no one at any time would know that the foot had ever been injured. In just three weeks I was back riding, with a boot on my right foot and a shoe on my left. I was still riding that way on the night the Texan was so disturbed by the aurora borealis.[14] . . .

Years passed by, and about 1920 or 1921, Charles W. Robertson was a coal, lumber and machinery merchant at Midland.[15] He kept writing me to go to Midland and go with him on a grouse-hunting trip up on Morphidite [Hermaphrodite] Creek. Being easily talked into that form of activity, I went to Midland, and we got plenty of grouse. You helped eat some of them. On the way out from Midland the next morning after my arrival, we went north through a country, which, in the raw, was entirely familiar to me. Now, with roads, fences, farms and dams, it was not even a caricature of itself. It was wholly unrecognizable. It was a wet, cold, blustery fall day, and, as we went along, I said, "Charlie, we can't be so very far from the old Bob Gray place at the trail crossing on Cottonwood."

He said, "No. It is just the other side of that little round hill." Sure enough, that made a perfect landmark when recognized, for it, of all the landscape, had not changed.

I asked, "Where are Bob and Mary now?"

Charlie answered, "They still live there."

I then told him of the last time I had seen Mary and how she fastened my cinch on that occasion. To my expressed wish to see her, Charlie answered by driving to the door. There were several saddle horses tied up close at hand, showing that some of the neighbors had come to visit. Charlie's knock on the door was answered by Mary coming to the door, greeting him, shaking hands and inviting him in. I stood behind him, and Mary very politely said to the stranger, "Won't you come in too?"

Charlie said that then I smiled, and a gleam of recognition shot into Mary's eyes, as she threw both arms around me, and said, "Georgie, I haven't seen you since the day I fixed your cinch." It was a relief to know that she, about the only one in the country who called me Georgie, still did so.

It is not often that matters of speculation can be reduced to a high measure of exactitude, but years afterward I measured the distance from

Fort Pierre to the crossing on Buzzard Creek where the Powell boys had their camp, and the speedometer registered seventy-four miles. It was a long, long trail that day on Blue Dog.

Maybe that was not a nice way to live, but it was free enterprise and an independent life, the like of which is not now known on the earth. We were young, and we loved it, evidenced by our unceasing complaint and criticism. Talk of free enterprise now is fairy story. Great political discussions take place over nonexistent free enterprise. Even Henry Ford, who still does not realize that even he is not a rugged individualist, is the most highly subsidized by government of any man on earth. National, state, county, township and municipal governments are taxed to the limit to furnish the runways for his products, without which his business would perish over night. Even the charges on our toll roads, and every foot of them comes in that class, are collected by government in the form of so many cents to the gallon on all the petroleum products we use or waste in running around. Everything is so tied into everything else in this complex world we have set up for our own comfort (or maybe our destruction) that we can have no free enterprise, no rugged individualism.

On the range we had no good roads and no bridges at all, but, with a good horse under you and nothing to circumscribe you but the horizon, there was a high measure of individual freedom, and plenty of room in which to exercise it. In that respect, if in no other, they were the good old days.

Affectionately,
Dad

CHAPTER 19

Working up an Appetite

January 14, 1941

My dear Geordie, Jean and Bob:

A short time ago there appeared in a popular periodical the following poem:

MEN ARE LIKE WILD HORSES
   by *Grace Noll Crowell*
Men are like wild horses; they will rear
And paw the air at certain sounds they hear;
A rein, a thing they do not understand;
They would be restive at a driver's hand;
They will not tolerate a chafing saddle,
And woe to any booted legs that straddle
Their quivering backs, and spurs are fiery swords;
But come to them with praise and honeyed words,
Reach out and pat their noses, touch their lips,
A lump of sugar in your fingertips,
Their rolling eyes will calm, their hoofbeats still,
And they will take you anywhere you will.
Learn early; men cannot be pushed and shoved,
But, like fine horses, can be led and loved.[1]

Just how much the lady knew about men may be problematical, but she seems to have had some experience with horses, and maybe range horses. A little sugar, sure enough, helps with either, and, when the need of it appears, food generally, without the refinement of a lump of sugar, has a common effect on each. "Feed the brute" does not apply to men only, for it likewise makes horses better natured and more useful.

One early summer, immediately after the completion of the spring roundup, the 73 outfit decided to make a roundup over the Rosebud Indian Reservation, which then included what now comprises the counties of Gregory, Mellette, Todd, and an area bounded on the south by the State of Nebraska, on the east by the Missouri River, on the north by White River, and on the west by the Pine Ridge Indian Reservation. That was a sizable territory, as a quartet of us was soon to find out.

Just what sort of telepathy, or jungle drums, brought us together has now completely gone from my memory, but sure it is that, at Tom Hill's place on Bad River, Charlie Hurst, a brother of my friend Bill, the roundup cook, Andy Feeney from down near the mouth of Bad River, and I met with the common purpose of going to join the 73 roundup, to which Tom Hill also was going. Charlie, as I recall was riding for La-Brecque, whose cattle ranged in the Ash Creek country on the south side of the Cheyenne River. Andy Feeney, a large, good-humored Irishman, a brother-in-law of Judge Hughes, and who afterwards served several terms as sheriff of Stanley County, was riding his own horses and was representing the owners on low Bad River. Tom Hill was riding for himself and was representing the cattle owners ranging generally in the central Bad River country.[2] I was riding a string of L-7 horses.

It made it nice to have four congenial fellows going together to join a roundup in a distant point on the range. We were off about the crack of day with our strings, about forty head of saddle horses. About midday we came to a throw-back wagon of the 73 camped on White Clay Creek, near the head and close to the White Clay Buttes. Cy Hiett was in charge of the throw-back wagon, which at the moment was holding no cattle. Naturally, we stopped and had dinner with the boys. Our plan was to go on to the Rosebud reservation in the hope of getting to the 73 roundup that night.

Each of us had a little money with us, and a rep far away from home was likely to need a little. It may be laid to ill fortune, but after dinner, someone of the 73 boys opened up a monte game, which was a smart move on his part. Tom Hill, Andy Feeney, Charlie Hurst and I joined in the general festivities of the same, but our blue bird was wearing dull gray that day, and so, in a very short time, we were on our way in high hopes that we would not go broke so quickly in the next monte game we found. The probabilities are that the combined losses of the four of us did not total twenty-five dollars, but being broke is being broke, no matter how much or how little you lose. It is too bad that some of the folks I know nowadays have always been deprived of the humbling, yet educating contact with personal bankruptcy.

Mention was made of a throw-back wagon, and maybe that should have some explanation. It sometimes happened that the winter storms were such that the cattle drifted in great numbers and for great distances from their usual range. In such cases a throw-back wagon would be run in conjunction with a big roundup outfit. A throw-back, or to throw back, meant the process by which cattle picked up on the range were taken back to that particular part of the range on which they were said to belong. When it was known that such cattle would be picked up in considerable numbers, the business of getting them back to their own range was expedited by the use of the throw-back wagon.

Sometimes a large outfit, and let us use the 73 for illustration, would rig up a throw-back wagon of its own, with its own men. They would meet up with the roundup outfit, take what cattle it would be carrying belonging farther north on the range, and drive them to the proper place to be turned loose. Then it would come back without cattle, meet the roundup, and repeat the performance. Sometimes, by prearrangement, another outfit, say the L-7, would act as a throw-back wagon for the 73. Of course this placing of the respective outfits is for illustration only. By reason of the cattle drifts, the throw-back wagons always went north with cattle and went south without any. When a throw-back wagon was not employed, then it became the task of a rep working with a roundup to work his cattle back to where they belonged. Such was the outfit at which we had lunch, and which, in a few days, under the direction of Cy Hiett, would move towards the 73 roundup and pick up its extra cattle.

It did not take us so very long to get over to the Forks of White River and on up Little White River. Somehow, Tom Hill and Charlie Hurst, who had worked through that country before, were possessed of a super confidence that we would certainly find that roundup wagon before dark. Andy and I, each making his first trip through that part of the country, made no pretensions of being anything but followers. When it got too dark to justify further movement, we rounded up our saddle horses, unpacked our beds, each picketed a horse, and Andy and Tom hobbled some of their horses. My horses and Charlie's were so sufficiently accustomed to be away from home that there was little purpose in hobbling any of them. Then we lay down for the night just about where the town of White River, the county seat of Mellette County, now is. It was then, of course, Indian reservation with little population, and that only along the better streams with which the Rosebud country abounded. There was no supper for us and no chance for any, although from off in the distance came the monotonous tom-tom of some Indian drums furnishing music for an Indian dance. Of course those drums can be heard for very considerable distances, and we were not so hungry as to feel in any way tempted to follow the sound to its source in order to get something to eat. We were missing only our first meal. Having had a fair amount of exercise, all of it in the open air, it was no task for us to fold up in dreams of the 73 wagon and the cook.

Bright and early the next morning we were up, and it took only a few minutes to get the horses rounded up. Packing our beds, and each catching a fresh horse for the day's ride, and not having the bother of a breakfast, we were soon on our way. Tom and Charlie kept up a fairly constant conference about where we were and the likelihood of where we would find the roundup outfit. Andy and I knew that we didn't know where we were, except that our directions were straight. It was hard to keep a man in the wide-open country with plenty of horseflesh permanently lost, so long as he knew he could point north. Later acquaintance with the Rosebud country, of which I had quite a little, definitely convinced me of the correctness of the suspicion that was at that moment beginning to fill Andy's mind and mine—that Tom and Charlie did not know the country.

There were two watercourses of which they persistently spoke, the Keyapaha River and Minnecaduza Creek, pronounced then by most of the cowpunchers as the Minnecadeuce. As a matter of fact, in our wanderings we never got into the watershed of either one of those tributaries of the Niobrara River. What we were seeking to find were the circling riders of a roundup. As our horses were being driven along in a general southeasterly or easterly direction, one or two of us would ride the ridges, thereby insuring detection of any riders. After a good view from one ridge, there was no need to look again until we approached a new ridge, or butte, or height of land, which would permit another good look. So it went for miles and miles and hours and hours.

By this time we had in a measure taken sides. Charlie and Tom were now defending with vigor their knowledge of the country, while Andy and I were equally vigorous in denouncing folks that would get other folks lost. Of course the Minnecadeuce entered into the joshing discussion. As we came up on top of a raise, directly in our forward path, Andy, the big, good-natured son of Erin, turned to me and, with a sweep of his hand toward the new stretch of country in front of us, said, "George, that must be the Minnecadeuce all right. It sure as hell looks like the deuce to me."

Although Tom and Charlie treated our efforts at humor at their cost with contempt, that country was, by that time, beginning to look like the deuce to each of us. It was now wearing into the afternoon, and our last food was at the throw-back wagon near the White Clay Buttes at noon of the day before. Although going without a meal now and then was far from unusual in the experience of any of us, we were now showing signs of missing too many in a row to suit any of us.

Although we could see no riders anywhere, nor any signs of our roundup outfit, a ray of hope was injected into the somber, hungry picture when we glimpsed a fence. Fences were scarce in that part of the country then, and this one could easily prove to be part of an Indian habitation. So it proved to be, and when we rode up, although dinner was over, the Indian lady agreed to get us something to eat. It so happened that she had a very nice, well-kept garden patch close to the house, and, while she was cooking something for us, we partook of her especially luscious carrots from the garden. Soon she announced it for us, and we set to and had a fine dinner. Dinner over, we could give her nothing but thanks, due to our unfortunate experience with the monte game in the 73 camp the preceding day. However, we thanked the lady, and, so far as I was concerned, that was genuine. There is no likelihood that it was otherwise with any of the other fellows.

Now we were well fortified for the ride, and we knew we would find the 73 wagon. As darkness settled down on us, it had not come into view, so we just located a place to water our horses, unpacked, caught a night horse apiece, hobbled two or three of the horses, and settled down for the night. It was easily time for another meal, but we were not so bad off, so we talked ourselves to sleep railing about the elusiveness and other qualities of the Minnecadeuce. That Minnecaduza really is a much finer creek than some of the things Andy and I had to say about it would indicate.

Next morning, not being bothered with any such folly as breakfast, we were off on the search for that roundup. Over the country, criss-crossing this way and that, making inspection from the top of every respectable eminence, we pursued our search fruitlessly, catching a change of saddle horses as fairness suggested. It seems past belief to anyone who has known that country since its settlement, and not before, that we could ride all that day and see neither person nor food, but so it was. That night we came to rest at a point on Oak Creek, and as we got ready for the night, just as we had prepared on the two preceding nights, we were in poor mood for joking. By now we were hungry and perfectly willing to say so, but there was little we could do about it.

Tom Hill was the first one to get his bed unpacked, and he took his night horse down over the bank to water him before picketing him for the night. Just as I was about through fixing my bed and was getting ready to take my horse to water, Tom's voice came floating up through the brush, as, in his drawling voice, he directed at me the question, "Say, Scotsman, do you like plums?"

Tom knew very well that I was especially fond of the wild plums that grew in profusion along some creeks in those days, although the march of civilization seems since to have cleaned them out. The thought of a few handfuls of good plums seemed to me a valuable dessert suggestion to follow up the complete nothingness of four successive meals. I immediately called back to Tom, "I'd tell a man I like plums." ("I'd tell a man" was a definite slang assurance among the cowpunchers, a phrase that now seems to have died out, like international honesty.)

Suiting action to the words, it was only an instant's job to pick up the loose coils of my picket rope, the end of which was already round the neck of my night horse, and be off down the bank to Tom, the water, and the plums. I knew Tom cared very little for wild plums, but his present apparent lack of interest seemed too much even for him. There he stood, listlessly watching his horse drink, his right hand holding his coiled picket rope, hanging limp against his leg. To my interested inquiry, "Where are those plums?" Tom drawled, without even the dignity of a smile, "Oh, George, I don't believe there are any plums on this creek. I just wondered if you like them."

My jaw dropped so badly that it took me the rest of the evening to get my mouth so it would stay shut. Although for many years, words have been my chief weapons of defense and offense, neither at the moment nor at any time since have they been adequate to express my feelings on that occasion. It was beyond me to understand how any person as kindly as Tom usually was could take the dearest feelings of an associate and trample them underfoot, knee-deep in gastric juice. There was nothing to say and nothing to do except to glare at Tom like a bull at a bastard calf, and it took no effort to do that. It just happened automatically. Charlie Hurst was much too dull witted to realize that Tom had done anything more than ask a simple question. Not so with the nimble-minded Irishman Andy Feeney. Quietly he made some suggestions on food that would have been comforting to one full of that commodity, but not to me then. The only comforting thing to me was the knowledge that they had not sneaked off to anybody's restaurant and indulged them-selves in a good twenty-five cent meal, the going price at the time. They were hungry, too. The joke was on me, and that meant that it was my turn to be good-natured, as good-natured as a hungry man can be. The heights of affability are not usually scaled in that condition, but there were no casualties. Soon we were all in our beds, plumless.

Next morning we were off with the dawn. There really was not any-thing to stay for, and we might find that roundup wagon. Looking from the ridges and high points brought no results. Along about ten o'clock in the forenoon, we sat on our horses atop a high pinnacle from which we could see no sign of the riders with the 73. Off in the distance to the north, beyond White River, we could see the eastern end of Lyman County, even then fairly thickly populated with Norwegian ranching farmers. White River was about fifteen or more miles to the north. North of the river was food, south of it was Rosebud Indian Reservation. Some-where on that reservation was the 73 wagon, for which we had searched in vain. It seemed the most logical thing in the world for me to burst out with the information that, no matter where the other fellows decided to go, there was no need to question my decision to ride over to the north side of White River and get something to eat.

Even Andy seemed now to join forces with Tom and Charlie and ap-peared assured that we must soon find the wagon. My point was pushed home hard that there was no harm in having some food in us when we should find it. To end the argument so far as I was concerned, I said, and please understand that there are some expurgations and deletions in the quotation, "The 73 wagon can go places, and you can go with it. You can go on hunting for it. I am going to the north side of White River. If you want to drive my horses along with yours, you can. If not, I will take them. I will find that wagon later, but not hungry."

We compromised by all of us heading for White River and making pretty fair time on the way. Our horses had not suffered on the trip. They were plentifully supplied with grass and water, and they had not been driven at any great rate of speed. Now we were out to make some fair time to White River, and we did. On arriving at the south bank of White River we discovered to our horror that, after we had crossed the river up at the forks and while we had been wandering around on the reservation vainly trying to locate the errant roundup wagon, there had been a heavy rain in the Badlands, and White River was running full from bank to bank with thick Badland mud and water. A little above us we saw a tent and a rope corral, so our immediate conclusion was that here was a line rider's camp. We immediately went up, put our horses in the corral, un-packed our bed horses, caught a fresh horse for each of us, and turned our horses loose to graze.

About that time the campers came along, and they turned out to be a couple of U+ (U cross) riders, Alex Meader and Bill Durkin, who had established a line camp there. I knew both of them well, and my recol-lection is that each of the six of us know every other member of the sex-tet.[3] . . . It was only a matter of a moment to tell them that we had been hunting for the 73 for several days, without success or food, and that we wanted something to eat now—not later. They knew as well as we did that hunger made poor fortification against hard riding, and we knew they sympathized with us. It gave no comfort to us to have Alex tell us in his slow, methodical way that they had eaten the last of their provisions that morning for breakfast. They had intended on that day to ride over to Peg Leg's store across White River to get some grub to tide them over, but they were not hungry enough to tackle that flooded river.

Well, it was different with us. We were going over to Peg Leg's and see what arrangements for trade and commerce could be made with him. Alex and Bill knew that the best place to ford the river was about half a mile above their camp, because there was a fairly easy place to get into the flood and a good pathway to make it out on the north side, provided you hit it. Accordingly, all six of us rode up to this fine place (God save the mark) of which they spoke. Just as we got to the jumping off place, Tom Hill inquired, "Now, has everybody got a good swimming horse?"

Then my amazing foresight appeared to view, for here was I, riding Mouse, the little horse that had previously that spring thrown me off after swimming Plum Creek near Bad River.

Tom then said, "All right, you stay on this side until Charlie, Andy, and I get across. Then you jump off into it. If you hit the path, all right. If you don't hit it, we will rope you and let your horse and saddle go down the river. He'll come out somewhere down below, and we can get him."

That arrangement was quickly made, and, in Indian file with a mod-erate distance between, Tom, Andy, and Charlie went off into the river. With no experience worth recording, each in turn hit the narrow pathway and went up the opposite bank. That was my signal, so I wasted no time in getting in, for across the river was food, of which there was none in me. Tom and Andy sat on their horses on the opposite bank, ropes down and loops made, all ready to catch me and haul me ashore if little Mouse failed to hit the pathway, but hit it he did, in perfect order, so we just went along through the cottonwood trees lining the river to Peg Leg's.

Now who and what was Peg Leg? He was a Norwegian by the name of Halvorson, who had a little bunch of cattle that he planned to keep close to his little ranch in that bend of White River. He was postmaster at the little country post office at Cavite, named by someone who had returned from military service in the Philippines, which was then just recently finished.[4] His nickname came from a wooden leg, which he used as a substitute for one he had lost in some manner (probably it was not bitten off). In a small log building, separate from the house and other buildings, were housed the post office of Cavite and a small general store run by Leg's two daughters, a pair of beautiful girls, one or the other of whom was the apple of many a cowboy's eye. Some cowboy or other was almost sure to return any of Peg Leg's straying cattle to his ranch, just to bask in the sunshine of a young lady's smile for a moment. Peg Leg's wife was a substantial sort of person who knew her way around a cook stove. That was my first introduction to the family, although I knew of them by reputation—all good.

When Mouse and I came out of the river, Tom and Andy were there, but Charlie was nowhere in sight. The three of us rode up the few hundred yards and got off our horses at the front and only door of Cavite post office. There was no sign of Charlie. Wet to the skin and bedraggled in Badlands water, we presented anything but a romantic picture of the North American cowboy. We were not bent on romance, and, even if White River had not been in flood, we would not have been so bent. I had neither information nor curiosity as to where Charlie had gone and, in fact, had not given it a thought. The three of us walked into this little store and immediately on entering, I said, "Now, let's see if we have any money at all left from that monte game."

A careful frisking of ourselves produced exactly twenty-six cents, eleven cents that I had and fifteen that Tom found in his pocket. Andy had none. Tom handed me his fifteen cents, and I, in turn, handed the twenty-six cents to Andy, who was sitting on the counter clicking his spurs against its front. Knowing that this sum would not go beyond a

box of crackers and that we would have to make additional arrangements for food, I said, "Now, buy something to eat, so we can start anyway."

With exasperating deliberation Andy sat there jingling his spurs against the counter, with that puny sum of money in his hand, as he said slowly, "All right." However, he made no move to buy anything, and Tom walked out of the store.

Waiting until patience seemed all out of place, and wholly unable to understand the nonchalance of those fellows whom I knew to be enthusiastically hungry, I said, "Well, Andy, for God's sake, buy something with that money."

Slowly Andy said, "All right. What do you think we ought to buy?"

Knowing that we had none to spare, I said, "Oh anything, just so it is something to eat."

Andy seemed to be doing a job of ponderous thinking, and finally he turned to one of the girls and said, "Now, you give us twelve-cents worth of peanuts and fourteen-cents worth of candy."

Of all the efforts at purchase that ever came across my path up to then, that seemed the most ridiculous. Here were four of us nearly starved, with twenty-six cents between us, and our purchasing agent proposed to invest all of it in candy and peanuts. Except for the diversion from food, and the fact that it would be bound to take a little unnecessary time and effort, I would have favored mayhem, if not murder, on Andy. Shouting profane and vulgar characterizations at him, even in the presence of those two lovely young ladies who were products of the Victorian age, I wound up my rapidly delivered tirade with the admonition, "And you'd better buy crackers with the whole damn cheese."

Knowing the characteristics of my associates and their willingness to play jokes even in tragic surroundings, it should have occurred to me that there was something going on beyond my comprehension, but deliberation never came easy for me on an empty stomach. As Andy was looking at me without rancor at my language, and as I was getting more and more in the mood to do some kind of damage to somebody, in walked Hurst and Tom. Charlie said, "Well, let's go down and get it. Mrs. Halvorson has a fine dinner ready for us."

Even that glad news scarcely obliterated my anger at the remembrance of Andy's prospective purchase of candy and peanuts. On the way to the house, I learned that Charlie knew the Halvorsons well, and immediately on his getting across the river, he had galloped up to the house to make arrangements for dinner. And that was a fine dinner served to appreciative guests.

After dinner we went back to the store, where it was plain and plainer that the girls appreciated the calm, gentlemanly bearing of Andy and that they disapproved of the crudities of Andy's victim. Of course, in that life someone had to be caught off base in order to furnish the fun, and on that occasion, I happened to be the one who was last across the river, giving the others a chance to do the required moment's worth of arranging as Charlie galloped off to get dinner going. Thus was I the victim of the ever present joke. . . . But we had to get going, and we had word that someone had come by Peg Leg's and had left the information that the 73 should be on Dog Ear Creek about that night. That made it simpler and sounded like sense.

We mounted our horses, rode down to the river, plunged in and swam across to the south side. Back at the U-Cross line camp, we quickly rounded up our horses, packed them, and were gone on what proved to be the last lap of our search, Bill and Alex being gone on a ride. Before supper we found the 73 working on Dog Ear Creek, camped just about where the prosperous city of Winner has stood for over thirty years. No one was interested in our wanderings, and none heard of them, except for a warped account of the unfortunate shortage of plums. We were immediately on the job and worked with the roundup outfit until it finished its work, but the details of that are blotted out from my mind.

It was a great life, with surroundings quite according to nature, and nature in the raw is seldom mild. Also she may not be kind, but, to the man who can read her book aright, she is eternally honest. The men that peopled it had to have a rugged sort of honesty in the main, but when the country was changed to a basis of everyone trying to sneak something to which he might not be entitled, those fellows "changed to men like you and me." As for me, if I could have that world back as it was then, I would gladly swap all the good roads and bridges, the shiny automobiles, the telephones, and all the other gew-gaws of this era of integrated economy for the country as it was, peopled as it was.

Of course there is always the danger that one would require a return of youth to take advantage of such a swap. Perhaps he would not dare make the deal without that. In those days there appeared to be a good deal of room, and sometimes to a hungry man there may have seemed a little too much, but you were not inspected and charged for everything. You could travel from place to place without paying toll or tribute through gasoline taxes or license plates. It would be refreshing to see some Republican politician putting a license plate, or anything else, on some of those ponies. If you made a winning in a poker game, it was not necessary to include the amount in an income-tax return. If every phase of human effort was covered by its own law, the cowboys did not know it, nor did they care. They knew that to understand and to respect the other fellow's right, in a positive and not a negative way, was the law of the range, and that law they proposed to follow to the end of the trail.

The overwhelming migration, known as the homesteader movement, turned everything topsy-turvy and even put the precious buffalo grass under, instead of over, the sod. Every newcomer tried to transplant a bit of Iowa, or Indiana, or New England into his new one-hundred-sixty-acre home on the range. That was a task that nature forgot to attempt, and she frowned on the efforts of those who planned to revolutionize her processes. Then it was not a kindly country, but it was an honest one, and vigorous young men loved it. For those who were willing to take what it had to give, it furnished a better form of life than any that has been offered in the succeeding transmutations. That was true even in a part of the country where plums were scarce.

Affectionately,

Dad

CHAPTER 20

Hot Irons on Live Hides

February 24, 1941

My dear Geordie, Jean, and Bob:

Years ago, when Bert Leston Taylor, B. L. T. of *Chicago Tribune* fame, wrote his line in that so-called World's Greatest Newspaper (or should that be Nuisance?) in one of his daily column contributions, he said:

> When men are calling names and making faces,
> And all the world's a-jangle and a-jar,
> I meditate on interstellar spaces,
> And smoke a mild cigar.[1]

Such meditation must have taken him into a consideration of units of distance, as it must take anyone today who considers such things as a relief from war talk. The parsec has come into vogue as a unit of distance. As a yardstick, it is equal to 3.26 light years, or 206,265 times the sun's distance from the earth. Those who try to master a concept of that single unit of distance should be enabled to give Hitler and his ilk an insignificant point in space. It can also be well calculated to minimize our conceits on other subjects. For instance, when the cowboys' unit of measurement was the mile, fairly accurately estimated across the face of the public domain, the free grass country, and that was multiplied by the number that went into a long, hard ride, it is relatively a humble offering to the gods of boastfulness.

That public domain, the free grass country, the cow country, extended over such an extensive area west of the Missouri River from the Gulf of Mexico to the Canadian line that its extent almost surpasses comprehension. From the close of the war between the states up to the time about 1904, when the grocery clerks, seamstresses, school ma'ams, and the like took the last of it over to make a new farming country, it was steadily di-minishing. The last of the open range was western South Dakota, with a little of eastern Montana and eastern Wyoming still available. The course of migration went westward to the Pacific, but to the south of what is now South Dakota. In the course of the passing years, the pioneers of the northwestern states of Washington and Oregon moved eastward to have more room. Thus Montana and Wyoming were settled by cattlemen and horsemen from the Northwest, as well as by the men who came up the trail with cattle from Texas and New Mexico. The last frontier to yield to migration was western (South) Dakota. With the opening of the Black Hills about 1876, with or without sanction of law, and the opening of the Great Sioux Reservation by the Act of March 2, 1889, that last frontier extended its invitation to migration.

The consequence is that the cattle business on the open range reached its highest state of development in western South Dakota by reason of the fact that the business then could profit by the experiences, the de-velopments, and the mistakes of the past. The law of the range became more settled, and a higher state of cooperation existed. Brands and marks, and the laws of the state relating to them, made it more difficult for roguery to flourish. Brand commissions under state law, brand in-spectors at the leading cattle markets, and alert stockmens' associations set the open-range cattle business on a more solid foundation. Even the roundups were the result of cooperative planning, and this was espe-cially so of the spring roundups, . . . where compliance with a prear-ranged program, and there was always compliance, would comb every nook and corner of the range.[2] Rare indeed were the animals that did not get into the roundups. Rare indeed were the calves that escaped the branding irons, and nearly all of the branding was done on the spring, or general, roundup, as was explained to you in my letter on "The Cowman" [1 June 1940].

Branding has for centuries been an evidence of ownership. Slaves, criminals and pathological persons have in past times been made to carry the mark that comes from application of the hot iron, even in Eng-land in the last century. Whether brands were made the subject of legis-lation in the Code of Hammurabi, or Khammurabi if you prefer, over two thousand years ago in the Babylonian realm, is too much for my limited knowledge to decide, but certain it is that they were well covered by law in South Dakota.[3]

There was no other evidence of ownership that was recognized as superior to an honest carrying brand. It was called by many the heraldry of the range, and a proud heraldry it was to the men who worked with the cows. In Mexico, where cattle and horses were branded before the country that is the United States was populated with persons or with cattle, strange conventional designs that resembled the fevered tortures of a futurist in his effort to make cubes and arcs look like pictures were adopted by Mexican cattle owners. They could not tell what their brands represented, for the very simple reason that they represented nothing in particular.

After the heraldry of the range extended northward into Texas, New Mexico, Arizona, and California, and any man who knew how to rope and tie an animal [could] run a brand on it with a red-hot cinch ring, men became more prosaic in their brand designs. Combinations of letters and figures became the main idea in identification, with back of it all the hope of evolving a brand that could not be "worked." Such evolution was not simple, because the man with the running iron was ingenious, as can be evidenced by the fact that the famous X I T brand of Texas worked over into a five-pointed star.[4] That was what brought about the statutory development, and it was the law in South Dakota that brands to be effective had to be registered, and no one could register a brand that could be made by running additions on an existing registered brand.

One of the famous brands was the "long rail and jingle bob" of John [Chisum] of New Mexico, whose herds suffered some depletion at the hands of Billy the Kid. This John [Chisum] is not to be confused, although that confusion does actually exist, with Jesse [Chisholm], the mixed-blood Indian cowman who established the historic [Chisholm] Trail.[5] The brand of John [Chisum] was a long mark made by running a hot iron from almost the point of the shoulder, along the left side, to the hipbone. That constituted the long rail part of the mark. The jingle bob was an earmark so cut that about half of the ear dangled fantastically, while the other part was natural. The unique earmark made the animals easy to identify in a mixed herd or bunch of cattle, and the long rail clinched the identification. Also, the brand seemed to defy all efforts to work it over into something else.

Another brand of fame was the Quien Sabe brand of Texas, pronounced by the cowpunchers as "kin savvy," Mexican for "Who knows?" or "I don't know." It appeared like two arcs or new moons in juxtaposition, with the horns pointing toward each other but not directly opposing, something like $\big(\!\big)$. It received its name from the answer the owner is said to have given when asked what his brand represented. In the vernacular of the range, where a good many Spanish words were used, particularly in the Southwest, he answered "*Quien sabe.*" The name stuck, and his brand became the kin savvy.[6]

Cattle were branded at any season of the year but usually in the spring on the general roundup. Looking back, it seems amazing that so few escaped branding. Of course there was the occasional unbranded animal, sometimes called a maverick, sometimes called a slick. When such an animal showed up, without brand or mark, there were usually those alert fellows on hand who were willing to run it off and quickly relieve it of its unadorned embarrassment by placing on its side or somewhere, with a hot iron, a crest or coat of arms that would indicate to the world that it belonged to somebody. The boss of a roundup had the right, and he exercised it, to have the brand of the outfit whose wagon was then working the country placed on any slick found, on the theory that that outfit had more cattle on that part of the range than any other outfit, and it had a better mathematical chance to be the owner of the slick than owners with fewer cattle. At that, it was quite a rare occasion.

An experience of my own can be used as an illustration of how a brand could be changed by adding parts to it. One spring roundup when I was riding for Scotty with the Bad River Pool wagon, we picked up a goodly number of Scotty's cattle on which the brand had been worked. His cattle brand was $\llcorner\!\!\!-\!\!\!\urcorner$ on the left side and a bar ▬ on the left thigh. Some acquisitive individual had gone to a lot of work to connect the top and bottom of the $\llcorner$ and the $\urcorner$ to extend the bar until it touched both the $\llcorner$ and the $\urcorner$, then ran a bar across the bar from the top to the bottom of the rectangular figure thus created. That changed the $\llcorner\!\!\!-\!\!\!\urcorner$ to a window-sash brand, ⊞. Also a bar was put across the bar on the thigh, converting it into a cross, ✝. That, of course, convinced an observer of the wisdom of the legislation against the use of a brand that could be made by adding to an existing brand.

Here were grown cattle, and manifestly range cattle, which were freshly branded. That was a contradiction on its face. That called for close observation of the brand, and the practical eye of a brand reader could detect the falsity almost at a glance. Of course an addition to a brand was never made by burning on only the added part and leaving the former brand as it was. The old brand had to be burned over, too, but there again the man who knew brands could at once detect the smooth burn of the branded part and the rough, coarse burning of the part put on over the former brand. So the L——⌐ could plainly be seen through the false window-sash brand and was instantly recognized as the holding brand.

There was another mark of identification on these cattle and on practically all range cattle. That was the earmark. There were numberless varieties and combinations of earmarks. Scotty's registered earmark was to "split the right and over slope the left." It was difficult to tamper with that earmark, except by full-cropping both ears close to the head. That was a cruel earmark, and one that was suspected. No tampering had been done with earmarks in this case, and anyone who had claimed that they were anything but L——⌐ cattle would have had something to overcome in the way of an argument. No such claim was made, and soon quite a few window-sash cows were suckling L——⌐ calves. That was about the most flagrant case of misbranding that came to my attention on the range.

At the time of branding, the brand was put on, the ears were marked, and the bull calves, on arising from the ordeal, could in fellowship mourn the fate of Abelard, but without any worries over progeny.[7] Other marks were sometimes placed on the animal. Occasionally an owner would mark the dewlap by cutting it so that a piece would be pendulously separate. Not infrequently an animal would be marked with a wattle, usually on the cheek but sometimes on the shoulder. A wattle was a rough protrusion caused by cutting back a piece of the skin so that it would grow apart, while fresh skin would form over the part that had been skinned off to form the wattle. The protuberance was always noticeable on the animal. Sometimes, but not often, animals were branded on both sides, but that detracted somewhat from the value on the market, although it did make it easy to pick them out among other cattle.

All in all, the branding was not a job to train a man for the presidency of the Society for the Prevention of Cruelty to Animals, and women did not participate in it at all. One day when we were branding, my old cowboy friend Bunk White said, as some of the fellows were discussing the pains and penalties the calves had to suffer, "When I was working for (and here he named a southwestern Texas outfit), we used to brand the calves on both sides, earmark them, dewlap them, wattle them on the

MICK
B.
HARRISON

left cheek, dehorn them, vaccinate them for blackleg, and castrate them. Dad blame, when we got through with them they'd just lie there and roll their eyes."

Such a continuity of immediate experiences almost makes one wonder how they had enough vitality left to roll their eyes. This much seems to be sure: when the calves were caught, they were in terror and made quite a fuss about the whole performance, but they seemed less sensitive to pain than one would suppose. Immediately on release the calf would return to an irate mother and partake of the next installment of a warm meal. They rarely seemed to suffer any incapacitating, or even impeding, effects from becoming standard bearers in the heraldry of the range.

Roundup on the Lower Brule

Something was said of the right of a roundup boss. He was as completely boss of a roundup outfit as the captain is of his ship. Sometimes that led to strange conclusions, and perhaps one can be recited.

In the fall of 1907, after I was engaged in the law business at Fort Pierre, Scotty came to me one Friday night and invited me to go with him the next morning to his ranch on the Lower Brule Indian Reservation. As we were leaving for the ranch on Cedar Creek the next morning, Scotty suggested that my saddle blanket and bridle be put in the back end of the buggy. His comment was, "You may want to take a ride."

When it was nearing sundown that late afternoon, and as we were approaching the ranch, he said, "I am going to start a beef roundup in the morning, and I want you to take charge of it. We will ship from Reliance three weeks from today."

Down went my heart to my boot soles. He had the whole reservation leased, and it was then a considerable area. I had not in four years done any riding that would toughen a fellow. I was trying to establish a law business in Fort Pierre. I did not want to ride through a roundup anyway. He had Bunk White working for him. Stanley Philip was working there. Other reasons came and went. They were met with final answers so far as Scotty was concerned: a fellow should always keep himself fit to do a lot of riding (something he never did); the law business would come some time, but roundups always had to be made now; it would be good for me to ride through a full beef roundup; Bunk White, although a splendid cow hand, was not available because of his color; Stanley was too young, having just turned seventeen. All my reasons went by the board. Scotty wanted me to take charge, so that settled it.

After we had been working about a week, Scotty came to our camp on Yellow Medicine Creek in his buggy. It was just at suppertime when he arrived and turned his team loose. By this time we were carrying a fair-sized beef herd. I went to the different fellows and told them who was to stand which guard. Scotty was not especially pleased to be told to get his saddle out of the back end of his buggy because he was to stand first guard with another rider, who was named. It was plain that his first inclination was to decline the assignment as soon as he saw that it was seriously intended. Then he realized that the law of the range still applied to a roundup, although, except within large leased pastures, the day of the roundup had passed. He knew there was no appeal from the decision of a roundup boss, not even to the owner. He knew that, under the law of the range, he could do one of three things: (1) he could hitch up his team and drive away; (2) he could fire the foreman and hire another; or (3) he could stand the guard. He stood the guard, which was only a mild bit of retaliation for the job he put up on me when he invited me down to the reservation. A strange experience occurred before the guard was concluded.

When North is Not North

The first guard had stood a little more than half its time when the herd, which had been bedded down three or four hundred yards from camp, took fright and started running from the bed ground. A storm had come up suddenly and violently. The ominous noise of the stampede awakened me. Quickly the other fellows were told to get on their horses and get out to the herd. By the time we got there the cattle were running badly in the rough brakes on the west side of Yellow Medicine. After a little while of trying to hold them, it became apparent that if they were held it would be at the expense of running many pounds off each animal, and of course beef cattle sold by the pound. They might run most of the night, and with disastrous results.

As the vision in the glare of the lightning flashes revealed from time to time the place of a galloping, yelling rider, I made for each in turn, telling him to turn them loose. This was with the knowledge that, if turned loose, they would scatter and get quiet, and it would be no great task to round them up next forenoon. As each man in turn was reached and told to turn them loose, he would quit the struggle and ride along. Soon, with several men accompanying me, we came to Scotty, who was still struggling to hold them. When he was told to turn them loose, he answered, "I think we can hold them."

There is no time to argue in such a situation, so I said, "We are turning them loose."

He immediately quit the effort and joined us. They were his cattle, but he had put me in charge of them. Picking up one man after another, after a considerable time, we got all the riders except one, and he was completely lost, finding his way to camp next morning. Knowing that the cattle were now turned loose, and without running off too much flesh, we halted for a little to take our bearings and get ready to go to camp. That was about two o'clock in the morning and at a point about three or four miles southwest of camp.

There is nothing more dreadfully confusing than to get lost on the prairie. In a country with which he is acquainted, a man is never lost by day or night so long as he knows he can point north. When that ability is temporarily suspended, he is so completely bewildered that often he cannot recognize landmarks or even buildings well known to him. Scotty was an old-timer on the prairie and an efficient one in getting around, but this night he was confused in the whirligig of activity. The heavy overhang of clouds barred all view of the stars. The rain had passed, the electric storm was over, but it was still unusually dark. As we sat on our horses, Scotty said, "Now what?"

The answer was, "We will go to camp."

He said, "All right," and turned his horse toward the south.

Fortunately, he was the only one who had lost his bearings, so when I said, "Hold on; camp is to the north of us," he said, "Certainly, and that is north," pointing to the south.

Convincing Scotty against his will was not a task to be undertaken lightly. We all participated in the discussion, but no one had any more proof of the correctness of his position than any other. Sometimes the right witness or the necessary piece of evidence will come to hand in the most unexpected fashion and in time to be of value. So it was for us on that occasion. Like a vast curtain drawn aside by an unseen hand, the clouds parted for a brief period, perhaps less than a minute, but long enough to see some stars. Of those celestial luminaries, all range riders had to be interested observers. Imagine our pleasure as those clouds parted to see the unmistakable guide post, the Big Dipper and the North Star. Scotty's attention was called to Polaris, and he looked at it intently until the clouds blotted it out again.

Then, in a final struggle to win the argument that he knew was lost, he pointed to the south, and said, "Well, I don't give a _____ _____. That's north."

Realizing the futility of convincing a man who already knows you are right, we all turned our horses in the direction where most of us believed we would find the camp, and Scotty went also. As luck would have it, we did not miss it, although that is easy to do.

In the morning we rounded up our beef herd, cleaned it of any strays accumulated during the nightly disturbance, and were away to a fresh start. The cattle were shipped on time from Reliance, and I rode with Scotty to Fort Pierre in his buggy. He pretended to believe it was a fine vacation for me, as opposed to my view that I had been working. In all my dealings with him, he was so grand a person that it was a pleasure in experience and in retrospect to do things for him or with him. That was the last time I ate, or slept, or worked at a roundup wagon, or even saw one.

Of course we branded anything that needed branding on that beef roundup, but my tale has been permitted to diverge from the heraldry of the range. The beef roundup, and indeed anything along that line after the general roundup in the spring, was a matter of the individual choice of the owner of the outfit or the foreman. The spring roundup, as you have seen, was based on agreement of collective opinion.

All must recognize that in the ambit of a country's life most things are regulable, and there must be an authorized directive force to permit the proper degree of regulation. That must be allowed to work in the wisdom of experience, and not in the penumbra of an eclipsing shadow thrown by some power ignorant of what must be done. It was so with cattle operations on the public domain, the open range. It is so with everything worthwhile.

In the hope that the foregoing may give you, and any others whom you wish to inform, some further light on what men did, and how they did it, in those days that now seem so long ago, I submit it to you.

Affectionately,
Dad

CHAPTER 21

Ailments of the Range

May 20, 1941

My dear Geordie, Jean, and Bob:

Only a strong-minded man can read the persuasive advertisement of a patent medicine without being convinced that he needs a bottle of it. The same goes for the women. With magazines and newspapers hurling their mendacities into our eyes, and the radios blaring their exaggerations into our ears, even the ladies feel short changed unless they can have a prostate-gland operation, and the men search for some use for Kotex and other similarly gifted commercial products. Truly, advertising doth make jackasses of us all.

It was not thus on the range. There were only men at work there, in the main, so any reference on that subject to the feminine would be much out of place. . . . Of course it must be borne in mind that we were a motley crew with work to do. We had very little to read and less chance to read it. We did not even have an almanac to guide us in our ailments, and there was no radio to tell us what was the matter with us. Consequently, by reason of abysmal ignorance, we simply stayed well and did not suffer from lack of calories or of vitamins. It was well that we did not, for in those days the doctors knew nothing about them either. It seems almost unbelievable that without all the myriad ailments and cures of today, the race was then able to produce a John L. Sullivan and, likewise, a man to conquer him. (Incidentally, I remember a very pleasant day and evening that Scotty and I put in at the buffalo pasture with John L. Sullivan and Jake Kilrain.)[1]

To show what had to be done on occasion, let me tell about Sim Reber's trip when he was driven in a lumber wagon down Bad River to Fort Pierre from his home. He was taken ill at his home, a few miles below where the city of Philip is, about seventy-five miles from Fort Pierre. Some terrific pains had taken him amidships. His wife, Gussie, did everything that misfortune could suggest, but the pain and suffering mounted to heights beyond the ken of that little lady. It was equally beyond Sim, but he was too beset with physical suffering and mental anguish to do more than attempt to control himself, without any efforts to analyze a pathology.

Sim Reber was a cowboy, who in his day was a whirlwind bronco rider. After he married Gussie Wilburn, he let up on the bronco busting a lot.[2] It was said of Sim and truthfully, as I can vouch, that he had a good eye for a slick, and, in short time after the discovery, it was almost sure to be sporting Sim's brand and earmark. On two occasions as I happened to be at Sim's place on my way through with a string of horses, I had opportunity to help him, and, being a believer in a good neighbor policy, I certainly did help him. Animals looked much better branded anyway. Sim and Gussie had a large family of small children, who just trod on each other's heels on their way into the world. Mrs. Sanger had not yet deluged the world with useful information.[3] I am telling you this much of Sim to let you know that he was not the type of man who would sit around feeling sorry for himself. He and I were very good friends, and I know that it took plenty to make him complain.

When Gussie saw that she was not going to be able to stop or even to halt momentarily the pain that seemed to be tearing Sim gut from entrail, she put her oldest boy, just a little fellow, on a horse and had him ride away for help. He went, as my memory tells, to the home of Ira Miller who then or soon after was married to Gussie's sister Eva. Ira knew that there was no help he could render by going over on horseback, so he hitched up a team to a lumber wagon and went over to see Sim. There he quickly agreed with the conclusion that Gussie had already reached, and that was that the case was of such gravity as to require the services of a doctor. The nearest doctor was in Fort Pierre, about seventy-five miles down Bad River.

Folks on the range may have lacked much—wealth, culture, and a long list of things—but very few of them lacked decision, the capacity to reach a conclusion, and that quickly. It took no time at all to decide that Sim must be started for Fort Pierre and for Dr. C. J. Lavery, a fine frontier physician, and without delay. Accordingly, Ira put some hay on the bottom of the lumber wagon, covered that over with some quilts that Gussie handed him. On the bed thus formed, the two of them helped the sick man to lie in the crude ambulance, and Ira started to drive his sick friend to Fort Pierre, a long and rough trail. He could not make fast time, but he went to the limit of his equipment.

When they got to the ranch, of George D. ("Dad") Mathieson, close to where the town of Wendte now is, Ira again changed teams, as he had done at several ranches on the way. This team was expected to take them to Fort Pierre, and in order to have all the help that could be made available on hand when they arrived there, a man on horseback made the ride to Fort Pierre, outdistancing the team. The intended destination was the hospital in Pierre, then in its infancy, but when Ira and his patient arrived at George D. Mathieson's house in Fort Pierre, it was night, with no chance to get across the Missouri River until next day. So there could be no hospital. Dr. Lavery was on hand at Mathieson's house, and it took that skilful man but a moment to know that Sim had an infected appendix and a strangulated hernia of several days.

Mrs. Mathieson was there. She was a pioneer of the pioneers. She raised a family of three daughters and seven sons, six of the latter with whom I at one time or another punched cows.[4] Quickly Mrs. Mathieson and Dr. Lavery got the desperately sick Sim undressed and on the kitchen table. Then, with Mrs. Mathieson doing the chloroforming and Dr. Lavery doing the carving, they soon had the operation performed and Sim in bed. Two or three days later, I happened to ride into Fort Pierre and was told the story by Dr. Lavery, who permitted me to have a visit with my friend being nursed by Mrs. Mathieson. The next summer Sim and I rode together on the range. Probably the same degree of care would be adequate for folks today if it were not for the frills the doctors have to sell. I do not recommend that, however.

Dragged

Lawrence Madsen, whose father T. M., had a ranch on Bad River about the mouth of Herd Camp Creek, was hurt on a fall roundup on Bad River.[5] Our boss had directed me to go to this roundup as a rep and thus came my acquaintance with the incident. Down on lower Bad River, about on Dan Powell Creek or Ash Creek, a horse fell with Lawrence. As soon as the horse got to his feet, and that was quickly done, it was noticed that Lawrence's left foot was hung fast in the stirrup. A falling horse always took fright and ran. This one proved true to the rule. As the frightened horse ran, he tried to kick away from him the burden suspended from the left stirrup. That was Lawrence. With men trying in desperation to get hold of that horse, it seemed certain that the hapless cowboy must be dragged to death, or kicked to death, or done to death by a combination of the two. When hope seemed gone, the horse kicked him loose from his entanglement with that madly galloping animal, and he lay on the ground, an inert and bloody mass.

It was not known for a bit whether he was already dead, but none there thought he could possibly survive. He was carried down to where the wagon was camped and placed on his bed, unrolled in the mess tent. It was quickly evident that he was still alive, but his head on all its parts, having been dragged along the ground at top speed for a long distance and vigorously kicked by a desperate horse, was battered out of all re-semblance to Lawrence Madsen. The complete unconsciousness that palled him forbade all realization of his late experience. In fact it was several days before he became conscious of his surroundings, and when he did, it served only to impress upon him the pains and miseries in every part and member of his frame.

The next morning after the dragging, while he was still wholly uncon-scious and battered into a most pitiable semblance of a human being, the outfit was going to move, and of course that called for moving Lawrence. The only place to carry him was on top of the beds on the bed wagon. Consequently he was lifted there, groaning in his unconsciousness, and securely fastened on top of the beds. The nighthawk was then instructed so to drive that he would not dump him off while on the move. On ar-riving at the scene of the next camp, the mess tent was set up; Law-rence was lifted down from the top of the bed wagon by the cook, the nighthawk, the horse wrangler, and the pilot. Then his bed was spread in a corner of the mess tent, and everybody went on about his business, leaving nature and Lawrence in the struggle for survival. At least there were no hampering ministrations, not even to the extent of washing the blood off him.

After three or four days of that he came to, and he was certainly a fit subject for the cleaners when he did. It was then certain that he was not going to die from the effects of that experience, and it was equally cer-tain that he was not going to be of any value around a cow outfit for long enough to insure that the roundup would be over before he could make a hand. Accordingly, a gentle horse was caught and saddled for him, and a man was assigned to ride with him to Pierre, not over fifteen miles away. Everyone had a joke or a razz to spring at the expense of Lawrence, and no one spoke his real feelings of sympathy, but I am sure that Lawrence did not fail to understand. Next spring he was back on roundup, working just as though nothing had happened. Nothing had happened.

Boils

You two boys will remember one spring when you were rather small youngsters and got infected with boils, supposedly in the shower baths at school. Dr. Jackson was kept on the run to and from our house, lancing boils on first one and then the other of you.[6] The notable time was when Geordie got a prosperous-looking one in the umbilical region, which made it out of the question to attempt to stand straight. The doctor surveyed the situation, and, as he cleaned the surrounding area, said, "Well, that is an inconvenient place to have a boil."

Soon it was lanced and started to drain. Then the doctor prepared to depart. All this time Bob, then only a little fellow, had been taking his turn as an observer. He stood around with a puzzled look on his face, and, as the doctor started down the stair, he stopped him by saying, "Say, Doc, where is there a convenient place to have a boil?" The doctor looked at me, shook his head, and walked downstairs, knowing that in all the lexicon of medical terminology there was no answer to that question. . . .

I, too, have had boils, and one in particular. Let me tell you about it, but first let me wipe off my brow the chill sweat that the recollection of the confounded thing causes. Also let me arise for a brief moment, just to make sure that it is not still there. . . . At the time I was working with a roundup on Bad River, of which my old friend George Jackson was foreman. Job, the prize pessimist of all time, who squawked worse than a Republican in a Democratic administration, was not justified in the calamity howling he shed forth, although it made him more famous as a squawker than Burton K. Wheeler.[7] Job really had little to complain about, for there is no record that he had to put in a twenty-hour day caressing with his boils the hard seat of a Gallup and Frazier saddle, on the backs of about five different jumping, dodging, running horses each day. Let me assure any anxious inquirers that the best place to have a boil is not between you and the seat of a cowboy saddle.

It was a long job to unlace and relace the stirrup straps on a cowboy saddle, and for months at a time there would be no change made in them when life ran the even boil-less tenor of its way. But during that ca-

MICK
B.
HARRISON

lamity, whenever the opportunity offered, my stirrup straps were laboriously unlaced and laboriously relaced again to offer a shorter stirrup.
After recurrent efforts, my stirrups were so short that I rode with that
boil pointing skyward, much after the fashion of a jockey who is trying
to boot the fifth horse into first place.

I had made a looking-glass survey, for every cowpuncher carried a
small mirror in the war sack in his bed. That boil, as can yet be attested
by other inspectors than myself, rested there (at the back and toward
the inner side where is the crease at the junction point of the right leg
with the right buttock) in its flaming beauty, about the size of half a
good-sized orange, but the smoothness of its surface contour was badly,
and painfully, marred by its nine heads pointing this way and that. Job!
What did he know about troubles? The bellyacher.

Should such a calamity sneak up behind me now and fasten itself to
my person, I would consult a physician, maybe two. Then would come
the advice, "You must be immobilized to prevent spread of infection. You
must go to bed and be sure not to move about at all. In order to insure
conformity to these instructions and to give you a fair chance to survive,
you must go to a hospital and get a special nurse. After consultation

locally, and by mail with the Mayo Clinic, we will determine whether surgery is indicated. How much money do you have? Have you any facilities for getting more?" . . .

Be all that as it may, the cowboy on the range could not be immobilized. He had to go along with the outfit. He had to ride something, either a horse or the bed wagon, to go along. There was no provision for care of casualties. If a man got killed by lightning or had a leg broken so he simply could not go, another man was dispatched on horseback to a ranch somewhere to borrow a spring wagon (or some wagon). He came back, picked up the casualty, and took him to town. That might be a long distance and a gruesome ride. Henry Hudson was so assigned at the time of the death of Bud Holcomb, who was killed on a roundup in the Badlands. After getting the wagon it was Henry's job to drive from down near Interior to Rapid City, about a hundred miles, and deliver the dead cattleman to his family.[8] But a boil, inconveniently located, could not be made to elicit even a decent percentage of the sympathetic attention it actually deserved.

My plight made itself known to the boss of the outfit, and he came riding up to me one day as we were working a roundup and asked what was the matter. With a brevity that would be a credit to the New Rules of Federal Procedure, in four words, the longest only four letters, I told him the exact nature of my ailment, with such a close approximation of its location that he at once had a very clear factual picture of the situation. He said, "You better go to camp because those things can be dangerous."

I said, "I don't want to go to camp. I have a lot of cattle to watch out for."

With a snort and a curse, each of them well within his capacity, George Jackson said, "Do you think you are the only fellow that knows the brands you represent? Don't you think there might be somebody else that can do that just as well as you? I said for you to go to camp. You can either do that, or you can pack your bed, cut your string, and get to hell out of here."

The boss was the boss, and I was repping with his outfit. I went to camp, which happened to be well up on Herd Camp Creek. Not long after my arrival in camp, as I lay really distressed and sick from my difficulty on a rolled out roundup bed in my tepee, George Jackson entered and made some pointed inquiries as to my ailment. He was a former Texan, with Missourian instincts, and had to be shown, for with him seeing was believing, and anything less than that failed of faith. Accordingly, as he sat on his heels in the flap of my tepee, my nether garments were farther lowered so the full effulgence of my boil flashed on his vision. To show that he was properly impressed, all one had to note was that he fell back into a sitting position as he luridly called on the Savior of mankind for witness. George Jackson was convinced.

Then followed his specific order that under no circumstances was I to get on a horse within a period of two weeks, and he warned that such a thing could easily poison a man to death. I was to ride on the bed wagon. Now that the order had come, it was really a relief to know that it was not going to be necessary to pound that particular thing all day long, and part of the night, on the hard seat of a stock saddle.

Next morning, when the bed rolls were piled on the bed wagon, I was helped up on top and lay there, face down in the beating sun, as we moved across rough country about ten miles to the next camp. That afternoon a similar ride, and again the next morning. Still that boil showed no inclination to relieve itself of any of its contents. A fellow under such circumstances has plenty of time to think, and his thinking is quite likely to be highly concentrated. Every kind of a remedy that he has ever heard is likely to be remembered and to have its possibilities assayed.

As we camped on Bad River that day and were not to make an afternoon move, I asked Hugh Schultz to stay in camp with me that afternoon, and we would see what could be done in the way of a remedy.[9] He did, and, being the type of a hand that was never much missed, no one said anything about it. After all the fellows were gone on circle, we began trying to evolve some effective medical plan, and we were quite dubious about the use of a knife. As luck would have it, Hugh's prayers for a bottle were answered when he found an empty quart whiskey bottle down by the creek. Now a remedy of which we had both heard could be applied.

Hugh and I soon got right down to the business in hand, which was the treatment of a nine-headed boil. One reason why the invitation to stay in off circle was sneaked to Hugh was that he was a gentle sort of soul, and one who would not be disposed to joke with the harrowed feelings incident to that sort of an ailment, nor seek to add further distress to an already agonizing and humiliating situation. After due inspection and thorough cleansing of the bottle, we were ready to test a remedy of which we had often heard but had never seen applied, which was sucking out a boil core with a bottle.

In a dumb sort of way, we understood the principle of it, which was to heat the bottle thoroughly by putting boiling water in it, pour out the water, and instantly apply the bottleneck over the head of the boil with sufficient firmness to prevent the admission of any air into the bottle. It was then held there until the heated, expanded air within the bottle began to cool and contract. As the cooling went on, a partial vacuum was created in the bottle, which of course sought to fill itself. The only available filling was the boil head in the neck of the bottle. As the air cooled and thereby reduced its own volume, the boil slowly (and, permit me to add, painfully) extended itself into the neck of the bottle. After a time, the pull of the vacuum in the bottle was greater than the resistance of the fevered, tortured skin enclosing the boil, and so "POP goes the weasel." Such was our theory.

After the proper measure of disrobing, my surgical field was laid bare to Hugh's inspection, and the bottle was prepared for application. Although the automobile manufacturers probably claim invention and development of the rear-view mirror, even then, before the days of automobiles, I too was able to make a careful survey of the field of operation in a rear-view mirror. Having borrowed from the cook a pot in which to heat our water, and a ladle with which to pour it, Hugh (gaily) and I (apprehensively) went down by the creek and lit our fire. As soon as the water was hot, we got at our job. With the bottle prepared, and the patient in due and proper position to receive it, Hugh firmly applied the neck of that bottle to the complete discomfort of his patient, who uttered many a fervent, muttered curse but kept physically still. Words of progress and encouragement came from Hugh, while it seemed to the patient that through a very definite part of his anatomy was being dragged a log chain, every other link of which had a hook in it. After a time, and not a short time, there seemed to be greatly increased vigor applied to the log chain, and soon Hugh announced the operation successful, for a boil core had been drawn.

Now the bottle must be washed and heated for another assault. Fortunately, the first had been a success, for not all of them were. The slightest relaxation of vigilant pressure on the part of Hugh or shrinking movement by the patient destroyed the forming vacuum by allowing air to enter the bottleneck. Persistent application of the remedy through a trying afternoon evacuated head after head until all nine were practically empty cells of former evil. It may have been a bit severe, but a remedy had been applied. Hugh was all worn out from the closeness of his application to his surgical duties. I didn't feel so good either, but it was a comfort to know that the pursuing demon that had attached itself to my person had been disemboweled.

An approach to a repetition of the experience, minus the horseback part, which could not be borne at all, would not be viewed with any sign of elation by me now. No, a self-indulgent softie would now get a hospital room, a doctor and a couple of nurses, knowing all the time that they would not be more effective than was Hugh with his empty, cooling whiskey bottle. Thus it was that a bottle, intended for man's delight (or maybe his destruction), was now transformed into an instrumentality of physical welfare.

The next day, unnoticed by George Jackson, I slipped out to the rope corral in the morning, caught my old –X [Bar X] sorrel saddle horse, and went on circle, a long ride. When we came in, George Jackson caught sight of me, and he gave me a bit of a range blessing.[10] I told him what Hugh and I had done to the boil. When I assured him in effect that an effort was being made to keep it antiseptic (neither one of us had ever heard the word then), no further mention was made of it, and I rode steadily with the others. Gradually my stirrups were lengthened to normal. Job was a piker.

That all happened back in the days of which Will Rogers said, "No one knew that grandma had legs, except grandpa and the family doctor." We didn't like to have embarrassing ailments advertised. Ben Sylva, whose beautiful sister Julia at that time was my polar star, was on that roundup. He knew all about my distress and told all about it to Julia just as soon as he got home from the roundup. Not so very long after that, as I was paying a visit to Julia and trying to make a good impression, along came Ben and, to my horror and chagrin, he said to me, "George, why don't you show Sis where your boil was?"

I would gladly have annihilated him on the spot, but Julia made some adroit comment that changed the subject. There are some things that a fellow wants to keep to himself, private as it were. Perhaps brothers have always been so.

Smallpox

Did you ever suffer from variola? No. Take my advice and escape it, for if you do become a victim of that devastating and loathsome infection, you will have smallpox. What we usually see depicted as the smooth, handsome and beatific face of George Washington was in reality the pock-marked, homely face of a wonderful human being, who was born near the beginning of the eighteenth century and died toward its close. In accordance with the accepted theory of his day toward the curse of smallpox, "Have it and get it over as soon as you can," Washington acquired the vile disease early in life on a visit to Barbados with his brother. An amazing percentage of the people in the world in the seventeenth and eighteenth centuries were survivors of the foul malady. Not until about three years before the death of George Washington did Dr. Jenner learn the effectiveness of cowpox in combating the plague-like evil of smallpox in human beings.[11]

How or where the accursed disease originated (probably somewhere in the Orient) we will leave to those who care to learn its source. It is sufficient for my purpose in this letter to know that in the Fort Pierre area, which in those days meant an area a hundred miles or so in radius west of the Missouri River centering at Fort Pierre and cut by the river on the east, in the winter of 1900-1901, there was an epidemic of small-pox, serious in type and unbelievably general throughout the area.[12] A large Indian population came within its sweep, with emphasis on the Cheyenne River Indian Reservation and especially in the Cherry Creek region. It is generally admitted by all, and assuredly without proof that I can furnish, that the dark-skinned races suffer worse in the assault of smallpox than do the fair-skinned people. Also, over the centuries of constant danger from the disease and frequent exposure to it, many races had built an ineffective sort of immunity to its ravages. Of course, too, from Jenner's day forward, vaccination played a prominent part in the combat.

Races without the partial immunity built by exposure over the ages, and wholly without the direct or indirect effects of vaccination, suffer incredibly in such an epidemic. So it was with the Cheyenne River Sioux Indians, dark-skinned and without any built-up immunity of any sort, when the smallpox broke loose among them during that winter. They died in families. It must be remembered that this was over forty years ago. Doctors were not considered as necessary then as now. The Indians still relied almost exclusively on their own medicine men, but their little dry rawhide sacks, with beans in them to rattle the evil spirits away, together with every amulet and talisman known to their trade, provided no defense at all against the smallpox. When that evil spirit took hold of family members, with its almost certainty of deadly effects, the Indians soon became so much the victims of their own panic that they would burn their little log houses, burning in them the dead and sometimes the dying. As they would flee their homes, they would take with them all the sick that could travel at all, thereby further spreading the contagion. I was not on the Cheyenne River Indian Reservation any time that winter, but while I worked for some time the next summer with the NSS outfit on a reservation roundup, Ed Lyman, the foreman, and others told me the story and showed the burned homes. It was a sad show. (Incidentally, it was on this roundup that Tommy McDonald and I took our horses on top of Rattlesnake Butte, but that has nothing to do with smallpox.)[13]

There are still those on earth who protest the value of vaccination for smallpox, and there were then. My uncle Scotty was not one of them. On one occasion, during the early winter, he sent word to me at our winter camp down near the mouth of Antelope Creek to be in Fort Pierre on a certain forenoon with a load of firewood. Not knowing nor caring the reasons for the specific instruction, I was on hand with the wood as directed. It then developed that the members of his family who had not previously been vaccinated were to be subjected to that precautionary measure that forenoon, and Dr. Ruble came over from Pierre for the purpose.

While Scotty was a realist in his own right, his two youngest children, Roderick and Annie, could talk him into or out of almost anything, and he knew it. Also, he was the last word in chicken-heartedness when it came to fear or suffering on the part of his children. It seemed, too, that little Annie, who could scarcely talk, had declared herself against any vaccination except in my presence.[14] Thus it came about that, not only was I present at the vaccination (and Scotty was not), but, in order to convince Annie of the validity of the procedure, it was required by her that I submit my arm to vaccination before hers. That was easy, and we were all quickly vaccinated. After lunch (dinner in those days), I started back for the winter camp, driving my team and riding the running gears of a wagon.

The vaccination took on all of Scotty's children, and none of them got the smallpox. It did not take on me, and I laid that to an immunity to vaccination and to smallpox, as well, due to a vaccination in early child-hood as shown by a well-defined scar. The books show many exceptions to the rule, and it is the rule that one attack of smallpox confers immu-nity from any recurrence. The same is true in greater measure of vacci-nation. Either is likely to reduce the number of vesicles, or pock spots, and to tone down the purulence of the pustules on the patient. There is no telling what the doctors may call it now, but in those days smallpox, in that somewhat modified form, was called varioloid.[15] It is doubtful if the symptoms of the approaching attack showed any modification, but its virulence after the onset differed.

Fortunately, coming events do not too much disturb our lives by cast-ing their shadows too far before. Let me explain our set up that winter. In my June 24, 1940, letter to you on "The Rooshian Wagon," explana-tion was made of the way we trailed the cattle in a three-days blizzard from Stony Butte Creek to the Fort George Bottom on the Missouri River for a turn-loose. Billy Hess, Fred Ervin, Posey and I stayed on and lived in a little log house on Antelope Creek, which Scotty had rented from Nick Hurst, a brother of my friend Bill Hurst, who had his own views on education, and of Charlie Hurst, who so hopefully looked for the Minnecadeuce. Al Martin, the cook, stayed on there to keep from riding grub line. With the rented log house went a log barn and small cow shed, corrals, and some prairie hay. There was a little water in Antelope Creek and plenty in the Missouri River about a mile and a half away.

It seems to me that Fred Ervin was gone for a while that winter, but he was back again in time for horse hunting. Knowing that we were in for intense work that spring, it was decided to do the saddle-horse hunting early. We knew we had to take a trail outfit and go down on the east side of the Missouri River to trail back from Wheeler, in Charles Mix County, a trainload of southern cattle that had been wrecked near there the year before and left there. We knew we had to take that herd back up through the farming country to a ranch in Buffalo County, near Gann Valley, and pick up several hundred head of cattle that had been wintered there and trail that whole herd to Pierre, there to ferry them across to the west side of the river, where we would drive them out on the range and turn them loose. We knew that we would have to make immediate return to Pierre to be on hand to receive, brand and care for about twelve thousand head of southern cattle that Scotty was shipping in. We knew that all that work would have to be fully completed before the general roundup commenced about May 15th or 20th. Later all that work was done on time, and a lot of it was a headache.

That was the reason it became necessary to gather the saddle horses early. Accordingly, in the early part of March, Billy Hess, Fred Ervin, and Posey took a couple of horses each and went off to the head of Bad River, a general distance of about a hundred twenty miles to the west, to look for the horses on their native range. Al Martin went to town to work. That left me to feed some calves and a hospital bunch and to get them daily to the Missouri River to water. About that time came Harry Read, a couple years younger than I, who was riding grub line. I was glad to have him stay for the company. He was glad to stay for the bed and board (I am informed that Harry is now living up near Faith).

A serio-comic incident occurred after the horse hunters had been gone a week or so. My work and Harry's (for the grub liner usually did some work too) was daytime work only, so we could do as we liked with our nights. It was just about twelve miles to Fort Pierre and there was to be a Masquerade Ball there on the 17th of March. Dick Curran and I had planned to go to the ball similarly masked, and he was to arrange for the costumes.[16] There was no general expectation that I would be in from the country, so my chance of disguise was fairly good. Accordingly, Harry and I rode to Fort Pierre, taking pains to see that we got there in the dark. Harry slipped both horses into Dan Powell's livery barn, while I sneaked my way to Curran's house and my costume. Harry then went to the dance and told the story we had agreed on, which was that I was lying down in the camp, sick with smallpox, and that a pock had broken out in my left eye, which caused more pain than all the rest.

Harry was a garrulous sort of chap, and he had made tremendous headway with his story before Dick and I showed up at the dance. The story completed the perfection of my disguise. No one suspected my presence. To my ears came many expressions of sympathy as to my plight down at the camp. Little did they know, as I knew, that I had been vaccinated and was immune from smallpox. It was a grand and glorious feeling for the whole evening. At midnight, the unmasking time, I got stationed close to my cousin Amy Philip. In her concern over my illness, she had long discarded all attempts to defy recognition in her mask as she talked freely with other maskers, most of whom were recognized as the evening wore on. At the unmasking, Amy looked toward me, her pity now changed to wrath as she smacked me hard, and said, "You old devil, you had me scared to death. Now I hope you get the smallpox." We had a lot of good laughs on Amy.

About two o'clock in the morning, mask off and riding gear on, I was on my horse on my way with Harry out to the camp. Arriving there about four in the morning, dark as the inside of a barrel, Harry and I turned our horses in the barn and went to get a couple hours of sleep. At about six I awakened, feeling miserable, went out to the barn, saddled my horse, threw out a little hay, and prepared to take the calves to the Missouri River for water. I got to feeling worse—and such a headache. Surely there never was another such headache. It still makes every bone in my head hurt. There was a raging fever, and, no matter what the doctors say, I was sweating at every pore.

There was no going on. There was no staying on a horse. I just got near the door on that horse and got off, making the rest of the way on my hands and knees into our hut and into my bed roll, unrolled on the dirt floor, without being sufficiently ceremonious even to take off my spurs. I mumbled to Harry to look after the livestock we had there. Although Harry gave me water to drink, I had nothing to eat during the bad spell. If there was any leaving of that bed until dark in the evening of the third day, it escaped me. There was no fear of death, but a decided longing for it. It still impresses me as being terrible.

With a bewildering suddenness, on the evening of the third day, I felt better. The headache had dwindled to a mild ache, which felt fine, and the fever subsided and may have gone completely. No one can ever know that. A sense of well-being came back, and hunger returned. I told Harry, who was by then in bed with me on the floor, that I was going to get a little something to eat. While I washed and fried some potatoes and bacon, dug up some cold biscuits and made some coffee, Harry told me how things had gone during my time of forgetfulness. Getting off my clothes, after eating a plentiful meal and washing my dishes, I crawled in alongside Harry. He told me of a deep snowstorm of that day, and soon we were asleep.

Not feeling too good, but realizing that a deep snow meant a ride, I had my breakfast and was gone about daylight in the morning. Probably about as real a case of fatigue as ever hampered my joints and muscles had settled itself down upon me by the time I came riding into that camp at dark that evening. I was really too tired to eat, and Harry put my horse away. Next morning I was quite refreshed and hungry. By this time some red spots on my forehead, a few on my cheeks, some on my body, and *one in my left eye* had appeared, but they never awakened the slightest suspicion in me. Besides, I smelled like something seined from the Chicago River. Crude though our facilities were, we could and did keep ourselves clean, so that was soon remedied.

Shortly after that, a couple of weeks or so, I was in Fort Pierre and dropped in for a little visit with my good friend Doc Lavery, not professionally, just socially. To his inquiry as to the state of my health, he got the answer that it had been fine. Then the recollection of that distressing experience prompted me to tell him I had been laid up for three days. Then he began inquiring into my symptoms, just as though he were reading them off, and he had every one correct, up to the cessation of the fever. Then the following conversation took place, almost, if not actually, verbatim:

"Then what did you do?"

"I got up and cooked me a good big meal."

"A meal of what?"

"Bacon, fried potatoes, biscuits and coffee."

"Then what?"

"Then I went to bed. Harry was already in bed."

"With you?"

"Sure. That was the only bed we had."

"Did he get sick?"

"No."

"What did you do the next day?"

"I got out before daylight and rode until dark in the snow."

"What did you do the next day?"

"I rode all day. I have ridden every day since then."

"Well. Isn't it a damn good thing that you don't have a sign of a brain in your head? If you had, you would be dead. You damn fool, you had smallpox."

Doc's irritation at my brainlessness soon passed, and then his professional interest compelled him to make examination of the nasty spots that remained, and particularly the one in my left eye. That confirmed his diagnosis. His failure to address me except with contumely on that occasion did not alter the fact that we were then, and ever since have been, good friends. (Some time I am going to ask some doctor if the terrific boil that Hugh Schultz worked on, as told earlier in this letter, may not have had its origin a couple of months earlier in that attack of smallpox.)

I may have been a poor patient, but I was hired to ride and not to lie around sick. I did the required riding.

Mumps

. . . Now the mumps, if not permitted to become too progressive and exploratory, are not so very painful. It does produce great disfigurement around the ears, jaws and neck. The greatest inconvenience lies in the effort to chew or swallow food or even drink. It sometimes does have other manifestations that are more inconveniencing, and indeed more painful, than the swelling about the head and neck.

The next winter after my experience with smallpox, for a time Billy Hess and I were holding forth in a small frame shack on the Missouri River Bottom, just below the upper Ree Indian Village, where afterwards was the buffalo pasture.[17] It was a flimsy shack without any basement or foundation—just put up on blocks set at the corners. The floorboards lacked a little, sometimes as much an inch, of coming together. Log houses were warm. Frame shacks were not comfortably warm in cold weather even when fairly put together, which was not so with that one. (By the way, that was the same shack that Fred Jones and I had occupied earlier that winter when my valor outran my discretion in telling him about the petrified birds.)[18]

That was where I got the mumps, and the entire crew at the time consisted of Billy Hess and me. It first started with a swelling near the right ear, quickly extending to the right jaw and neck. As if to balance incongruous disfigurement against incongruous disfigurement, the left side assumed the same proportions as the right to the intense merriment of Billy, whose sense of humor seemed to be extraordinarily distorted at the time. His laughter seemed as meaningless to me as that of the hyena or of that amazing Australian wonder bird, the laughing jackass. But he appeared to enjoy it.

After a day or two at effort to work, that was given up, and I retired to the comforts of my bed, which was a bedroll laid out on the rough cold floor and occupied jointly by Billy and me. In about five or six days, the head and neck had dwindled almost to their former size. That, however, did not quite spell the end of the mumps. The ailment was not content to attack and to disfigure temporarily the glands of the face and neck, but it seemed impelled to intrude its unwelcome presence into greater privacy. That gave great and greater play to Billy's orchitic humor. How could he come to have such a preposterous idea that you can cure an ailing human part and yet retain the swelling? It just does not sound reasonable.

The especial difficulty in getting around lasted for three or four days, and then [there was] rapid recovery. It is a gem of mild language to say that the disease called the mumps is a damned nuisance. Perhaps much more than that would be overstatement. I don't know. One cannot become an expert with one experience, although the parachute jumper has to be good the first time. . . .

It seems to me now that if one were intending to get the mumps for any reason, he could choose vastly better surroundings in which so to indulge himself than my haphazard, unwise choice. Although we were not unduly coddled in our ailments, and perhaps did not receive the acme of care, we seemed to get just as well as anybody. Neither did we regale others' ears with our ailments. We never enjoyed poor health.

Why this letter was ever written will defy solution, unless it be that news from the war zones is distressing.[19] That may be why my mind reverted to distress.

Affectionately,
Dad

Afterword by Richard W. Slatta

George Philip had the great good fortune to be a young man during the heyday of South Dakota's open-range cattle boom, the last in the nation. This exciting era witnessed huge influxes of cattle, horses, and people into the state's West River country (the area west of the Missouri River). Philip's candid and engrossing accounts of working on huge cattle roundups provide excellent details and insights into a period that existed but briefly both before and after his four years on the range. The disastrous winter of 1887 had set the stage for this last open-range era, which lasted until about 1908, a period sandwiched between two eras of much smaller ranches in South Dakota. The end date reflects adverse weather, the "Big Winter" of 1906–1907, when, as Ike Blasingame recalled, cattle drifted widely, "all of them starving, eating brush, willow sticks, anything that stuck up above the snow that buried everything for months."[1] In 1908, the government also opened western South Dakota reservation lands, which had been vital to the large open-range cattle ranchers, to white homesteaders. As historian Hazel Pulling put it: "By 1908 in South Dakota and 1904 in North Dakota, the free open range was no more. The small rancher, with a few straggling farmers, become the predominate feature of Dakota's vast cattle range."[2] The brief but exciting period that Philip recalls, with its immense cattle roundups and hundreds of cowboys, had lasted less than thirty years.

Ranching had developed gradually in southern Dakota Territory. The myth that the Great Plains were a "Great American Desert" had retarded early migration, but gradually firsthand knowledge replaced abstractions. By the 1860s, for example, road ranches had demonstrated that cattle could survive Great Plains winters. Early settlers, such as Hans Myron and his Norwegian immigrant parents, brought cattle into what is now Clay County in eastern South Dakota in 1859. The first territorial legislature, meeting in Yankton in March of 1862, passed a "Marks and Brands" law so that ranchers could register their brands for a modest fee, and many hoped that the grasslands of western Dakota Territory would soon be available to cattlemen. However, in 1868, the western half of what would become the state of South Dakota was set aside as the Great Sioux Reservation, which was to be held in reserve for the Lakota Indians. Meanwhile, the proliferation of military forts, with lucrative beef, horse, and cattle contracts, had generated markets for local ranchers in the eastern part of the territory. Nebraska beef initially supplied many Dakota forts, but local suppliers, sensing a great opportunity, quickly jumped in. High prices, eighteen to twenty dollars per head, and steady demand made for an inviting market, which included Forts Randall (1856), Sully (1863), Sisseton (1864), Bennett and Hale (1870).[3]

In western South Dakota, ranching began with the gold rush to the Black Hills, when many small stockmen established themselves in the region. During the mid-1870s, military and scientific expeditions into the Hills fueled national interest in both gold and pasture land. Expedition leaders George Armstrong Custer in 1874 and Richard I. Dodge in 1875 had praised the area's potential for ranching.[4] "The grass is splendid here," wrote Dodge. "As a grazing country it cannot be surpassed."[5] American Indians objected to the illegal invasion of white gold seekers and others into their territory, but government pressure led to the 1877 Sioux Agreement that opened the Black Hills to non-Indians. Soon, small cattle ranches occupied much of the grazing lands on the foothills to the east of the Black Hills, the bottomlands between the Cheyenne and Belle Fourche rivers, and much of what is today Fall River County. Cattle operators quickly noticed that the nutritious grasses and temperate climate of the northern ranges led cattle to grow bigger and more quickly than on southern ranges. The cattle also faced fewer diseases, such as black-leg or Texas fever.[6]

The herds grew gradually as cattle trails extended northward from Kansas and Texas. In 1876, brothers John, Dan, and Erasmus Deffenbach drove the first range cattle into western Dakota Territory from Wyoming and Nebraska and pastured them on the northern edge of the Black Hills. Joel Collins, a Texan, soon followed with a second herd. In 1878, Lank Forbes of Omaha moved a small herd of cattle to the Cheyenne River near Buffalo Gap in Custer County. W. B. Grimes augmented the Forbes herd a year later, raising the total to some eight hundred animals. The Shiner Brothers soon moved over twelve thousand cattle to graze east of the Grimes/Forbes herds. The establishment of Fort Meade (1878) in the northern Hills and the confinement of the Indians to the reservation offered lucrative new economic opportunities to these ranchers. To meet its treaty obligation of an allotment of 730 pounds of beef per capita per year on the reservation, the government also became a large purchaser of beef cattle, providing a handsome bonanza for local ranchers, some of whom were mixed white and Indian families based on the reservation itself. In 1880 alone, for example, the Rosebud and Pine Ridge Indian agencies purchased 12.5 million pounds of beef. According to census figures, the cattle population of Dakota Territory increased more than tenfold from 1870 (12,467 head) to 1880 (140,815).[7]

By 1887, overstocking, a parched summer, and the incredibly harsh winter of 1886–1887 brought huge livestock losses and economic disaster to many ranches in western Dakota. Harding County rancher W. H. Hamilton, who recalled the lack of strong spring rains in 1886, remarked that "it never rained a drop from the middle of June on." Blizzards next ravaged the region from November through March, driving many small outfits out of business. After this great "die-up" of 1886–1887, larger herds and larger ranches supplanted the small operations, as South Dakota became the scene of the nation's last big open-range cattle frontier. "Texas cattle began pouring in by the hundred thousand," Hamilton remembered. "The three-V, Hash-knife, B&B, 101, and Turkey-track, or E-6, were all running them in thick and fast, and they were eating everything they came to. . . . Things looked pretty black for small stockman."[8] The big drives brought in Longhorns from Texas, as well as eastern cattle, notably Shorthorns and Herefords. By 1900, South Dakota ranked ninth in the nation in cattle, with 933,000 head.[9]

The opening of Indian lands on the reservations created the big ranch boom. In 1889, the Great Sioux Reservation was subdivided into six smaller reservations: Standing Rock, Cheyenne River, Lower Brule, Pine Ridge, Rosebud, and, east of the Missouri River, Crow Creek. Nearly ten million acres of former reservation land came under federal control; much of the land was now available for leasing.[10] Writing in 1891, rancher Bruce Siberts summarized the attractiveness of using such public lands: "Borrow money at 10 percent, buy a few cows, and the herd will double every three years. . . . There was lots of grass in that 11,000,000-acre pasture taken from the Sioux in 1889, and there were very few settlers."[11] Will S. Hughes, who ranched with H. A. Dawson, quickly recognized the benefits of such leases: "Free grass, no income tax, no county tax, only a small state tax, no feed bills, small losses, open range from the reservation north to the state line and from the Black Hills to the Missouri River made it possible to build up the cattle numbers under this brand with just a foreman and one or two men, except during round-up time."[12]

By the mid-1890s, many large cattle outfits grazed tens of thousands of cattle, mostly on former reservation lands or leased reservation pastures. The "Turkey Track" (E6) Ranch ran as many as forty-five thousand cattle near Buffalo. The Hash Knife Ranch reached sixty-eight thousand head. G. E. ("Ed") Lemmon and associates leased 865,000 acres on the Standing Rock Indian Reservation, and in Old Stanley County, James ("Scotty") Philip presided over sizable herds of up to twenty thousand head for the "73 Outfit" (Minnesota and Dakota Cattle Company), as well as his own L-7 brand. In 1897, with Ed Lemmon as "boss," five roundups, including fifteen wagons and crews, gathered about forty-five thousand head of cattle on a wide tableland at the head of Bad River.[13] According to cowboy Fred Quinn, the roundup the next year "had 14 chuck wagons, and over 300 cowboys."[14] In 1902, the federal government levied a dollar-per-head fee for cattle grazing on what remained Indian-controlled land, precipitating a large roundup and movement of white-owned cattle off the reservations proper. The massive 1902 West River roundup on the Rosebud and Pine Ridge reservations became a fabled chapter in state history. Some who worked it insisted that it was "the biggest roundup anywhere, at any time."[15]

Into this heady mix of opportunity and adventure rode young George Philip in 1899. Within the large body of autobiographies, letters, and memoirs of cowboy life, George Philip's recollections rank among the best.[16] When I read frontier diaries, memoirs, interviews, or letters, I look for three things. First, I seek out the familiar—events, terms, people, places, attitudes that I recognize from prior research. Second, I look for the novel, the unusual—things that I have not encountered before and that therefore teach me more about ranch life. Third, I look for cowboy humor. George Philip's memoirs satisfy all three elements, thereby entertaining and enlightening the reader on every page. His depiction of range life rings clear and true, even though he wrote nearly four decades after the events took place. Given that he wrote these letters to his children, his candor is especially commendable. Unlike some "tall tale memoirs," he does not paint himself as some larger-than-life frontier hero, nor does he omit unsavory details. In fact, in many instances, Philip consciously debunks western mythology and sets the record straight.

Clear-eyed realism suffuses the Philip letters. He accurately explains the main jobs that cowboys performed: rounding up horses and cattle, branding, and working as a rep, nighthawk, or night guard. His unromanticized vision leads him to affirm that cowboys were "sweaty, dirty, tired, often sleepy, and sometimes frightened young men, who worked dreadfully long hours at times and in every sort of weather."[17] We can gauge the accuracy of his account by comparing it with that of other credible witnesses of the time. Some of his letters recount events that may sound like tall tales to anyone who has not lived on the northern ranges. Philip observed "Saint Elmo's fire" or "balls of fire" (also called foxfire) dancing across the horns of cattle at night. He also witnessed the impressive displays of the aurora borealis, or northern lights. Huge dens of rattlesnakes might seem implausible to the outsider, but many other observers, including W. H. Hamilton, described the same phenomenon. Roping and castrating old bull bison and hauling bison south to fight Mexican bulls sound equally improbable, but these bizarre occurrences actually happened.[18]

The mundane realities of life on the range come to life in these letters, as well. Philip numbered himself among the unlucky cowboys who suffered the "Texas itch," a painful condition that left him "scratching until the blood came." A boil on the wrong part of the anatomy could keep a cowhand out of the saddle for extended periods. Trying to travel through viscous gumbo mud turned Philip and his companions into "a quartet of water-soaked mud-plastered derelicts."[19] Many other sources corroborate the near impossibility of traveling through rain-soaked gumbo.[20]

Philip sets the record straight on a number of cherished fantasies and myths about range life. First, cowboys did not ride about armed to the teeth with a six-shooter or two, like some wild killers run amok. Handguns and ammunition belts, heavy and dangerous, had no place on the range, according to Philip, except "when riding in an area frequented by a bad, or attacking, stallion."[21] Most cowboys made poor marksmen, the famed deadly accuracy of the gunfighter being the exception. Contrary to popular notions of the cowboy, he seldom had the time or opportunity for religious worship. "This day was a Sunday," noted Philip, "which made no difference on the range." Horses and cattle did not observe a day of rest, and neither could the cowboy.[22]

Nor did most cowboys abstain from earthly pleasures, including gambling, tobacco, and alcohol. On generous consumption of alcohol, Philip corroborates candid accounts by others, including Bruce Siberts, who arrived in Dakota in 1890, and Ike Blasingame. In fact, Blasingame recounts how Murdo McKenzie, owner of the huge Matador Ranch, fired many cowboys, including his son and foreman Dode, for "staying drunk all fall" and thus neglecting their duties.[23] While remarkably complete and honest in his portrait of cowboy life, Philip did fail to broach another touchy topic, prostitution. Perhaps he made no such social calls during his cowboying years. In any case, the omission is understandable, given that he wrote these letters to his children. Other sources, however, including books by Blasingame and Edward Charles ("Teddy Blue") Abbott and newspaper accounts, attest to cowboy visitations with the "soiled doves" of the plains.[24]

The cowboy's peculiar and delightful sense of humor ran the gamut from pranks to tall tales to vulgar songs and poems. Cowboy Ed Lemmon put the matter succinctly: "I think it must've been born in cowboys to like a good joke."[25] Humor comes through clearly in Philip's letters, but in all cases, Philip distinguishes actual events from the windies, or tall tales, that cowboys loved to share. Putting one over on a companion represented great fun to cowhands, and Philip tells tales from both sides of the equation—both as the kidder in the petrified birds story and as the butt of the joke in "Working up an Appetite." For all the humor of Philip's final letter, however, the topic of range ailments stressed the hardships and the fleeting nature of the cowboy life on the open range. In fact, all Philip's letters foreshadow the change that had been coming on the open range even since its beginning.

Starting in the mid-1880s and coinciding with the open-range era, western South Dakota had been experiencing huge demographic, economic, and social changes. The disappearance of the immense herds of bison that had been purposely hunted to near-extinction and the shrinking of the reservations had freed up the Dakota prairies to other uses. Newcomers, such as the cattlemen, but also European immigrant farmers, had begun to adapt their social and work lives to the new plains environment. Farmers had learned to use new technologies, such as the John Deere plow, essential to breaking the tough sod of the virgin prairie, and Cyrus McCormick's self-binding reaper to harvest crops on the prairies and plains. The beef bonanza soon faltered in the face of growing numbers of farmers with political clout and barbed wire fences. As early as 1885, Dakota homesteaders pushed successfully for legislation that required cattlemen to fence their herds or pay for crop damages.[26] George Philip himself acquired painful experience with fences in "Mostly 'Cross County."

The Newlands Reclamation Act of 1902 further enticed farmers to relatively arid parts of the West by allowing them to irrigate their homesteads with water from federal reclamation reservoirs. Indian ranchers also lost ground to government policies. The Dawes Severalty, or General Allotment, Act of 1887, which had paved the way for the opening of the Great Sioux Reservation, had been ostensibly intended to convert reservation lands to individual Indian ownership by giving each person in the tribe an allotment of land, but it often ended up delivering more lands into white hands. Allotments of 160 acres to individual Indians proved woefully inadequate for sustainable agriculture or ranching. Reservation leaders and individuals often had to lease grazing lands to whites in order to generate income. Some Indians ended up working as cowboys for white ranchers instead of working their own herds.[27]

Between 1900 and 1910, more than one hundred thousand people used the 1862 Homestead Act and related legislation to gain lands in western South Dakota.[28] In 1908 when Mabel Stewart Worsley's family and some four thousand others homesteaded in Tripp County on lands made available from the Rosebud reservation, she remembered that cattle and crops did not mix. Cattle, frightened by an unwise blast from a farmer's shotgun, stampeded through their farm. "Their hooves made a regular roar, and their long horns were crashing too," she recalled. "They came through our potato patch and just missed the house. Some hit it hard enough to jar us up good."[29] Government actions that had once delivered lands to ranchers had also lured competing homesteaders and land speculators. In the end, farmers won the demographic and political tussle, bringing an end of open-range ranching. As Philip noted in his 14 January 1941 letter, "The homesteader movement turned everything topsy-turvy and even put the precious buffalo grass under, instead of over, the sod."

Other forces had also combined to end the open range and the cowboy's heyday. Beginning in the late 1870s, the expansion of railroads across the northern plains facilitated the movement of cattle, but also people. The Chicago & North Western Railroad reached Pierre in 1880 and Rapid City six years later.[30] Earl Martin wrote from Rapid City in 1908, "Every train has been bringing in scores of home steaders."[31] By 1911, the state had 4,420 miles of track. Belle Fourche, Evarts, and Le-Beau became major shipping points for cattle. Increasingly, ranchers put up hay, adding a new task to ranch work. Barbed wire encircled the cattle, and windmills or artesian wells brought them water, so cowboys no longer had to scour the open range locating and driving cattle from place to place. Fencing also permitted selective breeding, thus increasing the value of each animal. Cattle increasingly moved from place to place in railroad boxcars or trucks, some destined for faraway, fast-growing European markets.[32] A new era of smaller ranches had begun.

Despite the hardships, injuries, adverse weather, and financial setbacks of any size of ranching operation, the overwhelming majority of people involved would do it all over again. For many, like Philip, cowboying represented only a short interlude in life. For others, ranch work lasted a lifetime. Writer and rancher Linda M. Hasselstrom, whose grandfather homesteaded in western South Dakota in 1899, well captured the allure. "For me, ranch life was like slipping my foot into a perfectly fitting soft boot smelling of oil and good leather."[33] George Philip likewise reveled in his brief but memorable years on the open range. We all owe him a debt of gratitude for sharing his experiences with us.

APPENDIX

Roundup Program for 1901

As a sample of what the organization of the general, or spring, roundup meant, let me quote the plan adopted for the 1901 spring roundup, for which I am indebted to C. I. Leedy of Rapid City, who preserved an original copy:

ROUNDUP PROGRAM FOR 1901

No. 10. Lower Belle Fourche.—The roundup begins May 15th, at Bad Land Springs; thence to Timber Creek; then down the Cheyenne River to reservation line, circling south side; then across to Sulphur and up to mouth of Red Owl; thence up Red Owl to White Owl; then up White Owl to White Owl post office; then across to head of Bad Land Creek to roundup road; then follow roundup road to Elm Creek; then up Elm Creek to Shingle's ranch. Then roundup to divide, Sulphur division to cross over to head of Sulphur and down Sulphur to Brushy; then to Red Scaffold, Rattlesnake and Bear creeks; then to Morrow, at mouth of Thunder Butte Creek. Then roundup to again divide, one division working up Moreau to forks of Sand Creek; the other division to work Irish, Thunder Butte and Rabbit creeks to Slim Buttes; then Antelope Creek; then Sheep Creek and north Moreau to head; then Sand Creek to forks, joining other division; then work together to head of Moreau. Belle Fourche division to work Belle Fourche tributaries and Battle Creek to Miles City crossing. Foremen of respective ranges to act as roundup foremen.

No. 11. Roundup to begin May 17th at Dan Shine's ranch. Thence across to Viewfield, working Elk Creek divide and mouth of Alkali, joining No. 10 at Hay draw. Joe Irwin, Roundup Foreman

No. 12. This will be a continuation of the Lower Belle Fourche roundup, beginning at McQuillian's ranch on Alkali, and working up south side of Belle Fourche River to Minnesela.

No. 16. Box Elder Roundup. Will commence May 15th, at head of Box Elder, working down the creek to the mouth; thence up the Little Missouri to the Holben ranch, including Willow and Thompson creeks. Al. Taddiken, Foreman.

No. 17. Sandstone and Fallon Roundup. Commence May 15th at TD ranch, working back up Fallon to its head, working all its tributaries; thence to a point twenty or thirty miles below the mouth of Beaver Creek on the Little Missouri, working back up the Little Missouri and all its tributaries. Bob Devine, Foreman

No. [18.] Upper Cheyenne River. Begin at Hermosa, June 15. Work south to the Z Bell ranch; then down the Cheyenne River to Sage Creek; then working Cheyenne tributaries to Hermosa. Adolph Fiesler, Foreman

No. [19.] Indian Creek Roundup, commencing May 20th, at Hat Creek store, work down Indian Creek and tributaries; down Hat Creek to - -T ranch; thence west to Cottonwood; thence south of Cheyenne River to Moss Agate; thence west to mouth of Lance Creek, and up Lance Creek as far as necessary. Jas. Bell, Foreman

No. 1. Roundup to commence May 25th, at American Creek; thence to Oacoma; thence down Missouri to mouth of White River, then up White River to forks of White River, there meeting Willard Franklin's wagon; then to White Clay Buttes; then down Yellow Medicine to Missouri River; thence up Missouri to mouth of Cedar; thence up Cedar and down Antelope to Missouri; up Missouri to mouth of Bad River; then up Bad River till meeting 73 wagon.

[No. 2.] Franklin's wagon commencing work at east end of Rosebud reservation, working all of said reservation to forks of White River, meeting No. 1.

No. 3. Beginning work May 25th, on Cut Meat District, at Eagleman's working up to head of Cut Meat Creek; thence to Ironwood Creek; thence to Little White River, working both sides to mouth of Cut Meat Creek, up Cut Meat, working both sides to mouth of Grey Eagletail, working up said creek to Redleaf camp on Black Pipe; then joining Sullivan's wagon, working down both sides of Black Pipe to mouth; thence to Tom Larvie springs; thence to head of Cottonwood Creek; thence to Pine Creek school, there joining Robinson's wagon, working back to mouth of Cut Meat, working down both sides of Little White River to mouth, meeting Franklin's wagon at forks; thence up Big White river to Bartlett's ranch on White Willow. D. W. Thode, Foreman

No. 4. Will be a continuation of No. 3, work up White River from head of Willow Creek to head of Dave Creek. I. J. M. Brown, Foreman

No. 5. Begin at White Willow, after No. 3 reaches there, working all the range between the wall and forks of Bad River; then west to mouth of Sage Creek on Cheyenne River; then down Cheyenne to east fork of Deep Creek. Willard Franklin, Foreman

No. 6. Begin at forks of Bad River after No. 5 reaches there, working down Bad River till meeting No. 1; then north to Burnt Creek, at Black Hills road crossing; then west to east fork of Deep Creek, working all the range between Cheyenne River divide and Bad River. Jack Borden, Foreman

No. 7. Begin on east fork of Deep Creek after No. 6 reaches there and work east on south side of Cheyenne River to Leslie. Henry Hudson, Foreman

No. — Southern Black Hills roundup, to begin work at Edgemont, June 10, work up Red Canon and on to and around Custer; thence back by way of Bradleys Flatts taking in all of the southern Hills and meet Cheyenne River roundup at Sidney Crossing on Horsehead, June 20; thence proceed south as previous seasons, working Dry Creek, Lang Hollow and head of Horsehead. C. B. West, Foreman

NOTES

Introduction

1. George Philip to his children, 25 Dec. 1936, George Philip Letters, Philip Family Collection. All preceding direct quotations come from this letter.

2. George Philip, "James ('Scotty') Philip, 1858–1911," *South Dakota Historical Review* 1 (Oct. 1935): 5–47; "Dakota Images: James ('Scotty') Philip," *South Dakota History* 16 (Spring 1986): 88/back cover. For more on Scotty Philip, *see* Wayne C. Lee, *Scotty Philip, the Man Who Saved the Buffalo* (Caldwell, Idaho: Caxton Printers, 1975), and James M. Robinson, *West from Fort Pierre: The Wild World of James (Scotty) Philip* (Los Angeles: Westernlore Press, 1974).

3. Quoted in *Rapid City Daily Journal*, 15 Mar. 1948.

4. Ibid.; Philip to his children, 4 Mar. 1937.

5. For more on Great Plains cowboys in the era of the open range, *see* Richard W. Slatta, "Long Horns and Low Pay: Cowboy Life on the Northern Plains," *South Dakota History* 32 (Fall 2002): 194–216.

6. Philip to his children, 4 Mar. 1937, 1, 24 June 1940.

7. Ibid., 1 June 1940.

8. *See South Dakota Historical Review* 2 (Jan. 1937): 51–72, and Bert L. Hall, comp., *Roundup Years: Old Muddy to Black Hills*, Centennial ed. (Winner, S.Dak.: Western South Dakota Buck-a-roos, 2000), pp. 123–32. Copies of the unedited letters and related materials are available both at the State Archives, South Dakota State Historical Society, Pierre, and in the Richardson Archives, University of South Dakota, Vermillion.

9. *Rapid City Daily Journal*, 16 Mar. 1948.

1. The Open Range

1. California pants are described in *Western Words: A Dictionary of the Old West* (New York: Hippocrene Books, 1998) as "a style of pants used on the range, usually of striped or checked heavy wool of excellent double weave" (p. 27). Rancher Faye Longbrake noted, "They were dressy looking pants" (Longbrake to Cathie Draine, 11 May 2006).

2. *See* George Philip to his children, 16 July 1940.

3. Badger Clark, *Grass-Grown Trails* (Boston: Richard G. Badger, 1917), pp. 58–59.

4. A familiar patent medicine, Dr. Hostetter's Celebrated Stomach Bitters

was developed in Pennsylvania in 1853 by Dr. Joseph Hostetter and made popular by his son David. The concoction contained up to 44 percent alcohol. "Dr. Hostetter's Stomach Bitters," *California State Parks*, www.parks.ca.gov/default.asp? page_id=22424, accessed 10/20/06; "Drunkenness: Temperance Drinks?," *Digger Odell Publications*, www.bottlebooks.com/temperance/temperance.htm, accessed 10/20/06.

5. Robert W. Stewart, an Iowa native, began his law practice in Pierre in 1889 and was a state senator in 1898 and 1899. He developed a reputation as a competent attorney and moved to Chicago in 1907 to serve as western counsel for the Standard Oil Company. Stewart joined the company's board of directors in 1915 and was elected chairman in 1918. He rode with Grigsby's Rough Riders (Cowboys) during the Spanish-American War and attained the rank of colonel in the South Dakota National Guard. Paul H. Giddens, *Standard Oil Company (Indiana): Oil Pioneer of the Middle West* (New York: Appleton-Century-Crofts, 1955), pp. 103, 210; *Memorial and Biographical Record and Illustrated Compendium of Biography . . . of Central South Dakota* (Chicago: Geo. A. Ogle & Co., 1899), p. 315–16; *Christian Science Monitor*, 13 Apr. 1923. Captain Joseph B. Binder, who may or may not have been a riverboat captain, was a partner in the cattle business with Scotty Philip. He also owned a hardware store and was mayor of Pierre from 1918 to 1924. Harold H. Schuler, *Pierre since 1910* ([Pierre, S.Dak.]: By the Author, 1998), p. 267; James M. Robinson, *West from Fort Pierre: The Wild World of James (Scotty) Philip* (Los Angeles: Westernlore Press, 1974), p. 114.

6. Jack Borden was foreman of the 73 outfit. His daughter Ruth married Scotty Philip's youngest son, Roderick. Faye Longbrake to Cathie Draine, 11 Dec. 2005; Wayne C. Lee, *Scotty Philip, the Man Who Saved the Buffalo* (Caldwell, Idaho: Caxton Printers, 1975), p. 189. Alligator's reputation as an ill-tempered, dangerous horse was widepread, although stories suggest that both John ("Slim") Taggert and African-American cowboy Bunk White could master him. Slim Taggert, a Nebraska native, was also known as "73" Slim for his work with the 73 outfit. He married Louise Swarthout of Fort Pierre and after his cowboying days opened the 73 Saloon in the town of Philip. Clara Roseth, ed., *Prairie Progress in West Central South Dakota* (n.p.: Historical Society of Old Stanley County, 1968), p. 46. *See also* Bert L. Hall, comp., *Roundup Years: Old Muddy to Black Hills*, Centennial ed. (Winner, S.Dak.: Western South Dakota Buck-a-roos, 2000), pp. 252, 487.

7. Cyrus Hiett, mentioned frequently in these letters, was a native Minnesotan who had homesteaded on the Cheyenne River in the mid-1890s. He worked as a cowboy and rancher well into his seventies. *See* Hall, *Roundup Years*, pp. 296–97.

8. Cowboy Pete Ashley's D P sorrel may have been one of Dan Powell's horses. Powell and Scotty, friends and neighbors, had as young men been hired as gov-

ernment cowboys to trail cattle herds from Fort Robinson, Nebraska, to the Rosebud Indian Reservation. Longbrake to Draine, 11 Dec. 2005; Roseth, *Prairie Progress in West Central South Dakota*, p. 495.

9. This phrase was first uttered during World War I by Captain Charles E. Stanton at Lafayette's gravesite in the cemetery at Picpus in Paris, France, on 4 July 1917. "In their own Words," *World War I Trenches on the Web: An Internet History of the Great War*, www.worldwar1.com/dbc/ow_3.htm, accessed 2/24/06. The stratosphere flights were manned balloon flights that took place in 1934 and 1935 from a site eleven miles south of Rapid City. The balloon *Explorer II* and its United States Army Air Corps pilots set a world altitude record (13.7 miles) and paved the way for manned space flight. Gene Bauer, "On the Edge of Space: The Explorer Expeditions of 1934–1935," *South Dakota History* 12 (Spring 1982): 1–16.

10. Philip is referring back to Badger Clark's poem "The Passing of the Trail," which he quoted at the beginning of this letter.

11. In western South Dakota, these three partners are commonly known as the black-footed prairie dog (a member of the squirrel family), the burrowing owl, and the prairie (western) rattlesnake. For more information on plains wildlife, *see* Paul A. Johnsgard, *Great Wildlife of the Great Plains* (Lawrence: University Press of Kansas, 2003).

12. For a classic cowboy encounter with rattlesnakes denning up, *see* Philip to his children, 24 Aug. 1939.

13. Robert Philip's typewritten copy of this letter contains this handwritten note from his father:

This was written in the third person to you in the form of a letter, intended for the eyes of my children, and for no others. The real purpose was to give each of you the true story of the trip, inasmuch as so many fakers had been writing it up and claiming personal participation in the events of which they wrote, and which bore no similarity to the plain facts. Then, as you know, the State Historical Society got it, and published it in pamphlet form. It is put in here just for compactness of telling.

The South Dakota State Historical Society first printed the story as "South Dakota Buffaloes versus Mexican Bulls" in its quarterly magazine *South Dakota Historical Review* in January 1937. It was reprinted under the same title in *South Dakota Historical Collections* 20 (1940): 409–34. The third-person narrative style of this section is different from all Philip's other letters to his children, and how and when it was originally drafted is unknown, but clearly it was earlier than Christmas 1936 and the other letters in this series.

14. For more on the Scotty Philip buffalo herd and Bob Yokum's experiences training buffalo, *see* Lee, *Scotty Philip*, pp. 269–76. Bob Yokum's obituary in *West*

River Progress (Dupree, S.Dak.), 2 Feb. 1939, recalls that he had tamed a pair of buffalos that he drove around, "creating nothing less than a sensation, of course." Yokum, born in California in 1861, moved from frontier to frontier throughout his long life. He spent many years in early Fort Pierre and Dupree before moving to Wyoming to work in law enforcement.

15. Benito Juarez (1806–1892), a Zapoteco Indian, was president of Mexico from 1861 until French troops put Archduke Maximilian of Austria into power in 1864. In 1867, Juarez was reelected president, serving until his death in 1872. "History of Benito Juarez," *Mexonline.com*, www.mexonline.com/benitojuarez, accessed 11/08/06; "Benito Juárez," *Wikipedia, the Free Encyclopedia*, en.wikipedia.org/wiki/Benito_Ju%C3%Alrez, accessed 11/08/06.

16. According to his obituary, Eb Jones "was one of the few native born South Dakotans who came West to be a cowboy." He was born in Union County in the southeastern corner of the state. From age fifteen, he cowboyed in South Dakota, Wyoming, and Montana until the end of the open range, when he started a ranch near the town of Dupree in Ziebach County. *Ziebach County News*, 23 Feb. 1939. In the months before his death, Jones's memoirs ran as a series entitled "The Cowboy as He Was" in the *Ziebach County News*, 29 Dec. 1938–19 Jan. 1939.

17. Kansas law had prohibited liquor and saloons since the 1880s, but officials did not always enforce the prohibition. "Carrynationitis" is a reference to Carry Nation of Medicine Lodge, Kansas, who as a proactive temperance supporter attacked Kansas saloons with a hatchet in an attempt to get the owners to close down. Howard R. Lamar, ed., *The New Encyclopedia of the American West* (New Haven, Conn.: Yale University Press, 1998), p. 760. Saloon proprietor Bob Yokum had made sure that the party "left Pierre in a cab with a suitcase stocked full with the best brands of whiskey that Bob's saloon could procure" (*West River Progress*, 2 Feb. 1939). Philip, the lawyer, observes that this liquor remained "in the original packages," which is a reference to an 1890 United States Supreme Court ruling that allowed liquor to be transported across state lines—even those of prohibition states—if the original packaging was not removed or broken. *Aberdeen Saturday Pioneer*, 17 May 1890.

18. In freemasonry, the organization that confers degrees of the Ancient and Accepted Scottish Rite is officially known as the Consistory of Sublime Princes of the Royal Secret.

19. Jack Dempsey defeated Argentina's Luis Firpo, known as the "Wild Bull of the Pampas," by a knockout in a heavyweight championship fight at the Polo Grounds in New York City on 14 September 1932. "Enshrinees," *International Boxing Hall of Fame*, www.ibhof.com/dempsey.htm, accessed 11/22/06.

20. John Wesley Hardin (1853–1895), one of the Wild West's deadliest out-

law gunslingers, reputedly killed over twenty people. Lamar, *New Encyclopedia*, p. 468.

21. President Theodore Roosevelt appointed Thomas D. Edwards as consul to Juarez, Mexico, in 1905. Edwards came to the Black Hills of South Dakota in 1877, ran the first post office in Lead, and eventually became editor of the *Lead Tribune* for many years. After Edwards's stint in Mexico, Woodrow Wilson appointed him to a consulate in Canada, but ill health caused an early retirement. *Lead Daily Call*, 5 Aug. 1935.

22. President Roosevelt nominated Patrick Floyd Garrett to the position of customs collector at El Paso after obtaining a promise that Garrett would "abstain from the use of intoxicating liquors" during his term of office. Garrett was confirmed on 6 January 1902. President Roosevelt refused to reappoint him to the post in 1905 after Garrett introduced his friend Tom Powers to him as a cattleman when he was, in fact, a notorious gambler. The Coney Island Saloon was a well-known and infamous gathering place for many men of dubious reputation, but it is unlikely that Garrett was any longer visiting the place frequently after his dismissal as customs officer. Antonio Perez, Angel Villalobos, and Jeremiah J. Miranda, "Pat Garrett Enjoyed Controversy," *Borderlands: An El Paso Community College Local History Project*, www.epcc.edu/nwlibrary/borderlands/20 _garrett.htm, accessed 2/24/06. Tobe Driskill, Texas herder, and a group of cowboys tangled with Wyatt Earp in Dodge City in 1878. Beth Gibson, "Wyatt Earp," *AOL Hometown*, members.aol.com/Gibson0817/wearp.htm, accessed 2/24/06; Lamar, *New Encyclopedia*, pp. 326–27, 421. Robert Green Ingersoll (1833–1899), lawyer, political leader, and popular orator, was best known for his defense of agnosticism. "Robert G. Ingersoll," *Wikipedia*, en.wikipedia.org/wiki/Robert_ G._Ingersoll, accessed 2/24/06. For more on the life and times of Garrett, *see* Leon C. Metz, *Pat Garrett: The Story of a Western Lawman* (Norman: University of Oklahoma Press, 1974).

23. This line appears in Robert Burns's "To a Mouse, on Turning up Her Nest with the Plough, November, 1785," in *Seven Centuries of Verse, English and American, from the Early English Lyrics to the Present Day*, ed. A. J. M. Smith (New York: Charles Scribner's Sons, 1947), p. 276.

24. James McGarry's drugstore was in the town of Fort Pierre, where John W. Dickey was listed as physician in the 1910 federal census. U.S., Department of Commerce, Bureau of the Census, *Thirteenth Census of the United States, 1910*, Fort Pierre, Stanley County, S.Dak., in *AncestryLibrary.com* (subscription required). Dr. V. H. Ruble, a highly respected member of the Pierre community, graduated from the Bellevue Medical College of New York City in 1887. *Memorial and Biographical Record*, p. 610.

25. Clara, Scotty and Sally Philip's fifth child, had been born in 1888. She would have been about twelve years old. Lee, *Scotty Philip*, p. 160.

26. The Fort Pierre to Deadwood trail was a freighting route between the end of the railhead in Pierre and the Black Hills, plied by oxen-drawn wagons that left lasting ruts in the plains landscape. The 1877 agreement between the western Sioux, or Lakotas, and the United States government had allowed this corridor across what was then the Great Sioux Indian Reservation. Bob Lee, "It Started with a (Mining) Boom," *South Dakota History* 31 (Fall/Winter 2001): 273–74.

27. Louis ("Posey") Moran was Scotty Philip's stepson, the only child of Sally Philip's first marriage. Lee, *Scotty Philip*, pp. 249, 323n.9. For more about Bill Hess and Hugh Burgess, *see* Philip to his children, 24 Aug. 1939.

28. The Duprees were a ranching family similar to the Philip family. Fred Dupree, a French-Canadian trapper, married a Lakota Indian woman, and they and their children ranched from allotments on the Cheyenne River Indian Reservation. The Dupree and Philip families were friends and ran their cattle together on the open range between the Bad and Cheyenne rivers. Fred's children included his son Peter Dupree and his daughter Marcella, who married stockman Douglas L. Carlin in one of the range's biggest social events of the 1880s. In the early 1880s, Pete Dupree had taken in five buffalo calves after the last buffalo hunt along the Grand and Cheyenne rivers and nurtured them on the open range into a herd of fifty-seven animals by 1901, when they were sold to Scotty Philip. Robinson, *West from Fort Pierre*, pp. 74, 124–26; Lee, *Scotty Philip*, pp. 156–57; Doane Robinson, *History of South Dakota*, 2 vols. (n.p.: B. F. Bowen & Co., 1904), 2:1764–65. The 1900 federal census lists Paul Clogenson as a native of France who was working as a herder for Doug Carlin. *Twelfth Census, 1900*, Ziebach County.

29. For the story of the homesteaders in the region that was once the open range in South Dakota, *see* Paula M. Nelson's *After the West Was Won: Homesteaders and Town-Builders in Western South Dakota, 1900–1917* (Iowa City: University of Iowa Press, 1986).

2. A Few Days on the Range

1. Because the Philip and Dupree families ran their cattle together, the leasing or grazing arrangements were probably made through the Dupree family, whose members were affiliated with the Cheyenne River Indian Reservation. James M. Robinson, *West from Fort Pierre: The Wild World of James (Scotty) Philip* (Los Angeles: Westernlore Press, 1974), p. 74.

2. A Scotsman, George Philip knew the poetry of his fellow countryman

Robert Burns and the poem "Tam O'Shanter," which can be found in *Seven Centuries of Verse, English and American, from the Early English Lyrics to the Present Day*, ed. A. J. M. Smith (New York: Charles Scribner's Sons, 1947), pp. 279–85. In the poem, a drunken farmer runs afoul of a witch, a misadventure for which his horse pays the price.

3. By 1939, cowboy Hugh Burgess had moved to Rapid City, where he worked as a railway engineer. Bert L. Hall, comp., *Roundup Years: Old Muddy to Black Hills*, Centennial ed. (Winner, S.Dak.: Western South Dakota Buck-a-roos, 2000), p. 558.

4. The Frenchman Joseph Langlois had been a scout with George A. Custer in Kansas. He married Zoeie Kensler, who was part American Indian, and settled on the Cheyenne River reservation, where he ranched and raised a large family. Quill Ewing, who married Langlois's daughter Louise, was wagon boss for cattleman Narcisse Narcelle. J. W. ("Jim") Harrell, a well-educated Texas native who came north with the big herds, started a ranch near Lantry, South Dakota, after his cowboying days on the open range. He later moved to Idaho, dying there in 1939, the year this letter was written. *South Dakota's Ziebach County: History of the Prairie* (Dupree, S.Dak.: Ziebach County Historical Society, 1982), pp. 362, 390–91. Ovila ("Babe") LaPlante was the son of Louie LaPlante, a pioneer rancher on the Cheyenne River reservation. Babe LaPlante enlisted in the service during World War I, and he died at age seventy-three in 1954. Hall, *Roundup Years*, pp. 27, 270; *Hot Springs Star*, 2 Dec. 1954. The rest of this letter is a combination of two versions Philip told of the rattlesnake and Texas itch stories. The first version, which was much less complete, appeared in his 4 March 1937 letter.

5. The transient nature of a cowboy's life makes these men hard to place or track, but the 1900 federal census lists William R. Hess, "stock herder" in Stanley County, as a native of Pennsylvania. U.S., Department of the Interior, Census Office, *Twelfth Census of the United States, 1900*, Fort Pierre, Stanley County, S.Dak., in *AncestryLibrary.com* (subscription required). George Philip reported in 1939 that Hess had committed suicide in a small town in Montana "years ago." Likewise, cowboy Happy Jack Savage died in Fort Pierre in 1904 "when a horse fell over backwards with him, and drove the saddle horn into his abdomen," while Slim Sargent had moved to Redfield, where he died in a hack accident.

6. Technically, Texas itch was a disease that affected cattle only. The cowboys probably had scabies, a related parasite that affects humans and spreads quickly through close physical contact and the sharing of clothing or bedding with infected persons. As Philip relates, this "Texas itch" no doubt came north with the Texas cowboys who ran cattle on the northern range. Topical medications such as the one Jimmie used quickly killed the mites themselves, but the itching

persisted for weeks. N. S. Mayo, *Texas Itch*, Kansas State Agricultural College, Experiment Station Bulletin, no. 69 (Manhattan, 1897), pp. 103–4; "Scabies," *Centers for Disease Control, Division of Parasitic Diseases*, www.cdc.gov/NCIDOD/DPD/parasites/scabies /factsht_scabies.htm, accessed 12/1/06.

7. This line appears in Shakespeare's *Romeo and Juliet*, Act 2, scene 2, line 1.

8. Laches, a legal term, refers to negligence or undue delay in asserting a legal right or privilege. "Laches," www.answers.com/topic/laches-equity, accessed 11/20/06.

9. Dr. Charles J. Lavery, a New York State native, attended Starling Medical College in Columbus, Ohio, and worked in Fort Pierre from 1890 to 1893. He returned to medical school for post-graduate work before resuming his frontier practice in 1895. He worked in Fort Pierre for another decade and then relocated to Aberdeen, South Dakota. Doane Robinson, *History of South Dakota*, 2 vols. (n.p.: B. F. Bowen & Co., 1904), 1:821–23.

10. Because prairie rattlesnakes are cold-blooded and cannot maintain their own body temperature, they search for shaded areas to keep cool and seek sunny areas when they need warmth. Reptiles in South Dakota must hibernate to avoid the freezing cold of winter. Early fall frosts and shortening daylight encourage snakes to move together toward dens, normally found on hillsides with a southerly sun exposure so that the snakes can bask in the sun. They will congregate near the den until the lower temperatures drive them underground. South Dakota, Department of Game, Fish and Parks, Division of Wildlife, "Prairie Rattlesnake," www.sdgfp.info/Wildlife/Snakes/PrairieRattlesnake.htm, accessed 11/21/06.

11. Faye Longbrake, a long-time resident of Ziebach County, writes, "The snakes have a strong, musky odor when they gather up" (Longbrake to Cathie Draine, 11 May 2006).

12. From 1934 to 1938, Colonel Pope of the United States Fourth Cavalry commanded Fort Meade, an active military post in the northern Black Hills until 1944. [Herbert B. Cleveland], comp., *Fort Meade, D.T./S.D., 1878–1978* [Fort Meade, S.Dak.: Veterans Administration Hospital, 1978], pp. [17–18]. For a general history of Fort Meade, *see* Robert Lee, *Fort Meade & the Black Hills* (Lincoln: University of Nebraska Press, 1991). Robert S. Hill, a mining engineer, and his wife Maud resided in Rapid City, where he was the mayor in 1939. Eva Wortman was also a Rapid City resident. South Dakota, State Census, 1935, State Archives Collection, South Dakota State Historical Society (SDSHS), Pierre. For more on the Utes, who were in South Dakota from 1906 to 1908, *see* David D. Laudenschlager, "The Utes in South Dakota, 1906–1908," *South Dakota History* 9 (Summer 1979): 233–47.

13. In 1937, the South Dakota Department of Agriculture hired A. M. Jackley to head its newly-created Reptile Control and Eradication Division. In his reports, Jackley noted that over one thousand dens had been located in twenty-eight South Dakota counties in 1941 and that some dens had been occupied for over forty years. Jackley, "Report of Reptile Control Campaign," 1941, and untitled report, [ca. 1938], both in Vertical Files, s.v., "Rattlesnakes," State Archives Collection, SDSHS. The numbers of snakes in this era recalled to George Philip's mind the Robert Burns poem "To a Louse, on Seeing One on a Lady's Bonnet at Church" (*Seven Centuries of Verse*, pp. 278–79), which contains these lines regarding the louse:

There ye may creep, and sprawl, and sprattle,
Wi' ither kindred, jumping cattle,
   In shoals and nations;
Whare horn nor bane ne'er daur unsettle,
   Your thick plantations.

For more on rattlesnakes during this time period, *see* H. K. Gloyd, "The Problem of Too Many Snakes," *Chicago Naturalist* 7, no. 4 (1944): 87–97.

14. Ed Delehan, a Pennsylvania native, worked cattle in many parts of western South Dakota and, with partner Ben Ash, bought and sold southern cattle. In 1914, while branding on his ranch near Faith, he was gored in the eye by a steer and died a week later. *South Dakota's Ziebach County*, p. 332.

15. The term sunfishing describes a bucking horse that twists its body in such a way that he appears to be trying to turn his belly to the sun. Ramon F. Adams, *Western Words: A Dictionary of the Old West* (New York: Hippocrene Books, 1998), p. 159. Bert Hall's *Roundup Years* mentions an old-time cowboy named J. T. Singleton, who, in the roundups of the 1900–1902 era, worked as a rep for the Cheyenne River Pool, which he defined as "all the cattlemen east of the Limekiln pool outfit range, which was Spotted Bear Creek or thereabouts down the Cheyenne River to Sansarc Creek or thereabouts, and south from the Cheyenne River to the divide between Bad river and the Cheyenne river west" (quoted, p. 391). A roundup pool levied its members for the necessary gear to join the roundup. In 1939, Philip records that Henry Singleton died in Philip "a few years ago," and Terry lived on Cheyenne River, Plum Creek.

16. A Chet Calhoon was a member of the March Brothers Company, a smaller cattle outfit in the Bad River/Cheyenne River area, according to Hall, *Roundup Years*, p. 359. In 1939, Philip reported that Jet Calhoon, who had been a good horse rider on the open range, was now an underground miner for the Homestake Mining Company in Lead, South Dakota. A U-necked, or more accurately, ewe-necked, horse has a long, thin neck like that of a ewe.

17. George Jackson and William Hayes, early Stanley County stockmen, started their herd by purchasing several hundred head of cattle from John Rabideaux for sixteen dollars a head. Their brand, JR–, had developed from the initials of the original owner, with the bar added as a tally mark when he sold the cattle. Scotty Philip bought out Jackson, and Hayes would in turn buy the herd from Philip, eventually owning a thousand head on a ranch seventy miles from Pierre on Cherry Creek. Hayes had married Jessie Stewart from Highmore in 1899, and the couple maintained a home in Fort Pierre for the family. Bill Hayes died in Fort Pierre in 1934. Clara Roseth, ed., *Prairie Progress in West Central South Dakota* (n.p.: Historical Society of Old Stanley County, 1968), p. 535.

18. Arthur Conan Doyle, an English author, is best known for his Sherlock Holmes mysteries.

19. In 1939, A. L. Bodley had moved to Sioux Falls as an abstractor, while Dr. Bowen continued to practice dentistry in Pierre.

20. In a long paragraph that preceded this lament for the passing of the open range, Philip listed what he knew about the whereabouts of the people he mentioned in his letter; many were dead and that is all he knew. Where possible, I have added to his information and placed it in notes closer to the first mention of individuals.

21. The McAdam and McDonald families played important roles in the early development of Wind Cave National Park in Custer County. Jesse McDonald, Tommy's father, began managing the property for the South Dakota Mining Company in April 1890 with his sons Elmer and Alvin. Alvin McDonald systematically explored and named features of the cave, recording his finds in a diary. Alvin died 15 September 1893 of "walking typhoid fever," supposedly complicated by pneumonia that he contracted while exploring the cave. John W. Bohl, "Seventy-five Years at Wind Cave: A History of the National Park," *South Dakota Historical Collections* 31 (1962): 365–468.

22. William O. Borst came to Fort Pierre from Wisconsin in 1877 and raised cattle in Meade County from 1883 to 1889, when he established a ranch in Ziebach County. Robinson, *History of South Dakota*, 1:825–26.

23. Narcisse Narcelle, whose brand was NSS, was one of the earliest big cattlemen of the open-range era in South Dakota. The son of a French fur trader and a Lakota woman, Narcelle headquartered his cattle operations on the Circle Dot Ranch, halfway between Philip and Faith in west-central South Dakota. Sometime after 1900, he moved his operations farther north onto the Cheyenne River Indian Reservation. He usually had ten or more cowboys working for him, including Quill Ewing, who was mentioned earlier. "Narcisse Narcelle, Ran

Thousands of Cattle and Horses," *South Dakota Heritage* 16 (Fall 1990): 22–23. Ike Blasingame, who knew Narcelle around 1906, referred to him as "a great Indian humorist," who "loved to tell stories around the campfire" (Blasingame, *Dakota Cowboy: My Life in the Old Days* [New York: G. P. Putnam's Sons, 1958], p. 215).

3. The Ghouls

1. The traditional Sioux Indian burial practice was to wrap the body of the deceased in a robe or blanket and place it on a scaffold or in a tree along with some of the individual's personal items. In the early 1900s, taking objects from these graves was not an uncommon practice. Under the 1990 federal Native American Graves Protection and Repatriation Act, American-Indian cultural items thus stolen and now in museum collections or held by federal agencies must be offered back to the appropriate tribe. *See* Stephen Huffstetter, *Lakota Grieving: A Pastoral Response* (Chamberlain, S.Dak.: Tipi Press, 1998), p. 17; Ike Blasingame, *Dakota Cowboy: My Life in the Old Days* (New York: G. P. Putnam's Sons, 1958), pp. 69–70; "Frequently Asked Questions," National NAGPRA, www.cr.nps.gov/nagpra/FAQ/INDEX.HTM, accessed 11/28/06.

2. Never a large community, Stamford had a store, hotel/café, and a blacksmith shop. It was located between present-day Okaton and Belvidere. In 1910, it boasted a population of 157, but it is now a ghost town. *Jackson-Washabaugh Counties, 1915–1965* ([Kadoka, S.Dak.]: Jackson-Washabaugh County Historical Society, [1966]), p. 17; U.S., Department of Commerce, Bureau of the Census, *Thirteenth Census of the United States, 1910*, Stanley County, in *AncestryLibrary.com* (subscription required).

3. John F. Hughes, an Iowa native who settled in Pierre in 1883, was a civil and criminal lawyer known for his meticulous case preparation. He served as city attorney for Fort Pierre and states attorney in Stanley County before he was named a judge of the sixth judicial circuit, a position he held for thirty-five years until his death in 1946. George W. Kingsbury, *History of Dakota Territory*, and George M. Smith, *South Dakota: Its History and Its People*, 5 vols. (Chicago: S. J. Clarke Publishing Co., 1915), 4:1200–1203; *Pierre Daily Capital Journal*, 8 Jan. 1946. Little is known of Clyde Whiting beyond his death. He is not recorded in the 1905 South Dakota state census, but court records indicate he was in Stanley County during the fall of 1905. *State of South Dakota v. Gus A. Tusha*, File no. 453, Stanley County Clerk of Courts Office, Fort Pierre, S.Dak.

4. Gus A. Tusha, a Czech immigrant, was a twenty-six-year-old painter living in Hanson County in 1905, according to the South Dakota state census, and so had only recently moved to Stanley County when he was accused of killing

Whiting. South Dakota, State Census, 1905, Microfilm ed., State Archives Collection, South Dakota State Historical Society, Pierre. An infernal machine is "an explosive device designed to harm or destroy, especially with criminal intent" (Your Dictionary.com, www.yourdictionary.com/ahd/i/i0128200.html, accessed 11/30/06). Loring Ellis Gaffy practiced law in Deadwood, South Dakota, before moving to Pierre in 1884. He was elected states attorney of Hughes County in 1888 and appointed judge of the sixth judicial circuit in 1894. Kingsbury, History of Dakota Territory, 4:56–57; Pierre Daily Capital Journal, 20 Feb. 1936. Julius Haugen Johnson practiced law in Fort Pierre from 1905 to 1916, serving as both city attorney and Stanley County states attorney. Doane Robinson, South Dakota, Sui Generis, Stressing the Unique and Dramatic in South Dakota History, 3 vols. (Chicago: American Historical Society, 1930), 3:194–96. Lyman T. Boucher came to South Dakota from Illinois in 1883 and practiced law in Leola and Eureka before he was elected to the sixth judicial circuit in 1904. Doane Robinson, History of South Dakota, 2 vols. (n.p.: B. F. Bowen & Co., 1904), 2:1745–46. See also Philip to his children, 1 Aug. 1940.

5. Joseph Mark Walsh, who was born in Yankton, Dakota Territory, received his medical training at the University of Illinois in 1905. He practiced medicine in Fort Pierre until 1917, when he moved to Rapid City. He died in 1939. Kingsbury, History of Dakota Territory, 4:749; Pierre Daily Capital Journal, 27 June 1939.

6. W. David Giddings settled in Stanley County with his parents in 1896. He worked at a variety of jobs including automobile mechanic, construction worker, hack driver, and farmer. He also operated the first sawmill on the Bad River. Irene Caldwell, ed., Bad River (Wakpa Sica), Ripples, Rages, and Residents (Fort Pierre, S.Dak.: Bad River Women's Club, 1983), pp. 87–88; Pierre Daily Capital Journal, 21 Jan. 1936.

7. Dutch Van Metre was likely Charles Luther Van Metre, the son of Arthur C. Van Metre who first settled in southeastern Dakota Territory in 1858. Arthur and his Dakota Indian wife came to Fort Pierre in 1883, establishing a large and prosperous ranch with the help of their children, one of whom was Jane Van Metre Waldron, mother of Alice ("Isle") Waldron, George Philip's wife. Charles Van Metre was thus Jane's brother and Isle's uncle, and the soubriquet "Dutch" probably refers to the family's Dutch ancestry. Mary H. Powell LeBeau, A Multi-Racial Tree (n.p.: By the Author, 1975); Robinson, History of South Dakota, 2:1408–10.

8. Robert Burns, "To a Mouse, on Turning up Her Nest with the Plough, November 1785," in Seven Centuries of Verse, English and American, from the Early English Lyrics to the Present Day, ed. A. J. M. Smith (New York: Charles Scribner's Sons, 1947), p. 276.

9. The full transcript of the trial is available in *South Dakota v. Tusha*. The *Murdo Coyote*, 28 Sept. 1906, indicates Whiting had been drying dynamite in his cabin.

4. Let There Be Light

1. This line comes from Franklin Delano Roosevelt's First Inaugural Address, given on 4 March 1933 in the depths of the Great Depression as he was preparing to take corrective measures. The full text can be found at http://odur.let.rug .nl/~usa/P/fr32/speeches/fdr1.htm, accessed 11/29/06.

2. Saint Elmo's fire is the glow accompanying the discharges of atmospheric electricity. It usually appears in stormy weather around church spires, sailing masts, and airplane wings. It is commonly accompanied by a crackling or fizzing noise. During thunderstorms, the air between the clouds and the ground becomes electrically charged, and this electricity is drawn to the closest conductor. *New Encyclopaedia Britannica*, 15th ed. (2005), s.v. "Saint Elmo's fire."

3. Philip is once again quoting from Robert Burns's "Tam O' Shanter."

4. By 1939, Philip himself had lost track of this Texas cowboy.

5. Ramon F. Adams, *Western Words: A Dictionary of the Old West* (New York: Hippocrene Books, 1998), p. 87, defines the "killpecker guard" as "the period of herding from sundown until 8 P.M."

6. Ike Blasingame describes the coonskin coats that he and his fellow cowboys wore as "full length, with high collars, and they cost us fifty dollars apiece" (Blasingame, *Dakota Cowboy: My Life in the Old Days* [New York: G. P. Putnam's Sons, 1958], p. 159). Faye Longbrake also recalls: "It was not uncommon for cowboys who could afford them to wear coonskin coats (made from the hides and fur of many raccoons). No cold air could penetrate those coats" (Longbrake to Cathie Draine, 5 May 2006).

7. Jesse Knight, a veteran cowboy, had been foreman for the 73 outfit as early as 1894. He ran roundup wagons for the L-7 and would later work for Captain Burton C. ("Cap") Mossman's Diamond A Cattle Company in what is now Stanley and Dewey counties. Bert L. Hall, comp., *Roundup Years: Old Muddy to Black Hills*, Centennial ed. (Winner, S.Dak.: Western South Dakota Buck-a-roos, 2000), p. 367; James M. Robinson, *West from Fort Pierre: The Wild World of James (Scotty) Philip* (Los Angeles: Westernlore Press, 1974), p. 94; and Blasingame, *Dakota Cowboy*, p. 208.

8. Auroras are luminous phenomena of the upper atmosphere, and auroras in the Northern Hemisphere are called aurora borealis, or northern lights. They are caused by the interaction of energetic particles (electrons and protons) from outside the atmosphere with atoms of the upper atmosphere. Auroras take many

forms, including luminous curtains, arcs, bands, and patches in colors of red or greenish blue. The uniform arc is the most stable form of aurora, sometimes persisting for hours without noticeable variation. *New Encyclopaedia Britannica*, s.v. "Aurora."

5. Who Knows?

1. Bill Hurst was born in Yankton in 1860 and moved to Fort Pierre with his parents in 1867. In 1914, he married and moved to Spearfish, where he operated a café and served as cook at Spearfish Normal School (now Black Hills State University). *Spearfish Queen City Mail*, 4 Feb. 1940. In a later notation on this letter, Philip writes, "My friend Bill Hurst was buried in Spearfish, South Dakota, in January, 1940." John L. Lewis was president of the United Mine Workers of America from 1920 to 1960. He advocated worker's rights and helped organize labor unions in other industries. "John L. Lewis," *United Mine Workers of America*, www.umwa.org/history/jll1.shtml, accessed 12/4/06.

2. A running iron is a straight branding iron used to "write" a brand freehand. Ramon F. Adams, *Western Words: A Dictionary of the Old West* (New York: Hippocrene Books, 1998), p. 134. *See also* Philip to his children, 1 June 1940, 24 Feb. 1941.

3. *Out Our Way* was a series drawn by J. R. Williams, cartoonist and humorist in the first half of the twentieth century. His best-known cowboy characters were Wes and Curly. "J. R. Williams," *Lambiek.Net*, www.lambiek.net/artists/w/williams_jr.htm, accessed 3/11/06).

6. Happy Landing?

1. As cowboy J. T. Singleton explained, the members of a roundup pool "made a small levy on what cattle they estimated were in that territory. This fund was used to purchase a cook tent, stove, and stove cart, cooking utensils, rope, corral, and cash enough to buy grub and to pay a foreman, cook, night hawk" (quoted in Bert L. Hall, comp., *Roundup Years: Old Muddy to Black Hills*, Centennial ed. [Winner, S.Dak.: Western South Dakota Buck-a-roos, 2000], p. 391). In addition to money, pool numbers also provided wagons and horses to pull wagons and mount the horse handlers.

2. Harry F. Briggs was born in Yankton, Dakota Territory, in 1887 and moved with his mother to Fort Pierre as an infant. He worked on the Louis and George LaPlante ranch and ran his own operation on the Bad River before becoming a partner in the Briggs-Melady Cattle Company. In 1936, he began working for the Farm Security Agency in Philip, where he died in 1940. *Philip Pioneer-Review*, 8 Aug. 1940.

3. A native of Ireland, John Holland lived in New York City and Canada before settling in Sully County, Dakota Territory, in 1880. He was a scout with the United States Army at the time of the battle at Wounded Knee, reaching the rank of second lieutenant. He maintained his ranch in Sully County until his death in 1926. *Pierre Daily Capital Journal*, 1 May 1926.

4. In professional rodeo, the rider is only required to stay on the horse for eight seconds, and even then the rider often has to use his spurs to entice the horse to buck. Faye Longbrake to Cathie Draine, 6 May 2006.

5. Victor T. Jepsen was a Rapid City commissioner from 1926 to 1931 and served as the city's mayor in 1927. He was involved in real estate and insurance in Deadwood and Rapid City. *Rapid City Daily Journal*, 11 May 1959.

7. The Cowman

1. During his experiences in Kansas with his uncle Alex and cousin George, Philip visited Ellis, "which was then a Union Pacific division point about thirteen miles west of Hays." While in Ellis, Philip met "a young chap working in the Union Pacific machine shop, by the name of Walt Chrysler," the future automobile mogul. On another occasion, Philip arrived in Ellis "pitifully dirty, and travelworn," and the first person he met on the street was Chrysler. "Walt, after some profane inquiry as to why my appearance was as it was, took me up to his room, cleaned me up, and gave me a ticket to Hays." Philip concluded, "Others may since have been 'cleaned' by Walt Chrysler, but he still has my gratefulness for that particular cleaning he gave me, together with the opportunity to ride the cushions into Hays, like any other affluent citizen" (Philip to his children, 25 Dec. 1936).

2. Orlin Holcomb was the son of Gene Holcomb, who owned the OHO outfit north of the Belle Fourche River, and could "handle a rope much better than his old dad" (Bert L. Hall, comp., *Roundup Years: Old Muddy to Black Hills*, Centennial ed. [Winner, S.Dak.: Western South Dakota Buck-a-roos, 2000], p. 121).

3. A wind knocker was simply throwing a calf to the ground with such force that the breath was knocked out of him.

4. Wattles are "a mark of ownership made on the neck or the jaw of an animal by pinching up a quantity of skin and cutting it, but not entirely off. When the wound is healed, a hanging flap of skin is left" (Ramon F. Adams, *Western Words: A Dictionary of the Old West* [New York: Hippocrene Books, 1998], p. 175). Some ranchers mark their cattle by cutting in addition to branding them. "Irons," *Buckaroos in Paradise: Ranching Culture in Northern Nevada, 1945–1982*, memory.loc. gov/ammem/ncrhtml/crviewo8.html, accessed 12/06/06.

5. Billy Pressler is best remembered as one of the foremen at the 1902 roundup

on the Rosebud Indian Reservation, which was considered by some to be the "world's largest." Pressler worked for the Bar X outfit near Chamberlain. Hall, *Roundup Years*, pp. 23, 489. *Also see* Philip to his children, 30 Sept. 1940.

6. The BXB brand was owned by the Vermont Cattle Company that ran twelve thousand cattle on the Moreau River. The town of Bixby was named for its brand. Early settler Sarah Wilson recalled that Bixby was settled around 1892 or 1893. *Bison Courier*, 22 Jan. 1931; Nellie Snyder Yost, ed., *Boss Cowman: The Recollections of Ed Lemmon, 1857–1946* (Lincoln: University of Nebraska Press, 1969), p. 216.

7. Lewis Wallace, a Union general during the Civil War, was the author of *Ben-Hur: A Tale of the Christ*, published in 1880. He encountered Billy the Kid (William Bonney) in 1879 when, as governor, Wallace offered Bonney a pardon in exchange for information against persons involved in a dispute in Lincoln County, New Mexico Territory. Bonney reneged, and the pardon was withdrawn. "Lew Wallace," *Wikipedia*, en.wikipedia.org/wiki/Lew_Wallace, accessed 12/06/06.

8. Philip's letter of 10 November 1939 explains what constituted "the wagon." Ira Miller also cowboyed for the U-Cross ranch near Smithville and by 1905, when he was thirty-eight years old, owned a ranch near Philip, South Dakota. Hall, *Roundup Years*, p. 303; South Dakota, State Census, 1905, State Archives Collection, South Dakota State Historical Society (SDSHS), Pierre.

9. On 15 June 1815, the Duke of Wellington was attending a ball hosted by the Duchess of Richmond when the unexpected news reached him that the French had invaded Belgium as far as Quatre Bras and were about to split his forces. Wellington rallied and defeated Napoleon's army three days later at Waterloo. Peter Hofschröer, "Wellington on Waterloo," www.achart.ca/Wellington/waterloo2.htm, accessed 12/06/06.

10. This line appears in Robert Burns's "Tam o' Shanter."

11. Paul Prairie Chicken, the son of Paul First Hawk, had been educated at Hampton University in Virginia from July 1885 to January 1887. Prairie Chicken died in 1939, and his obituary lauded his athletic prowess, remarking that he was "known almost as a legend to hundreds of central South Dakotans, was massive like a huge tree and as ancient as any man can remember in this section of the state." After his schooling, he had returned to central South Dakota, where he had a reputation as a pow-wow dancer, interpreter, and a man of "philosophical wisdom" that "took but few words to express" (Hall, *Roundup Years*, p. 524). *See also* Jon L. Brudvig, comp., "Hampton Normal & Agricultural Institutes, American Indian Students, 1878–1923," www.twofrog.com/hamptonmale3.txt, accessed 5/29/06.

12. Van Francis Moore, who was also called Francis Van Moore, was prone to trouble. His penitentiary records show that his incarceration for murder was

his third time in jail. "Van Moore," Penitentiary Files, State Archives Collection, SDSHS. George Tackett spent most of his life as a roundup cook in western South Dakota and eastern Montana. *Winner Advocate*, 17 Apr. 1924.

13. The Tin Cup family lived on the Bad River. Tin Cup's wife was a black woman named Fannie. *Bad River (Wakpa Sica), Ripples, Rages, and Residents* (Fort Pierre, S.Dak.: Bad River Women's Club, 1983), p. 257. In addition to owning a hardware store in Fort Pierre, Fred S. Rowe served two terms in the South Dakota State Senate and was a candidate for lieutenant governor and secretary of state. At the time of his death in 1929, he was a member of the Custer State Park board. *Fort Pierre Times*, 7 Feb. 1929.

14. Spotted Crow was born in about 1853 and lived on the Bad River with his wife Deer Lucs [Looks] Good. U.S., Department of the Interior, Census Office, *Twelfth Census of the United States, 1900*, Stanley County, in *AncestryLibrary.com* (subscription required).

15. Martin Patrick Kennedy came to Stanley County from Minnesota in 1890. He was the county's third sheriff and held other offices including county auditor. *Fort Pierre Times*, 18 Nov. 1937.

16. Bill Brown was foreman for the U-Cross ranch, owned by Henry A. Dawson, which was considered to be one of the largest operations in the southwestern part of South Dakota. Bob Lee and Dick Williams, *Last Grass Frontier: The South Dakota Stock Grower Heritage* (Sturgis, S.Dak.: South Dakota Stock Growers Assoc., 1964), pp. 245–46. Fred Ervin worked as a teamster in Fort Pierre and then as a merchant in Van Metre before moving to Sioux Falls to work for the railroad. Although Philip writes that Ervin was a conductor, census documents record his occupation as switchman. South Dakota, State Census, 1905, 1935, 1945, State Archives Collection, SDSHS; *Thirteenth Census of the United States, 1910*, Van Metre Township, Stanley County, S.Dak. Van Moore's mother was Mary Dolphus, who died in 1912. "Van Moore," Penitentiary Files.

17. Faye Longbrake commented, "I think it was Van Moore's sister, not his mother, who pressed him to turn himself into the law" (Longbrake to Cathie Draine, 11 Dec. 2005).

18. Vermont native William G. Porter received his law degree from Drake University in Iowa in 1884. He moved to South Dakota in 1889 and served as Custer County state's attorney from 1890 to 1895 and as United States district attorney from 1907 to 1910. He was in private practice in Sioux Falls when he died on 11 August 1927. Doane Robinson, *History of South Dakota*, 2 vols. (n.p.: B. F. Bowen & Co., 1904), 1:624–26; *Sioux Falls Daily Argus Leader*, 11 Aug. 1927.

19. James H. McCoy began his law practice in Britton, South Dakota, in 1885 and was elected fifth district circuit court judge in 1901. He was appointed to

the state supreme court in 1909. George W. Kingsbury, *History of Dakota Territory*, and George M. Smith, *South Dakota: Its History and Its People*, 5 vols. (Chicago: S. J. Clarke Publishing Co., 1915), 4:562–63.

20. Charles Evans Hughes was an associate justice of the United States Supreme Court from 1910 to 1916. He returned to the court when he was appointed chief justice by President Herbert Hoover in 1930 and served until 1941. "Members of the Supreme Court of the United States," *Supreme Court of the United States*, www.supremecourtus.gov/about/members.pdf, accessed 12/8/06. In *United States v. Pelican*, regarding the 1913 murder of Ed Louie by Sam Pelican and Tony Ponterre on the Colville Indian Reservation in Washington State, the court ruled that "commission of a crime . . . upon Indian lands . . . was punishable under the laws of the United States" (*United States v. Pelican*, 232 U.S. 442 [1914], *FindLaw for Legal Professionals*, caselaw.lp.findlaw.com/scripts/printer_friendly .pl?page=us/232/442.html, accessed 12/8/06).

21. Iowa native James D. Elliott practiced law in eastern Dakota Territory until 1897, when he was appointed United States district attorney, a position he held for ten years. In 1911, President William Howard Taft appointed Elliott a United States district judge, a position he held until his death in 1933. Kingsbury, *History of Dakota Territory*, 4:630–34; *Sioux Falls Daily Argus Leader*, 31 Dec. 1933.

22. "The way Van Moore disappeared is the way I always heard it told," wrote rancher Faye Longbrake. "Van Moore's headstone sets in the Mossman Cemetery among the Dolphus family graves . . . between Ridgeview and Eagle Butte along Highway 212" (Longbrake to Cathie Draine, 11 Dec. 2005).

23. Stanley Philip, born in 1891, was Scotty Philip's second son and the first to survive infancy. Wayne C. Lee, *Scotty Philip, the Man Who Saved the Buffalo* (Caldwell, Idaho: Caxton Printers, 1975), pp. 174–75.

24. Faye Longbrake recalls that "Buff" was a regular at Scotty's, and he was close to Scotty's wife, Sarah. He did possess the urge to "over" on other people's horses, Longbrake also remembers, and after his times spent in the South Dakota penitentiary, he eventually "migrated to Montana and went by the alias of Joe Cobb. . . . He couldn't resist stealing horses there either and also did some time in the MT penitentiary" (Longbrake to Draine, 11 Dec. 2005).

25. For more on the "McCanles Massacre" and the life of James Butler ("Wild Bill") Hickok, *see* Joseph G. Rosa, *Wild Bill Hickok: The Man and His Myth* (Lawrence: University Press of Kansas, 1996), pp. 113–16.

26. Julius Wickert had a ranch on the Bad River near Wendte that he settled in 1898. There is no record of Dick Wickert, but he may have been a relative. *Bad River (Wakpa Sica)*, pp. 246–49.

27. John Charles ("Charlie") Russell opened a trading post in 1890 near the

site that became the town of Midland. His business grew into a general store that he ran until 1933. Russell died in 1941. Hall, *Roundup Years*, pp. 67–68; *Midland Mail*, 20 Mar. 1941. In 1905, Leo T. Hollis was a twenty-five-year-old ranch hand living in the Midland area. As with many cowboys of this era, he may have moved on after working for the L-7 outfit. He is not recorded in any state census after 1905. South Dakota, State Census, 1905.

28. Originally from Tennessee, Fay or Faye Gentry lived with his wife, Mary, and seven children in Pennington County, having arrived in South Dakota around 1889. South Dakota, State Census, 1905; *Thirteenth Census*, Township 1, Pennington County. John E. Reddick established a ranch along Battle Creek in the mid-1880s and brought in cattle from Texas and Mexico to fatten and sell. In 1919, he sold that ranch and worked another one near Fruitdale until 1924. Reddick died in 1935. *Belle Fourche Bee*, 5 June 1935.

29. These lines are from Thomas Hood's poem "The Bridge of Sighs." Philip changed the sex of the subject of the poem in the last four lines. *See* "The Bridge of Sighs," in *The Oxford Book of English Verse*, ed. Arthur Quiller-Couch, www.bartleby.com/101/654.html, accessed 12/11/06.

8. The Rooshian Wagon

1. Here and elsewhere, Philip makes no effort to temper his strong feelings about the Axis leaders in World War II. For more on the politics of the era, *see* Piers Brendon, *The Dark Valley: A Panorama of the 1930s* (New York: Alfred A. Knopf, 2000).

2. According to the 1905 state census, about a dozen Russian-born residents were living in Stanley County near a small town named Meers, located north and west of Fort Pierre. The Alexander Meers living there at that time was only nine years old. Two adults, Martin Meers, who gave his occupation as stockman, and Anton Meers, a farmer, were also residents. In the 1870s and 1880s, several hundred Russian Mennonites, mostly farmers, had also settled in Dakota Territory, primarily in the eastern portion. Among other religious practices, the Mennonites owned their property communally. As Philip notes, the Meers family and neighbors apparently did not belong to the Mennonite church. Alan H. Patera, John S. Gallagher, and Kenneth W. Stach, *South Dakota Post Offices* (Lake Grove, Oreg.: The Depot, 1990), p. 341; South Dakota, State Census, 1905, State Archives Collection, South Dakota State Historical Society (SDSHS), Pierre. For more on the Mennonites, *see* John David Unruh, "The Mennonites in South Dakota" (master's thesis, University of South Dakota, 1933), and Rod Janzen, *The Prairie People: Forgotten Anabaptists* (Hanover, N.H.: University Press of New England, 1999).

3. John J. Hilger and his brother Anson built one of the first frame buildings in Pierre, which was used as a clothing store, post office, church, and saloon. Anthony D. Hengel worked as a clerk in Hilger's store and ultimately bought out his employer. The store was a popular gathering place for cattlemen when they came to Pierre. *Hughes County History* (Pierre, S.Dak.: Office of the County Superintendent of Schools, 1937), p. 42; *Pierre Daily Capital Journal*, 12 Dec. 1927.

4. Bunk White was born about 1859 in Texas and came to Dakota Territory around 1891. Prior to working for Scotty Philip, White worked for the Wells Brothers's Quarter Circle W horse outfit on the Moreau River. He was a half-brother to another black cowboy, Tom Simms. Philip indicates in this letter that White was not dark-skinned, and the record shows that White was at times listed as white in census documents. Even so, friction occurred concerning his race. Ike Blasingame recorded that some people would not work with him, while others, like Philip, respected him highly. Another contemporary of White's, Jake Handley, wrote, "Wherever Bunk was laid to rest, [I] would like to mark on the stone, 'Cow Boy Extraordinary' " (quoted in Clara Roseth, ed., *Prairie Progress in West Central South Dakota* [n.p.: Historical Society of Old Stanley County, 1968], p. 46). *See also* South Dakota, State Census, 1905; Roseth, *Prairie Progress in West Central South Dakota*, p. 46; Bert L. Hall, comp., *Roundup Years: Old Muddy to Black Hills*, Centennial ed. (Winner, S.Dak.: Western South Dakota Buck-a-roos, 2000), p. 365; Blasingame, *Dakota Cowboy: My Life in the Old Days* (New York: G. P. Putnam's Sons, 1958), p. 180.

5. When white settlers moved westward, they depleted most of the big game animals that had been the wolves' prey. Wolves then preyed on sheep and cattle, resulting in financial losses for livestock owners. As Philip observed, wolves tend to concentrate on the bigger muscles of animals rather than the tendons on the back of the leg, where a predator risks getting kicked in the face by an animal's sharp hooves. After bounty programs were initiated, wolves became nearly extinct in the lower forty-eight states in the early part of the twentieth century. Three Toes, a gray wolf that prowled northwestern South Dakota, was credited with at least fifty-thousand dollars worth of livestock killings. He had lost one toe in a trap, hence his nickname. An estimated one hundred fifty men tried to capture him over a thirteen-year period before Clyde F. Briggs, a hunter hired by the federal government, successfully trapped him in July 1925. U.S., Fish & Wildlife Service, "Gray wolf, *Canis lupus*," revised Mar. 2006, http://www.fws .gov/midwest/wolf/biology/biologue.pdf, accessed 12/19/06; Bud Dalrymple, *The Gray Wolf of South Dakota* (Altoona, Pa: Altoona Tribune Co., 1919), p. 27; "Wolves: The Basics of Wolf Biology and Taxonomy," *Defenders of Wildlife*, http://www

.defenders.org/wildlife/wolf/wolfbio.html, accessed 12/19/06; Archer B. Gil-fillan, *Sheep* (Boston: Little, Brown, & Co., 1929), pp. 181–96.

6. Big Mouth Thompson may or may not have been a cowboy named Charley Thompson. Guy W. Moulton worked as a cowboy during his youth, but in 1906, he and his father opened a cigar store in Pierre. Moulton later worked in various retail operations and served as Hughes County auditor. Harry Hoyt had a ranch on Red Woman Draw and also worked as a cowhand for the Native Cattle Company. *Pierre Daily Capital Journal*, 5 Apr. 1957; Roseth, *Prairie Progress in West Central South Dakota*, p. 190; Hall, *Roundup Years*, pp. 145–46, 471.

7. These cowboys left little trace of themselves in the historical record. Fred Ervin, age thirty, lived with his wife and family near Van Metre in 1910. Alvin Martin, a twenty-eight-year-old Texan, worked as a farmhand in Harding County in northwestern South Dakota in 1905. W. P. ("Pat") Oakes served as sheriff of Stanley County and eventually moved to Eagle Butte, South Dakota. U.S., Department of Commerce, Bureau of the Census, *Thirteenth Census of the United States*, 1910, Van Metre, Lyman County, in *Ancestry Library.com* (subscription required); South Dakota, State Census, 1905; *Fort Pierre Times*, 7 Apr. 1927. For more on Oakes, *see* Philip to his children, 24 July 1940.

8. Winchell Smith and Frank Bacon were coauthors of the comedy, *Lightnin'*, which opened on Broadway in 1918 with Bacon in the lead role and ran for 1,291 performances. "Winchell Smith," *Answers.com*, www.answers.com/topic/winchell-smith, accessed 12/15/06.

9. At its height, the settlement of Meers had only about one hundred residents. It had a post office starting around 1904, along with a saloon and general store. By 1923, the post office was closed and the Russian immigrants and other settlers had moved on. Patera, Gallagher, and Stack, *South Dakota Post Offices*, p. 341; Vertical Files, s.v. "Ghost Towns I," State Archives Collection, SDSHS. At age sixty in 1920, White was working as a ranch hand in California. *Fourteenth Census*, 1920, Willow Town, Glenn County, Calif.

9. The Law of the Range

1. Philip may be referring to N. W. Goodell, a Wisconsin native born around 1863, who listed his occupation in 1905 as a ranch man in Stanley County. South Dakota, State Census, 1905, State Archives Collection, South Dakota State Historical Society, Pierre.

2. This jingle, which describes promises made and rarely kept in moments of duress and panic, is firmly anchored in folk wisdom with no known author.

3. George Philip to his children, 24 Aug. 1939.

4. Zay Jeffries, who became one of the nation's most distinguished metal-lurgists, was born at Willow Lake, Dakota Territory, in 1888. He clerked in his uncle's store in Fort Pierre before earning degrees in mining and metallurgical engineering from the South Dakota School of Mines and Technology and a doctorate from Harvard University. Jefferies was on the faculty of Case Institute of Technology and was a vice-president of General Electric Company. Jeffries's daughter suggests that the trip from Fort Pierre to Rapid City took her father seven days and that he sold the horse along with the tack. Zay Jeffries File, Alumni Office, South Dakota School of Mines and Technology, Rapid City, S.Dak.

5. For the firing of Tom Beverly in just this fashion, *see* Philip to his children, 1 June 1940.

6. The reference here is probably to Saint Joseph, who is generally regarded as guardian protector of Jesus and Mary in Christian tradition.

10. Practical Joking

1. Originally from Wisconsin, Carson Clay Williams worked in the livestock business in Philip and Pierre. Cowboy Manuel Sylva came in on the first cattle drive from Texas to Fort Pierre in 1879. *Pierre Daily Capital Journal*, 14 Feb. 1930; Clara Roseth, ed., *Prairie Progress in West Central South Dakota* (n.p.: Historical Society of Old Stanley County, 1968), p. 473.

2. Alvira Van Metre Oakes was one of the children of Mary Aungie and Arthur Van Metre. Her sister was Jane Van Metre Waldron, the mother of Alice ("Isle") Waldron Philip. Her husband, Pat Oakes, was an early sheriff of Stanley County. *Fort Pierre Times*, 7 Apr. 1927.

3. James B. Cox learned the cattle business in Texas, then came to Dakota Territory in 1881 and began a freighting company. He later established the Spanish Five ranch in Meade County and had one of the largest herds in the state. Cox also worked as a scout and commissary to soldiers in the 1890s. *Pierre Daily Capital Journal*, 20 Mar. 1939.

4. Vermont native Cassius C. ("Cash") Bennett moved to Pierre in 1883 and became president of the First National Bank in 1888. He also was a member of the state senate in 1894 and 1902. *Memorial and Biographical Record and Illustrated Compendium of Biography . . . of Central South Dakota* (Chicago: Geo. A. Ogle & Co., 1899), pp. 215–515; *Biographical Directory of the South Dakota Legislature, 1889–1989*, 2 vols. (Pierre: South Dakota Legislative Research Council, 1989), 1:81.

5. Daniel P. Sherwood served from 1861 to 1863 with Company I, 18th Wisconsin Infantry during the Civil War. Thirty-seven years old when he joined the military, he died at age seventy-six on 17 July 1900. Veterans Records, Stanley

County, WPA Graves Registration, Microfilm ed., State Archives Collection, South Dakota State Historical Society, Pierre.

11. That Game of Poker

1. George Edgar McIntire, a Kentucky native, had a ranch about twenty miles north of Fort Pierre. *Pierre Daily Capital Journal*, 12 Feb. 1945. *See also* Philip to his children, 16 Aug. 1940.

2. Henry Walcott, originally from Iowa and proprietor of a saloon in Stamford, Old Stanley County, had "matters of business" to attend to in Fort Pierre on 24 September 1910, according to the *Stock Growers News* (Fort Pierre), 29 Sept. 1910. The business matter in question might have been his appearance in front of Justice McGuire. *See also* U.S., Department of Commerce, Bureau of the Census, *Thirteenth Census of the United States, 1910,* Fort Pierre, Stanley County, S.Dak., in *AncestryLibrary.com* (subscription required). For more information on Johnson and Boucher, *see* Philip to his children, 27 Sept. 1939.

3. George S. Huston was elected sheriff of Stanley County in 1906 and re-elected in 1908. He and his wife, Lizzie, ran the Huston House in Fort Pierre for sixteen years, and he was a director of the Fort Pierre National Bank. *Fort Pierre Times,* 27 Nov. 1925. An Iowa native, Hugh C. McGuire was a contractor and builder in Pierre and Philip in addition to serving as justice of the peace. *Fort Pierre Times,* 6 Nov. 1930.

12. Plenty O' Nuttin'

1. Charles J. Buell was born in Minnesota in 1865, attended law school at the University of Michigan, and practiced in Saint Paul until 1889, when he moved to Rapid City. Buell spent 1902 to 1906 as the state's attorney of Pennington County and was a member of the South Dakota legislature in 1919, 1921, and 1923. In the 1920s, Buell partnered with Albert R. Denu and George Philip. *Doane Robinson's Encyclopedia of South Dakota* (Sioux Falls, S.Dak.: By the Author, 1925), p. 100. William Gardner Buell, eldest son of Charles, served in World War I and returned to practice law in his father's company. He married Theresa Fayel Bennett in Rapid City in October 1920. At the time of this adventure, William A. Dilger found official employment as a real-estate agent. *Rapid City Journal,* 15 Oct. 1920, 25 July 1938; U.S., Department of Commerce, Bureau of the Census, *Fourteenth Census of the United States, 1920,* and *Fifteenth Census of the United States, 1930,* Rapid City, Pennington County, S.Dak., in *AncestryLibrary.com* (subscription required).

2. The Barren Lands is the region in Canada's Northwest Territory where there are no inhabitants and no trees.

3. Louis Edward Saunders, a Wisconsin native, homesteaded north of Interior in 1906, operating a ranch and a hardware store in town for almost forty years. George W. Mitchell was a banker in Winner, South Dakota, where the First National Bank closed in 1922. Millay is probably Lloyd (or Loyd) Millay, who was listed as an assistant cashier at a bank in Gregory in the 1920 census. Ten years later he is listed as a bookkeeper for a lumberyard in Winner. *Rapid City Journal*, 26 Feb. 1952; *The History of Tripp County, South Dakota* (Winner, S.Dak.: Winner Chamber of Commerce, 1984), p. 137; Robert J. Maule, "A History of Tripp County, South Dakota" (master's thesis, University of South Dakota, 1954), p. 48; *Fourteenth Census*, Gregory, Gregory County, S.Dak.; *Fifteenth Census*, Winner, Tripp County, S.Dak.

4. These lines come from the song "Fou' the Noo" or "Something in the Bottle for the Morning," words and music by Gerald Grafton and Harry Lauder, 1905. "Fou" is an old Scottish word for "drunk or tipsy." "Noo" is an abbreviation of "noodle" and means "head." "Fou the Noo," *Traditional Scottish Songs*, www.rampantscotland.com/songs/blsongs_fou.htm, accessed 1/8/07.

5. John Wolcot, an eighteenth-century satirist who wrote under the pseudonym Peter Pindar, was a prolific writer whose works attacked such prominent figures as Thomas Paine and George III. The lines Philip quoted come from Pindar's "Ode XV," *Expostulatory Odes* (1789). A copy can be found in E. Cobham Brewer, *Dictionary of Phrase and Fable* (1898), www. bartleby.com/81/11878.html, accessed 12/26/06. Chambers Kellar, who practiced law first in Hot Springs and then in Deadwood, was general counsel for the Homestake Mining Company. Kellar's wife, Florence, was the daughter of lawman Seth Bullock. *Rapid City Daily Journal*, 19 May 1950. For more on Pindar, see Robert L. Vales, *Peter Pindar (John Wolcot)*, Twayne's English Authors Series (New York: Twayne Publishers, 1973).

6. Alecia, born in 1908, was the only daughter and youngest child of Charles J. Buell and his wife Maude Mitchell Buell. *Fourteenth Census*, Rapid City, Pennington County, S.Dak.

7. At the turn of the century, Archibald K. Gardner practiced law in Rapid City, South Dakota, with Charles J. Buell until he became general solicitor for the Chicago & North Western Railway and moved to Huron. President Herbert Hoover appointed him in 1929 to be one of five circuit judges of the United States Court of Appeals for the Eighth Circuit. Doane Robinson, *South Dakota, Sui Generis, Stressing the Unique and Dramatic in South Dakota History*, 3 vols. (Chicago: American Historical Society, 1930), 2:232–33. In the 1920s, Albert R. Denu formed part of the law partnership of Buell, Denu, and Philip. Elected judge of the Seventh Circuit Court of South Dakota in 1936, Denu still held that position when this letter was written. South Dakota, *South Dakota Legislative Manual*, 1937, 25th Leg. Sess.

(Pierre, 1937), p. 572, and *South Dakota Legislative Manual*, 1941, 27th Leg. Sess. (Pierre, 1941), p. 505.

8. A Father O'Hare was the priest at Saint Mary's Catholic Church in Piedmont from 1920 to 1928, according to John R. Honerkamp, *At the Foot of the Mountain* (Piedmont, S.Dak.: By the Author, 1978), p. 110.

9. The picturesque Buell Building is situated on the corner of Saint Joseph and Seventh streets in Rapid City, South Dakota. The famous onion-domed tower section on the corner was built in 1888, and additions were made in 1901, 1915, and 1925. The building is considered one of South Dakota's best examples of commercial Queen Anne style. Jay D. Vogt, Stephen C. Rogers, and Scott Myers, *Picturing the Past: South Dakota's Historic Places*, Historical Preservation Series, no. 3 (Pierre: South Dakota State Historical Society Press, 2006), p. 48; David Erpestad and David Wood, *Building South Dakota: A Historical Survey of the State's Architecture to 1945*, Historical Preservation Series, no. 1 (Pierre: South Dakota State Historical Society Press, 1997), p. 132.

10. Philip is referring to the White River Badlands of southwestern South Dakota. American Indians called them *Mako Sica*, which translates as "land, bad," and early French explorers called them *Les Mauvaises Terres à Traverser*, or "bad lands to travel across." The Badlands, formed by mountain uprisings, sea deposits, and wind and water erosion over millions of years, are characterized by buttes, mudstone hills, and tables that rise as much as one thousand feet above the White and Cheyenne river valleys. The Badlands Wall, which is the northeastern rim of the area, forms a natural border between the upper grasslands on the northern side and the lower grasslands to the southeast in Badlands National Park. In some places the Wall reaches up to four hundred fifty feet above the lower grassland areas. Sven G. Froiland, *Natural History of the Black Hills and Badlands*, rev. ed. (Sioux Falls, S.Dak.: Center for Western Studies, Augustana College, 1990), pp. 177–79; Mary Durant and Michael Harwood, *This Curious Country: Badlands National Park* (Interior, S.Dak.: Badlands Natural History Association, 1988), pp. 8, 15–16.

11. Homesteading near Interior in 1910, Harlan Carlyle Snodgrass also worked as a banker for fourteen years at the State Bank of Interior. After his banking career, he moved into the real-estate business at Martin until the fall of 1925, when he moved to Batesland in Shannon County. Robinson, *South Dakota, Sui Generis*, 3:417–18.

12. Albert G. Granger was a Jackson County rancher and a lawyer based in Kadoka. Robinson, *South Dakota, Sui Generis*, 3:229.

13. Hotel owner Frank L. Hafner was a Michigan native. *Fifteenth Census*, Kadoka, Jackson County, S.Dak.

14. Originally from Iowa, Clem Coverston bought the Matson Brothers Mercantile Company in Imlay around 1922. At that time, the town had a school, a blacksmith shop, a dance hall, and a small church. It is now a ghost town. *A History of Pennington County, South Dakota* (Rapid City, S.Dak.: Pennington County History Book Committee, n.d.), p. 244; South Dakota, State Census, 1925, State Archives Collection, South Dakota State Historical Society, Pierre.

15. By the mid-1920s, Pete Lemley owned a large and successful ranch on the Cheyenne River, about thirty miles east of Rapid City. *See* Margaret Lemley Warren, *The Badlands Fox* (Hermosa, S.Dak.: By the Author, 1991).

16. Maude Mitchell, the daughter of Judge William H. Mitchell of Rapid City, married Charles J. Buell on 5 May 1892. The couple had four children. She died in 1931. George W. Kingsbury, *History of Dakota Territory*, and George M. Smith, *South Dakota: Its History and Its People*, 5 vols. (Chicago: S. J. Clarke Publishing Co., 1915), 5:409; *Rapid City Journal*, 25 July 1938.

17. Philip is quoting "I Got Plenty O' Nuttin,'" a song from *Porgy and Bess*, music by George Gershwin, lyrics by DuBose Heyward and Ira Gershwin, 1935. For the lyrics, *see* Gershwin, Heyward, and Gershwin, *Porgy and Bess* (New York: Gershwin Publishing Corp./Chappell & Co., [1935]), pp. 197–200. For the story of Gershwin's opera, *see* Hollis Alpert, *The Life and Times of Porgy and Bess: The Story of an American Classic* (New York: Alfred A. Knopf, 1990).

13. Rough Play

1. Today, as in 1940, the Days of '76 is the annual celebration of the gold-rush era held in Deadwood, South Dakota, each summer. For more on the celebration, Deadwood, and the Black Hills gold rush, *see* Bob Lee, ed., *Gold, Gals, Guns, Guts: A History of Deadwood, Lead, & Spearfish, 1874–1976* (Pierre: South Dakota State Historical Society Press, 2004).

2. Mike Dunn was Scotty Philip's brother-in-law. Dunn had married Sarah Larabee Philip's sister Susie. Sarah and Susie were the daughters of Joseph Larabee, a French fur-trader who married a Cheyenne Indian woman. The Larabees had a large family, and the oldest daughter, Helen, had married Crazy Horse, the famous Oglala Lakota warrior. Wayne C. Lee, *Scotty Philip, the Man Who Saved the Buffalo* (Caldwell, Idaho: Caxton Printers, 1975), p. 116.

3. Philip gives more details about this pasture in his article "James (Scotty) Philip, 1858–1911," *South Dakota Historical Review* 1 (Oct. 1935): 37–38, explaining that the 1906 act set aside an area of roughly thirty-five hundred acres on the west bank of the Missouri. Scotty Philip rented the land "exclusively for the pasturing of native buffalo" (p. 38).

4. This tribute to strength and courage appears in Rudyard Kipling's poem

"The Ballad of East and West" (1889), in *Rudyard Kipling's Verse*, Definitive ed. (Garden City, N.Y.: Doubleday & Co., 1940), pp. 233–36.

5. *Selah* is an obscure Hebrew word, derivation unknown, spoken to conclude a verse in the psalms.

14. Old Dishrag

1. John Horton Slaughter, rancher, cowboy, Texas Ranger, and gunfighter, learned his cowboy skills from the Mexican *vaqueros*. His life inspired a Disney television series entitled *Texas John Slaughter*, which ran from 1958 to 1961. Texas State Historical Association, *The Handbook of Texas*, http://www.tsha.utexas.edu/handbook/online/articles/SS/fsl110.html, accessed 1/2/07.

2. There was a Francis E. Morrison listed as a farmer in Philip in the 1910 census. Whether or not this man was the Humpy Morrison that George Philip knew is unknown. U.S., Department of Commerce, Bureau of the Census, *Thirteenth Census of the United States, 1910*, Philip, Stanley County, S.Dak., in *AncestryLibrary. com* (subscription required). John Curington worked as a rep for various outfits, including the Sheidley Cattle Company for five years. A renowned horseman, Curington was reportedly able to "ride anything that wore hair" (Bert L. Hall, comp., *Roundup Years: Old Muddy to Black Hills*, Centennial ed. [Winner, S.Dak.: Western South Dakota Buck-a-roos, 2000], p. 121). *See also* p. 336.

3. Richard W. ("Dick") Mathieson, Bad River cowman and rancher, reportedly acted as a sutler on the 1874 George A. Custer Expedition to the Black Hills. The Iowa native then worked as a freighter to the Black Hills until 1882, when he and his brother took up cattle raising. His son Kenneth would have been twelve years old in 1902. Hall, *Roundup Years*, p. 335; *Thirteenth Census*, Fort Pierre, Stanley County, S.Dak.

4. D. W. ("Dan") Bastion and his wife Sophia came to the Midland area in partnership with C. Bradshaw in 1892. When Bradshaw moved to Fort Pierre a decade later, Bastion and his wife operated a horse ranch several miles east of Midland. They built a roadhouse there in 1905 and then the Bastion Hotel in Midland in 1907. *Midland Mail*, 5 Mar. 1936.

5. In Matthew 8:28 Revised Standard Version, Jesus cast two demons into a herd of swine in the country of the Gadarenes. The herd then rushed headlong into the sea or lake, destroying the demons.

6. In an aside later in this letter, Philip alludes to the tragic fate that would overcome the Hill family later in the summer of 1906. The story was later pieced together that one day in Hill's absence, the hired man, Clarence Johnson, went to clean the bottom of the well and was overcome by gas. Julia Hill went to help him and suffered the same fate, only to be followed by her son Frank. Two

younger children survived until their father returned home. Early newspaper accounts suggested that Frank fell into the well and Johnson tried to save him, only to be asphyxiated by the gas. Faye Longbrake to Cathie Draine, 5 May 2006; *Pierre Daily Capital Journal*, 27 June 1906.

7. "The Strawberry Roan" was a popular cowboy ballad about an unrideable horse, "a sunfishing son of a gun." The song was recorded by numerous country and western singers in the 1920s and 1930s. The coloring of a strawberry roan begins with a chestnut base and can on occasion have a pink hue. Tom Isern, *Plains Folk*, www.plainsfolk.com/songs/song9.htm, accessed 1/10/07.

8. See Philip to his children, 16 July 1940.

9. Henry Livermont, who was a Stanley County stockman, moved to Timber Lake in Dewey County around 1910. He had two sons, Jack and Henry Alexander, and two daughters. South Dakota, State Census, 1905, State Archives Collection, South Dakota State Historical Society, Pierre; *Timber Lake Topic*, 31 Aug. 1944.

10. For the conclusion of this story, *see* Philip to his children, 30 Sept. 1940.

11. Cattleman John Hayes, one of the men for whom the town of Hayes was named, published the *Sioux Stock Journal* in Fort Pierre and helped found the Missouri River Stockmen's Association in 1894. He acted as secretary of that group from 1903 until 1906, when he left the organization to join the Western South Dakota Stock Growers Association. Bob Lee and Dick Williams, *Last Grass Frontier: The South Dakota Stock Grower Heritage* (Sturgis, S.Dak.: South Dakota Stock Growers Assoc., 1964), pp. 209, 226; Virginia Driving Hawk Sneve, *South Dakota Geographic Names* (Sioux Falls, S.Dak.: Brevet Press, 1973), p. 62.

12. Toward the end of the cowboy era, from 1904 to 1909, Pat Gallagher owned and operated Gallagher Brothers Livery and Feed in Midland with his brother Martin. From 1908 to 1910, Pat Gallagher held the post of editor for the *Western Star* in Midland. On occasion, he also worked as a hired hand for Scotty Philip. Faye Jones, et. al., eds., *Historic Midland, 1890–1986* (Midland, S.Dak: Midland Pioneer Museum, 1986), pp. 52, 57, 105.

13. Philip recalled that in the summer of 1939 Gallagher was back from Portland, Oregon, where he then practiced law, to attend a funeral, and they reminisced about old times. Gallagher's version of another such experience appears in *Roundup Years*, where he recalls that, when George Philip left to go to law school, "I got to pick his string and took 'Dishrag.' . . . Well, one day we started to make a roundup in Frozenman country. A lot of 'school marms' were homesteading there by that time and as we were riding past a bunch of cabins, Frank Calhoon, who was riding near me, let out a whoop and cut in ahead of me, thus giving Dishrag a good excuse to go into a demonstration of what he could do

when given a chance. Being caught off guard, I lasted about eight or ten jumps and then landed on my head while Dishrag kept up the performance by himself. It took a long time to live that one down but I got to know one of the school marms afterwards and she told me she thought it was a great exhibition. It was, for Dishrag" (quoted in Hall, *Roundup Years*, pp. 357–58).

14. Hiram Ellsworth ("Hite") Brisbine, a member of the Elks and masons, was a merchant and prominent stockholder in Yankton. Brisbine spoke five languages, which he claimed to have acquired while working in his dry-goods store. George W. Kingsbury, *History of Dakota Territory*, and George M. Smith, *South Dakota: Its History and Its People*, 5 vols. (Chicago: S. J. Clarke Publishing Co., 1915), 4:738–39.

15. The Sacred City of Anuradhapura is located in modern-day Sri Lanka and is listed as a World Heritage Centre by UNESCO. Established in the third century B.C., Anuradhapura flourished as a political and religious capital for more than thirteen hundred years before being abandoned in A.D. 993. "Sacred City of Anuradhapura," UNESCO, whc.unesco.org/pg.cfm?cid=31&id_site=200, accessed 1/3/07.

16. Author Adelaide Anne Procter (1825–1864) was an English poet best known for her poem "A Lost Chord" (1860). The lines Philip is quoting come from her poem titled "Judge Not," in *Legends and Lyrics–First Series* (1858), which can be found as a Project Gutenberg ebook, www.gutenberg.org/file/2303/2303-h/2303-h.htm, accessed 1/3/07. *See also* "Adelaide Anne Procter," *Wikipedia, the Free Encyclopedia*, en.wikipedia.org/wiki/Adelaide_Anne_Procter.

15. An Indian Roundup

1. In 1900, Johnnie Burnett, his wife Amelia, and children Grover and Ella lived and worked on the Rosebud Indian Reservation, where they were large stock raisers. Both Burnett and his wife were the offspring of white fathers and Sioux Indian mothers, and they built a large ranch on their joint allotments. U.S., Department of the Interior, Census Office, *Twelfth Census of the United States*, 1900, Rosebud Indian Reservation, Meyer County, S.Dak., in *AncestryLibrary.com* (subscription required); William Red Cloud Jordan, "Eighty Years on the Rosebud," ed. Henry W. Hamilton, *South Dakota Historical Collections* 35 (1970): 352–53.

2. George D. Mathieson was a fifty-seven-year-old stockman in Stanley County in 1905. He served as vice-president of the Missouri River Stockmen's Association in 1903. His son John, or Jack, was born in 1882 and gave his occupation as ranch hand in 1905. Bob Lee and Dick Williams, *Last Grass Frontier: The South Dakota Stock Grower Heritage* (Sturgis, S.Dak.: South Dakota Stock Growers

Assoc., 1964), p. 226; South Dakota, State Census, 1905, State Archives Collection, South Dakota State Historical Society (SDSHS), Pierre.

3. In the biblical account, Ananias sold some property and lied to the apostles about the amount of the proceeds. When his lie was revealed, he fell down and died. Acts 5:1–5 Revised Standard Version. In a well-known but likely apocryphal story, a young George Washington said, "I cannot tell a lie," when asked who chopped down a cherry tree. "Washington and the cherry tree," Answers.com, www.answers.com/topic/Washington-and-the-cherry-tree, accessed 1/3/07.

4. Philip may be referring to Irish-born Frank McGrath who settled on the Big White River in 1884. McGrath had a store in Westover and was the postmaster there. His nickname may have been Pat because Robert Parks refers to the Westover postmaster as Pat in Bert L. Hall, comp., Roundup Years: Old Muddy to Black Hills, Centennial ed. (Winner, S.Dak.: Western South Dakota Buck-a-roos, 2000), p. 33. See also Murdo Coyote, 4 Dec. 1924.

5. The Rosebud Indian Reservation was established in 1889, and around the turn of the twentieth century, the United States government hired Indian workers to construct a barbed wire fence to enclose the reservation pasture lands to keep white-owned cattle out. The effort was not terribly successful. In the cattle roundup of 1902, sixty-two thousand head of white-owned cattle were collected. Jordan, "Eighty Years on the Rosebud," p. 356.

6. Charles McChesney, a New Jersey native, was agent on the Rosebud Indian Reservation, where he lived with his wife, Helen, and daughter, Mary. Charles P. Jordan spent his adult life among the Sioux Indians, operating a trading post at the Rosebud Agency and serving as interpreter for the Indians, including Red Cloud, before presidents and various commissions. Mark Marston was a partner with John L. Dawson in a store on the Rosebud Indian Reservation. Twelfth Census, Rosebud Indian Reservation, Meyer County, S.Dak.; Jordan, "Eighty Years," pp. 327–28. For more on life on the Rosebud reservation in the early 1900s, see Henry W. Hamilton and Jean Tyree Hamilton, comps., Remington Schuyler's West: Artistic Visions of Cowboys and Indians (Pierre: South Dakota State Historical Society Press, 2004).

7. George W. Bowley was the son of Freeman Mayo Bowley, Jr., who came to Stanley County with John Rea in 1890. They established ranches near Van Metre, and the families were also merchants. Abram J. Bunker had a ranch near Hayes and was a partner in Keyser and Bunker, a lumberyard. Irene Caldwell, ed., Bad River (Wakpa Sica), Ripples, Rages, and Residents (Fort Pierre, S.Dak.: Bad River Women's Club, 1983), pp. 182–83; Hall, Roundup Years, p. 585.

8. The quotation from Alexander Pope comes from his "An Essay on Man, Epistle I," a copy of which can be found in Ian Lancashire, ed., Representative

Poetry Online, www.rpo.library.utoronto.ca/poem/1637.html, accessed 1/4/07. The concept of American Indians as a vanishing race evolved from the social theory that certain dominant races would assimilate other races. An accurate count of the American Indian population is always problematic, but in general, Philip was correct in saying that the number of Indians has increased since 1900. *See* Brian W. Dippie, *The Vanishing American: White Attitudes and U. S. Indian Policy* (Lawrence: University Press of Kansas, 1991), pp. xv–xvii.

9. Robert N. Adams was sentenced to seven years in the South Dakota State Penitentiary for the murder of Ed Sanchez in February 1902. The killing took place at the Northwestern Stage Barn along the Fort Pierre to Deadwood Trail. Hall, *Roundup Years*, pp. 375, 594; "Robert N. Adams," Penitentiary Files, State Archives Collection, SDSHS.

10. Nick L. Janis was a thirty-eight-year-old stock raiser from the Pine Ridge Indian Reservation. Lee, *Last Grass Frontier*, pp. 23, 57; *Twelfth Census*, Pine Ridge Indian Reservation, S.Dak.

11. Adam Smith, a German immigrant who served in the United States Army and worked as a freighter, raised cattle on the Big White River on the Rosebud Indian Reservation. He married Mary Burnette in 1877. *Twelfth Census*, Rosebud Indian Reservation, S.Dak.; *Martin Messenger*, 21 Aug. 1930.

12. For more on Van Moore, *see* Philip to his children, 1 June 1940. In a long aside omitted from this letter, Philip conceded that Sammy Dolphus could be dangerous when cornered and actually shot a man a couple of months after this roundup.

13. J. E. ("Corny") Utterback married Zoe Larabee and was therefore Scotty Philip's brother-in-law. Utterback was an army blacksmith before becoming a rancher. His brand was an anvil in recognition of his days as a blacksmith. Wayne C. Lee, *Scotty Philip, the Man Who Saved the Buffalo* (Caldwell, Idaho: Caxton Printers, 1975), pp. 116, 194–95.

14. This stanza is the first of Rudyard Kipling's "Together," *Rudyard Kipling's Verse*, Definitive ed. (Garden City, N. Y.: Doubleday & Co., 1940), pp. 724–25.

15. A copy of this poem appears as "Sleepin' Out," in *Songs of Men: An Anthology*, ed. Robert Frothingham (Boston: Houghton Mifflin, 1918), p. 173, where it is unattributed.

16. The Swinging Cinch

1. Philip is paraphrasing Alfred, Lord Tennyson's "Locksley Hall," which reads, "In the spring a young man's fancy lightly turns to thoughts of love" (*The Poetical Works of Tennyson*, ed. G. Robert Strange, Cambridge ed. [Boston: Houghton Mifflin Co., 1974], p. 90).

2. This line is the title of a song in the stage production of *Stubborn Cinderella* (1909). *Internet Broadway Database*, www.ibdb.com/ProductionSongs.aspx?ShowN o=1292&ProdNo=5101, accessed 1/4/07.

3. In Shakespeare's *Richard III*, Act V, Scene IV, King Richard fights on foot after his horse is killed, declaring "A horse! a horse! my kingdom for a horse."

4. Willie Heston, an All-American halfback, played for the University of Michigan from 1901 to 1904. Tom Harmon, who played halfback for the University of Michigan from 1938 to 1940, was an All-American and Heisman Trophy winner in 1940. *Bentley Historical Library*, bentley.umich.edu/athdept/football/fballam/ aaheston.htm, and bentley.umich.edu/athdept/football/fballam/aaharmon.htm, both accessed 1/4/07.

5. For more on Pecos Bill, *see* Philip to his children, 12 Dec. 1940.

6. For this story, *see* Philip to his children, 1 June 1940.

7. William C. ("Bogus") Mathieson, the son of George D. Mathieson, owned a ranch on the Bad River above the mouth of Lance Creek in Stanley County. Bogus Mathieson became postmaster at Fort Pierre from 1914 until 1931. Clara Roseth, ed., *Prairie Progress in West Central South Dakota* (n.p.: Historical Society of Old Stanley County, 1968), p. 738; Bert L. Hall, comp., *Roundup Years: Old Muddy to Black Hills*, Centennial ed. (Winner, S.Dak.: Western South Dakota Buck-a-roos, 2000), pp. 303–4; Alan H. Patera, John S. Gallagher, and Kenneth W. Stach, *South Dakota Post Offices* (Lake Grove, Ore.: The Depot, 1990), p. 339.

8. During Tom Jones's career on the open range, he found employment as a roundup man for Scotty Philip and as the head of Richard Mathieson's W M herd. In 1904, he took the position of range foreman for the Native Cattle Company, which ran up to five thousand head of cattle in the area and sold cattle mostly to the government for use on the Indian reservations. When Philip sold his stake in that company in 1908, he and Jones partnered to purchase land on the Lower Brule Indian Reservation. Wayne C. Lee, *Scotty Philip, the Man Who Saved the Buffalo* (Caldwell, Idaho: Caxton Printers, 1975), pp. 202, 214, 249, 258, 297; James M. Robinson, *West from Fort Pierre: The Wild World of James (Scotty) Philip* (Los Angeles: Westernlore Press, 1974), p. 310; Hall, *Roundup Years*, p. 441.

9. W. I. Walker's outfit was the ZT brand, which was part of the Native Cattle Company, of which he was also a stakeholder. Lee, *Scotty Philip*, p. 258.

10. David R. Crippen, born in 1828 in Massachusetts, moved to Dakota Territory in 1883. South Dakota, State Census, 1905, State Archives Collection, South Dakota State Historical Society, Pierre.

11. Captain Edward P. Pearson and the Seventeenth United States Infantry established Fort Bennett sixty miles north of Fort Pierre on 17 May 1870. It served as the Indian agency for the Cheyenne River Indian Reservation until being aban-

doned in 1889. Its location, approximately nine miles below the mouth of the Cheyenne River near the Missouri River, is now covered by Lake Oahe. Clara Roseth, ed., *Prairie Progress in West Central South Dakota* (n.p.: Historical Society of Old Stanley County, 1968), p. 389–90.

12. Philip to his children, 16 Apr. 1940.

13. "Whoever exalts himself will be humbled, and whoever humbles himself will be exalted" appears in Matthew 23:12 Revised Standard Version.

17. Fixing the Wheel

1. The name William Broderick does not appear in South Dakota in any United States or South Dakota census of the time.

2. The South Sea Bubble was a famous British trading scam of 1711, in which a company formed to trade with Spanish South America actually funded government debt following the British involvement in a war over the Spanish succession. Likewise, Crédit Mobilier of America was established by an official of the Union Pacific Railroad to limit stockholder liability and maximize construction profits for the railroad. The company also sold shares at reduced prices to those members of Congress who supported federal subsidies to the railroad. The public learned of the scandal in 1872. "The South Sea Company," *Wikipedia, the Free Encyclopedia*, en.wikipedia.org/wiki/The_South_Sea_Company, accessed 1/5/07; "Crédit Mobilier of America scandal," *Wikipedia*, en.wikipedia.org/wiki/Cr%Cr%3A9dit_Mobilier_of_America_Scandal, accessed 1/8/07.

3. Harry D. Hopkins had married Dora May Feezer of Fort Pierre in 1896. In 1903, they moved to a ranch near Meers, where the couple raised cattle and had a store and road ranch. Harry moved back to Fort Pierre in 1928. *Fort Pierre Times*, 16 June 1938.

4. The 1900 federal census includes a twenty-five-year-old Bradshaw whose first name may be Joe, who was a saloonkeeper in Fort Pierre. John Hack was a native of Germany whose occupation was laborer. U.S., Department of the Interior, Census Office, *Twelfth Census of the United States*, 1900, Stanley County, Fort Pierre, S.Dak., in *AncestryLibrary.com* (subscription required); South Dakota, State Census, 1905, State Archives Collection, South Dakota State Historical Society, Pierre.

5. Sir Walter Scott actually says of his hero Lochinvar's adventure: "There was racing and chasing on Cannobie Lee/But the lost bride of Netherby ne'er did they see" (Scott, *Marmion*, in *The Complete Poetical Works of Sir Walter Scott*, ed. Horace E. Scudder, Cambridge ed. (Boston: Houghton Mifflin Co., 1900), p. 130.

6. In two sentences, Philip refers to Shakespeare's play *Love's Labor's Lost* (1597) and Robert Burns's poem "To a Mouse, on Turning up Her Nest with the

Plough, November, 1785," which contains the line, "The best laid schemes o' mice an' men/Gang aft a-gley" (*Seven Centuries of Verse, English and American, from the Early English Lyrics to the Present Day*, ed. A. J. M. Smith [New York: Charles Scribner's Sons, 1947], p. 276).

7. Joseph Jagger was likely the first man to take advantage of a flaw in a roulette wheel and "break the bank at Monte Carlo" in 1873. Charles Wells, who broke the bank several times, inspired the 1892 song "The Man that Broke the Bank at Monte Carlo." "Monte Carlo," *Wikipedia*, en.wikipedia.org/wiki/Monte_ Carlo, accessed 1/8/07.

18. Mostly 'Cross Country

1. The anonymous "Sunday School Song," which takes a satirical view of the major events occurring in the Bible, exists in many variations. See "Young Folks Old Folks, or The Sunday School Song," www.whitetreeaz.com/yfof/yfof.htm, accessed 1/5/07.

2. Scotty Philip held both shares and the position of director in the Stockgrower's National Bank of Fort Pierre, which in 1903 built the impressive building that still stands on a corner in downtown Fort Pierre. Wayne C. Lee, *Scotty Philip, the Man Who Saved the Buffalo* (Caldwell, Idaho: Caxton Printers, 1975), pp. 218, 253, 288; Jay D. Vogt, Stephen C. Rogers, and Scott Myers, *Picturing the Past: South Dakota's Historic Places*, Historic Preservation Series, no. 3 (Pierre: South Dakota State Historical Society Press, 2006), p. 56.

3. Frank ("Carload") Cottle opened his store in 1887. He received his nickname from his habit of purchasing goods in large quantities. Bert L. Hall, comp., *Roundup Years: Old Muddy to Black Hills*, Centennial ed. (Winner, S.Dak.: Western South Dakota Buck-a-roos, 2000), pp. 435, 566.

4. Rex A. Terry would serve as lieutenant governor of South Dakota in 1948 and 1950, following four terms in the South Dakota State Senate from 1941 to 1947. He would also become managing officer of the Fort Pierre National Bank, president of the Fort Pierre Commercial Club, and city commissioner of Fort Pierre. South Dakota, *South Dakota Legislative Manual*, 1949, 31st Leg. Sess. (Pierre, 1949), p. 395; Irene Caldwell, ed., *Bad River (Wakpa Sica), Ripples, Rages, and Residents* (Fort Pierre, S.Dak: Bad River Women's Club, 1983), p. 234.

5. The Black Hills/Bear Lodge Uplift, a roughly circular mountainous region in western South Dakota and northeastern Wyoming, formed approximately sixty million years ago. The Cheyenne River flows out of the Thunder Basin National Grassland in northeastern Wyoming and through the southern edge of this uplift in South Dakota, draining the Black Hills and emptying into the Missouri River in the central part of the state. U.S., National Park Service, "Geo-

logic Setting,"www2.nature.nps.gov/views/Sites/DETO/HTML/ET_GeoOverview
.htm, accessed 1/5/07.

6. Philip is slightly misquoting Sir Walter Scott's "The Lay of the Last Min-
strel," in *The Complete Poetical Works of Sir Walter Scott*, Cambridge ed. (Boston:
Houghton Mifflin Co., 1900), p. 54.

7. The Germans invaded Norway on 9 April 1940, and Norwegian and British
troops withdrew on 2 May. Germany occupied Norway until 1945. Hell is a small
town situated approximately nineteen miles east of Trondheim in the hilly farm-
land area of Trøndelag in central Norway. "The Invasion of Norway, April 9–May
9, 1940," *World War II Multimedia Database*, worldwar2database.com/html/norway
.htm, accessed 1/5/07; "Mainly Heaven, and a Tiny Bit of Hell," *Visitnorway.com*,
www.tourist.no/templates/NTRarticle.aspx?id=168919, accessed 1/8/07.

8. Michael Quinn arrived in Dakota Territory in 1877 and soon began trans-
porting goods between Pierre and the Black Hills. In 1881, he established a ranch
on the Cheyenne River, moving the concern to the Bad River in 1892. Michael
Quinn gave his name to the town of Quinn in Pennington County, which was
established on, or near, his Bad River ranch in 1906 or 1907. Hall, *Roundup Years*,
p. 352; Bob Lee and Dick Williams, *Last Grass Frontier: The South Dakota Stock Grower
Heritage* (Sturgis, S.Dak: South Dakota Stock Growers Assoc., 1964), p. 60; *Eastern Pennington County Memories* (Wall, S.Dak.: American Legion Auxiliary, Carrol
McDonald Unit, n.d.), p. 264.

9. William Hopkins owned and operated a "road ranch," or hotel, and store
in Hayes from 1899 onwards. In 1907, he was elected to the Stanley County Board
of Commissioners and served in that position for four years. Ella B. Porterfield,
Hopkins's sister, later moved to Rapid City but continued to make lengthy trips
to visit her brother in Hayes, dying there in 1935. *Fort Pierre Times*, 15 Aug. 1935, 11
Nov. 1943.

10. Ed Olney ranched on the upper Bad River near Philip and used the ONY
brand. Buzzard Creek, where Philip ran afoul of Olney's barbed wire, is a few
miles west of Nowlin in Haakon County. Hall, *Roundup Years*, p. 31; *Van Dersal's
Stock Growers' Directory of Marks and Brands for the State of South Dakota*, 1902 (Aberdeen,
S.Dak.: *Dakota Farmer*, [1902]), p. 46; *South Dakota Atlas & Gazetteer* (Yarmouth,
Maine: DeLorme, 1997), p. 40.

11. William Powell, son of the elder Dan Powell, was born in 1886 near Powell,
South Dakota, and died 22 July 1968. Billy Powell ranched with his father on the
family's Bad River ranch and later served as county sheriff for Stanley County
from 1940 to 1944. *Fort Pierre Times*, 25 July 1968; James M. Robinson, *West from
Fort Pierre: The Wild World of James (Scotty) Philip* (Los Angeles: Westernlore Press,
1974), p. 73; Caldwell, *Bad River (Wakpa Sica)*, pp. 175–77; Clara Roseth, ed., *Prairie

Progress in West Central South Dakota (n.p.: Historical Society of Old Stanley County, 1968), p. 743.

12. For the earlier cinch episode, *see* Philip to his children, 27 Nov. 1940.

13. The Rosenbaum Brothers Commission Company was established in Chicago in 1874 by Joseph Rosenbaum and his brother, both born in Bavaria. Among other enterprises, the company owned banks and acted as loan agent for cattlemen across the West. *Time*, 1 Aug. 1927, p. 1; "Rosenbaum, Joseph," www .livestockexpo.org/ssclub/ssbook_pdfs/pqr.pdf, accessed 1/9/07.

14. *See* Philip to his children, 24 Oct. 1939, for this episode.

15. A long-time resident of Midland, Charles W. Robertson owned or ran at various times a lumberyard, a farm equipment dealership, a livery, and a movie theater. Faye Jones, et al., eds., *Historic Midland, 1890–1986* (Midland, S.Dak: Midland Pioneer Museum, 1986), pp. 20, 110.

19. Working up an Appetite

1. Iowa-born Grace Noll Crowell (1877–1969) became poet laureate of Texas in 1938. This poem appeared in the *Saturday Evening Post*, 27 July 1940, p. 40. "Crowell, Grace Noll," *The Handbook of Texas Online*, www.tsha.utexas.edu/handbook/online/articles/cc/fcr57.html, accessed 1/12/07.

2. Charlie Hurst worked as a cowboy for Henry Angel, a ranchman from Dewey County. Irish-born Andrew Feeney immigrated to America as a young boy. He ranched on the Bad River fifteen miles southwest of Fort Pierre. Feeney was elected sheriff of Stanley County in 1905. Ludger LaBreque was born in Quebec, Canada, and immigrated to Dakota Territory as a young man, working first as a bullwhacker for a freighting company. He became a successful cattle rancher in Stanley County and often worked as a wagon boss for roundup pools. Bert L. Hall, comp., *Roundup Years: Old Muddy to Black Hills*, Centennial ed. (Winner, S.Dak.: Western South Dakota Buck-a-roos, 2000), p. 600; *Fort Pierre Times*, 10 May 1956; *Pioneers of the Open Range: Haakon County, South Dakota, Settlers before January 1, 1906* (Midland, S.Dak., Pioneer Club of Western South Dakota, n.d.), pp. 124–25; Clara Roseth, ed., *Prairie Progress in West Central South Dakota* (n.p.: Historical Society of Old Stanley County, 1968), p. 45.

3. Bill Durkin worked for J. Q. Anderson, whose ranch was between Presho and Vivian. Alex Meader, a young horse wrangler during the roundup years, eventually moved to California. James M. Robinson, *West from Fort Pierre: The Wild World of James (Scotty) Philip* (Los Angeles: Westernlore Press, 1974), pp. 185–87; Hall, *Roundup Years*, p. 146. Philip goes into a long aside about these two men that is reproduced here:

Bill Durkin not so long after that got into some horse-stealing difficulty with Buffalo George, and it seems to me through the haze of years that Bill about that time decided to swell western Canada's then rapidly growing population. I hope he prospered because Bill was really a good sort of fellow. Not so long after that, Alex Meader was with Bob Adams, a crack six-shooter shot, at Mexican Ed's place on the North Fork of Bad River. They had an altercation, apparently fostered by Bob Adams who irritated old Ed until he pulled a gun. Much too quick from careful cultivation of the art of the draw, Bob pulled and shot Mexican Ed right in the eye, the bullet coming out at the back of his head.

I saw Mexican Ed's body at the time of the inquest in Fort Pierre. Bob Adams claimed self-defense at his trial, but the jury found him guilty of manslaughter, and he got seven years for it. Alex was a witness at the trial. It may be interesting to note in passing that Alex Meader, a short, stubby, duck-legged sort of a chap, was a cracker-jack bronco rider. Alex never had to leave the country, and he still lives about Elm Springs in the east end of Meade County. He was a nice fellow, and it is still a pleasure to meet up with him once in a while in Rapid City and have a visit with him about old times. Such were the two fellows we found in the line riders' camp.

4. Svend Halvorsgard (also Halvardsgaard) was born in Norway in 1853. He taught school and worked at a sawmill where his right leg was crushed between two logs and had to be amputated below the knee. He and his family left Norway in 1881, settling first in the Canton, South Dakota, area and moving to Lyman County in 1893. The family ran several head of cattle and built the Halvardsgaard Store near their home buildings in Cavite, a small town named for the Filipino province of the same name, probably by someone who had served with the South Dakota National Guard in the Spanish-American-Cuban-Filipino War (1898–1901). Halvorsgard was postmaster of Cavite from 1901 to 1916. In addition to three sons, Svend and his wife Margit actually had three daughters: Martha born in 1882, Anna born in 1884, and Betsy born in 1892. *"Winds of Change" in Lyman County* (Presho, S.Dak.: Lyman County Historical Society, 1997), pp. 167–69; Alan H. Patera, John S. Gallagher, and Kenneth W. Stach, *South Dakota Post Offices* (Lake Grove, Ore: The Depot, 1990), p. 237; Steven J. Bucklin, ed. "We were all mustered in Uncle Sam's Army: The Journal of Thomas H. Briggs in the Philippines, 1898–1899," *South Dakota History* 34 (Fall 2004): 237.

20. Hot Irons on Live Hides

1. Bert Leston Taylor's daily column was titled "Line o' Type or Two" for the *Chicago Tribune* from 1910 until his death in 1921. "Newspapers," *Encyclopedia of Chicago*, www.encyclopedia.chicagohistory.org/pages/889.html, accessed 1/9/07.

2. At this point, Philip inserted a copy of the prearranged plan for the 1902 spring roundup, which is reproduced in its entirety as an appendix to this book. *See* pp. 305–7.

3. Created in around 1760 B.C., the Babylonian Code of Hammurabi set out two hundred eighty-two rules and laws. The state of South Dakota enacted its first legislation related to brands in 1861 and, in 1897, required statewide registration. A brief survey of the state law can be found in Manfred R. Wolfenstine's *The Manual of Brands and Marks*, ed. Ramon F. Adams (Norman: University of Oklahoma Press, 1970), pp. 207–8. *See also* South Dakota, State Brand Board, "'A Tale of the Hot Iron Brand': The Evolution of Brands, the South Dakota Brand Board, and Livestock Ownership Inspection" (Pierre, 1994).

4. The Capitol Freehold Land and Investment Company registered the XIT brand in 1882. It could be found in up to nine counties in Texas. David Dary, "Cattle Brands," *The Handbook of Texas Online*, www.tsha.utexas.edu/handbook/online/articles/CC/auc1.html, accessed 1/10/07. For more on Texas brands and the XIT brand in particular, *see A Century of Texas Cattle Brands* (Fort Worth, Tex.: Fair Publishing Co., 1936) and J. Evetts Haley, *The XIT Ranch of Texas and the Early Days of the Llano Estacado* (Norman: University of Oklahoma Press, 1967).

5. John Simpson Chisum, known as the "Cow King of New Mexico," helped establish the cattle trade in New Mexico. Chisum himself estimated that rustlers stole over ten thousand head of cattle from him. Jesse Chisholm was a Scottish and Cherokee trader and interpreter who blazed the Chisholm Trail, which ran from Fort Leavenworth, Kansas, to Oklahoma City, Oklahoma, in 1865. Howard R. Lamar, ed., *The New Encyclopedia of the American West* (New Haven, Conn.: Yale University Press, 1998), pp. 208–9; T. C. Richardson, "Chisholm, Jesse," *The Handbook of Texas Online*. Philip himself had the two last names transposed in his original letter; for clarity, I corrected his spellings.

6. The Quien Sabe brand belonged to W. H. Funk of Briscoe County, Texas. "Famous Texas Cattle Brands poster," FrontierTimes.com, frontiertimes.com/poster_info.html, accessed 1/10/07; David Dary, "Cattle Brands."

7. Pierre ("Peter") Abelard was a twelfth-century philosopher and theologian, whose liaison with a young woman named Heloise resulted in her pregnancy. Her uncle then had Abelard castrated, but the couple had a son, whose career they monitored from the monastic institutions to which they retired after the castration and birth. *See* Elizabeth Radice, ed., *The Letters of Abelard and Heloise* (New York: Penguin Books, 1974), and Jeff Brower and Kevin Guilfroy, eds., *The Cambridge Companion to Abelard* (New York: Cambridge University Press, 2004).

21. Ailments of the Range

1. John L. Sullivan fought John ("Jake") Kilrain in the last bare-knuckle heavyweight championship in 1889 in a fight that went seventy-five rounds. The two fought exhibition bouts throughout the country following their championship fight. "Jake Kilrain" and "John L. Sullivan," *Wikipedia, the Free Encyclopedia,* en.wikipedia.org/wiki/Jake_Kilrain and en.wikipedia.org/wiki/John_L._Sullivan, accessed 11/8/06.

2. Illinois native Seymour ("Sim") Reber settled on the Bad River east of Philip in 1892 where he ranched with his wife Augusta ("Gussie") Wilbern of Kansas, who had homesteaded with her parents near Philip in 1890. The couple had twelve children and ranched until 1915. *Pioneers of the Open Range: Haakon County, South Dakota, Settlers before January 1, 1906* (Midland, S.Dak., Pioneer Club of Western South Dakota, n.d.), pp. 74–75.

3. Margaret Sanger, an advocate for contraception and women's health, founded the American Birth Control League in 1921 and coined the term "birth control." "Margaret Sanger," *Wikipedia,* en.wikipedia.org/wiki/Margaret_Sanger, accessed 1/5/2007.

4. George D. ("Dad") and Kate Congleton Mathieson settled in Fort Pierre in 1879. Their children, some of whom are mentioned elsewhere in this story, were: Joseph D., Robert B., Willie C., Mabel, George D., Richard W., John, Kate, Margaret, Charles S., Clarence, and Joseph. U.S., Department of the Interior, Census Office, *Tenth Census of the United States, 1880,* and *Twelfth Census of the United States, 1900,* both in AncestryLibrary.com (subscription required).

5. Lawrence Madsen was one of eleven children born to Danish immigrants Truels ("T. M.") and Caroline Madsen, who raised cattle and sheep on a ranch twenty-two miles west of Pierre on the Bad River. *Pioneers of the Open Range,* p. 38.

6. Hair follicles infected with *Staphylococcus* bacteria form boils. If the bacteria enter the bloodstream, septicemia (blood poisoning) can result. A native of Canada, Robert J. Jackson obtained his medical degree from Michigan Medical College in 1902 and moved to Yankton before moving to Rapid City, where he also served as coroner. "Boils and carbuncles," *MayoClinic.com,* www.mayoclinic.com/boils-and-carbuncles/DS00466/DSECTION=3, accessed 1/11/07; *A History of Pennington County, South Dakota* (Rapid City, S.Dak.: Pennington County History Book Committee, n.d.), p. 140.

7. In the Old Testament (Job 2–3 Revised Standard Version) account, God allowed Satan to afflict Job with painful sores. Job at first refused to complain, but after seven days he began to lament his condition. Burton K. Wheeler was a

United States senator from Montana who advocated isolationism during World War II and opposed aid to Britain. "Burton K. Wheeler," *Wikipedia*, en.wikipedia .org/wiki/Burton_K._Wheeler, accessed 1/11/07.

8. Born in Missouri, Henry Hudson came to Stanley County in 1898 and worked for several different ranchers, including Fred Holcomb, George Mathieson, Scotty Philip, and Lewis LaPlante. Bud Holcomb may be a reference to Algernon L. Holcomb, who died after he was thrown from a horse on 11 October 1891 on his ranch on White River. Clara Roseth, ed., *Prairie Progress in West Central South Dakota* (n.p.: Historical Society of Old Stanley County, 1968), pp. 455–57; Bert L. Hall, comp., *Roundup Years: Old Muddy to Black Hills*, Centennial ed. (Winner, S.Dak.: Western South Dakota Buck-a-roos, 2000), p. 268.

9. Minnesota-native Hugh Schultz married Olive Philip, Scotty Philip's daughter, on 24 July 1906. By 1920, the couple was living with and working for Stanley Philip. Sometime between 1920 and 1923, the couple apparently divorced. Hugh Schultz died in Huron in 1937, and his obituary mentions only his wife Marie, whom he married in 1923. Olive Philip died 22 May 1950 in New Mexico. Her obituary makes no mention of Hugh Schultz. *Fort Pierre Stock Growers News*, 26 July 1906; *Fort Pierre Times*, 26 Aug. 1937, 8 June 1950; Fourteenth Census, 1920, Lyman County.

10. A range blessing is a profane scolding.

11. In 1762, surgeon's apprentice Edward Jenner first learned the folk belief that those who had cowpox would not get smallpox. The Englishman tested the theory in 1796, injecting a subject first with tissue from a cowpox lesion and then with matter from a smallpox lesion. By 1800, vaccination with cowpox was an accepted procedure. Stefan Riedel, "Edward Jenner and the History of Smallpox and Vaccination," *Baylor University Medical Center Proceedings* 18 (Jan. 2005): 21–25. For more on George Washington's experience with smallpox, *see* " 'More to dread . . . than from the Sword of the Enemy,' " *George Washington's Mount Vernon Estate & Gardens*, www.mountvernon.org/visit/plan/index.cfm/pid/237/, accessed 1/12/07.

12. Smallpox first appeared in the Upper Missouri River region in the 1780s, following the trading routes, and periodic epidemics through the 1830s nearly eliminated the Arikara, Hidatsa, and Mandan Indians—sedentary tribes of farmers and hunters who once controlled the river in what would become South Dakota and North Dakota. Ironically, the outbreak in 1901 that began on the Cheyenne River Indian Reservation spread to many residents of Fort Pierre when infected Indians visited the town to do their trading. Quarantine camps and vaccination programs were quickly set up to halt the disease. R. G. Robertson, *Rotting Face: Smallpox and the American Indian* (Caldwell, Idaho: Caxton Press, 2001), pp.

158, 164; U.S., Department of the Interior, Office of Indian Affairs, *Report of the Commissioner of Indian Affairs, 1901*, pt. 1 (Washington, D.C.: Government Printing Office, 1902), p. 359.

13. The NSS brand belonged to Narcisse Narcelle, who operated on the lower Moreau River. Narcelle's foreman, Ed Lyman, was originally from the Yankton Indian Reservation and had an allotment on the Cheyenne River reservation. *Boss Cowman: The Recollections of Ed Lemmon*, ed. Nellie Snyder Yost (Lincoln: University of Nebraska Press, 1969), p. 218; *Faith Country Heritage, 1910–1985* (Faith, S.Dak.: Faith Historical Committee, 1985), p. 234. For the Rattlesnake Butte story, *see* Philip to his children, 24 Aug. 1939.

14. Annie Philip, who was born in 1897, was the youngest of Scotty and Sarah Philip's ten children. She died in 1902 at the age of five after being injured in a fall. George Philip, "James (Scotty) Philip, 1858–1911," *South Dakota Historical Review* 1 (1935): 29.

15. Philip is correct in stating that *Variola minor*, or varioloid, is a milder form of the smallpox virus, a strain that evolved after the advent of vaccination and modern treatments. *Variola major*, the deadly original variety, came in two forms: *Variola vera* and *Variola hemorrhagica*, with *Variola vera* being the most common. The highly contagious disease is airborne, entering through the respiratory system. Robertson, *Rotting Face*, pp. 37–38.

16. R. E. ("Dick") Curran was born in Wisconsin in 1881 and moved to Fort Pierre with his parents as a young boy. He worked with his father and brothers in the contracting and building business. *Fort Pierre Times*, 28 May 1942.

17. The upper Ree Indian Village had once been a fortified assemblage of more than thirty earth lodges belonging to the Arikara (Ree) Indians who farmed and hunted along the Missouri River in the late 1700s. Explorers Meriwether Lewis and William Clark noted the presence of the village in 1804, mentioning that it had been abandoned a few years earlier. The waters rising behind Oahe Dam inundated the site in 1959. Donald J. Lehmer and David T. Jones, *Arikara Archeology: The Bad River Phase*, Smithsonian Institution, River Basin Surveys, Publications in Salvage Archeology, no. 7 (Lincoln, Nebr., 1968), pp. 3, 5, 47–48; Charles E. DeLand, "The Aborigines of South Dakota," pt. 1, *South Dakota Historical Collections* 3 (1906): 542–44.

18. This episode appears in Philip to his children, 4 Mar. 1937.

19. At the time Philip was writing, Yugoslavia and Greece had surrendered to the Nazis and the Germans were bombing London. Norman Polmar and Thomas B. Allen, *World War II: America at War, 1941–1945* (New York: Random House, 1991), pp. 4–5.

Afterword

1. Ike Blasingame, *Dakota Cowboy: My Life in the Old Days*. (New York: G. P. Putnam's Sons, 1958), p. 228.

2. Hazel Adele Pulling, "History of the Range Cattle Industry of Dakota," *South Dakota Historical Collections* 20 (1940): 507.

3. Richard W. Slatta, *Comparing Cowboys and Frontiers: New Perspectives on the History of the Americas* (Norman: University of Oklahoma Press, 2001), pp. 8–9, 104–5; Richard W. Slatta, *The Cowboy Encyclopedia* (New York: W. W. Norton, 1994), p. 29; Harry F. Thompson, ed., *A New South Dakota History* (Sioux Falls, S.Dak.: Center for Western Studies, Augustana College, 2005), pp. 257–58; Pulling, "History of the Range Cattle Industry, p. 470; Warren A. Beck and Ynez D. Haase, *Historical Atlas of the American West* (Norman: University of Oklahoma Press, 1989), pp. 50–51. For a look at how one fort affected the area and the people around it, *see* Jerome A. Greene, *Fort Randall on the Missouri, 1856–1892* (Pierre: South Dakota State Historical Society Press, 2005).

4. Thompson, *New History of South Dakota*, pp. 260–61.

5. Quoted ibid., p. 261.

6. Herbert S. Schell, *History of South Dakota*. 4th ed., rev. John E. Miller (Pierre: South Dakota State Historical Society, 2004), p. 156; Paula M. Nelson, *After the West Was Won: Homesteaders and Town-Builders in Western South Dakota, 1900-1917* (Iowa City: University of Iowa Press, 1986), p. 6.

7. Schell, *History of South Dakota*, p. 250; Thompson, *New South Dakota History*, pp. 257–62; Ed Lemmon, *Boss Cowman: The Recollections of Ed Lemmon, 1857–1946*, ed. Nellie Snyder Yost (Lincoln: University of Nebraska Press, 1969), pp. 210–12; Pulling, "History of the Range Cattle Industry," pp. 471–72, 477; Edward Everett Dale, *The Range Cattle Industry: Ranching on the Great Plains from 1865 to 1925*, new ed. (Norman: University of Oklahoma Press, 1960), p. 76.

8. W. H. Hamilton, *Dakota: An Autobiography of a Cowman*, Intro. Thomas D. Isern (Pierre: South Dakota State Historical Society, 1998), pp. 28–29.

9. John Hudson, "Two Dakota Homestead Frontiers," *Annals of the Association of American Geographers* 63 (Dec. 1973): 453–54; Pulling, "History of the Range Cattle Industry," p. 486; Dale, *Range Cattle Industry*, p. 95.

10. Herbert T. Hoover, "The Sioux Agreement of 1889 and Its Aftermath," *South Dakota History* 19 (Spring 1989): 58.

11. Bruce Siberts and Walker D. Wyman, *Nothing but Prairie and Sky: Life on the Dakota Range in the Early Days* (Norman: University of Oklahoma Press, 1954), p. 30.

12. Hughes, quoted in Peter Iverson, *When Indians Became Cowboys: Native Peoples*

and Cattle Ranching in the American West (Norman: University of Oklahoma Press, 1994), p. 39.

13. Pulling, "History of the Range Cattle Industry," p. 479; Lemmon, *Boss Cowman*, p. 229; Schell, *History of South Dakota*, p 251; Thompson, *New South Dakota History*, p. 267.

14. Quinn, quoted in Bert L. Hall, comp., *Roundup Years: Old Muddy to Black Hills*, Centennial ed. (Philip, S.Dak.: Western South Dakota Buck-a-roos, 2000), p. 19.

15. Hall, *Roundup Years*, pp. v, 19, 34.

16. For other prominent firsthand accounts, *see* Slatta, *Cowboy Encyclopedia*, pp. 16–21, and compare with the experiences of other South Dakota cowboys in Hall, *Roundup Years*.

17. Philip to his children, 24 Aug. 1939. For more ranch realism, *see* Elsie Carlson Stokes, "A History of the AU7," *Bits and Pieces* 7 (Jan./Feb. 1971): 21–28.

18. Philip to his children, 4 Mar. 1937, 24 Aug., 24 Oct. 1939. Compare to Slatta, *Cowboy Encyclopedia*, p. 348; Hamilton, *Dakota*, p. 141.

19. Philip to his children, 24 Aug. 1939, 14 Aug. 1940, 20 May 1941.

20. *See* Hamilton, *Dakota*, pp. 66–67, 99–100; Nelson, *After the West Was Won*, pp. 39–40.

21. Philip to his children, 30 Sept. 1940. *See also* Richard W. Slatta, *Cowboy: The Illustrated History* (New York: Sterling, 2006), pp. 59–60.

22. Philip to his children, 24 Aug. 1939. *See also* Richard W. Slatta, *Cowboys of the Americas* (New Haven: Yale University Press, 1994), p. 227.

23. Blasingame, *Dakota Cowboy*, p. 274. *See also* Siberts and Walker, *Nothing but Prairie and Sky*, pp. 140–49, and Slatta, *Comparing Cowboys and Frontiers*, pp. 110–12.

24. Blasingame, *Dakota Cowboy*, p. 202; Edward Charles ("Teddy Blue") Abbott and Helena Huntington Smith, *We Pointed Them North: Recollections of a Cowpuncher*, new ed. (Norman: University of Oklahoma Press, 1955), p. 108; Slatta, *Comparing Cowboys and Frontiers*, pp. 115–16.

25. Lemmon, *Boss Cowman*, p. 224. For examples of the full range of cowboy humor, *see* Slatta, *Cowboy*, pp. 152–60.

26. Richard W. Slatta, "Long Hours and Low Pay: Cowboy Life on the Northern Plains," *South Dakota History* 32 (Fall 2002): 194–95; Pulling, "History of the Range Cattle Industry," pp. 479, 507; Lori Ann Lahlum, "'Everything was changed and looked strange': Norwegian Women in South Dakota," *South Dakota History* 35 (Fall 2005): 189–216; Thompson, *New South Dakota History*, p. 226. On immigration, *see also* Shirley Fischer Arends, *The Central Dakota Germans: Their*

History, Language, and Culture (Washington, D.C.: Georgetown University Press, 1989).

27. Howard R. Lamar, ed., The New Encyclopedia of the American West (New Haven, Conn.: Yale University Press, 1998), p. 784; Hoover, "Sioux Agreement of 1889," p. 65; Iverson, When Indians Became Cowboys, pp. 34–39.

28. Paula M. Nelson, The Prairie Winnows Out Its Own: The West River Country of South Dakota in the Years of Depression and Dust (Iowa City: University of Iowa Press, 1996), p. xix.

29. James J. Balakier, ed., "Homesteading on the Rosebud: The Reminiscence of Mabelle Stewart Worsley," South Dakota History 35 (Fall 2005): 229–30.

30. Nelson, Prairie Winnows Out Its Own, p. xx; Schell, History of South Dakota, pp. 159-67; Thompson, New South Dakota History, p. 484.

31. Earl Martin, " 'Plenty of Work and Fair Wages': A Cowboy's Letters from the Range," ed. Molly Kruckenberg, Montana, the Magazine of Western History 56 (Autumn 2006): 65.

32. Thompson, New History of South Dakota, pp. 273, 484; Slatta, Cowboy Encyclopedia, p. 121. For an account of haying as ranch work, see the letters of Remington Schuyler in Jean Tyree Hamilton and Henry W. Hamilton, comps., Remington Schuyler's West: Artistic Visions of Cowboys and Indians, Afterword Brian W. Dippie (Pierre: South Dakota State Historical Society Press, 2004), pp. 32–39.

33. Linda M. Hasselstrom, Feels like Far: A Rancher's Life on the Great Plains (New York: Lyons Press, 1999), pp. 3, 16.

INDEX

When required for clarity, page references for end notes may include the chapter number (e.g., 322:5n1 indicates page 322, chapter 5, note 1)

Abbott, Edward Charles ("Teddy Blue"), 302
Abelard, Pierre, 272, 346n7
Accidents and injuries: from barbedwire, 246–54; being dragged, 280–82; being gored, 317n14; being thrown, 227–28, 348n8; from cactus, 86–87; from falling horse, 56–57, 118–19, 209–11, 315n5. *See also* Health
Adams, Robert N., 201, 339n9, 345n3
African Americans: Bunk White, 115–23; Fannie Tincup, 325n13; George Philip defends, 5–6; as railroad porters, 27; Sam Baker, 181; Tom Beverly on, 92
Ailments. *See* Health
Alcohol/alcoholism: American Indians and, 98–99, 199; cowboy use of, 301–2; Cy Hiett and, 11–13, 16–17; frontier medicine and, 42; Hostetter's bitters, 12, 112, 309n4; and prohibition, 25–28, 312n17; Tom Beverly and, 91–92, 94–98, 111–13; women and, 178
American Birth Control League, 347n3
American bison. *See* Buffalo
American Indians: alcohol/alcoholism and, 142, 199–200; Arikara (Ree) Indian village, 294, 349n17; assimilation of, 338n8; burial practices of, 319n1; as cattle owners,

59, 183, 299, 303, 337n1; cowboy work ethic of, 198–99; education of, 324n11; and General Allotment Act of 1887, 303; intermarriage of with whites, 6, 176–78, 314n28, 315n4, 318n23, 320n7, 334n2, 337n1; mixed-blood, 198, 204, 270; smallpox epidemic and, 288–89, 348n12; South Dakota reservations, x–xi, 299; government land acquisitions from, 45, 297–98; *United States v. Pelican*, 107, 326n20. *See also* individual reservations
Amonett, Billy, 22, 24, 35
Anderson, J. Q., 344n3
Angel, Henry, 344n2
Anuradhapura, Sacred City of, 189, 337n15
Ash, Ben, 317n14
Ashley, Pete, 16, 182–84, 310n8
Aurora borealis, 70–76, 253, 321n2, 321n8

Bacon, Frank, 122, 329n8
Badlands, White River, 151–55, 175, 262–63, 284, 333n10
Baker, Sam, 181
Bar Bell horse outfit, 240–44, 248
Bastion, Dan W., 177, 335n4
Bastion, Sophia, 335n4
Battle of Waterloo, 95, 324n9
Bell, James, 306
Belle Fourche, S.Dak., 303

Belvidere, S.Dak., 155–56, 158, 175, 209, 319n2

Ben Hur: A Tale of the Christ (Wallace), 324n7

Bennett, Cassius C. ("Cash"), 134, 330:10n4

Bennett, S. Dak., 298

Benthine, Jim, 183

Berry, Tom, 5

Beverly, Frank, 88

Beverly, Tom, 5–6, 88–106, 109–13, 222, 225

Binder, Joseph B., 13, 310n5

Bixby, S. Dak., 91, 324n6

Black Hills: Custer Expedition to, 335n3; formation of, 241, 342n5; gold rush in, 298; opening of to whites, 269; range cattle in, 298

Black Hills General Hospital, 5

Black Hills Power and Light Company, 5

Black Hills State University, 322:5n1

Blasingame, Ike, 297, 301–2, 321n6, 328n4

Blizzards. See Weather

Bodley, A. L., 318n19

Boils, 282–87, 293, 347n6

Bonney, William ("Billy the Kid"), 35, 93, 270, 324n7

Borden, Jack, 13, 306, 310n6

Borst, William O. ("Billie"), 59, 318n22

Boucher, Lyman T. ("Old Bouch"), 62, 140–42, 319n4

Bowen, T. E., 58, 318n19

Bowley, Freeman Mayo, Jr., 338n7

Bowley, George W., 198, 338n7

Bradshaw, C., 335n4

Bradshaw, Joe, 341n4

Brands/branding: Bar Bell, 240; BXB, 299, 324n6; D P, 16, 174, 310n8; earmarks, castration, and wattles,

90, 272–73, 323:7n4; as evidence of ownership, 269–73, 323n4; Hashknife, 299–300; as heraldry of the range, 269–70; hind-foot roping for, 88; horses, 84, 117, 174–75, 179; JR–, 318n17; law of 1862, 297; L-7, 4, 94, 300; "long rail and jingle bob," 270; of mavericks & slicks, 271, 279; NSS, 318n23, 349n13; 101, 299; ONY, 343n10; Quien Sabe, 270–71, 346n6; reading of, 78, 182; registration of, 297, 346n3; running iron and, 322n2; Russian wagon, 114–15; 73 outfit, 4, 300; spring roundup for, 88–90; XIT, 270, 346n4; ZT, 340n9

"The Bridge of Sighs" (Hood), 113, 327n29

Briggs, Clyde F., 328n5

Briggs, Harry F., 84–87, 118, 137–39, 179, 185, 215–16, 228, 322:6n2

Briggs, Mamie, 221

Briggs-Melady Cattle Company, 322:6n2

Brisbine, Hiram Ellsworth ("Hite"), 189–90, 337n14

Broderick, William ("Pecos Bill"), 221–22, 231–37, 341n1

Broncobuster/bronc peeler, 174

Brown, Bill, 106, 325n16

Brown, I. J. M., 306

Buell, Alecia, 146, 332n6

Buell, Charles J. ("Judge"), 144–62, 169–70, 332n7, 331:12n1

Buell, Charles T., 112

Buell, Denu and Philip (law firm), 145

Buell, Maude Mitchell, 161–62, 334n16

Buell, Theresa Fayel Bennett, 331:12n1

Buell, William Gardner, 144, 149–62, 331:12n1

Buffalo: Mexican bullfighting with,

22–40, 311n13; roping and cas-
trating of, 164–73; Scotty Philip
purchase of, 42–43, 314n28; Scotty
Philip role in preserving, 4, 22
Buffalo, S.Dak., 300
Buffalo County, 290
Buffalo George (Joe Cobb), 108,
326n24, 345n3
Buffalo Ranch, 216, 271–72; 334n3
Bullfighting with buffalo, 22–40
Bullock, Seth, 332n5
Bunker, Abram J., 338n7
Burgess, Hughie, 47, 49–50, 109, 122,
235–38, 315n3
Burnett, Amelia, 205, 337n1
Burnett, Johnnie, 192, 205–7, 213,
337n1
Burney, Charley, 29
Burns, Robert, 313n23, 315n2,
317n13, 341n5
Burrowing owl, 18–19, 311n11
Butts, Charlie, 137
BXB brand, 91, 299, 324n6

Calhoon, Frank, 336n13
Calhoon, Jet (Chet), 57, 154, 317n16
California pants, 6, 9, 309n1
Canada: Barren Lands of, 331:12n2
Canton, S.Dak., 345n4
Capa, S.Dak., 106, 177
Capitol Freehold Land and Invest-
ment Company, 346n4
Carlin, Douglas L., 42–43, 314n28
Carlin, Marcella Dupree, 314n28
Carr, Robert V., 213
Carroll, Bill, 181
Case Institute of Technology, 330:9n4
Castration: of buffalo, 164–73; of
cattle, 90, 272–73, 323:7n4
Cattle companies: Briggs-Melady
Cattle Co., 322:6n2; BXB Cattle
Co., 91, 324n6; Capitol Freehold

Land & Investment Co., 346n4;
Circle Dot Ranch, 318n23; Diamond A Cattle Co., 321n7; Dupree
family, 42–43, 314n28; Hash Knife
Ranch, 299–300; JR– outfit, 57,
318n17; LaBrecque, 256; March
Brothers Co., 317n16; Matador
Ranch, 301–2; McQuillian Ranch,
305; Native Cattle Co., 329n6,
340n8; Oglala Cattle Co., 13; OHO
outfit, 323:7n2; Quarter Circle W,
328n4; Rea and Bunker, 198; Sheid-
ley Cattle Co., 335n2; 6 L outfit,
125–26; Spanish Five, 122, 330n3;
TD Ranch, 305; Turkey Track (E-
6) Ranch, 299–300; U Cross out-
fit, 125–26, 262, 324n8, 325n16;
Vermont Cattle Co., 324n6; W. I.
Walker outfit, 226, 340n9; W M
wagon, 225–26, 340n8. See also
Cow outfits; L-7 cattle company;
Roundup outfits; 73 outfit
Cavite, S.Dak., 262, 345n4
Cedar Butte, S.Dak., 156
Chamberlain, S.Dak., 140
Charles Mix County, 290
Cheyenne Bill (cowboy), 109–10
Cheyenne River Agency, 106, 340n11
Cheyenne River Indian Reservation:
cow outfits on, 45–46, 59, 314n1,
318n23; creation of, 299; Fort
Bennett and, 340n11; smallpox
epidemic on, 288–89
Chicago, Milwaukee & St. Paul Rail-
way Company, 61
Chicago Tribune, 268, 345n1
Chisholm, Jesse, 270, 346n5
Chisholm Trail, 270, 346n5
Chisum, John Simpson, 270, 346n5
Chrysler, Walter P., 88, 323:7n1
Churchill, Winston, 127
Circle Dot Ranch, 318n23

Clark, Badger, 10–11, 91
Clark, William, 349n17
Clay County, 297
Clogenson, Paul ("Pollyvoo"), 42–44, 314n28
Clower, John, 113
Cobb, Joe. *See* Buffalo George
Code of Hammurabi, 269, 346n3
Collins, Joel, 298
Conata, S.Dak., 159–60
Coney Island (saloon), 22, 24, 35, 38–39, 313n22
Cooks, roundup, 56, 78–79, 82, 118, 205
Cottle, Frank ("Carload"), 240–41, 342n3
Cottonwood, S.Dak., 243
Coverston, Clem, 160, 334n14
Cowboy code: bedroll and the, 49, 57–58, 128; betting as principle of, 23, 36, 51; customs of, 119; for firing a cowpuncher, 112; regulation of saloons and, 141; roundup as a fraternity of, 196, 210–11, 242; Russian settlers and, 115; traditions and, 130. *See also* Law of the range
Cowboy jargon: augured on guard, 73–74; being on circle, 59–60, 119; broke to ride, 179–82; bronco-buster/bronc peeler, 174; California pants, 6, 9, 309n1; cheeking, 207–8; cotton pickers, 48; day herd/beef herd, 79; fell back, 210–11; fence-line riders, 48; "ga'nt," 116–17; greenhorn/tenderfoot, 91; "I'd tell a man," 259; kilpecker duty, 72, 321n5; knot-head/buzzard-head, 227; mavericks/slicks, 271, 279; nester rancher, 111; range blessing, 348n10; reps, 45–47, 114, 174–75, 182–83, 198, 280; ride like an Indian, 199; riding grub

line, 290–91; road ranch, 235, 297, 341n3, 343n9; 'round the rim-rock, 119; saddle-horse strings, 13–16, 56; soiled doves, 302; sunfishing, 56, 181, 317n15; throw back cattle, 46–47, 256–57; thumbing a horse, 17; U-necked (ewe-necked) horse, 317n16; waddies, 163; war sack, 128; windknocker, 323:7n3; windmill tenders, 48; winter men, 19; working a brand, 270–72; working the watch, 205–9
Cowboy lore: cattle stampede, 275–76; cowboy and his boots, 246–48; cowboy and his hat, 228; cowboy and his horse, 190, 211; cowboy as race of kings, 18; George Philip's preservation of, 6–7, 300–302; men as horses, 255; practical jokes, 131–36, 302; profanity in, 127–28, 242; rodeo and steer riding, 163–64; stereotyping the cowboy, 9, 93–94; wearing six-shooters, 200–203, 301. *See also* Law of the range
Cow country. *See* Open range; Range country
Cow outfits: boom times for, 297–300; gambling and, 137–39, 231–32; Indian reservations and, 299; nester ranch and, 111; Norwegian settlers and, 297; outside men of (reps), 45–47, 114, 174–75, 182–83, 198, 280; ranch hand at, 203; ranch headquarters of, 48; saddle-horse strings of, 13–16, 56; winter men, 19. *See also* Brands/branding; Roundup outfits; Wagon, the
Cox, James B., 133–34, 330n3
Coyotes, 118
Crazy Horse (Sioux Indian), 334n2
Crippen, Dave, 42, 227, 340n10
Crow Creek Indian Reservation, 299

Crowell, Grace Noll, 255, 344n1
Curington, Johnnie, 175, 335n2
Curran, R. E. ("Dick"), 291, 349n16
Custer, George Armstrong, 298, 315n4, 335n3
Custer County, 298, 318n21, 325n18

Dakota Territory. See North Dakota; South Dakota
Dalhart, Tex., 26–27
Dawson, Henry A., 299, 325n16
Dawson, John L., 338n6
Deadwood, S.Dak., 109, 145, 163, 334n1
Death in the Afternoon (Hemmingway), 30
Deffenback brothers (John, Dan, Erasmus), 298
Delehan, Ed, 56, 193, 317n14
Dempsey, Jack, 32, 312n19
Denu, Albert R., 147, 332n7, 331:12n1
Denver, Colo.: gambling in, 234
Devine, Bob, 306
Dewey County, 321n7, 336n9, 344n2
Diamond A Cattle Company, 321n7
Dickey, John W. ("Doc"), 40–42, 313n24
Dilger, William A., 144–62, 331:12n1
Dodge, Richard I., 298
Dolphus, Mary, 106, 325n16–17
Dolphus, Sam ("Black Sam"), 203–4, 339n12
Douglas, Bret, 176
Doyle, Arthur Conan, 318n18
D P brand, 16, 174, 310n8
Drake University, 325n18
Driskill, Tobe, 35
Drunkenness. See Alcohol/alcoholism
Dunn, Mike, 164, 227–28, 334n2
Dunn, Susie Larabee, 334n2
Dupree family, 42–43, 314:1n28, 314:2n1

Dupree, Peter, 42–43, 314n28
Dupree, S.Dak., 46, 311n14, 312n16
Durkin, Bill, 262, 344n3

Eagle Butte, S.Dak., 76, 134, 176, 326n22
Eagles, Fraternal Order of, 26, 337n14
Earmarks, 90, 272–73
Earp, Wyatt, 35
Edwards, Thomas D., 34–35, 38, 313n21
Elliott, James D., 107, 145, 326n21
Ellis, Kans., 88, 323:7n1
El Paso, Tex., 22, 24–25, 28–29, 34–35, 38, 313n22
Ervin, Fred, 3, 106, 122, 176, 290–91, 325n16, 329n7
Evarts, S.Dak., 303
Ewing, Louise Langlois, 315n4
Ewing, Quill, 48, 315n4, 318n23
Explorer II, 17, 311n9

Faith, S.Dak., 291, 317n14, 318n23
Fall River County, 298
Feeney, Andrew, 256–66, 344n2
Fields, W. C., 232
Fiesler, Adolph, 306
Fighting the Underworld (Van Cise), 234
First Hawk, Paul, 324n11
First National Bank: of the Black Hills, 163–64; of Pierre, 134, 330:10n4; of Rapid City, 237; of Winner, 145, 157, 332n3
Fletcher's drug store, 96, 252
Forbes, Lank, 298
Ford, Henry, 254
Fort Bennett, 228, 340n11
Fort Leavenworth, Kans., 346n5
Fort Meade, 53, 298, 316n12
Fort Pierre, S.Dak., 3–4, 22, 79, 106
Fort Pierre National Bank, 331:11n3
Fort Randall, 298

Fort Robinson, Nebr., 4, 310n8
Frankfurter, Felix, 124
Franklin, Willard, 306
Fraternal Order of Eagles, 26, 337n14
Freemasonry. *See* Masons
Funk, W. H., 346n6

Gaffy, Loring Ellis, 62, 106, 217, 227,
    319n4
Gallagher, Martin, 336n12
Gallagher, Pat, 187–89, 336n12–13
Gambling: betting, 23, 36, 51; buck-
    ing the wheel, 231–38, 342n7;
    cheating at, 233–37; in Deadwood,
    58; Mexican monte, 231–32; regu-
    lation of saloons and, 140–43;
    roundup camps and, 137–39, 256
Gann Valley, S.Dak., 290
Gardner, Archibald K., 147, 332n7
Garrett, Patrick Floyd, 35, 313n22
Gas Belt Expositions, 39, 58
Gentry, Faye, 93, 112, 327n28
Gentry, Mary, 327n28
Gershwin, George, 334n17
Giddings, W. David, 62–69, 320n6
Goodell, N. W. ("Win"), 127, 329n1
Gordon, George, 95
Granger, Albert G., 155, 333n12
Grant, Colo., 3
Graves: digging up of, 61–69; rob-
    bing, 319n1
Gray, Bob & Mary, 250, 253
Gray wolves, 13, 116–18, 328n5
Great American Desert, 297–98
Great Sioux Reservation: cattle boom
    and, 269; Fort Pierre to Deadwood
    trail across, 235, 244–45, 314n26;
    and General Allotment Act of 1887,
    303; homesteading on, 4, 297–98;
    subdividing the, 299
Gregory County, 256

Grigsby's Rough Riders, 310n5
Grimes, W. B., 298

Haakon County, 21, 57, 61
Hack, John, 235, 341n4
Hafner, Frank L., 155
Hale, S.Dak., 298
Hall, Bert, 7, 317n15
Halvorson, Svend ("Peg Leg"), 262–
    66, 345n4
Hamilton, W. H., 299
Hammurabi, Code of, 269, 346n3
Hampton University, 324n11
Handley, Jake, 328n4
Hanson County, 319n4
Hardin, John Wesley, 34, 312n20
Harding County, 118, 299, 329n7
Harmon, Tom, 220, 340n4
Harrell, Billie, 22
Harrell, J. W. ("Jimmie"), 47–48, 50,
    56–58, 128, 315n4
Harrell, Loretta, 58
Harvard University, 79, 330:9n4
Hash Knife Ranch, 299–300
Hasselstrom, Linda M., 304
Hayes, Bill, 57, 233
Hayes, Jessie Stewart, 318n17
Hayes, John, 184, 336n11
Hayes, Mary, 57
Hayes, William, 318n17
Hayes, S.Dak., 12, 138, 244, 336n11,
    338n7, 343n9
Hays, Kans., 2–3, 8, 185, 323:7n1
Health: appendicitis and hernia,
    278–80; boils, 282–87, 293, 347n6;
    exercise and sun for, 164–73; and
    frontier medicine, 12, 40–42, 112,
    278, 309n4; mumps, 294–95; and
    snakes, 52–53; smallpox (vario-
    loid), 288–94, 348n11, 349n15;
    Texas itch, 48–50, 57–58, 315n6;

treatment of injuries, 56–57; tuberculosis, 2. *See also* Accidents and injury; Alcohol/alcoholism

Hemmingway, Ernest, 30

Hengel, Anthony D., 328n3

Hess, Billy, 3, 41, 48–49, 51–53, 56, 114, 122, 225–26, 290–91, 294, 315n5

Heston, Willie, 220, 340n4

Hickok, James Butler ("Wild Bill"), 109

Hiett, Cy, 11–13, 16–17, 72–76, 222, 256–57, 310n7

Highmore, S.Dak., 318n17

Hilger, John J., 115, 328n3

Hill, Frankie, 178, 335n6

Hill, Julia Ducheneaux, 177–78, 335n6

Hill, Robert S., 53, 316n12

Hill, Tom, 177–79, 256–66

Hitler, Adolph, 7, 141

Holcomb, Bud, 284, 348n8

Holcomb, Gene, 323:7n2

Holcomb, Orlin, 88, 323:7n2

Holland, John, 85, 323:6n3

Hollis, Leo T., 112, 327n27

Homestead Act of 1862, 303

Homesteading: effect on cowboy life, 58–59; free range days before, 45, 268–69; impact on the open range, 5, 9–11, 106, 267; Norwegian settlers and, 261; opening Indian lands to, 297–98; Russian settlers and, 122

Hood, Thomas, 327n29

Hopkins, Dorothy Feezer, 235, 341n3

Hopkins, Harry ("Hop Lee"), 235, 341n3

Hopkins, William, 12, 243, 250, 343n9

Horses and cowponies: Blue Dog, 249–54; branding/naming of, 84, 117, 179; breaking to ride, 179–82; cowboy and his, 190, 211; cowboy (Cy Hiett) riding skills, 16–17; horse roundups, 174–79, 240–44; horse wrangler duties, 82; knothead/buzzard-head, 227; men are like, 255; and method for firing a cowboy, 112; nighthawk duties with, 72; Old Alligator, 13, 16–17, 310n6; Old Dishrag, 179, 181–90, 226–27, 336n13; practical jokes and, 131–36; range country damage from, 110; roping duties of, 166–67; roundups of, 174–75; saddles and cinch ring for, 214–19, 250; strings of, 13–16, 56, 84–86, 191–92, 221–230; Tamarack, 41–42; "The Strawberry Roan," 181, 336n7; thumbing of, 17; treatment of, 186, 208, 211–12, 220, 228–29; Watcheye, 183, 191–95, 207–9, 211–13; well-trained, 51, 117, 185–86

Hostetter, Joseph, 309n4

Hostetter's bitters, 12, 112

Hoyt, Harry, 118, 120–22, 329n6

Hudson, Henry, 284, 307, 348n8

Hughes, Charles Evan, 107, 326n20

Hughes, John F., 62, 319n3

Hughes County, S.Dak., 319n4, 329n6

Humor and practical jokes: as entertainment, 131–32, 302; on George Philip, 263–66; of George Philip, 291–92; law of the range and, 132–34; of Narcisse Narcelle, 318n23

Huron, S.Dak., 147, 332n7

Hurst, Bill, 77–83, 256, 290, 322:5n1

Hurst, Charlie, 256–66, 290, 344n2

Hurst, Nick, 290

Huston, George S., 140, 331:11n3

Huston, Lizzie, 331:11n3

Imlay, S.Dak., 160, 334n14
Ingersoll, Robert, 35
Interior, S.Dak., 145, 151–55, 158, 284, 333n11
Irwin, Joe, 305

Jackson, George, 57, 84, 229, 282–87, 318n17
Jackson, Robert J., 282, 347n6
Jackson County, 21, 61
Jagger, Joseph, 342n7
Janis, Nick L., 201–2, 339n10
Jefferies, Zay, 129, 330:9n4
Jenner, Edward, 348n11
Jepsen, Victor T., 87, 323:6n5
Johnson, Clarence, 335n6
Johnson, Julius Haugen, 62, 140–43
Jones, Eb, 23–24, 39, 48, 312n16
Jones, Fred ("Rawhide"), 20–22, 43, 294
Jones, Tom, 225, 340n8
Jordan, Charles P., 197–98, 338n6
JR- outfit, 57, 318n17
Juarez, Benito, 312n15
Juarez, Mex., 22–24, 29–39, 313n21
"Judge Not" (Procter), 190, 337n16

Kadoka, S.Dak., 151, 155–56, 158
Kansas: cattle trails from, 298; Chisholm Trail in, 346n5; and beer, 25–26; George Philip in, 2–3, 323:7n1; Scotty Philip in, 4; temperance movement in, 312n17; James Butler ("Wild Bill") Hickok in, 109
Kellar, Chambers, 145, 332n5
Kellar, Florence Bullock, 332n5
Kennedy, Martin Patrick, 105–6, 325n15
Kilrain, Jake, 278, 347n1
Kipling, Rudyard, 211, 334n4
Knight, Jesse, 74, 76, 240, 249, 321n7

L-7 Cattle Company: on Cheyenne River Indian Reservation, 45–46; formation of, 4; George Philip as rep for, 46–47, 56, 114; horse roundup of, 174–79; Ira Miller as foreman of, 105, 111–12; Scotty Philip and, 94, 300; Tom Beverly as foreman of, 94–98
LaBreque, Ludger, 256, 344n2
Langlois, Joseph, 48, 315n4
Langlois, Zoeie Kensler, 315n4
Language, cowboy. See Cowboy jargon
LaPlante, George, 322:6n2
LaPlante, Louis, 315n4, 322:6n2
LaPlante, Ovila ("Babe"), 48, 315n4
Larabee, Helen, 334n2
Larabee, Joseph, 334n2
Larabee, Sarah ("Sally"). See Philip, Sarah ("Sally") Larabee
Larvie, Tom, 306
Lauder, Harry, 145
Lavery, Charles J., 49, 57, 96, 154, 252, 279–80, 293, 316n9
Lawmen: Earp, Wyatt, 35; Feeney, Andrew, 256, 344n2; Garrett, Pat, 35; Huston, George S., 331:11n3; Indian police, 196–97; Kennedy, Martin Patrick, 325n15; Mexican rurales, 34, 38–39; Oakes, W. P. ("Pat"), 329n7; Powell, William, 176, 343n11
Law of the Range: brands/branding and, 269–70; as code of conduct, 124–25, 130; and cow country, 9, 93; and gray wolves, 13, 116–18, 328n5; honesty and, 125–27, 193–94; killing rattlesnakes as, 52, 56; lost saddle horses and, 216; man's past and property and, 128; neighbor's livestock and, 128–29; practical jokes and, 134–36; wagon-boss

authority and, 119–22, 129, 273–75; women and, 129–30. *See also* Cowboy code

Lead, S.Dak., 35, 163, 313n21, 317n16

LeBeau, S.Dak., 303

Leedy, C. I., 305

Lemley, Pete, 161, 334n14

Lemmon, G. E. ("Ed"), 300, 302

Leslie, S.Dak., 183

Lewis, John L., 322:5n1

Lewis, Meriwether, 349n17

Lightnin' (Smith and Bacon), 122, 329n8

Livermont, Henry Alexander, 183, 191–95, 211–13, 336n9

Livermont, Jack, 336n9

Longbrake, Faye, 316n11, 321n6, 326n22, 326n24

"The Lost Chord" (Procter), 190

Lower Brule Agency, 122

Lower Brule Indian Reservation: cow outfits on, 47, 340n8; creation of, 299; overwintering cattle on, 114

Lyman, Ed, 289, 349n13

Lyman County, 261, 345n4

Lynching, 104–5

McAdam, Bob, 59, 318n21

McAdam, Mack, 59, 318n21

McChesney, Charles, 197–98, 338n6

McCoy, James H., 107, 325n19

McDonald, Alvin, 59, 318n21

McDonald, Elmer, 318n21

McDonald, Jesse, 318n21

McDonald, Tommy, 59–60, 289, 318n21

McGarraugh, Gib A., 163–64

McGarry, James, 40, 42, 313n24

McGrath, Frank ("Pat"), 195–96, 338n4

McGuire, Hugh C., 140, 331:11n3

McIntire, Eddie, 163–64

McIntire, George Edgar, 137, 331:11n1

McKenzie, Dode, 301

McKenzie, Murdo, 301

Maclaren, Catherine. *See* Philip, Catherine Maclaren

McLaughlin, S.Dak., 164

McPherson, Kans., 25–26

McQuillian Ranch, 305

Madsen, Lawrence, 280–82, 347n5

Madsen, T. M., 280

March Brothers Company, 317n16

Marmot. *See* prairie dogs

Marston, Mark, 198, 338n6

Martin, Al, 122, 290–91, 329n7

Martin, Earl, 303

Masons, 312n18; George Philip membership in, 5, 189; in Juarez, Mex., 29; lodge as social gathering, 135; in South Dakota, 240, 337n14

Matador Ranch, 301–2

Mathieson, George D. ("Dad"), 193, 280, 337n2, 340n7, 347n4

Mathieson, George (Mrs.), 280

Mathieson, Jack, 193, 337n2

Mathieson, Kate Congleton, 347n4

Mathieson, Kenneth, 177, 335n3

Mathieson, Richard W. ("Dick"), 176–77, 225, 335n3, 340n8

Mathieson, William C. ("Bogus"), 222–23, 340n7

Mavericks, 271, 279

Meade County, 318n22, 330n3

Meader, Alex, 262, 344n3

Medical care/medicine. *See* Health

Meers, Alexander, 115, 119, 327n2

Meers, Anton, 327n2

Meers, Martin, 327n2

Meers, S.Dak., 327n2, 329n9

Mellette County, 256

"Men Are Like Wild Horses" (Crowell), 255

Mexico, 22–40, 311n13

Midland, S.Dak., 21–22, 112, 253, 327n27, 335n4, 344n15
Millay, Lloyd, 145, 332n3
Miller, Eva Wilburn, 279
Miller, Ira, 94, 105, 111–12, 222, 279–80, 324n8
Minnesota and Dakota Cattle Company. See 73 outfit
Missouri River: Arikara (Ree) Indian Village on, 294, 349n17; Fort Pierre shipping point on, 79; overwintering cattle on, 114, 122; steamships on, 3
Missouri River Stockmen's Association, 336n11, 337n2
Mitchell, George W., 145, 332n3
Mitchell, William H., 334n16
Montana: as cow country, 9, 269
Moore, Van Francis, 98–109, 204, 324n12, 325n16–17, 326n22
Moran, Louis ("Posey"), 48–49, 122, 290–91, 314n27
Morgan, Ed, 251
Morrison, Humpy, 175, 335n2
Mossman, Burton C. ("Cap"), 321n7
Moulton, Guy W., 118, 228, 329n6
Mount Rushmore National Memorial, 5
Mullen, M. ("Pat"), 13, 16
Murdo, S.Dak., 47, 62–65, 195
My Early Life: A Roving Commission (Churchill), 127
Myron, Hans, 297

Narcelle, Narcisse ("Savage"), 59, 315n4, 318n23, 349n13; NSS brand of, 101, 299, 318n23, 349n13
Nation, Carry, 25–26, 312n17
Native American Graves Protection and Repatriation Act, 319n1
Native Cattle Company, 329n6, 340n8

Nebraska: as cow country, 9, 298; roundup in, 192, 198; selling horses in, 241; James Butler ("Wild Bill") Hickok in, 109
Newcastle, Wyo., 213
Newlands Reclamation Act of 1902, 302–3
New Mexico, 93, 269, 270, 324n7, 346n5
Nichols, Billie, 235–37
Nordvold, Ort, 163–64
North Dakota, 9, 297
Northern Great Plains, 5, 297–98. See also Open range; Range country
Norway, 261, 297, 343n7, 345n4
Norwegian settlers, 261, 263, 297
NSS brand, 318n23, 349n13

Oakes, Alvira Van Metre, 132, 330n2
Oakes, W. P. ("Pat"), 122, 132–36, 329n7, 330n2
Oglala Cattle Company, 13
O'Hare (priest), 147, 333n8
OHO outfit, 323:7n2
Okaton, S.Dak., 319n2
Oklahoma, 346n5
Old Stanley County, 21–22, 300
Olney, Ed, 246, 252, 343n10
Olson, John, 3
Open range: cattle boom in, 297–300; cowboy pay in, 229; homesteading and the end of, 5, 268–69; law of the range in, 9; preserving the cowboy lore of, 6–8; romantic stereotype of, 239–40; writing the record of, 114, 300–302. See also Range country
Oregon, 269
Out Our Way (Williams), 79, 322:5n3
Outside men. See Reps
Owanka, S.Dak., 151
Owens, Elias, 99–101

"The Passing of the Trail" (Clark), 10–11, 91

Pearson, Edward P., 340n11

Pecos Bill (William Broderick), 221–22, 231–37, 341n1

Pelican, United States v., 107, 326n20

Pennington County, 327n28, 343n8, 331:12n1

Perkins County, 91

Petrified forest tale, 19–22, 294

Philip, Alex, 2–3, 323:7n1

Philip, Alice Island ("Isle") Waldron, 4, 6, 320n7, 330n2

Philip, Amy, 291–92

Philip, Anne, 3, 289–90, 349n14

Philip, Catherine Maclaren, 1

Philip, Clara, 314n25

Philip, George: birth and childhood, 1–2; cowboy years, 2–4, 300; death, 7; education, 4, 62, 106; and horses, 184–87, 189–90, 195, 207–9, 211–13, 217–30; illness, 291–95; injuries/accidents, 209–11, 246–54; the last roundup of, 273–77; law career, 61–69, 107–9, 144–45, 331:12n1; marriage and family, 4–5; photographs, xiv, 4; and the Texas itch, 48–50; turned in his string, 44, 71–72, 187

Philip, George (cousin), 185, 187, 323:7n1

Philip, George, Jr. (son), 4, 7, 282

Philip, James ("Scotty"): 73 outfit and, 13; as banker, 342n2; cow outfits of, 300; emigration from Scotland, 3–4; family of, 289–90; as government cowboy, 310n8; JR– outfit and, 57, 318n17; Mexican bullfighting and, 22–24, 311n13; and preservation of the buffalo, 164–73; standing night guard, 274–77

Philip, Jean, 4

Philip, Olive, 348n9

Philip, Robert (father), 1

Philip, Robert (son), 4, 7, 282

Philip, Roderick ("Rod"), 289, 310n6

Philip, Ruth Borden, 13, 310n6

Philip, Sarah ("Sally") Larabee, 4, 314n27, 326n24, 334n2

Philip, Stanley, 108, 228, 274, 326n23, 348n9

Philip, S.Dak., 4, 175, 279, 310n6, 318n23

Piedmont, S.Dak., 147, 333n8

Pierre, S.Dak., 3, 303

Pine Ridge Indian Reservation: cattle operations on, 47; creation of, 299; roundups on, 192, 300

Politics: in free enterprise and individualism, 254; George Philip and, 5, 21–22; homestead movement and, 303

Pope, Alexander, 199, 338n8

Pope, W. R., 53, 316n12

Porgy and Bess (Gershwin), 334n17

Porter, Frank, 240–44

Porter, William G., 107, 325n18

Porterfield, Ella B., 245, 343n9

Powell, Billy, 176, 245, 247–49

Powell, Dan (father), 174–75, 310n8, 343n11

Powell, Dan (son), 175–76, 229, 245, 247–49

Powell, William, 343n11

Powell, S.Dak., 111

Powers, Tom, 22, 24, 35, 313n22

Prairie Chicken, Paul, 98–105, 324n11

Prairie dogs, 18–19, 311n11

Presho, S.Dak., 344n3

Pressler, Billy, 91, 93, 198, 202–3, 208–11, 213, 222, 323:7n5

Profanity and weather, 127–28

Prostitution, 302
Pulling, Hazel, 297

Quarter Circle W, 328n4
Quien Sabe, 270–71, 346n6
Quinn, Fred, 300
Quinn, Michael, 243, 343n8
Quinn, S.Dak., 151, 243

Rabideaux, John, 318n17
Racism: African-American cowboys and, 115–16; American Indians and, 198–200; custom of the range and, 119–22; George Philip attitude toward, 5–6, 121; Tom Beverly on, 92
Railroads: bison trip to Mexico on, 23–29, 311n13; Chicago, Milwaukee & St. Paul Railway Co., 138; Chicago & Northwestern Railway, 222, 237, 332n7; end of open range and, 303–4; Fort Pierre shipping point, 79, 137–38; influence peddling scam of, 341n2; *Nashville, Chattanooga & St. Louis Railway v. Browning*, 124; Walter P. Chrysler and, 323:7n1
A Rainy Morning in a Cow Camp (Russell), 240
Range country: barbed-wire fences in, 246–47, 259, 303–4, 338n5; winter of 1906-1907, 297; code of conduct in, 124–27; cow outfit operations in, 45–46; cowboy deaths on roundup in, 284; free enterprise in, 254; George Philip's life as record of, 1, 5–8; growth of cattle industry in, 297–300; homesteading and end of, 9–11, 44, 58–59, 189–90, 267; of Texas, 48, 71; winter of 1887 in, 297, 299. *See also* Open range

Rapid City, S.Dak.: Air Corps balloon flights near, 311n9; arrival of railroad in, 140, 303; Buell Building in, 333n9; George Philip relocation to, 4–5, 108; George Philip's death in, 7
Rapid City Daily Journal, 8
Rattlesnake Butte, 59–60, 289
Rattlesnakes: in cowboy lore, 17–19, 311n11; love-locked, 110–11; on Rattlesnake Butte, 59–60; in South Dakota, 316n10–11, 317n13; on Thunder Butte, 46, 50–56
Rea, John, 338n7
Rea and Bunker, 198
Read, Harry, 122, 291–92
Reber, Augusta ("Gussie") Wilburn, 279, 347n2
Reber, Seymour ("Sim"), 278–80, 347n2
Reddick, John E., 112, 327n28
Redfield, C. C., 108
Religion: day of rest and, 301; gambling and, 232; power of prayer, 220; practical jokes and, 134–36; profanity and, 127–28; Russian Mennonites and, 327n2
Reps: cowboys as, 45; George Philip as, 46–47, 56, 114, 198, 240, 280, 284; horse roundups and, 174–79; Pete Ashley as, 182–83; roundup duties of, 119–22
Ricker, Cliff, 246
Road ranch, 235, 297, 341n3, 343n9
Robert, Felix, 22, 29, 33, 36–38
Robertson, Charles W., 253, 344n15
Rocky Mountain oysters, 90
Rodeo: bronc riding in, 323:6n4; as everyday business, 85, 229; steer riding in, 163–64
Rogers, Will, 287

Roosevelt, Franklin D., 5, 70, 321n1
Roosevelt, Theodore, 35, 313n21–22
Rosebud Indian Reservation: cattle
operations on, 47, 337n1; creation
of, 299; fencing of, 195–96, 338n5;
law enforcement on, 196–98;
roundups on, 192, 256–67, 300,
323:7n5
Rosenbaum Brothers Cattle Commission Company, 251, 344n13
Roundup cooks, 56, 78–79, 82, 118,
205
Roundups and roundup outfits: Bad
River pool, 84, 222, 229, 271; bed
wagons and mess wagons, 78–82;
castration, 90; Cheyenne River
Pool, 317n15; day herders, 72;
foreman/pilot of, 79–80; horse
roundups, 174–79; horse wrangler duties, 82; Indian roundup
wagon, 192, 198–200, 213; injury
and death on, 284; 1901 program,
305–7; 1902 West River roundup,
300, 338n5, 323:7n5; night guards,
70–76; nighthawks, 72, 78; operations of, 45–46, 59; pooled wagons, 322:6n1; reps (outside men),
119; Rosebud Indian Reservation
roundup, 192; Russian wagon, 114–
15, 290; stockmen's associations
and, 269, 336n11, 337n2; throw
back wagons, 256–57; wagon boss
authority, 119–22, 129, 273–75,
284–85. See also Brands/branding;
Reps
Roundup wagon: components of,
79–80; defined, 11–12; 1901 roundups and, 305–7; rep operations
and, 45–46; cattle boom and, 300.
See also Cow outfits; Roundups and
roundup outfits
Roundup Years (Hall), 7, 317n15

Roush, Walter, 27
Rowe, Fred S., 99, 108, 325n13
Ruble, V. H., 40, 289, 313n24
Russell, Charles M., 228, 240
Russell, John Charles ("Charlie"), 112,
326n27
Russian colony, 114–15, 122, 327n2

Saloons: Bob Yokum owns, 22,
312n17; Coney Island, 22, 24, 35,
38–39, 313n22; gambling at, 235–
36; George Gordon owns, 95–96;
in frontier towns, 135; in Kansas,
312n17; in Midland, 21–22; 73
saloon, 310n6; in Stamford, 140,
331n2; Sunday closing law and,
140–43
Saint Elmo's Fire, 70–76, 253, 321n2
Sanchez, Ed ("Mexican Ed"), 201,
339n9, 345n3
Sanger, Margaret, 347n3
Sargent, Slim, 48–53
Saunders, Louis Edward, 145, 159,
332n3
Savage, Happy Jack, 48–49, 51–53,
184, 315n5
Scenic, S.Dak., 161
Schneider, Jimmie, 84–87, 229
Schultz, Hugh, 165–73, 285–87,
348n9
Schultz, Olive Philip, 348n9
Scotland: Philip family in, 1–4, 7–8
73 outfit: George Philip with, 221;
Jesse Knight as foreman of, 321n7;
on roundup, 256–67; Scotty Philip
and, 4, 13, 94, 300
73 Saloon, 310n6
Sheep, 110
Sheidley Cattle Company, 335n2
Sherwood, Daniel P., 134–36,
330:10n5
Shriner Brothers, 298

Siberts, Bruce, 299, 301
Simms, Tom, 328n4
Singleton, Henry, 57, 317n15
Singleton, J. T. ("Terry"), 56–57, 154, 317n15, 322:6n1
Sisseton, S.Dak., 298
6 L outfit, 125–26
Slang. See Cowboy jargon
Slaughter, John Horton, 175, 179–82, 335n1
"Sleeping Out" (Carr), 213
Slicks, 271, 279
Smallpox, 288–94, 348n11, 349n15
Smith, Adam, 203, 339n11
Smith, Mary Burnette, 339n11
Smith, Winchell, 329n8
Smithville, S.Dak., 324n8
Smoky Tom (gambler), 237–38
Snodgrass, Harlan Carlyle, 151, 158–59, 333n11
South Dakota: as cow country, 9, 297–300; end of open range in, 268–69, 297; George Philip as U. S. attorney for, 5; map of, x–xi; Norwegian settlement in, 261, 297; regulation of saloons and gambling by, 140–43; Russian settlers in, 114–15, 122, 327n2; territorial legislature of, 297, 346n3; Wall of the Badlands in, 151, 175, 243, 333n10; West River country of, 84, 297, 300
South Dakota Cement Commission, 5
South Dakota State Historical Society, 311n13
South Dakota Mining Company, 318n21
South Dakota National Guard, 310n5, 345n4
South Dakota School of Mines, 129, 330:9n4

South Dakota State Hospital for the Insane, 123
South Dakota State Penitentiary, 326n24, 339n9
Spanish-American War, 310n5, 345n4
Spanish Five, 122, 330n3
Spearfish, S.Dak., 322:5n1
Spotted Crow (Sioux Indian), 100–105, 325n14
Stamford, S.Dak., 61, 140, 319n2, 331:11n2
Standard Oil Company, 13, 310n5
Standing Rock Indian Reservation, 299–300
Stanley County, Old, 319n4; cow outfits in, 300; law enforcement in, 106, 140, 176, 256, 325n15, 329n7, 343n11, 344n2, 331:11n3; map of, ix; politics in, 21–22; Russian settlers in, 327n2; settlement of, 61
Stanton, Charles E., 311n9
Stewart, Robert W. ("Bob"), 13, 310n5
Stock Growers Bank (Fort Pierre), 240, 243, 342n2
Stuebe, Charles, 13
Sturgis, S.Dak., 53, 164
Sullivan, John L., 278, 347n1
Sully County, 298, 323:6n3
Sylva, Ben, 287
Sylva, Julia, 215–17, 287
Sylva, Manuel, 131, 215, 330n1

Tackett, George, 99–105, 324n12
Taddiken, Al, 305
Taft, William Howard, 326n21
Taggart, Louise Swarthout, 310n6
Taggart, Slim ("Slobbering Slim"), 13, 16, 310n6
"Tam O'Shanter" (Burns), 46, 315n2

Taylor, Bert Leston, 268, 345n1
Taylor, King, 93
TD Ranch, 305
Terry, Rex A., 240–44, 342n4
Texas: brands/branding, 270–71;
    cattle trails, 298; cow outfits,
    346n4; end of open range in, 48,
    71, 269, 299
Texas itch, 48–50, 57–58, 315n6
Thode, D. W., 306
Thompson, Big Mouth, 118, 329n6
Throw-back cattle, 46–47
Thunder Basin National Grassland,
    342n5
Thunder Butte, 46, 50–56, 59
Tincup, Fannie, 325n13
Tincup, Frank, 98–99, 101, 325n13
"To a Mouse, on Turning up Her Nest
    with the Plough" (Burns), 313n23,
    320n8, 341n6
Todd County, 256
Tripp County, 303
Tuberculosis, 2
Turkey Track (E-6) Ranch, 299–300
Tusha, Gus A., 62, 319n4, 321n9

U Cross ranch, 125–26, 262, 324n8,
    325n16
Union County, 312n16
United States Army, 311n9, 323:6n3
United States government: federal
    court at Deadwood, 145; Gen-
    eral Allotment Act of 1887, 303,
    314n26; George Philip as U. S. at-
    torney, 5; Homestead Act of 1862,
    303; Indian policy and, 338n8; and
    Indian lands, 45, 297–98, 300–303;
    as purchaser of beef, 298–99
United States v. Pelican, 107, 326n20
University of Michigan, 3–4, 106,
    340n4, 331:12n1

Utterback, Ben, 209
Utterback, J. E. ("Corny"), 209–10,
    339n13
Utterback, Zoe Larabee, 339n13

Van Cise, Philip, 234
Van Metre, Arthur C., 320n7, 330n2
Van Metre, Charles Luther ("Dutch"),
    63–69, 320n7
Van Metre, Mary Aungie, 330n2
Van Metre, S.Dak., 47, 62–63, 84,
    183, 325n16, 329n7, 338n7
Vermont Cattle Company, 324n6
Vivian, S.Dak., 122, 344n3

Wagon, the: cattle boom and, 300;
    components of, 79–80; defined, 11–
    12; 1901 roundups and, 305–7; rep
    operations and, 45–46. See also Cow
    outfits; Roundups and roundup
    outfits
Walcott, Henry, 140, 331:11n2
Waldron, Alice Island ("Isle").
    See Philip, Alice Island ("Isle")
    Waldron
Waldron, Jane Van Metre, 6, 320n7,
    330n2
Walker, W. I., 226, 340n9
Wall, S.Dak., 151, 175, 242–43
Wallace, Lewis, 93, 324n7
Walsh, Joseph Mark, 62–69, 320n5
Washington, George, 288
Washington (state), 269, 326n20
Wasta, S.Dak., 151
Waterloo, Battle of, 95, 324n9
Wattles, 90, 272–73, 323:7n4
Weather: "balls of fire," 70–76; bliz-
    zards, 19, 122, 290; cattle stam-
    pede and, 275–76; flooding, 48;
    in open-range era, 297; profanity
    and thunderstorms, 127–28; winter

of 1887, 297, 299; winter of 1906-1907, 297
Wells, Charles, 342n7
Wendte, S.Dak., 84, 193, 280
West, C. B., 307
Western South Dakota Stock Growers Association, 336n11
Westover, S.Dak., 196
West River country, 84, 297, 300, 338n5
Wheeler, Burton K., 282, 347n7
Wheeler, S.Dak., 290
Whiskey. See Alcohol/alcoholism
White, Bunk, 5, 115–23, 165–73, 225, 272–74, 310n6, 328n4
White River, S.Dak., 156–58, 257
White River Badlands, 151–55, 175, 262–63, 284, 333n10
Whiting, Clyde G., 62–69, 319n3, 321n9
Wickert, Dick, 111, 326n26
Wickert, Julius, 326n26
Wilburn, Eva, 111
Williams, Carson Clay, 131, 330n1
Williams, J. R., 322:5n3
Willow Lake, S.Dak., 330:9n4
Wilson, Sarah, 324n6
Wilson, Woodrow, 5, 313n21
Wind Cave, 59, 318n21
Winner, S.Dak., 145, 155, 266, 332n3
Withers, Bob, 71–76, 249
Witten, S.Dak., 157

W M wagon, 225–26, 340n8
Wolcot, John (Peter Pindar), 145, 332n5
Wolves, gray, 13, 116–18, 328n5
Women: African-American, 325n13; and birth control, 347n3; changing roles of, 205, 238; cowboy courting of, 215–17; in cowboy life, 245, 272, 278; Indian intermarriage and, 6, 176–78, 314n28, 315n4, 318n23, 320n7, 334n2, 337n1; law of the range and, 129–30; marriage and, 92–93; practical jokes and, 131–32; prostitution and, 302; smoking and drinking by, 178, 194
World War I, 311n9, 331:12n1
World War II, 7, 242, 268, 295, 327n1, 343n7, 347n7, 349n19
Worsley, Mabel Stewart, 303
Wortman, Eva, 53, 316n12
Wyoming, 9, 269, 298, 342n5

XIT brand, 270, 346n4

Yankton, S.Dak., 123, 189, 297, 320n5, 337n14, 347n6
Yankton Indian Reservation, 349n13
Yokum, Bob, 22–24, 29–30, 36–39, 311n14, 312n17

Ziebach County, 46, 312n16, 318n22